The Northern Region of Korea: History, Identity, and Culture

SUN JOO KIM, Editor

The Center for Korea Studies Publication Series published by the University of Washington Press is supported by the Center for Korea Studies and the Academy of Korean Studies.

The Center for Korea Studies Publication Series is dedicated to providing excellent academic resources and conference volumes related to the history, culture, and politics of the Korean peninsula.

Clark W. Sorensen | Director & General Editor
| Center for Korea Studies

THE Northern Region of Korea

HistoryIdentityCulture
☙

EDITED BY

SUN JOO KIM

A CENTER FOR KOREA STUDIES PUBLICATION

UNIVERSITY OF WASHINGTON PRESS | SEATTLE & LONDON

This book is published by the Center for Korea Studies at the University of Washington with the assistance of a grant from the Academy of Korean Studies.

CENTER FOR KOREA STUDIES
Henry M. Jackson School of International Studies
University of Washington
Box 353650, Seattle, WA 98195-3650
http://jsis.washington.edu/Korea

UNIVERSITY OF WASHINGTON PRESS
P.O. Box 50096, Seattle, WA 98145 U.S.A.
www.washington.edu/uwpress

LIBRARY OF CONGRESS CATALOGING-IN-PUBLICATION DATA
The northern region of Korea : history, identity, and culture / edited by Sun Joo Kim. — 1st ed.
   p. cm. — (Center for Korea Studies publication)
   Includes bibliographical references and index.
   ISBN 978-0-295-99041-5 (acid-free paper)
   1. Hwanghae-bukto (Korea)—History. 2. Hamgyong-bukto (Korea)—History. 3. P'yongan-bukto (Korea)—History. 4. Regionalism—Korea (North)—Hwanghae-bukto. 5. Regionalism—Korea (North)—Hamgyong-bukto. 6. Regionalism—Korea (North)—P'yongan-bukto. 7. Ethnicity—Korea (North)—Hwanghae-bukto. 8. Ethnicity—Korea (North)—Hamgyong-bukto. 9. Ethnicity—Korea (North)—P'yongan-bukto. I. Kim, Sun Joo, 1962-
   DS936.H85N67 2010
   951.93—dc22   2010004169

The paper used in this publication meets the minimum requirements of American National Standard for Information Sciences-Permanence of Paper for Printed Library Materials, ANSI Z39.48-1984.

Contents

Maps, Figures, and Tables

Acknowledgments

The inception of this project in 2003 under the working title "The Northern Region, Culture, and Identity in Korea" was much encouraged by my dearest colleague, Carter J. Eckert. Without his rather forceful "push," I would not have dared to initiate this project, which I knew would take years to complete. I am most thankful for his steady support and faith in me. Professors Yi Taejin and Oh Soo-chang resided in Cambridge while I struggled to develop concrete plans for the project. Together with my colleagues David R. McCann and Edward J. Baker, they served as members of the advisory committee for the project, which first met in January 2004, and helped me establish useful directions for the project. Since then, numerous people, in particular Peter K. Bol, supported the project throughout the past seven years. I am greatly indebted to their warm guidance.

The project convened two workshops on June 14, 2004 and February 18–19, 2005 respectively, and one conference on October 20–21, 2005. Altogether twenty-four papers were presented at these three occasions, but this present volume carries only eleven. Those scholars, who participated in and enriched the project, but whose papers are not included in this book because of various reasons, including the protracted publication process, are: Kyung Moon Hwang, "Northern Koreans in the Chosŏn and Early Modern Eras"; Jeon Bong-hee, "A Preliminary Study on the Characteristics of Architectural Heritages in the Northern Region in Korea,"; Sun Joo Kim, "An Investigation of Elite Culture and Society of Chŏngju, P'yŏngan Province, in the Late Chosŏn Period"; Oh Soo-chang, "Expectations and Policies of P'yŏngan Province in the Early Nineteenth Century: Perspectives from the Local and the Center"; David R. McCann, "Kim Sowŏl and His Poetic World as a

Northerner"; Ann Y. Choi, "United Nation: The Poetry of Kim Sowŏl and Kim Yŏngnang"; Lee Jung Sook, "Kim Sa-ryang's Literary Connection with P'yŏngyang"; Kim Kuen-Tae, "The Characteristics of the Financial Policy in P'yŏngan Province as seen through Household Registers in Mid-Nineteenth Century Korea"; Ko Seung Hee, "The Characteristics of Regional Development in Hamgyŏng Province in Late Chosŏn"; Chong Bum Kim, "Jerusalem is Doomed: Kil Sŏn-ju and Christian Millennialism in Northwest Korea" and "For God and Country: The Osan School in Colonial Korea"; Kim Gwi-Ok, "Life Experience and Culture of the People from Hamgyŏng Province during Japanese Colonial Rule"; and Seung-Hee Jeon, "Korean History from the Late Nineteenth to Mid-Twentieth Century from the Perspective of a Kaesŏng Merchant Family in Pak Wansŏ's Kkum endŭl ich'iriya."

Many other scholars from near and far joined these meetings as commentators and moderators; their critical views and encouraging comments were enormously helpful in revising the papers and tightening arguments. They are: John B. Duncan at UCLA, Vipan Chandra at Wheaton College, Gari Keith Ledyard at Columbia University, Kyung Moon Hwang at the University of Southern California, Christine Kim at Georgetown University, Kwon Youngmin at Seoul National University, Sung-Yoon Lee at Tufts University, and Peter K. Bol, Elizabeth J. Perry, David R. McCann, Carter J. Eckert, Mikael Adolphson, Sang-Suk Oh, and Wesley Jacobsen at Harvard University. I am grateful for their intellectual generosity. A number of students at Harvard lent enthusiastic hands for the project: Jungwon Kim, Aeri Shin, Sue-Jean Cho, and Junghwan Lee as assistants; Ellie Choi, Peter Wayne de Fremery, Jungwon Kim, Ji-Eun Lee, Junghwan Lee, Javier Cha, and Aeri Shin as translators; Jaeyoon Song, Ellie Choi, Victoria Kim, and Mia You as simultaneous interpreters; and Joe Wicentowski and Tae Yang Kwak in managing the conference website. Susan Lee Laurence, Myong-suk Chandra, Kathryn Maldonis, Susan McHone, and Melanie Wang all provided essential services in various administrative capacities. I owe all of them a huge hug and many thanks.

All three meetings and the publication itself would have been impossible without the generous financial support of a number of organizations. I would like to thank the Korea Research Foundation, the Korea Foundation, the Harvard-Yenching Institute, and Harvard's Asia Center and Korea Institute. From the beginning, Clark Sorensen showed genuine enthusiasm, embraced the book, and took great care of it through every step of the publication process. Victoria Scott and Tracy Stober magically transformed a manuscript of twelve different writing styles into a much more consistent and readable form. I would like to offer my heartfelt appreciation to them. I would also like to note that Ross King generously assisted me with the editing of Chapter 5, which required expertise in linguistics.

Diverse topics and disciplines were represented at the workshops and conference and many shared the themes and academic agendas discussed in my introductory chapter. I am truly sorry that all of these great papers could not be published in this limited volume; at the same time, it is my great pleasure to report to readers that the regional approach of this project did provide an unique opportunity for scholars to delve into dynamic and diverse aspects of Korea's past. It is apparent that this book is only the beginning of much deeper and broader studies on the northern region's history and culture and I would feel honored if this volume inspired further future studies and generated more exciting and critical scholarship, not only in the field of Korean studies, but also all other relevant fields.

Editor's Note

The Korean terms and names in the text are rendered in McCune-Reischauer Romanization, the Chinese terms and names in Pinyin, and the Japanese in the Hepburn system. Korean, Chinese, and Japanese names in the text, notes, and bibliography are given in Korean order (surname first, without comma), except for those authors who have published in English. The references to Chosŏn rulers use their posthumous titles. Lunar calendar dates appear as year/month/day (1945/8/15), and Roman calendar dates appear in "American style" (August 15, 1945).

All references to Kuksa p'yŏnch'an wiwŏnhoe [National Institute of Korean History] ed., Chosŏn wangjo sillok [The Veritable Records of the Kings of the Chosŏn Dynasty], 48 vols. (Seoul: Kuksa p'yŏnch'an wiwŏnhoe, 1955–58), are noted according to the sillok of each king. The page reference is to the volume of this reprint edition, followed by year/month/day, e.g., Injo sillok, 34:511a, 1633/1/8.

The Northern Region of Korea

History, Identity, and Culture

CHINA

North
Hamgyŏng

South
Hamgyŏng

North
P'yŏngan

•Ŭiju

Hamhŭng•

East Sea

South
P'yŏngan
P'yŏngyang•

KOREA

Hwanghae

Kangwŏn

Kaesŏng•

•Seoul
Kyŏnggi

North
Ch'ungch'ŏng

South
Ch'ungch'ŏng

North
Kyŏngsang

Yellow
Sea

North
Chŏlla

South
Kyŏngsang

South
Chŏlla

•Pusan

N

Tsushima Is.

0   50 miles
0   50 km

Cheju Is.

JAPAN

Korea at the Turn of the Twentieth Century

Introduction

Thinking Through Region

SUN JOO KIM

Numerous men and women of prominence in modern Korea—Syngman Rhee, Kim Kyusik, Kim Ku, Yi Sŭnghun, Yi Kwangsu, Kim Tongin, Hwang Sunwŏn, Kim Sowŏl, Mo Yunsuk, No Ch'ŏnmyŏng, Kil Sŏnju, Ham Sŏkhŏn, Han Kyŏngjik, Mun Sŏnmyŏng, Kim Hwallan, Hwang Sindŏk, Kim Maria, Kim Okkil, Kim Chunhyŏp, Paek Nakchun, Chang Chunha, Yi Yŏnghŭi, Yi Tonghwi, An Chunggŭn, An Ch'angho, and Chu Sigyŏng, to name a few—came from the northern region.[1] We cannot discuss Korea's modern era without mentioning their thoughts and activities in the fields of history, literature, religion, medicine, education, politics, the military, and independence and dissident movements. Yet how many Koreans know these influential figures and their regional affiliation and ponder whether their regional background has anything to do with their fame and contributions to modern Korea? This collective scholarly investigation of the northern region, its history, culture, and identity addresses this silence about the historical depth of regional identity in Korean history.

Historical study in the modern world has been dominated by grand paradigms such as modernization theory, the positivist perspective, and Marxism. In her examination of modern European historiography, Celia Applegate points out that the paradigm of modernization has obscured our view of Europe's regions more than any other conceptual model. She goes on to argue that writing history in the modern era has been closely interwoven with the making and legitimating of nation-states, and that the devaluation of regions and their pasts has emerged naturally alongside the triumph of national historiographies. Not only has this trend subjected the study of regions and local places to a national history project, but the study of regional history and regionalism has often been expressed in terms of reactionary parochialism and separatism.[2] The net result has been the subordination of the local to the national, diversity to homogeneity, and place to class, as Kären Wigen insightfully informs us.[3]

Korea's modern historiography has also been subjected to a nation-centered framework, which apparently tends to suppress scholarly attention to the significance of region and regional diversity. Recent studies using the methodology of micro-history spatially limit investigations to a province, a district, or even a village, yet the ultimate aim of such studies has often been to extract a "national" trend from local experiences and to answer general questions about the nation. Even in such microscopic studies, the northern region has been marginalized for unspecified reasons, which ought to be a matter of scrutiny in itself. This book thus proposes that we turn our scholarly orientation toward regional history, culture, and literary production and acknowledge the agency of a given locale.

The regional approach that emphasizes place is, of course, not new to the fields of world history and culture. Criticizing the evolutionary historical view of nationalism, which claims nationalism as a unitary consciousness or identity, Prasenjit Duara, in his monumental study of modern China, proposes viewing the histories of nations contingently, since nations are themselves contingent. After noting that there are multiple nation-views and that nationalism is best seen as a relational identity, he argues that "potential others" deserve the most attention because "they reveal the principle that creates nations—the willing into existence of a nation which will choose to privilege its difference and obscure all of the cultural bonds that had tied it to its sociological kin."[4]

In Sinology, the call to pay attention to regional differences, diversity, and uniqueness has been made for many decades. The enormous size of China's territory, diverse environmental factors such as climate and terrain, ethnic and linguistic complexity, and resultant differing historical experiences naturally led to the critical view that a national narrative would not do justice to its peripheries. As early as 1947, when China's future was critically obscured by struggles between the Chinese Communist Party and the Nationalist Party (Kuomintang), J. E. Spencer declared that "Chinese culture is not a tightly homogenous matter" and surveyed regional varieties in food, clothing, physical appearance and temperament, language, and landscapes. More insightfully, he stated that regionalism is "a vital factor in Chinese affairs" and is frequently "at the root of some of the political and social happenings" in China.[5] William Skinner's macro-regional framework provided a more systematic tool with which to analyze such Chinese affairs, producing a critical impact on Sinologists and resulting in many regionally focused monographs over the years.[6]

Sinologists widely acknowledge that consideration of the different cultural and social clusters that make up an empire, particularly the pluralism and great diversity of the Qing Empire (1644–1912), would enrich national history.[7] China's tumultuous modern transformations could also be explicated by probing its regional particularities. For example, in a study of militarism and separatism in Szechwan Province, Robert Kapp sees republican militarism after the demise of the Qing in 1911 not only as something arising from a post-imperial context—intellectual and political instability and disorganization following the destruction of the Qing—but also as a new expression of the ancient problem of local differentiation and local autonomy, which were deeply rooted in anti-centralism in China.[8]

Even in more contemporary affairs, Edward Friedman, in his analysis of China's capitalist transformation, discusses the clashes between the northern, anti-imperialist, Han-race-centered Maoist national narrative and the rise of different nationalisms emphasizing economic growth and multiethnic, regionally diverse national cultures. He argues that the conflict between two meta-narratives in China—political legitimation from the north and economic dynamism from the south—is deeply embedded in China's history.[9] Indeed, the roots of regionalism and intra-regional identity conflict seem to run deep. Xiaofei Tian's recent study of literary identities in medieval China shows that the origin of regional competition goes back as far as the Period of Disunion (220–589) and the Tang Dynasty (618–907).[10] Regional conflict within Ming China (1368–1644) was readily noticed by Koreans, when the northern and southern Chinese armies deployed to Chosŏn (1392–1910) to help fight Japanese invaders from 1592–98 showed clear signs of discord stemming from regional rivalry.[11]

The facts that the Korean peninsula (1) is relatively small in territorial terms, and (2) has been under one ruling structure for a long period of time have rationalized the writing of Korean history as a single narrative in which variances have been effectively buried. Yet regionalism and regional diversity are not analytical tools reserved only for territorially large countries. The study of regionalism in Italy, which is about 1.4 times the size of Korea, is instructive. In his several-decades-long research and analysis of regional governments in Italy, Robert D. Putnam argues that historical and social conditions have had a critical impact on the success and failure of the new regional governments that were instituted in the 1970s. In other words, historical conditions that had emerged by the beginning of the fourteenth century—feudal monarchy in the south and communal republicanism in northern and central Italy—resulted in different political cultures in modern Italy. The former produced a highly autocratic and hierarchical social structure, while the latter nurtured civil involvement and social solidarity. Putnam finds that the north's historical and cultural heritage was largely conducive to the success of efficient, democratic, regional governments and to economic development in that region, in contrast to the failure of the south, which had lacked a civic tradition.[12] The argument that cultural antecedents are vital to economic development and civic government is provocative, as Putnam himself acknowledges, yet the evidence he uses remains compelling.

In studies of Japan, which is about 1.6 times larger than Korea, scholars have noted that the different historical and cultural trajectories present in each regional enclave provide a powerful explanation for the dynamic development of modern Japan. In a classic study of the Meiji Restoration, Albert Craig specifically asks why Chōshū Domain played a leading role. In answering his own question, he emphasizes traditional strengths within Chōshū—its large size in terms of land as well as samurai class, long-standing hostility to the Bakufu, its special relation to the court, the relatively affluent financial conditions and high morale of its samurai, and healthy and flexible domain politics.[13] Bernard S. Silberman's study of elite mobility in post-Restoration Japan, between 1868 and 1873 (a time of great political, social, and economic change), also finds that pre-Restoration conditions explain why a majority of the new elite in this period came from the lower samurai status group from relatively few domains. He argues that this particular group of samurai had suffered from increasing socio-economic expansion and responded to such status deprivation by developing innovative behaviors such as the acquisition of Western knowledge, which became instrumental to its political rise. He points out that the few domains that supplied the majority of the post-Restoration elite had gone through more dynamic socio-economic changes during the Tokugawa period than had other domains, thus heightening the degree of status deprivation felt by lower samurai from those regions.[14] Research on the Meiji Restoration since these pioneering studies has produced a large number of works, most of which look at individual domains and investigate why certain domains were active in this monumental "revolutionary" process while others were not.[15]

Kären Wigen's study of Shimoina County truly exemplifies a regional approach. Although her larger pursuit is the origins of Japan's phenomenal transformation from a decentralized state to a strong, unified imperial state, she investigates the course of transformation through the changing landscapes of the region. Proposing to "reconceive Japan's modern metamorphosis in spatial terms," she richly documents the developments, stagnation, and decline of the regional economy in relation to the environment and the political and economic relations with the world surrounding it, including national and world markets.[16]

These works by scholars of China, Japan, and Italy emphasize both the importance of regional variations and the lasting effects of these variations even today, in the seemingly quite different world in which we now live. Korea's historical experiences are certainly different from those of China, Japan, and Italy. Its political system was more highly centralized for almost a millennium than were those of Italy and Japan. Modern history from the late nineteenth century until today has been conditioned by imperialism, colonialism, the cold war, and division, all of which seem to have made its national framework make more sense. Yet the authors of the present volume share the views that (1) regional differentiation did emerge in premodern Korea, and that (2) the workings of "global" historical forces on the Korean peninsula in the modern period can best be understood when we take various internal historical and cultural dimensions, including regionalism and regionality, into serious consideration.

DEFINITION AND BRIEF HISTORY OF THE NORTHERN REGION

What do we mean by the northern region of Korea? The word "region" often refers to an administrative unit such as province. Nonetheless, as aptly displayed in China, an administrative division of land does not always form a culturally and economically meaningful region. In our discussion, the northern region encompasses the three northern provinces (Hwanghae, Hamgyŏng, and P'yŏngan) during the Chosŏn Dynasty, which were further divided into five provinces (Hwanghae, North and South Hamgyŏng, and North and South P'yŏngan) in 1897 and remained that way during the colonial period (1910–45). Kaesŏng—located right next to the southern border of Hwanghae Province, a special district under the rule of a junior second rank magistrate during the Chosŏn period—was also included as a part of the northern region. The unifying identification that grouped these separate administrative units into a single region was their shared historical fate as a spatial object of political discrimination in the late Chosŏn period. Jung Min's selection of anecdotes portraying the sad fates of talented northerners (Chapter 4) represents the culturally constructed nature of this region, which we uphold as an analytical unit. We recognize the diversity within the region, as Jang Yoo-seung (Chapter 3) articulates in his discussion of the divergent literati identities of P'yŏngan and Hamgyŏng provinces. Furthermore, we stress that the cultural content and context of regional identities are fluid and flexible rather than fixed and unchanging.

The territorial boundaries of the northern region, especially its northern border, fluctuated widely until they were "settled" in the fifteenth century along the two rivers, the Yalu and Tumen, originating from Paektu Mountain. Although the territory of the Old Chosŏn period (?–108 BCE) is as controversial as is its historicity, historians and archeologists often situate Old Chosŏn in the northwestern part of the Korean peninsula and southern Manchuria. Historical records tell us that Han China (194 BCE–220 CE) established four commanderies in the territory of Old Chosŏn, and that one of them, the Lelang commandery (K. Nangnang, 108 BCE–313 CE) in the low reaches of the Taedong River, seems to have been the most influential in the subsequent formation of ancient states in Korean history. A number of "confederate kingdoms" and "walled-town" states rose and fell on the Korean peninsula while its northwestern part remained under the rule of the Lelang commandery. Okchŏ and Eastern Ye occupied the northeastern part of the peninsula until they were incorporated by the Koguryŏ kingdom (37 BCE?—668 CE). Often imagined as a mighty military kingdom in Korea's history, Koguryŏ, at its height, occupied vast lands in Manchuria and the northern part of the Korean peninsula. Yet when the Silla kingdom (57 BCE?–935 CE) "unified" the three kingdoms in 668, its territory reached only as far north as the

Taedong River to the northwest and Wŏnsan to the northeast. "Nationalists" from the late Chosŏn, and more visibly in the twentieth century, have claimed that the Parhae state (C. Bohai, 698–926), located in Manchuria and the northern part of the Korean peninsula, was a Korean kingdom, for it was founded by a Koguryŏ general and is thus a part of authentic Korean history. This line of argument, however, cannot be applied to the period after the demise of Parhae early in the tenth century because Manchuria had long been lost in Korea's historical narrative until it was rediscovered in the nationalist discourses in the twentieth century.

From early in the tenth century, the northernmost territory of the Korean peninsula had in fact been under contention, with various polities formed by the Mohe, Khitan, Jurchen, and Mongols. Even in the early Chosŏn period, not every place along the two rivers was populated and not all living in the area were Chosŏn people. Although lower and middle reaches of the Yalu River were inhabited as early as the mid-Koryŏ period, the upper reaches of the Yalu did not provide a habitable environment. Therefore, within a few decades four districts established in the fifteenth century in the area northeast of Kanggye were abandoned due to the inhospitable terrain. The area south and north of the Tumen River served as the stage for a group of people known as the Jurchen. The porous and contentious nature of the border region and how the Jurchen and Chosŏn negotiated distinct notions of culture and territory in the early Chosŏn period are well discussed by Kenneth R. Robinson (Chapter 1).

Border problems, including dealing with people living in the area, were not settled in the early Chosŏn period, nor did the geographical investigation and political agreement between Chosŏn Korea and Qing China in 1712 bring a solid resolution to border disputes.[17] The migration of the Chosŏn populace toward the hinterlands along the upper reaches of the Yalu River and all along the Tumen River eventually changed the entire landscape of the area from that of a barren, uninhabitable place to a land of opportunity for extracting various natural resources and reclaiming hillsides and valleys.[18] This newly populated area was not confined to the land south of the two watersheds but spilled over into territory farther north, despite legal prohibitions against such migration by both governments, thus creating a source of border disputes in contemporary Korea and China. These unsettled border issues—and the frequent movements of Korean people into the area known as "Kando" in the late nineteenth and

early twentieth century—were noted by the first Russians who visited northeastern Korea at the time, as Chapter 10 by German Kim and Ross King reveals.

The position of the northern region as a frontier and periphery in
Confucian cultural discourse imparted an enormous disadvantage to the
region and its residents. According to Confucian cultural discourse, any land
far from the center was deemed to be less civilized than the center itself. In
addition, the history of the Korean populace's interaction (mixed marriage
and cohabitation) with Jurchen people under Chosŏn's administration, which
left distinguishable cultural imprints on the region's various customs, provided sources for the negative construction of the region and people during
the late Chosŏn period. As Jang Yoo-seung and Jung Min note (Chapter 3 and
4), the cultural construction of the region as uncivilized, militaristic, and
barbaric found its way into the late Chosŏn popular consciousness. Such
cultural discourse legitimized social marginalization and political discrimination against northerners whose culture was judged to be not up to the standard set by orthodox central Confucians.[19]

REGIONAL DISCRIMINATION, DEVELOPMENT, AND TRANSFORMATION

This book, then, explores how the northern part of the Korean peninsula
developed and changed historically from the early Chosŏn to the colonial
period. Regions in Korea have long been neatly and conveniently divided by
provincial demarcations which have been set by geographical features such
as rivers and mountain ranges, and which have presumably created discrete
linguistic and cultural traits. Although it is true that the relatively small size
of Korea's dynastic territory and its long history as a unified state under one
ruling structure and ideology shaped a fairly well-integrated identity and cultural practices, the concentration of power and authority—not just political
but also cultural, social, economic, and ideological—at the center promoted
the development of subjective expressions of regional belonging by insiders,
as well as equally subjective expressions of regional stereotyping by outsiders.
One of our goals here is to trace northern regional identities as constructed
and negotiated in reaction to outsiders' views, and to locate such regional
identities and politics in relation to the center, during the Chosŏn Dynasty
and the colonial period. Because identity politics is not a one-way process

from the center to the margin but works the other way around, we also investigate various efforts of the central court and "national" elites to civilize,
manipulate, and mobilize the marginal and alienated region of the country,
and examine how their policy orientation and attitudes toward the north
became conditioned by northerners' reactions and demands.[20]

The dynamic interactions in identity politics between the center and the
margin stemmed from social and political discrimination developed against
the northern region in the late Chosŏn period. The problem of native-place
identities and discrimination based purely on geographical origin has been
discussed in Chinese historiography. Emily Honig's intuitive study on the
Subei people looks at the specific problem of spatially assigned prejudice; the
author catalogs the Subei people as a culturally constructed ethnic group even
though they are of Han ethnicity. The development of this particular perception also had to do with this migrant community's involvement with low-
paying, dirty urban jobs, and with its shack settlements. Interestingly, disdain
against this particular group of migrants soon found its own trajectory, turning into systematic alienation and marginalization of people from the Subei
Region.[21]

The circumstances by which prejudice and discrimination against northerners developed in the late Chosŏn period differed from the circumstances
of the Subei people in China. Yet the construction of cultural rhetoric against
a group of people based on their place of origin and cultural practices is quite
similar. Numerous anecdotes from this period testify to unfair yet widely held
cultural bias against northerners, and their resultant social and cultural marginalization. (As mentioned above, Jung Min colorfully showcases the sad lot
of northerners in Chapter 4). Prejudice and consequent offenses against
northerners were felt most bitterly by northern literati who had bureaucratic
ambitions. Even when they had obtained the honor of passing the country's
most prestigious state examinations, the *munkwa*, their bureaucratic advance-
ments were effectively blocked by a number of discriminatory screening systems at the court. Furthermore, social and cultural abuses that the northern
literati experienced while living in the capital as central officials or when in
search of employment and promotion drove them to become extremely
resentful. Sources tell us that central elites regarded and treated northern
elites as professional entertainers (*kisaeng*) or eunuchs (*chunggwan*).
Northerners themselves were angered that even the servants of central elite

households addressed them with debasing words and rudeness. They were also snubbed at the court by their colleagues, and even by junior officials, solely on the basis of their native-place origins.[22]

No satisfactory and acceptable reasons for regional discrimination, or explanations of when it began, seem to have been offered by either northerners or non-northerners of the late Chosŏn period. Sun Joo Kim suggests that the development of regional discrimination was embedded in social and political arrangements laid out in the early Chosŏn period, when both conscious and subconscious self-control of the size of the central elite resulted in discrimination and exclusion of the most powerful competitors.[23] Such power politics had spilled over not only to northerners but also to most local elites by the eighteenth century. Yet the fact remains that discriminatory discourses constructed by central elites against northerners involved not only political dimensions but also social and cultural ones.

Therefore, we view identity politics in relational and contextual terms that are made, remade, and unmade by actors of various levels. And in understanding the development of identity politics, the growth in regional cultural capital is critical. As Kwon Naehyun in Chapter 2 and Ko Sŭnghŭi in her conference paper argue, the economic growth and territorial expansion of P'yongan and Hamgyŏng provinces since the beginning of the Chosŏn Dynasty, and especially after international conditions became stabilized in the mid-seventeenth century, were quite impressive.[24] It is apparent that the wealth created by economic growth in the region provided a material basis for the cultural growth of regional elites, who made every effort to be a part of the national elite simultaneously, and began to imagine and construct their own cultural identities, as Jang Yoo-seung's work clearly shows (Chapter 3). The collective voice to undo the injustice against northerners, especially that against P'yŏngan literati, was powerful by the nineteenth century. Policy makers' dilemmas in dealing with regional demands and problems, both at the provincial level as well as at the central court, are succinctly described in O Such'ang's work.[25]

The dimension of regional identity as a social force that promotes social and political mobility and engagement is a crucial one. Sinologists and Japanologists have been interested in it for some time, and we are too. Elizabeth Perry, for example, has specifically noted that the politics of place is "a two-edged sword that both opened possibilities and set boundaries to the development of collective action."[26] Through analysis of the native-place origins of Shanghai's labor force (mostly domestic immigrants from other regions of China), she argues that native-place identities determine workers' politics to a large degree. She found that the close relationship between native-place identity and job opportunities promoted the formation of occupational groupings along the line of native places, and that divisions among Shanghai laborers by native-place origins generated systematic and long-standing solidarities. Immigrants of the same native place and gender engaged in common lines of work, thereby creating a potent basis for collective action.[27] In a similar vein, we examine how presumably local, parochial, and even backward regionalism unfolded in Korea in the vortex of colonialism and nation-building in the first half of the twentieth century. In the past, the mere possibility of localism leading to beneficial contributions to the nation-building project had been seriously questioned because regionalism had been perceived as bringing divisionism and parochial interests to the fore. But building a nation can be advanced by and drawn from local attachments, for positive regional identity can transform itself, as a form of cultural capital, into coin that contributes to the invention of a larger imaginary—namely, that of a nation.[28]

A number of chapters in this volume richly document the multifaceted manifestations of regionalism and regionality in the tumultuous, critical decades of the 1890s through the 1940s when Koreans were faced with internal as well as external challenges that ultimately led to the collapse of traditional dynastic structures, the colonization of Korea, and subsequent intellectual and popular movements to rethink Korea's pasts and invent new Korean identities. As already indicated, one question we pose is what made some northerners so receptive to modern Western ideologies and practices. Silbermann's concept of a sense of status deprivation may partly explain why northerners, whose economic and cultural capital was not effectively translated into political power in the late Chosŏn period, quickly and readily found Western learning beneficial. Of course, not all northerners turned to new cultural waves and opportunities. There were certainly conflicts between traditionalists and innovators, as described, for example, in Bruce Fulton's analysis of Hwang Sunwŏn's short stories (Chapter 8). Fulton discovers the rich but unique cultural tradition and identity constructed by the P'yŏngan people, and discusses how their regional identity pushed some of them to jump into modern transformation and others to hold onto their proud past. Moreover, Yumi Moon's heroes in Chapter 7—Tonghak followers, Christians, and Ilchinhoe members—exemplify the popular confusion and struggles between localist and nationalist goals during the short but extremely turbulent years between 1903 and 1908 when the national government was losing its authority and legitimacy, and Japan's colonial ambitions were casting an ever darker shadow over the Korean peninsula. The localism expressed in the anti-tax movements did have nationalist pretensions, yet it also inhibited the effective extension of central power to the local scene to mobilize critical financial resources for the nation's reform efforts.

What most dramatically reveals the regionalism in action in this period is how northerners quickly adopted new cultural capital—namely, Christianity and Western education—as examined by Donald N. Clark (Chapter 9). Again it is enlightening to learn that regionalism has unexpected effects. We know that the early modernizers listed at the beginning of this introduction found modern education valuable as it became available to Koreans. Most of them also belonged to the first group of Koreans who converted to Christianity. We believe that regional backgrounds provide clues explaining why native northerners took the initiative to accept Protestantism even before Western missionaries set foot in Korea, and also why Protestantism's totally unfamiliar ideas took root rather easily in the north, as Western missionaries later testified. Yet northerners' modern conversion did not remove their regional affiliation. Their regional language identity—which has a long, important history in itself, as argued by Paek Doo-hyeon in Chapter 5—was vociferously expressed in the national debates on Korean vernacular standardization during the colonial period, as vividly portrayed by Ross King (Chapter 6). Apparently, since the early modern period and even in the latter part of the twentieth century in Western Europe regional dialect has been taken up as a distinctive cultural heritage to represent a region and has become a critical political tool frequently used by regionalist movements against centralization efforts by the nation-state.[29] Colonial imposition of Shinto worship also sparked the divisive nature of regional identity and further fragmented Christian groups along regional and denominational lines, indelibly marking the development of Christianity in South Korea during the post-liberation period.[30]

While we do not intend to produce a neat, single narrative that explicates the place of a region in Korean history, it turns out to be apparent that there are strong links between the earlier (late Chosŏn up until the late nineteenth century) and the later period (late nineteenth and early twentieth centuries) in terms of how and why regionalism played out. Some contributors discern a long-term continuity in the development of the regional economy, which promoted cultural and intellectual growth throughout the period under scrutiny in this book. Those wealthy merchants who traveled as far as Australia in 1901 (Chapter 7) were offspring of Ŭiju merchants who frequented Qing China in late Chosŏn (Chapter 2). Northerners who had made regular contacts with other ethnic groups (Chapter 1 and 2) were willing to venture beyond Korea's borders and were not hesitant to step out of their ideological and ethical prescriptions, which did not provide much benefit to them in late Chosŏn, and were ready to learn new ideas and religious practices (Chapter 9). Although a majority of northern elites of late Chosŏn were vigilant to identify themselves as practitioners of dominant Confucian ethics and culture, and desired to be a part of the central elites (Chapter 3), some were also keen to highlight their own distinct historical and cultural legacy (Chapter 3 and 5). Likewise, as northerners had gone through drastic changes in identity politics, from Confucian practitioners to national subjects, some of the new intellectuals and Christian converts, whose conversions must have shocked other more conservative seniors and colleagues, clung to the traditional garb, for example, the originality of their dialect—one of the key regional identifiers developed by their forefathers—in establishing a new national language identity (Chapter 6).

The present volume is further enriched by two more studies—one on Japanese views on northern Korea and Korean people by Mark E. Caprio (Chapter 11), and one on Russian views by Ross King and German Kim (Chapter 10). These foreign visitors and residents came to the Korean peninsula with certain political and cultural agendas conditioned by their own times and cultures. Although their records look "biased" from our point of view, they nevertheless inform us of useful aspects of regional practices and development. Last but not least, Kim Gwi-Ok's work, although not included in this volume, is based on the oral histories of refugees from Hamgyŏng Province, who left their homes, whether by accident or intention, during the chaotic post-liberation period in divided Korea, a period further complicated by the emerging cold war.[31] The cultural and social landscape that these refugees transmit to us is invaluable to understanding how quickly we can lose our tradition while simultaneously reinventing it. In particular, it is eye-opening to discover that native-place networking and identity had been critical for the Hamgyŏng refugees' survival in the south, even though homogenizing national discourses, especially those with anti-northern sentiments, have put a muzzle on the self-expression of Koreans originally from the northern region.

We do not touch on how the distinctive northern identity swirled into near oblivion in the whirlpool of Korean nation-building in the latter half of the twentieth century. Nor do we extend our discussion into the post-liberation period, the Korean War, division, and subsequent paths of South and North Korea, or address how the northern region's history and identity have played out. However, recent scholarship on nation-building has increasingly emphasized fragmentation, contingencies, and multiplicity. As a result, categories that have heretofore been marginalized such as regional identity (as well as women and laborers) await innovative scholarly probes in the near future. Did regionalism, regional identity, and regionality contribute in any way to the division of the Korean peninsula? What imprints will the distinctive paths taken by South and North Korea leave on the future Korea, if it is ever reunified? These are great questions to stimulate curious minds.

NOTES

1. Academic works that pay attention to the relationship between regionalism and modernization include Yi Kwangnin, "Kaehwagi Kwansŏ chibang kwa kaesin'gyo"; Chang Kyusik, *Ilcheha han'guk kidokkyo minjok chuŭi yŏn'gu*; and Kyung Moon Hwang, *Beyond Birth: Social Status in the Emergence of Modern Korea.*

2. Applegate, "A Europe of Regions: Reflections on the Historiography of Sub-National Places in Modern Times."

3. Wigen, "Culture, Power, and Place: The New Landscapes of East Asian Regionalism."

4. Duara, *Rescuing History from the Nation*, 15–16.

5. Spencer, "On Regionalism in China."

6. For the debates about Skinner's framework, see Little and Esherick, "Testing the Testers"; and Lavely, "The Spatial Approach to Chinese History." For a succinct review of works addressing regional issues in Sinology, see Wigen, "Culture, Power, and Place." More recent studies that are not discussed in Wigen's article are in Crossley, Siu, and Sutton, *Empire at the Margins*; and Ong, "Men of Letters within the Passes."

7. Naquin and Rawski, *Chinese Society in the Eighteenth Century*, 138–39.

8. Kapp, *Szechwan and the Chinese Republic*.

9. Friedman, "A Failed Chinese Modernity."

10. Tian, *Beacon Fire and Shooting Star*, 310–66.

11. Yu Sŏngnyong, *The Book of Corrections*, 157–58 and 172.

12. Putnam, *Making Democracy Work*.

13. Craig, *Chōshū in the Meiji Restoration*.

14. Silberman, *Ministers of Modernization*.

15. Examples are Ishimitsu Mahito, ed., *Remembering Aizu*; Baxter, *The Meiji Unification through the Lens of Ishikawa Prefecture*; and Koschmann, *The Mito Ideology*.

16. Wigen, *The Making of a Japanese Periphery*.

17. Ledyard, "Cartography in Korea."

18. Ko Sŭnghŭi, "The Regional Characteristics of Development in Hamgyŏng Province during the Late Chosŏn Period."

19. Hwang, "From the Dirt to Heaven"; and Sun Joo Kim, "Negotiating Cultural Identities in Conflict."

20. O Such'ang, "19 segi ch'o P'yŏngan-do sahoe munje e taehan chibangmin kwa chungang kwalli ŭi insik kwa chŏngch'aek." This paper was presented at the conference on "The Northern Region, Identity, and Culture in Korea" held at Harvard University on October 2005, but not included in this book because it was published in the Korean journal, *Han'guk munhwa*, in 2005.

21. Honig, *Creating Chinese Ethnicity*.

22. For an episode in 1822 when northern officials were insulted by a junior official from a renowned central elite family, see Sun Joo Kim, "Negotiating Cultural Identities in Conflict."

23. Sun Joo Kim, "Negotiating Cultural Identities in Conflict."

24. Ko Sŭnghŭi, "The Regional Characteristics of Development in Hamgyŏng Province during the Late Chosŏn Period."

25. O Such'ang, "19 segi ch'o P'yŏngan-do sahoe munje e taehan chibangmin kwa chungang kwalli ŭi insik kwa chŏngch'aek."

26. Perry, *Shanghai on Strike*, 30.

27. Ibid., 1–31.

28. For an exemplary study of how native-place lodges and ties in Beijing in late imperial China facilitated the emergence of a modern state based on loyalty to the nation, see Belsky, *Localities at the Center*.

29. Mény and Wright ed., *Centre-Periphery Relations in Western Europe*.

30. Chung-shin Park, *Protestantism and Politics in Korea*, 148–57.

31. Kim Kwi-Ok, "Life Experiences and Culture of the People from Hamgyŏng Province during Japanese Colonial Rule."

1

Residence and Foreign Relations in the Peninsular Northeast During the Fifteenth and Sixteenth Centuries

KENNETH R. ROBINSON

The Chosŏn government engaged in foreign relations with individuals living in Hamgyŏng Province into the late sixteenth century.[1] Jurchens (K. Yŏjin, Yain) from several tribes, including the Odoli, Uryangkhad, and Hurhan Wudiha, concentrated in the peninsular northeast, particularly in Hoeryŏng and further to the north and east. Aware of the Ming China government's approach to managing interaction with Jurchens based north of Chosŏn, many of whom belonged to tribes whose members also lived in the peninsular northeast, the Korean government similarly treated state-sponsored interaction as domestic administration.

The peninsular northeast was a multicultural frontier, a zone of interaction where Koreans and Jurchens commingled, collided, and cooperated.[2] The territorial and jurisdictional spaces named "Chosŏn" and "Hamgyŏng Province," though, may not be the most appropriate locations for placing the interactions between the Chosŏn court and Jurchens who resided there.[3] In "Hamgyŏng Province," many Jurchens lived in communities that were not fully incorporated into the Korean state, and they were not subjects of the King of Chosŏn as Koreans were subjects of the King of Chosŏn.

The concepts of territorial sovereignty and jurisdictional sovereignty borrowed here from Peter Sahlins' study of the making of a state boundary between France and Spain in the seventeenth and eighteenth centuries help to draw more sharply the disjuncture in the King of Chosŏn's rule in Hamgyŏng Province.[4] As Korean kings and their officials did not treat all Jurchens residing in the northeastern province the same as the Koreans living there, it seems clear that the court understood that the monarch's authority did not fully extend into all Jurchen communities.

Interaction illuminates complexities of administration in the peninsular northeast and Chosŏn. Seeking to encourage and maintain quiet in the northeast, from the mid-1420s the Chosŏn court appointed Jurchen elites to military posts and permitted them, but not Korean military officials holding the same posts, to trade in the capital. The Chosŏn court treated these Jurchens as both subjects and guests. Such Korean government policies suggest that Chosŏn was not a singular administrative space in the peninsula northeast from 1392 into the late sixteenth century.[5]

RESHAPING CHOSŎN

Jurchens moved into the peninsula during the Koryŏ period, and more resettled there in the late fourteenth century and the early fifteenth century. Their villages concentrated in the northeast corner, with different tribes generally residing in separate areas. Many of these Jurchens did not sever ties with communities north of the Yalu (K. Amnok) and Tumen (K. Tuman) rivers.

Jurchens who resided in the peninsula in the late fourteenth, fifteenth, and sixteenth centuries may be broadly divided into two groups, immigrant (hyanghwa; t'uhwa; kwihwa) Jurchens and Jurchens who had not immigrated. The contours of the first group can not always be sharply defined, but, in general, these were people who had sought the Chosŏn court's permission to immigrate into Korean society. Some Jurchen immigrants lived in the capital area, others in the northeast and elsewhere. The focus here will be on Jurchen elites who had not immigrated into Korean society and resided in the northeast area of the peninsula.

Korean officials distinguished the area north of the Tumen and Yalu rivers from the area south of the two rivers. North of the rivers was the "kangoe," or "the land beyond the river(s)." Jurchens lived there, and the Chosŏn court considered "there" to be China. For example, Korean officials referred to the kangoe area as "sangguk," or "the superior country," "the country to the north," and "Ming China."[6] From Chosŏn, immigrant Jurchens with government permission could cross the Tumen River and visit their family (pon'ga) or their home village (pont'o). Crossing the river and going ashore constituted crossing a territorial boundary and a jurisdictional boundary, and the wish to do so triggered regulations that the Korean government expected to be followed. This imposition of state oversight offers an example of spatial socialization through the expression of state administration. Other immigrants, though, abandoned their residences and moved north across the river or elsewhere in the peninsula.[7] Jurchens who had not immigrated also travelled north.

Korean officials referred to royal territory as "south of the river(s)" (*kangnae*) or as the "main land" or "Chosŏn" (*naeji*). The island ring was the area close to the peninsula's edge (*yŏnbyŏn*).[8] The expanse of the offshore area was fluid as the court incorporated unpopulated islands in the fifteenth century.[9] The maritime boundary was zonal rather than linear, knowable by presence in royal territory rather than by the point of entry into royal territory.

In the north, the "country's boundary" (*kukkyŏng*) separated the "*kangoe*" and the "*kangnae.*"[10] For the Chosŏn court, the boundary seems to have followed the northern shores of the Yalu and Tumen rivers. To the south, the zonal boundary encompassed islands and the surrounding waters, as regulations regarding Japanese presence in Korean waters and Chosŏn government policies for the island called Tsushima in Japan and Taema-do in Chosŏn and this island's residents suggest.

Important for the reshaping of Chosŏn to be outlined below were Jurchens that resided in "Hamgyŏng Province" but who had not immigrated into Korean society. From 1434 to 1444 the Chosŏn court built six garrisons (*yukchin*) in the province's northeast, in Puryŏng, Hoeryŏng, Chongsŏng, Onsŏng, Kyŏngwŏn, and Kyŏnghŭng. The garrisons were constructed near Jurchen communities. The establishment of Korean administration centers, especially of these garrisons, in northeast Hamgyŏng Province typically is accepted in historical scholarship as resulting in administrative control over the area. Such analyses help identify expressions of jurisdiction. However, they overestimate the Korean government's ability to oversee Jurchen communities. The opening of the garrisons did not result in the equal extension of royal jurisdiction throughout Hamgyŏng Province.

From 1392 there was not one Chosŏn. Two "Chosŏns" may be identified: a territorial Chosŏn and a jurisdictional Chosŏn.[11] The territorial Chosŏn was the royal realm, the area claimed by the Korean king. The territory extended from the islands of Cheju-do and Tsushima (Taema-do) in the maritime south to the northern shores of the Tumen and Yalu rivers.

The jurisdictional Chosŏn was the area within the royal territory that the state administered. However, the jurisdictional Chosŏn did not coincide perfectly with the territorial Chosŏn. That is, royal jurisdiction was incomplete within the territorial Chosŏn. In its first decades, the court added external means of Chosŏn state administration to local forms of administration in Tsushima and Cheju. These included the issuance of Tsushima travel permits (munin) by the governor of Tsushima (J. Shugo) and the dispatch of Korean officials assigned to posts used within Chosŏn to both islands.[12] In the peninsular northeast, the administrative reach of the Korean government into Jurchen villages varied from policy to policy, from community to community, and from family to family where immigrant families lived among non-immigrant families.

There is no evidence available which shows the Chosŏn government in the fifteenth and sixteenth centuries taxing northeastern Jurchens as it taxed Koreans. Immigration brought a three-year exemption from submitting taxes,[13] but how Korean officials collected levies from immigrants or from descendants living among non-immigrant Jurchens is not clear. Royal jurisdiction, however, clearly extended into communities through the court's management of travel to the capital. In other words, the jurisdictional Chosŏn expanded and contracted according to the state's ability to extend administration into each Jurchen village. The mutable jurisdictional Chosŏn in Hamgyŏng Province display the disjuncture between territory and jurisdiction.

Various forms of contact shaped frontiers in the peninsular northeast. For example, the northeast was an economic frontier where Jurchens traded with Korean villagers and with the Korean government for items not readily available otherwise. It was a linguistic frontier of languages spoken by Jurchens and Koreans, and possibly by Chinese (if the people referred to by Korean officials as yangniin were indeed Chinese), and multilingual abilities could serve many purposes. It was a status frontier where Jurchens added status markers bestowed by others—the King of Chosŏn and, in some instances, the Emperor of Ming China—to markers generated within their own communities. Some frontiers extended across the Tumen River and the Amur River and into Jurchen communities. Status and economic frontiers informed each other such as through the linkage between status markers collected externally and trade at the Korean capital. The northeast also was an environmental frontier where Koreans relocated from the south introduced crops and farming methods. Such frontiers were, as is frequently noted in studies of North American history, sites of negotiation, accommodation, and cultural production. Movement back and forth across the rivers also shaped transboundary frontiers in the borderlands into the late sixteenth century.

The boundary between Chosŏn and China did not separate Jurchens from their homelands, relatives, and exchange opportunities. Neither did it prevent the Chosŏn court from permitting Jurchens residing north of the Tumen River, in Ming China, to engage in interactions with the Korean government. The extension of Korean interaction policies into this territory, as during the reign of King Sejo (r. 1455–1468), suggests that Korean officials believed that Chinese expressions of jurisdiction were ineffective. Boundaries were "contextual phenomena" that people and governments inscribed with different meanings in different contexts.[14]

Frontiers could be mobile, too. Korean elites often suggested that exposure to civilized behavior could change Jurchens and Japanese.[15] Demonstration of civilized behavior and its repetition, or the performance of civilization in acts of diplomacy and guest ritual, occurred as Jurchens travelled through regulations up to the King of Chosŏn and through space down to the capital of Chosŏn.

JURCHENS IN INTERACTION POLICIES OF THE CHOSŎN COURT

The multiple Chosŏns may also be identified through the Korean government's interaction policies. The recognition of the distance of Jurchens from royal jurisdiction contributed to the construction and adjustment of regulations for regularized contact. So too did the court's preference not to challenge Jurchens forcefully and not to contest their cultural practices directly. The Chosŏn court decided in the mid-1420s that state finances were better invested in trade than in military defense considering the latter's economic and social costs (such as recruitment). Stated differently, Korean categories of ethnicity in the fifteenth century contributed to the establishment, and later revision of interaction policies.

From the mid-1420s the Chosŏn court permitted Jurchens to engage in sanctioned trade in the capital through a Korean military post bestowed by the monarch. That presentation enrolled individual Jurchens into a hierarchical relationship with the King of Chosŏn. The military post and the regulations for gatherings, gifts, and "promotions" to higher military offices and posts, among other facets of the interaction, placed the recipients in new hierarchical relationships vis-à-vis other Jurchens in their village, in other villages, and in other tribes.

The Korean government adapted this approach from the Ming government's policies toward Jurchen communities in the northeast (and north of Chosŏn) and trade missions sent to the Chinese capital. In the early 1400s the Ming government began reconstituting Jurchen communities as guards, or commanderies (C. *wei*). Elites in those communities received appointments to Chinese military posts; the leader of each new guard gained the highest military post and a seal. All such appointees could visit the Ming capital and trade there.[16] Although the Chosŏn court did not reconstitute Jurchen communities as Korean military institutions, it deployed the military administration system as a foreign policy and as a means of defense. As an element of defense, the appointments encouraged quiet in the northeast in part through the monarch's implicit invitation to trade.

The Chosŏn court's issuance of military posts to Jurchens followed the same regulations as the appointments to Koreans. Kings and the Ministry of Military Affairs (Pyŏngjo) presented an office warrant (*kosin*) to the Jurchen. If the military post was of the junior fourth rank or higher, the king bestowed the office warrant. If the post was of the senior fifth rank or lower, the Ministry of Military Affairs issued the office warrant upon royal approval.[17] There appear to be no extant office warrants issued to Jurchens. The contents of extant office warrants for Japanese issued military posts did not differ in form or content from those presented to Korean officials, and evidence suggests the same for office warrants issued to Jurchens.[18] From the next visit to the Korean capital, the Jurchen always had to present the office warrant in order to appear before the King of Chosŏn. The office warrant became the key to access to the capital and opportunities for sanctioned and illicit trade.[19]

From the mid-1420s the Chosŏn court opened for Jurchen appointments the Five Military Commands (Owi) and the Manho series of provincial military posts: Tomanho, Manho, and Pumanho. In the mid-1450s the court began regularly issuing posts in the Office of Ministers-without-Portfolio (Chungch'ubu or Chungch'uwŏn).[20] As did the Ming court, the Korean government "promoted" Jurchens through a hierarchy of offices and posts. Most initial grants enrolled them in the Five Military Commands. The court frequently promoted recipients to higher-ranking posts in the Five Military Commands and from the Five Military Commands into the Manho series. However, the Chosŏn government advanced Jurchens from the Manho series into the Office of Ministers-without-Portfolio less often. The Office of Ministers-without-Portfolio posts opened to Jurchens were of ministerial rank (tangsanggwan).

The court demarcated status within the appointment system through these offices and their post ranks. Among the Five Military Commands posts, the most important division occurred at the junior fourth rank. At the senior fifth rank and below were the military officer posts, or those for which the Ministry of Military Affairs issued the office warrants. Most Jurchens received their initial appointment to one of these military officer posts. Superior to the military officer posts were the four deputy commander posts in the Five Military Commands from the fourth rank to the senior third rank. As of 1455/3, at least fifty-six Jurchens held one of the deputy commander posts and at least 127 Jurchens held one of the military officer posts.

The Tomanho and Pumanho posts were not listed among the army or navy posts in the Kyŏngguk taejŏn (Great Code of Administration); they had been eliminated or renamed by early 1485, when the law code was printed.[21] Despite their removal from the military bureaucracy, kings continued to appoint Jurchen elites as Tomanho and Pumanho. However, the monarch bestowed the Tomanho post grant primarily upon Uryangkhad and Odoli chieftains leading communities in the Hoeryŏng area.[22] That is, the Korean government used military posts as a means to identify and demarcate Jurchen forms of status.

The court further accentuated distinctions and lengthened the status hierarchy by regularly placing Jurchen elites in Office of Ministers-without-Portfolio posts. At least twelve Jurchens active in the mid-fifteenth century gained these appointments; eight of them were chieftains or sons of chieftains. Seven of these eight individuals received posts in the Five Military Commands, the Manho series, and the Office of Ministers-without-Portfolio over their careers. As the Korean government promoted Jurchens through the military posts, officials paid careful attention to their status in the home community and to the court's patterns of bestowal.

According to an incomplete count, the Chosŏn court appointed 675 Jurchens to at least twenty-two different posts between 1395/12 and 1554/5.[23]

The court issued the highest number of posts to the Uryangkhad and Odoli communities near Hoeryŏng. This stemmed from factors that included the population surge which had resulted from the return of the powerful Odoli chieftain, Tong Mongke Temur, and his community to the Hoeryŏng area in 1423, the increase in interaction that followed, and the concern for Uryangkhad and Odoli violence. It thus was soon after the return of this Odoli community that the court chose trade over constant military readiness and coupled the nominal post with sanctioned trade at court. As an element of defense the bestowals encouraged quiet in the northeast, in part through the court's implicit guarantee of exchange.

While these Jurchens could travel to the capital, meet the monarch, and conduct trade at court, the Korean government did not extend the same privileges to Korean military officials. Furthermore, unlike Koreans who held the same military posts, the Jurchens did not perform military duties for the Korean government. Their appointments were nominal. These appointments could also be honorary, as were the rewards for assistance during the 1460 campaign against an Uryangkhad community in Hadongnyang, near Musan. At the same time, the court applied regulations designed for Korean military men to Jurchen post recipients. For example, Jurchens holding posts in the Office of Ministers-without-Portfolio received a stipend (nokpong).[24] And like Korean military men, Jurchens holding a Manho series post did not receive a stipend.[25]

TRAVELING UP TO THE KING

Unable to recognize Jurchen community leaders as rulers, the court used the military posts as a means to structure foreign relations and compose hierarchical relationships. As these Jurchens moved through regulations and guest rituals up to the king and through space southward to the capital, the Korean government conducted diplomacy under the guise of dealings with royal subjects. The use of government posts for organizing foreign relations blurred distinctions between domestic administration and diplomacy.

When traveling to the Korean capital, Jurchens had to follow Korean government regulations in order to trade at court. They also had to perform appropriately at the gatherings in the guest ritual itinerary. Continued movement through space was dependent upon the continued permission of progress through guest ritual.

The Chosŏn court in 1445/11 limited the annual number of passages to the capital per tribe.[26] In 1474/9, the court introduced a policy of seasonal travel in which Jurchens could depart only in the eighth lunar month, and they were permitted only two or three missions per month. That policy came under revision less than two weeks later. The revision dictated that Jurchen missions could now depart only after the harvest had been completed.[27] And by or in 1528/2 the court introduced quotas for departure from five garrisons based upon each year's harvest. In years of good harvest, a total of seventeen missions could proceed to the capital, four each from Hoeryŏng and Chongsŏng and three each from Onsŏng, Kyŏngwŏn, and Kyŏnghŭng. The total number of Jurchens in these seventeen missions was not to exceed 120 people. In years of lean harvest, only twelve missions could depart, three each from Hoeryŏng and Chongsŏng, and two each from Onsŏng, Kyŏngwŏn, and Kyŏnghŭng. The number of Jurchens in the total of twelve missions was not to exceed ninety people.[28] The court shifted from travel quotas based upon tribes, to travel quotas based upon the garrisons of departure.[29] The higher totals for Hoeryŏng and Chongsŏng bespeak the larger Jurchen populations there than in other districts.

As the departure sites suggest, the court assigned Jurchen communities to nearby garrisons. When a post recipient wanted to proceed to the Korean capital, he, together with other community members, went first to the garrison. There the post holders presented the office warrants. Jurchens continued from the village to the garrison without direct Korean oversight, but their movements began with the acceptance of certain requirements: (1) carry the office warrant (and court clothing, if issued, for the appearance before the king) and (2) arrive at the specified administration center. The office warrant enabled transit at state expense and trade in the capital. This document also functioned as a kind of travel pass to the capital.

A military installation served as the point of entry into full Korean oversight of the passages up to and down from the King of Chosŏn. The presiding military official met the Jurchens outside the garrison, in the "Yain'gwan," or Jurchen Hall. These gatherings outside the walls of the administration center distanced the guests from local populations, hid administrative and military details, and reduced security concerns.[30] From the garrison the Jurchens moved along Korean government post roads (yŏngno) that took them to Hoeryŏng or to Puryŏng. They continued southward along the post road to

Kyŏngsŏng. From Kyŏngsŏng, they proceeded southward into Kangwŏn Province, turned westward in Yangyang, headed toward Kyŏnggi Province, and eventually entered the capital.[31] The travelers were to rest at administration centers and not stay overnight in villages.[32] It would seem likely that other Chosŏn government officials, in addition to local interpreters (hyang t'ongsa), guided these retinues.[33]

As they proceeded up to the king, Jurchen recipients of Korean military posts participated in receptions (chŏptae) hosted by various Korean government officials. These gatherings combined diplomacy and domestic governance. The placement of participants began with the highest-ranking Chosŏn government official present. Concerns of rank among Koreans, among Jurchens, and between Koreans and Jurchens had to be carefully considered and spatially expressed through the placement of the participants. The court organized the seating hierarchy for Jurchens according to their Korean military post and, when relevant, the Chinese military post.[34]

In regulations introduced in 1442/10 (or as recommended—the entry in the veritable records does not indicate King Sejong's response to the Ministry of Rites' Memorial), the Jurchen Tomanho sat superior to other Jurchen post recipients. For example, when a Korean provincial official (oegwan) in a post of the second rank or higher sat at north, the Tomanho sat at east, Jurchens holding Chinese military posts sat at west, and the Manho sat at south. When the highest-ranking Korean official present was a military official (pyŏnjang) of the fourth rank or higher, he sat in the east, the Tomanho sat at west, and the Manho and Jurchens holding Chinese military posts sat at south. If a Tomanho was not present, the Korean military official sat at north and Jurchens holding Chinese military posts and the Manho sat at west. Also, when a county magistrate (suryŏng) of the third rank or lower was present, he sat at west, the Tomanho sat at east, and Jurchens holding Chinese military posts and the Manho sat at south. If the Korean provincial official was of the fourth rank or lower, he sat at east and the Manho and Jurchens holding Chinese military posts sat at west.[35]

The spatial arrangement of Jurchens at these state gatherings followed a hierarchy starting with the government post held by the Korean host. The location of the host depended in certain cases upon the presence or absence of a Jurchen Tomanho. That is, in 1442/10, the Tomanho post was the highest Korean military post to which the court appointed Jurchens. The Jurchen

Tomanho official always sat separate from other Jurchens. The seating arrangements embedded Jurchen recipients among Korean officials. The Chosŏn court also recognized and constituted, in a Korean venue, both the hierarchy of Jurchen post recipients within the Korean military administration system and the hierarchy within Jurchen communities.

The seating arrangements introduced in 1472/3 (or recommended by the Ministry of Rites) reflected changes in the court's military post appointments. This reform occurred after two years of revisions to the maritime reception system for Japanese and Ryukyuans and approximately three months after King Sŏngjong had accepted the Haedong chegukki (Records of Countries across the Seas to the East), a handbook for relations with Japan and Ryukyu that included regulations for travel and seating. In the 1472/3 arrangements, the court placed Jurchens holding posts in the Office of Ministers-without-Portfolio, but did not place Jurchens holding Chinese military posts. This most certainly was because Jurchens with Chinese military posts no longer appeared at court regularly, if at all.

This time the Ministry of Rites mapped the physical dispositions and chairs for eight placements in the room. Positioning the Jurchens had become more complicated since 1442/10 because people bearing a wider range of Korean military posts at a broader range of ranks could be present. That is, Jurchens now held posts of ministerial rank in the Office of Ministers-without-Portfolio. The ministry expanded the space available for seating (if not in 1472/3 then earlier) and arrayed the participants to reflect more finely the proprieties of rank as expressed through the appointments.

For example, at meetings presided over by the army commander, who was in charge of that province's military forces (Pyŏngma Chŏltosa, Jr. 2), or by the provincial governor (Kwanch'alsa or Kamsa, Jr. 2), the host sat at north and Jurchens holding posts of ministerial rank sat at west, but in a row behind Korean officials also of ministerial rank. When hosted by a district magistrate of ministerial rank, the Korean official sat at north and Jurchens holding posts of ministerial rank sat at west. Also, the court separated Jurchens holding posts of the fourth rank and higher from those holding posts of the fifth rank and lower. Differing from the procedures outlined in 1442/10, in none of the mappings from 1472/3 were Jurchens to be seated in the chair (kyoŭi) of higher status.[36]

In the capital, the court lodged Jurchens at the Hall of Northern Peace (Pukp'yŏnggwan). Upon appropriately performing the prescribed activities, movements, and vocalizations at the royal audience, which were requirements that both reiterated a discourse of power which distinguished the guests from Koreans and underlined the interaction as foreign relations, Jurchens could engage in sanctioned trade with the government.[37] It may perhaps be assumed, though, that not every Jurchen participant fully accepted the physical and verbal expressions of subordination demanded of them by the King of Chosŏn. The preference among some Jurchens for trade over expressions of respect is described below.

An important feature of interaction in the capital was, of course, the exchange of gifts. In 1446/1, Korean officials calibrated return gifts for Jurchens according to the source of the military post and that military post's rank. This hierarchical division of Jurchens followed the hierarchies of offices and posts in the Chinese and Korean militaries. The gifting regime organized Jurchens into three grades based upon their Korean or Chinese posts. The grades determined the court clothing, shoes, and other items to be bestowed upon the individual. Grade 1 encompassed Jurchens holding the Tomanho post or any of the three posts comprising the Ming government's Regional Military Commission (C. Duzhihuishisi), which were of the senior second rank, junior second rank, and senior third rank, respectively. Grade 2 included Jurchens appointed to posts in the Korean deputy commander series—first deputy commander (Sanghogun, Sr. 3, lower), second deputy commander (Taehogun, Jr. 3), and third deputy commander (Hogun, Sr. 4), and the next two posts in the Manho series, Manho and Pumanho. Grade 3 included Jurchens appointed as fifth rank military officers, sixth rank military officers, seventh rank military officers, and eighth rank military officers (Sajik, Pusajik, Sajŏng, and Pusajŏng), and individuals without military posts.[38] The absence of posts in the Office of Ministers-without-Portfolio suggests that despite at least one earlier bestowal the court had not yet begun to systematically issue those appointments.

The Jurchens departed the capital upon completing the guest ritual calendar and other events that may have been included in their schedule. Little information is available about the movement down from the king and up to the garrison in Hamgyŏng Province, but it may be assumed that a local interpreter and perhaps other government officials escorted the Jurchens. The same or similar regulations and schedules for state gatherings likely punctuated the return. However, some Jurchens who moved through the guest rituals and bowed to the King of Chosŏn claimed to be other people.

MANIPULATING KOREAN MILITARY POSTS

The mobile frontier, of Korean officials seeking to impress civilized forms of behavior upon Jurchen elites as the guests proceeded up to and down from the king and to and from the capital, may not have been as successful as Korean officials hoped. For some Jurchens the intersection of the economic and status frontiers, particularly in the Office of Ministers-without-Portfolio, proved enticing. Such men explored ways of stretching regulations so to gain entry into the capital, to collect stipend disbursements, and to engage in exchange in the capital.[39] Trade and its utility in the community almost certainly inspired these explorations. While there were many individual strategies, the discussion below will focus broadly on three tactics by which Jurchens utilized Korean regulations.

In the first approach, members of the Hurhan Wudiha tribe took advantage of the Chosŏn court's limited knowledge of Jurchen guards in Ming China. They invented guards, affixed names to those guards, and posed as Jurchens holding Chinese posts and serving in those non-existent guards. One measure of success was the sudden increase in missions in the late 1430s and early 1440s.[40] The Ministry of Rites complained in 1439/4 that it was difficult to determine who was being truthful and who was not, and that receptions at court had become a problem.[41] Hurhan Wudiha Jurchens deployed both Chinese and Korean regulations to increase the frequency and the amount of exchange in the Korean capital.

New trends in Hurhan Wudiha trade appeared in 1461. After 1443, Hurhan Wudiha elites had stopped sending trade missions to the capital. Eighteen years later, contacts identifying themselves as Hurhan Wudiha tribal members began regularly sending missions and receiving military posts. Kawachi Yoshihiro suspects that Uryangkhad elites created these identities and sent missions in the guise of Hurhan Wudiha elites.[42] Following Kawachi in suggesting that those contacts were not members of Hurhan Wudiha communities, one possible reason for the appropriation of these distant communities may be the ceiling on the number of trade missions that communities could send each year. The quotas imposed by the court in 1445/11 for yearly missions restricted Uryangkhad to ten retinues and Hurhan Wudiha and Odoli each to seven.[43] Those who traded through forged Hurhan Wudiha identities in the 1460s may have been tapping the unused quota for the Hurhan Wudiha. If they did, the participants added to the frequency and the volume of trade that could be conducted annually. A second possible contributing reason for these missions may have been the lack of current information about the Hurhan Wudiha communities and elites among Korean officials in Hamgyŏng Province and at court.

Finally, Jurchens maneuvered solely within Korean regulations. In some instances, individuals exposed by court officials had presented office warrants that had been purchased, borrowed, or obtained through other means.[44] In one case, an Uryangkhad called Numuhe presented an office warrant that had been altered. This writ of appointment included the military prestige title Pogong Changgun, which was at the junior third rank, lower and the military post of first deputy commander. The Ministry of Rites noted that this post could not be attached to a prestige title, and later stated that the holder had purchased the office warrant from another Uryangkhad.[45] A desire for trade and benefits from the goods obtained in the capital almost certainly inspired this forging of a superior deputy commander post, one that presumably provided better perquisites. Depending upon the context in which individuals gained an office warrant, they may also have claimed and posed as a status above their standing in the community.

A case of fraudulent identification exposed in 1485/11 displays promotion practices at court and document preservation practices among Jurchens. That year, the Ministry of Rites discovered that a visiting Jurchen had presented an office warrant which had been issued to another Jurchen in 1459. The recipient of that 1459 warrant, an Uryangkhad named Yuandousha, visited in 1457 bearing a military post warrant issued by the Ming court. He departed with a Pumanho appointment.[46] Yuandousha returned in 1459, and received a prestige title and the post of first deputy commander in the Five Military Commands. At that time, Yuandousha stated that he did not know his father's name.[47] Yuandousha traveled to the Korean capital again in 1483. He received a promotion to a higher-ranking prestige title and promotion to fifth minister in the Office of Ministers-without-Portfolio, a senior third rank post. This time, Yuandousha stated that his father was Dayangjie, who had received the post of fifth rank military officer. The man posing as Yuandousha who arrived in late 1485 made the mistake of not presenting the 1483 office warrant. Instead, he presented the 1459 office warrant, which was no longer valid. Further, he stated that his father was General (*sangjang*) Choujiayingju. The Ministry of Rites believed that the man had borrowed an old office warrant and pronounced that office warrant "fraudulent" (*sawi*).[48]

Jurchens continued to greet the King of Chosŏn through office warrants issued to others. According to Korean officials in 1527/1, in Onsŏng only three or four of some seventy writs of appointment reviewed by court officials were valid. Moreover, of nearly one hundred Jurchens whom officials in Hamgyŏng Province had recently sent up to the king, about thirty presented themselves as holders of posts in the Office of Ministers-without-Portfolio. One Korean official recognized the plight of those provincial officials, noting that officials who sent imposters to the capital would be punished, but if they halted the missions of fraudulent post recipients the provincial officials would have invited disturbances "day and night."[49] These examples indicate that the Korean government could not control the circulation or improper use of fraudulent office warrants in the peninsular northeast.

In such instances Chosŏn government officials met with the "subjects of the King" who carried office warrants that were not their own. These Jurchens exercised the appointment for the economic and other benefits that could accrue. Similar intentions may be revealed in the preservation of office warrants for the Office of Ministers-without-Portfolio posts. The large number of those office warrants available suggests that bestowal had expanded beyond tribal chieftains and their sons to a broader range of community elites. The large number strongly suggests that the Chosŏn court provided better gifting and trade privileges for holders of Office of Ministers-without-Portfolio posts than for holders of the Manho series or Five Military Commands posts. Trade attracted Jurchens to the Korean capital. Significant for a more complex and more complete history of the peninsular northeast are such manipulations of Chosŏn court policies. Status, economic, and administrative frontiers merged in these strategies.

To summarize, military post appointments were instruments by which Chosŏn royal authority and royal jurisdiction reached into Jurchen communities. The bestowal of these titles inserted the recipients into domestic administration policies designed for Korean recipients of military posts. Second, appointments permitted recipients to engage in trade in the Korean capital. The policy brought these Jurchens physically before the King of Chosŏn and manufactured opportunities for monarchs and high-ranking officials to meet, communicate with, and potentially influence tribal members, as well as collect information from them. The Chosŏn court treated Jurchen post recipients as royal subjects and as non-Koreans. This provided Jurchen elites with privileges because of their presence in Chosŏn and their standing outside of Korean society. The absence of military duties underscored the nominal nature of the appointments and the limited nature of the individuals' relationship with the King of Chosŏn as his "subject." The Chosŏn court marked ethnicity by distinguishing privileges that accompanied appointments to military posts. Jurchens accepted this extension of royal authority into their villages and into their families for several possible reasons including trade and the accumulation of other benefits that would follow.

CONCLUSION

"Hamgyŏng Province," in particular the northeastern corner where Jurchen communities concentrated, was a frontier zone of interaction. Significantly, the Chosŏn state did not attempt to impose cultural transformation upon Jurchens. Stated differently, in the eyes of the Chosŏn government, the presence of multiple ethnic groups did not pose problems that required immediate solutions.

Jurchen residence necessitated that the Chosŏn court design ways to channel contact into acceptable forms and observable locations. The first two centuries of Chosŏn government rule in the northeastern province can be distinguished in part by sanctioned, managed interaction with non-Korean residents. The court had no alternative but to continue encouraging trade, having, as in the south, chosen trade over constant military readiness.

The Jurchen communities in the northeast were multi-localic places inscribed with meanings by Jurchens and by Koreans.[50] Further, with the frequent crossing into Chosŏn and (back) into China, what was "north" or "northern" to Koreans likely was "south" or "southern" to Jurchens for whom relatives, home villages, ancestral communities, allies, enemies, and other connections were north and/or south of the Tumen and Yalu rivers. "Hamgyŏng Province" can also be spatialized in terms of cultural and economic zones that stretched across the Tumen River. During these two centuries the peninsular northeast was unlike any other region in "Chosŏn," its multiple histories unlike other regional histories in the peninsula.

NOTES

*Parts of this chapter were first presented as "Distinguishing Local and Central in 'Hamgyong Province' in the 'Early Choson Period': Jurchens, Koreans, and Foreign Relations in the Peninsula" at the New Dimensions in Korean Historiography conference, P'ohang, Republic of Korea, October 10–13, 2002. This conference was sponsored by the Research Center for the Humanities, Sogang University and the Center for Korean Studies, University of Hawai'i at Manoa. I would like to thank the organizers of the 2002 conference again for that opportunity.

1. The Chosŏn court called this province by different names in the fifteenth and sixteenth centuries. For the sake of simplicity, it will be referred to here as Hamgyŏng Province.

2. See Forbes, "Frontiers in American History and the Role of the Frontier Historian," 203–35.

3. For early English language contributions see Robinson, "From Raiders to Traders," 94–115; Duncan, "Hyanghwain: Migration and Assimilation in Chosŏn Korea," 99–113; and Kyung Moon Hwang, "From the Dirt to Heaven," 135–78.

4. Sahlins, Boundaries, 1–7.

5. For a recent example of scholarship that treats Chosŏn as a complete administrative space, as the space depicted in textbook maps and other texts, see Pang Tong'in, Hanguk ŭi kukkyŏng hoekchŏng yŏn'gu 219–28

6. Sejong sillok, 4:113, 1437/11/3; Sejong sillok, 4:646, 1445/12/4; Sŏngjong sillok, 9:555, 1477/5/1; and Sinjŭng Tongguk yŏji sŭngnam, 42:32a–b.

7. For an example see Sŏngjong sillok, 10:314, 1482/4/4.

8. Munjong sillok, 6:419, 1451/8/9.

9. Chang Hakkŭn, "Sejong-Sŏngjong nyŏn'gan ŭi sindo sut'am chŏngch'aek," 17–19.

10. Munjong sillok, 6:482, 1452/4/7.

11. This paragraph and the next are from Robinson, "An Island's Place in History," 42–43. A geomantic Chosŏn is also discussed in this article.

12. For Cheju see Takahashi, "Chōsen gaikō chitsujo to Higashi Ajia kaiiki no kōryū," 68–69; and Pettid, "Vengeful Gods and Shrewd Men," 171–75.

13. Kyŏngguk taejŏn, 2:16a.

14. Paasi, "Boundaries as Social Processes: Territoriality in the World of Flows," 72.

15. For an example see *Sŏngjong sillok*, 11:203, 1487/4/15.

16. In English see Rossabi, *The Jurchens in the Yüan and Ming*, 16–18.

17. *Kyŏngguk taejŏn*, 3:52b–53a.

18. *Sŏngjong sillok*, 11:74, 1485/11/15; and *Chungjong sillok*, 16:546, 1527/1/11.

19. For an example of illicit trade in Seoul see *Sŏngjong sillok*, 9:199, 1475/2/17. Also see Yi Inyŏng, *Han'guk Manju kwan'gyesa ŭi yŏn'gu*, 40–48.

20. The earliest confirmed appointment of a Jurchen to the Office of Ministers-without-Portfolio occurred in 1441. *Sejong sillok*, 4:342, 1441/5/11. The next confirmed assignment was in 1454. *Tanjong sillok*, 6:715, 1454/12/27. All other confirmed appointments appear in records from 1455 and later.

21. *Kyŏngguk taejŏn*, 4:6b–15a. The court renamed the Tomanho navy post in the 1466/1 reform of the military bureaucracy. *Sejo sillok*, 8:2, 1466/1/15.

22. Woodruff, "Status and Lineage among the Jurchens of the Korean Northeast in the Mid-fifteenth Century," 131.

23. Yu Pong'yŏng, "Wangjo sillok e nat'anan Yijo chŏn'gi ŭi Yain," 93.

24. *Sejo sillok*, 7:299, 1458/10/17 and 8:2, 1466/1/10.

25. *Sejo sillok*, 8:2, 1466/1/10.

26. *Sejong sillok*, 4:643, 1445/11/1.

27. *Sŏngjong sillok*, 9:149, 1474/9/27 and 9:152, 1474/10/7.

28. *Chungjong sillok*, 16:625, 1528/2/5; and Ŏ Sukkwŏn, *Kosa ch'waryo*, 2:42b–43a.

29. Annual retinue quotas based upon the year's harvest may have been introduced prior to 1528/2. The court seems to have permitted Jurchens a total of twelve retinues during years of good harvests and a total of nine during years of lean harvests, with seven or eight individuals in each retinue. *Chungjong sillok*, 16:5, 1527/1/11.

30. Yi Inyŏng, *Han'guk Manju kwan'gyesa ŭi yŏn'gu*, 36; Yi Hyŏnhŭi, "Chosŏn wangjo sidae ŭi Pukp'yŏnggwan Yain: kŭ sumuch'aek iltan," 128–33; and *Munjong sillok*, 6:419, 1451/8/9; *Sejo sillok*, 7:371, 1460/2/19.

31. *Sejong sillok*, 119:6b, 1448/1/28.

32. *Kyŏngguk taejŏn*, 3:33b.

33. *Sejong sillok*, 3:44, 1426/9/22; *Kyŏngguk taejŏn*, 3:33a; and *Sŏngjong sillok*, 11:75, 1485/11/17.

34. *Sejong sillok, Orye pillye ŭisik yŏn inguksa ŭi*, 5:354–55.

35. *Sejong sillok*, 4:442, 1442/10/25. The Ming government post cited in this entry was a generic term for a series of military posts in the Regional Military Commission and Guard. The posts ranged from senior second rank to senior fourth rank. See *Da Ming huidian*, 118:2b.

36. *Sŏngjong sillok*, 8:642, 1472/3/10; *Kyŏngguk taejŏn*, 3:50a–b.

37. For movement and vocalizations at Chinese guest ritual see Hevia, *Cherishing Men from Afar*.

38. *Sejong sillok*, 4:649, 1446/1/10; and Kawachi, *Mindai Joshinshi no kenkyū*, 434. The English language translations of the posts in the military officer series reflect the posts' ranks prior to the 1466/1 reform of the military bureaucracy. The translations provided by Edward Willett Wagner in *The Literati Purges: Political Conflict in Early Yi Korea*, 126, are for the military series posts after the 1466/1 reform. The Ming court, presumably at an earlier date, divided Jurchens into five grades for gifting purposes. Grade 1 included senior first rank and junior first rank posts in the highest military office. Grade 2 included senior second rank posts in the Five Chief Military Commissions and the Regional Military Commissions. Grade 3 included posts from junior second rank through senior fourth rank in the Regional Military Commissions and the Guards. Grade 4 included the lowest-ranking post, at junior fifth rank, in the guards and the brigades. The lowest grade included guests without a military appointment. *Da Ming huidian* 111:16b.

39. See Kawachi, *Mindai Joshinshi no kenkyū*, 443–44.

40. Kawachi, *Mindai Joshinshi no kenkyū*, 300–21.

41. *Sejong sillok*, 4:209, 1439/4/27.

42. Kawachi, *Mindai Joshinshi no kenkyū*, 293–300.

43. *Sejong sillok*, 4:643, 1445/11/1.

44. *Sŏngjong sillok*, 11:74, 1485/11/15 and 11:575, 1490/2/26.

45. *Sŏngjong sillok*, 11:74, 1485/11/15 and 11:575, 1490/2/26; and *Kyŏngguk taejŏn*, 4:1b.

46. *Sejo sillok*, 7:164, 1457/1/7 and 7:180, 1457/2/29. Yuandousha's Ming government military post is given as "Zhihui" in the Korean veritable records. As Pumanho was of the junior fourth rank, this term may refer to "Zhihuishi," or the guard commander in the Guards, a post which was of the senior third rank.

47. *Sŏngjong sillok*, 11:74, 1485/11/15 and *Sejo sillok*, 7:352, 1459/10/21.

48. *Sŏngjong sillok*, 11:74, 1485/11/15.

49. *Chungjong sillok*, 16:546, 1527/1/11.

50. Rodman, "Empowering Place: Multilocality and Multivocality," 643–44 and 647; and Douglass, "A Western Perspective on an Eastern Interpretation of Where North Meets South," 90.

2

Chosŏn-Qing Relations and the Society of P'yŏngan Province During the Late Chosŏn Period

KWON NAEHYUN

INTRODUCTION

Envoys traveling between Chosŏn (1392–1910) and Qing (1644–1912) in the late Chosŏn period moved along a route between Seoul and Beijing that passed through P'yŏngan Province. The remaining seven provinces of the Chosŏn Dynasty did not participate in the tributary missions as actively as P'yŏngan did. The people of the southern provinces were largely excluded from relations with China, and although a portion of Hamgyŏng Province had trade relations with China, this area did not include the important routes of envoys and merchants. Kyŏnggi and Hwanghae provinces were also on the route of the embassies, but given the short distances over which envoys traveled in these provinces, this activity was of relatively modest importance.

P'yŏngan Province had been a strategically important region that was the first line of defense against invasion from northern peoples. After Chosŏn was defeated by the Later Jin[1] (1616–1636), however, the military importance of the region was greatly reduced. By the time the defense system was restored, Chosŏn and Qing had entered into a long period of peaceful relations. Thus in the late Chosŏn period the role of P'yŏngan Province in diplomatic and commercial affairs grew in importance while its military functions diminished.

The people of P'yŏngan Province had to bear enormous burdens in providing support for diplomatic and trade relations with the Qing, but these very burdens also presented opportunities for regional economic growth. Residents of the province took advantage of their geopolitical location and were able to accumulate wealth through trade and commercial enterprise. Their economic resources consequently supported cultural growth. This in turn frustrated the P'yŏngan elite because they were politically and socially discriminated against by the central elite in the capital (see the discussion in Chapters 3 and 4).

This chapter examines the effects of the development of Chosŏn-Qing relations on the society of P'yŏngan Province. What were the regional burdens imposed by the diplomatic and trade relations between the two countries, and what did the P'yŏngan people receive in return? How did these diplomatic and trade dynamics change the regional economy and the lives of the people? The answers shed light on the nature of P'yŏngan society and its connections to Chosŏn-Qing relations, providing insight into the background of the rebellions of the early nineteenth century.

CHOSŎN-QING RELATIONS
AND THEIR IMPACT ON P'YŎNGAN PROVINCE

Chosŏn faced China across its northern border, and it was P'yŏngan Province that was most affected by its relations with the Chinese dynasties and the Jurchen tribal people. The expansion of the Later Jin and two subsequent Manchu invasions in the early seventeenth century placed great military and financial burdens on the region. Chosŏn's relations with the Manchus were based on disdain, distrust, and military confrontation, especially after King Injo (r. 1623–1649) and his supporters took power in 1623, resulting in Chosŏn's humiliating subjugation to the Qing in 1636. From the time the Qing defeated Chosŏn to the time it occupied Beijing in 1644, the Manchu court sent more envoys to Chosŏn than in any other period, in an effort to maintain surveillance there. As it came to rule over the Chinese mainland, the Qing loosened its controls over Chosŏn, though the frequency of Qing embassies remained high into the early eighteenth century. Chosŏn could not but respond in kind by dispatching frequent envoys to the Qing court as well.

The situation had begun to change by the middle of the eighteenth century. The Chosŏn court saw that the Qing would not fall easily and had little reason to again invade Chosŏn territory. Increasingly confident in its control of the mainland and the much-enhanced state power, the Qing court maintained only a minor interest in Chosŏn affairs and did not even object to Chosŏn's attempts to strengthen its own defenses. This marked the beginning of a very long period of peace between the two countries, and the frequency of embassies between the two states dropped dramatically as a result. Because it profited considerably from the trade that went on in association with the embassies, however, Chosŏn sought to maintain a set frequency of missions.[2]

Chosŏn-Qing relations in this period gradually shifted from military clashes and diplomatic tension to long-term peace. How did this change affect Chosŏn's domestic society? Military and diplomatic affairs were generally managed by the central government, but in Chosŏn some responsibilities were relegated to provincial and district governments as well. When Later Jin power had first been on the rise, Chosŏn military planners had expected an invasion through Hamgyŏng Province, but as the Later Jin turned its attention to China, P'yŏngan Province became the focus of defensive considerations.[3] Moreover, when the military operations of Ming General Mao Wenlong were physically based in P'yŏngan Province, this region directly faced the crisis of war and resulting financial burdens. Two Manchu armies ultimately passed through on route from Ŭiju, a border town, to Seoul, leaving the P'yŏngan Region in ruin.

The same route was also used by diplomatic missions of the two countries in times of peace. Although the route passed through P'yŏngan, Hwanghae, and a part of Kyŏnggi Province, P'yŏngan played a central role not only as the border province but in a diplomatic capacity as well. This can be confirmed in part by the number of days embassies spent in each province. Table 2.1 shows the number of days Qing envoys spent in each province during the course of their missions to Chosŏn.[4] The most notable aspect of Table 2.1 is the dramatic decrease in the number of Qing embassies. From the immediate postwar period to the eighteenth century, the frequency of embassies dropped by half, and almost stopped entirely during the first half of the nineteenth century. The number of days each embassy spent in Chosŏn also dropped precipitously.

The Qing embassies to Chosŏn spent the most time in P'yŏngan Province. Although diplomatic matters were discussed in the capital, activities to welcome envoys as they arrived and to send them off as they departed took place in P'yŏngan. The entire province, even those areas not directly on the route between Ŭiju and Chunghwa, had to be mobilized to provide men, horses, and supplies to the embassies as they passed through.[5] Hwanghae Province had fewer responsibilities than P'yŏngan for hosting and supplying Qing embassies; Kyŏnggi had fewer still because envoys traveled only the short distance from its northern provincial boundary to Seoul, the capital. The regions south of the capital, especially the three southern provinces, were not directly affected by the Qing embassies.[6]

Table 2.1 Qing Embassies to Chosŏn

Time period	Average length of mission in days	Average number of embassies per year	Annual average sojourn by region in days			
			P'yŏngan	Hwanghae	Kyŏnggi	Seoul
1637–1656	44.6	2.30	36.1	22.3	16.8	27.4
1717–1736	32.4	1.15	14.4	8.9	6.6	7.5
1837–1856	28.2	0.30	3.7	2.3	1.7	0.8

The route traveled by Qing envoys between Ŭiju and the capital was the same one traveled by Chosŏn envoys on their way to the Qing court, so the role of P'yŏngan Province was doubly important in Chosŏn-Qing relations. The length of Chosŏn embassies to the Qing are given in Table 2.2.

Table 2.2 shows the itinerary of Chosŏn embassies traveling to and from Beijing based on data taken from the diaries of envoys.[7] The Chosŏn envoys stayed for more than a month in Beijing and spent considerable time traveling the long road between Zhamen (K. Ch'aengmun) and Beijing.[8] Within Chosŏn, they spent the most time in P'yŏngan Province. Moreover, the journey from the Yalu River to Zhamen was undertaken with men and supplies from the town of Ŭiju in P'yŏngan.

Table 2.2 Chosŏn Embassy's Sojourn in Days by Region

Year	Kyŏnggi	Hwanghae	P'yŏngan	Yalu River ↔ Zhamen	Zhamen ↔ Beijing	Beijing	Total
1656	5	7	22	3	58	36	131
1712	5	7	28	2	56	47	145
1777	5	8	32	2	61	43	151
1828	6	10	35	2	64	39	156

Unlike the Qing embassies to Chosŏn, the Chosŏn embassies to the Qing became longer as time went on. Comparing the embassy of 1777 to that of 1656, Table 2.2 shows that the itinerary had increased by twenty days, with ten of those additional days spent in P'yŏngan Province. The amount of time spent in other provinces changed little, indicating the growing importance of P'yŏngan Province in the execution of the embassies. The increased responsibility that the province took on during this period was related directly to matters of trade.

Within P'yŏngan Province, the embassies stayed the longest in the town of Ŭiju. The Chosŏn embassy of 1656 stayed in Ŭiju for three days, whereas the embassy of 1777 stayed ten. From this time onward, the stay in Ŭiju continually increased. Located south of the Yalu River, Ŭiju was the entry port where official documents were prepared, personnel and horses inspected, and welcome and farewell banquets held. Thus embassies spent more time there than any other place within Chosŏn. The principal reason for lengthening the stay in Ŭiju, however, was the inspection of merchandise belonging to private Ŭiju merchants (mansang). Much time was spent monitoring the merchants' provisions and merchandise in an effort to prevent illegal trade.

At the core of the Qing trade were the transactions carried out during the course of the Chosŏn embassies. This embassy trade was conducted in various ways in Zhamen, Shenyang, and Beijing. Interpreters (yŏkkwan) initially dominated this trade but gradually yielded ground to private merchants (sasang) and lost their commanding position. The private merchants, who profited enormously through this trade, either legally or otherwise, were primarily from Ŭiju and Kaesŏng.[9]

The P'yŏngan Provincial Governor's Office (Kamyŏng), the Provincial Military Command (Pyŏngyŏng), and the Ŭiju Magistracy all had the authority to conduct embassy trade in Shenyang. The Ŭiju Magistracy was especially active in the trade at Zhamen as a means of augmenting its fiscal resources. The magistrate's office charged a fixed sum in silver for each packhorse that traveled between Ŭiju and Zhamen to transport the luggage and provisions of the embassies. The number of packhorses, however, was not limited. Private merchants took advantage of this and engaged in a brisk trade in Zhamen. Five to six hundred men would cross the Yalu River to meet the returning Chosŏn embassies, yet the number of pack animals was commonly several

Map 2.1 Road Used by Chosŏn Envoys to Visit the Qing

times that figure.[10] Many of these animals were used for private trade in Zhamen with the tacit approval of the Ŭiju magistracy.

The embassy trade was conducted largely to satisfy economic demands within Chosŏn, while the Chunggang market, held at an island in the Yalu River, was established to meet economic demands of Qing local government officials and ordinary people in Manchuria.[11] The Chosŏn court gained little profit from this market, which opened twice a year, on the fifteenth day of the second and eighth lunar months. Many P'yŏngan merchants, especially those from P'yŏngyang, Anju, and Yongch'ŏn, participated in this state-sanctioned market. Once it closed, however, some of them also made profits from outside transactions.[12]

There were at least two Chosŏn embassies to the Qing court every year, and each one stayed in P'yŏngan for more than a month. Thus the province hosted Chosŏn embassies for at least two to three months a year, year in and year out, which meant it had to constantly scramble for the necessary supplies and personnel to accommodate them. In addition, P'yŏngan had to host the Qing embassies to the Chosŏn court, and organize and manage the Chunggang market. Thus P'yŏngan Province clearly played a pivotal role in Chosŏn-Qing diplomatic and trade relations.

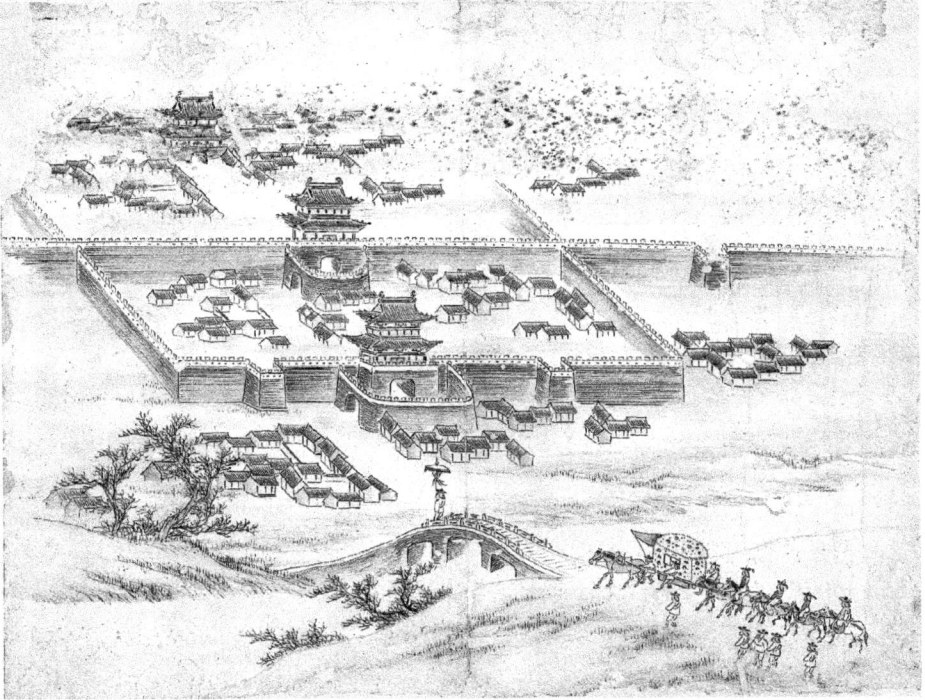

Fig. 2.1 Illustration of the Chosŏn Envoy to Qing (*Yŏnhaengdo*), attributed to Kim Hongdo (1745–?), who accompanied the Chosŏn diplomatic mission to Qing in 1789. This is one of the thirteen album illustrations that depict the Chosŏn envoy's route to Beijing and its activities. 34.4 x 44.7 cm. Used by permission of the Korean Christian Museum at Soongsil University.

THE FINANCIAL LANDSCAPE OF P'YŎNGAN PROVINCE

Tax Administration

Before discussing in detail the financial burdens P'yŏngan Province incurred due to diplomatic relations between Chosŏn and Qing, it is helpful to lay out certain features of the financial structure of the province. With its enormous diplomatic and commercial roles to play in peacetime and crucial military role in wartime, P'yŏngan was in a unique fiscal situation. In recognition of this, the central government allowed taxes assessed on land and people to be retained within the province to cover diplomatic and military expenditures. Local tax revenues were sometimes used for local administrative costs in other regions as well, but in P'yŏngan all appropriations, including land taxes, tribute, and corvée, remained with the province.[13]

Land tax revenues had been retained within the province since the beginning of the Chosŏn Dynasty. And tribute tax had been retained as the western provisions tax (sŏryang), a temporary surcharge to assist military provisioning of Ming troops stationed on Ka Island, off the coast of P'yŏngan, during the confrontation with Manchu forces in the early seventeenth century.[14] Even after the Qing invasion of 1636–1637, tribute tax was renamed the rice surtax (sumi) and was continuously collected by the local governments. After the end of hostilities with the Qing, these revenues were used to compensate for the expenses incurred by diplomatic affairs. The retention of tax revenues within the province also arose from the recognition of P'yŏngan's poor agricultural productivity and difficulty with transportation. A more fundamental reason, however, was the need for funds to actively address the political situation in China and Manchuria. Table 2.3 shows the land tax revenues collected by province in 1807.[15]

The number of kyŏl in P'yŏngan steadily increased after the Qing invasions.[16] With fewer wet fields, however, agricultural productivity tended to be lower than before. P'yŏngan had 10.5 percent of the cultivated land in the country, but its land tax revenues amounted to only 4.1 percent of the national total. In contrast, Chŏlla had only 25.2 percent of the cultivated land and contributed 32.6 percent of the national land tax revenues because of the much higher proportion of the more productive wet rice fields there. The rates of taxation were also lower in P'yŏngan than in other areas. Wet-field

Table 2.3 Cultivated Land and Land Tax Revenues by Province in 1807

	Land				Land Tax		
	Wet fields	Dry fields	Total	%	Total grain revenue	Cash equivalent	%
Kyŏnggi	14,907	22,637	37,544	4.6	10,018	21,592	3.2
Ch'ungch'ŏng	58,719	62,114	120,833	14.9	43,893	108,455	16.0
Chŏlla	133,574	71,186	204,760	25.2	84,580	221,129	32.6
Kyŏngsang	99,692	101,861	201,553	24.9	77,436	195,506	28.9
Kangwŏn	3,911	7,658	11,569	1.4	5,164	12,166	1.8
Hamgyŏng	4,986	61,553	66,539	8.2	7,451	17,101	2.5
Hwanghae	11,106	57,442	68,548	8.5	30,314	65,121	9.6
P'yŏngan	12,070	72,840	84,910	10.5	13,426	27,569	4.1
Four special magistracies	6,863	7,700	14,563	1.8	11,365	8,859	1.3
Total	345,828	464,991	810,819	100	283,647	677,498	100

NOTE: Land is expressed in kyŏl, grain in sŏm, and cash in yang. Revenue figures for Kyŏngsang and Hwanghae include cotton. 1 sŏm of hulled rice = 3 yang; 1 sŏm of hulled millet = 2.5 yang; 1 sŏm of beans = 1.6 yang; 1 p'il of cotton = 2 yang.

taxes in P'yŏngan were assessed at only 67 or 83 percent of the rates in other provinces.[17] Moreover, the people of P'yŏngan were not required to pay the special military surtax called samsumi. They also bore a lighter tribute burden. Their rice surtax of five to six mal per kyŏl was similar in nature to the rice payment according to the Uniform Land Tax Law (taedongbŏp) in other provinces. However, the taedong tax was generally assessed at twelve mal per kyŏl—more than twice the rate of the rice surtax in P'yŏngan Province.

The people of P'yŏngan did have greater corvée and military service obligations than residents of other provinces. According to the eighteenth century Yangyŏk silch'ong (Actual Assessment of Military Taxation), each Chosŏn household provided on average 0.37 to 0.47 men for corvée or military service.[18] This rate increased to 0.78 for Hwanghae Province and 1.22 for P'yŏngan. The higher service requirements were a result of military necessity, fiscal conditions, and the mobilization of human resources to host embassies. Soldiers in P'yŏngan were not attached to the capital divisions; rather, they were assigned to provincial garrisons. And finally, the military cloth tax collected in P'yŏngan remained within the province.

Financial Burdens vs. Privileges

P'yŏngan Province bore considerable responsibility for the routine diplomatic and trade relations between Chosŏn and the Qing. First, the province was responsible for the cost of mobilizing the men and horses, preparing the provisions, and giving the gifts that were all necessary parts of hosting Qing embassies. While the central government offset such expenses to a degree in other provinces, P'yŏngan had to meet these costs independently. This distinguished P'yŏngan as a special diplomatic zone and constituted recognition of provincial independence in fiscal management.

Qing embassies bearing imperial edicts to the Chosŏn court generally included two high-ranking envoys and four interpreters. For such missions the P'yŏngan provincial government had to mobilize 412 men and 127 horses, to provide both security and the appropriate dignity and pageantry to the procession.[19] When the men and horses needed to attend the other members of the embassy were included, the numbers increased astronomically. When the embassies traveled back to Qing, P'yŏngan also had to mobilize 500 horses to transport their baggage from Chunghwa to Ŭiju.[20] The men needed to tend to the Qing embassies were drawn from among corvée laborers, while the horses were taken from the post station stables. Military cloth tax revenues were often used to hire privately owned horses.

Expenses were also incurred in giving gifts to the envoys and interpreters of the Qing embassies. As the Qing envoys passed through important places, they received many kinds of offerings, most notably silver. Though this was a matter of diplomatic protocol, whenever Chosŏn submitted a special request to the Qing court or there was friction between the two states, the quantity of silver given rose dramatically.[21] The amount of silver given to Qing envoys in the three northern provinces and the capital during the course of their journeys during the second half of the eighteenth century is shown in Table 2.4.[22]

With the exception of Kyŏnggi Province, each region gave approximately the same amount of silver to the Qing embassies. The cash equivalent of the

**Table 2.4 Silver Presented to Qing Envoys
and Interpreters in the Late Eighteenth Century by Province, in *Yang***

	P'yŏngan	Hwanghae	Kyŏnggi	Seoul
Ch'ŏn silver	8,174	2,031	726	7,540
Chŏng silver	1,018	8,834	—	—
Cash equivalent	21,653	22,542	1,742	22,620

NOTE: Ch'ŏn-grade silver (*ch'ŏnŭn*) was pure, whereas *chŏng*-grade silver (*chŏngŭn*) was 70 percent silver, 30 percent lead; 500 *yang* of *chŏng*-grade silver was equivalent to 416.67 *yang* of *ch'ŏn*-grade silver, and 1 *yang* of *chŏng*-grade silver had a cash value of 2 *yang*.

silver given by P'yŏngan Province is somewhat less than that given by Hwanghae, but most of the P'yŏngan silver was of the pure *ch'ŏn* grade. If other gifts are considered, P'yŏngan expenses far outweighed those of Hwanghae. In Hwanghae Province, the highest-ranking Qing interpreter received eight kinds of gifts, such as silk and paper, but in P'yŏngan Province, the same interpreter might receive as many as thirty different kinds, including such expensive items as pure silver stirrups and deerskin shoes.[23] The total expenses for gifts was clearly higher in P'yŏngan Province.

In addition, the cost of feeding a Qing embassy in the late eighteenth century was 23,079 *yang*. Other miscellaneous expenses added another 14,486 *yang*.[24] These figures do not include Ŭiju, where these expenditures were the highest. Located on the Chosŏn-Qing border, the Ŭiju magistracy was responsible for providing food and shelter for the Qing embassies when they passed through the uninhabited region north of the Yalu River, and also had to host the Qing guard units that escorted the embassy to the Chosŏn border. With the Ŭiju expenses included, the total cost of hosting a Qing embassy in P'yŏngan exceeded 60,000–70,000 *yang*.

The monies spent to host a Qing embassy in Seoul during the same period may have approached 80,000–90,000 *yang*.[25] It is difficult to know the total Hwanghae and Kyŏnggi provincial expenditures, but P'yŏngan Province likely bore the brunt of hosting Qing embassies on their way to and from the capital. Since Chosŏn-Qing diplomatic relations took place within the context of the tribute-investiture system (*chogong ch'aekpong che*), the reception of Qing embassies was of enormous importance to the Chosŏn government, warranting vast expenditures of money, time, and manpower by each region from Ŭiju to Seoul.

Since the embassies were reciprocal, it is also necessary to examine the costs of hosting Chosŏn embassies to the Qing court. Chosŏn embassies generally lasted from 130 to 150 days during the late Chosŏn period. A month or more of this time was spent in P'yŏngan. The vast amounts of money and provisions used by members of the Chosŏn embassies were provided either by the offices of the central government, such as the Ministry of Taxation (Hojo), or by the provincial government offices, but the mobilization of men, horses, and food along the way nevertheless increased the total costs. Eighteenth-century Chosŏn embassies consisted of more than three hundred people and required more than two hundred horses. In addition, more than one hundred packhorses, used to transport baggage, had to be requisitioned from the P'yŏngan Provincial Governor's Office, the Ŭiju magistracy, and Hwanghae Province. The three southern provinces provided forty horses, but if there were problems in meeting this quota, P'yŏngan had to make up for the difference.[26] The packhorses also required drivers, who were mobilized within P'yŏngan as well.

It is difficult to calculate the total expense of mobilizing men and horses, though we know that in the late eighteenth century provincial authorities had to provide 116 men and thirty-four horses to attend to the Winter Solstice Embassy (Tongjisa).[27] A special agency in P'yŏngyang called the Pumago was maintained especially to provide men and horses for the two or more annual Chosŏn embassies to the Qing. Ŭiju also supplied a portion of the horses needed to transport Chosŏn's tributary goods to Zhamen. The cost of entertaining the high-ranking members of the embassies in the places through which they passed was also the responsibility of the Ŭiju magistracy.

Although the direct costs of hosting embassies were borne by the provincial government, there were also some indirect costs. Chosŏn embassies had funds allotted to them to cover the costs of information gathering, gifts, and social functions. These funds were called kongyongŭn (silver for public use). Embassy interpreters made disbursements of kongyongŭn and in return secured large loans of silver for use in commercial transactions. At this time the interpreters borrowed silver from the P'yŏngan Provincial Governor's Office and the P'yŏngan Military Command. P'yŏngan thus provided both the funds that covered the direct costs of the Chosŏn embassies and the capital for the trade mediated by the interpreters.

Table 2.5 shows silver lent to Chosŏn embassies by central and provincial government offices during the 1710s and 1720s.[28] Central government offices included the Ministry of Taxation and the Ministry of Military Affairs

Table 2.5 Central and Provincial Government Silver Loans to Chosŏn Embassies, in *Yang*

	Winter Solstice Embassy (1714)	Condolence Embassy (Chinwisa) (1723)	Obituary Embassy (Kobusa) (1725)	Embassy Expressing Gratitude for Imperial Grace (Saŭnsa) (1725)	(1726)
Central government offices	11,700	2,000	2,000	14,000	3,500
Central military offices	4,300	4,000	10,000	27,000	6,500
P'yŏngan	4,000	4,000	8,000	29,000	8,000
Hwanghae	0	0	0	0	0
Kyŏnggi	0	0	0	0	0
Total	20,000	10,000	20,000	70,000	18,000
% lent by P'yŏngan	20	40	40	41	44

(Pyŏngjo). Central military offices included the Military Training Command (Hullyŏn togam), the Royal Guards Command (Ŏyŏngch'ŏng), and the Capital Garrison (Kŭmwiyŏng). P'yŏngan was the only province to provide silver loans. In addition, the proportion of loans provided by P'yŏngan grew throughout the period. This indicates that P'yŏngan possessed the largest silver reserves outside the central government and military offices.

Not only was P'yŏngan the largest silver-producing region in Chosŏn, but large quantities of silver were in circulation there in connection with the Qing trade. The production of silver and the collection of silver taxes in P'yŏngan were the highest in the country; indeed, the total amount in P'yŏngan was higher than the total in the remaining seven provinces. A considerable amount of the silver used for diplomatic and trade relations was Japanese silver, but it was locally produced silver—especially P'yŏngan silver—that supplemented the loans. The amount of silver loaned by government offices varied greatly according to the size and purpose of the embassies, though the proportion supplied by P'yŏngan Province remained steady at around 40 percent. In 1710, the Ministry of Taxation supplied the largest share of silver, but through the 1720s the P'yŏngan provincial and military offices provided the largest proportion of silver loans, becoming the largest sources of silver for the Chosŏn embassies.

Table 2.5 does not include data for all years, although P'yŏngan provided silver loans every year—sometimes several times a year—to the interpreters of the Chosŏn embassies. When the principal and interest on these loans were repaid smoothly, government offices stood to make a profit, but when *kongyongŭn* expenditures were high and trade was poor, the interpreters could not repay the loans. During the 1720s, direct trade between the Qing and Japan and the expansion of private trade weakened the dominant position the interpreters had previously enjoyed, making the repayment of silver loans increasingly difficult leading to financial losses for P'yŏngan government offices.

One of the most profitable kinds of trade was carried out in Shenyang, the early capital of the Qing. It was referred to as the *p'alp'o* trade—literally, "the trade of eight bags"—because each authorized member of an embassy was allowed to carry eight bags of ginseng for trade.[29] One bag held 10 kŭn of ginseng, so the total amount allowed was 80 kŭn. In general, 1 kŭn of ginseng was worth 25 yang of silver, making 80 kŭn of ginseng worth 2,000 yang of silver as a trade fund. The original purpose of such official trade using valuable ginseng was to cover expenses for an envoy, but some portion of profit made through this trade was appropriated by those government offices that participated in this trade. Thus this trade opportunity attracted the attention of Chosŏn government offices outside the Ŭiju magistracy and even outside P'yŏngan Province. The offices that were permitted to participate in this trade differed over time, as Table 2.6 illustrates.[30]

As shown in Table 2.6, *p'alp'o* trade privileges were granted to those places closely associated with the Chosŏn embassies, such as the Ŭiju magistracy, the P'yŏngan Provincial Governor's Office, the P'yŏngan Military Command, the Hwanghae Provincial Governor's Office, and the Kaesŏng magistracy. For

**Table 2.6 Shenyang P'alp'o Trade Privileges
by Province, in Number of P'alp'o Granted**

Year	Ŭiju	Military escorts	Pyŏngan Provincial Governor's Office	Provincial Military Command	Hwanghae Provincial Governor's Office	Kyŏnggi Kaesŏng	Kanghwa
1718	4–5	—	—	—	—	3	—
1720	4–5	—	—	—	—	—	1
1722	8	3	—	—	—	—	—
1723	6	2	—	—	—	—	—
1726	6	2	2	2	1	2	—
1727	3	1	1	1	1	1	—
1728	—	—	—	—	—	—	—

example, in 1722, the Ŭiju magistracy was granted the right to trade at Shenyang with eight p'alp'o, which was 640 kŭn of ginseng, or 16,000 yang of silver. The Ŭiju magistracy held the greatest share in the Shenyang trade among the Chosŏn government offices. The military escorts (Tallyŏnsa) responsible for coordinating men and horses for the Chosŏn embassies between Shenyang and Ŭiju were attached to the Ŭiju magistracy, and their p'alp'o were a further favor granted to P'yŏngan by the central government in recognition of the special burden that this region bore.

These government offices appointed special commanders (Pyŏlchang) to serve as commercial agents supervising market transactions in the Shenyang market. These posts were often sold to private merchants, despite the fact that the latter were prohibited from participating in the Shenyang trade for fear that this would increase the size of the market transactions beyond the scope of state control. It was the sale of these appointments that gave private merchants access to both the Shenyang and Zhamen markets.

It is difficult to calculate just how much profit private merchants were able to accrue in this trade, but in 1726, when p'alp'o privileges had expanded greatly, the P'yŏngan provincial government offices obtained twelve p'alp'o— namely, the right to transport to Shenyang as capital 24,000 yang of silver with a cash value of 72,000 yang. The central government granted the p'alp'o in recognition of the special circumstances in P'yŏngan Province. When private merchants took advantage of these favors to amass their own wealth, however, embassy interpreters did not stand idly by. They lodged complaints at the court and their sabotage led to the abolition of the p'alp'o trade in 1728.

Given the deficit incurred by interpreter-led trade after the p'alp'o system was abolished, the Chosŏn government had instituted a new method called the official hat system (kwanmoje) in 1758, granting interpreters the right to import large numbers of winter hats for resale within Chosŏn for the purpose of securing a kongyongŭn fund. The government supplied 40,000 yang to support this new trade; 20,000 yang of this sum came from P'yŏngan, while the rest was provided by the Ministry of Military Affairs and the capital military divisions.[31] But hats turned out to be not so profitable, and the government soon realized that it was difficult to supply silver for such a trade. Thus, in 1777, the government granted the rights to the hat trade to Ŭiju and Kaesŏng merchants (songsang). In return for the privilege of importing 1 million hats per year, these merchants paid a hat tax (mose) of 40,000 yang. The Ŭiju merchants largely controlled this trade, and when the Qing trade stagnated, this tax obligation had the potential to force them into very difficult situations. The hat tax had to be paid regardless of any fall in the actual number of hats imported. As domestic consumption fell from the levels of the early period of the hat trade, hat imports continually decreased. Moreover, Seoul hat merchants gained the favor of the central government and were granted tax exemptions. By the early nineteenth century, hat imports were as low as 200,000–300,000 a year, and tax receipts no more than 4,000 yang. Between 1796 and 1806, the Ŭiju merchants took on hundreds of thousands of yang of debt as the hat trade collapsed.[32]

Though the hat trade turned out to be unsuccessful, private merchants from Seoul and Ŭiju found that red ginseng (hongsam), which was valued greatly in China, provided lucrative commercial opportunities. As exports of red ginseng and profits increased, tax revenues also grew. Despite improving business, the Ŭiju merchants still had to pay the 40,000 yang hat tax and were thus forced to depend on large loans from the P'yŏngan Provincial Office, as they had done before. Competition intensified as private merchants sought to take over the embassy trade from the interpreters, but Ŭiju merchants, saddled with the hat tax, could not effectively compete with Seoul merchants (kyŏngsang).

What, then, of the role of the Chunggang market in the embassy trade? Products purveyed at Chunggang were procured in P'yŏngan, Hwanghae, and Kyŏnggi provinces. Hwanghae and Kyŏnggi did not loan silver but they did share responsibility for the Chunggang market. Provincial quotas for the products sold at the Chunggang market are shown in Table 2.7.[33]

Common necessities (cattle, marine products, cloth, paper) and agricultural implements were traded at the Chunggang market, which catered to the Qing population and was of little benefit to Chosŏn. The Qing paid for the goods with low-quality hemp cloth, which embarrassed the Chosŏn side. Approximately 50 percent of the products came from P'yŏngan and 30 per-

Table 2.7 Products Traded at the Chunggang Market, by Province

Product (unit)	P'yŏngan	Hwanghae	Kyŏnggi	Total	Percentage by Province		
					P'yŏngan	Hwanghae	Kyŏnggi
Cattle (su)	101	78	21	200	50.5	39.0	10.5
Seaweed (kŭn)	9,200	4,300	2,300	15,300	58.2	27.2	14.6
Sea cucumber (kŭn)	1,000	600	600	2,200	45.5	27.3	27.3
Salt (sŏm)	210	100	0	310	67.7	32.3	0
Superior cloth (p'il)	202	113	58	373	54.2	30.3	15.5
Standard cloth (p'il)	117	58	0	175	66.9	33.1	0
Large paper (sŏm)	400	200	0	600	66.7	33.3	0
White paper (sŏm)	2,800	4,000	1,600	8,400	33.3	47.6	19.1
Porcelain (chuk)	330	0	0	330	100	0	0
Ploughshares (kae)	194	0	0	194	100	0	0

cent from Hwanghae. Kyŏnggi provided products in half the categories traded at the Chunggang market, but only in small quantities.

Officials and private merchants who participated in the Chunggang market gathered in Ŭiju and then during a fixed period conducted business at Ŏjŏk Island in the Yalu River. Since the market was within its jurisdiction, the Ŭiju magistracy was charged with hosting both the Chosŏn and the Qing officials connected with the management of the market. In return, Ŭiju was granted the authority to tax the Chunggang "after-market" (husi), where merchants continued doing business after the formal Chunggang market closed.[34] Merchants profited by dealing in various goods in the Chunggang after-market, though the central government tried to restrict such informal trade and suspended the market completely in 1700.

There was also an after-market at Zhamen, held when Chosŏn envoys passed through. Most of this activity consisted of illegal trade strictly prohibited by the government. Seeing potential tax revenues, however, the Ŭiju magistracy secured official recognition of the Zhamen after-market in the early eighteenth century. Large numbers of P'yŏngan merchants then paid fees in Ŭiju for the privilege of participating in the Zhamen after-market, which eventually grew to a significant degree. The Chosŏn government shut down the after-markets in 1727, but this only produced a resurgence in illegal trade by private merchants. The Zhamen after-market was allowed in the mid-eighteenth century, closed down again in 1787, and finally reopened in 1795.

Governmental protection of the interpreters' trade had the effect of expanding illegal trade by private merchants, yet granting official recognition to private trade functioned to constrict the interpreters' commercial operations. This dilemma was not easily resolved within the embassy trade structure, as seen in the fluctuating government policy toward after-markets. The central government continued to privilege interpreters in the embassy trade, even though private merchants of Ŭiju and Kaesŏng eventually changed the structure of interpreter-centered trade as they began to dominate both officially sanctioned and illegal trade in the area.[35]

In sum, P'yŏngan Province bore a considerable share of the expense of maintaining Chosŏn-Qing diplomatic and commercial relations. The province mobilized the men and horses to attend the Qing embassies, prepared gifts for envoys and interpreters, and provided the necessary supplies for the Chosŏn embassies as they made their way to and from the Qing border.

Moreover, half of the silver loans and products needed for embassy trade and the Chunggang market came from P'yŏngan. In return, P'yŏngan merchants enjoyed more trade opportunities with China and provincial offices reserved the right to collect commercial taxes. The special dispensation that P'yŏngan had once enjoyed, however, was gradually lost. The Shenyang *p'alp'o* trade was abolished after the interpreters complained about it, and the government's position toward the Zhamen after-market swung back and forth. Moreover, the central government began to support the commerce of the licensed Seoul merchants, cutting into Ŭiju merchants' profits and reducing local access to provincial tax revenues, while continuing to provide official recognition to the interpreters as primary agents in the embassy trade.

Aside from the Qing trade, there were other changes afoot in P'yŏngan during the eighteenth century, brought on by the long-term stability of Chosŏn-Qing relations. With the continuing peace, the diplomatic and military expenditures traditionally borne by P'yŏngan decreased dramatically, and the dispensations that had been granted by the central government began to disappear. Moreover, as the central government grew stronger and appropriated resources that had once stayed within P'yŏngan, the province's fiscal circumstances lost their uniqueness. Even the most productive silver mine in the province came under the control of the Ministry of Taxation.[36]

CONCLUSION: ECONOMIC GROWTH AND REGIONAL SOCIETY

P'yŏngan's economic growth in the late Chosŏn period was primarily connected with the Qing trade relationship. The size of taxable land increased, as did the absolute area of cultivated land, becoming second only to the three southern provinces. As Chosŏn-Qing relations stabilized, border regions, starting with "the four abolished districts" (*p'yesagun*), were opened to cultivation and there was an influx of population.[37] Even so, the relatively small number of wet fields prevented agricultural productivity from reaching the levels of the three southern provinces. In 1807, the population of Chosŏn was 7,561,403, of whom 1,305,969 lived in P'yŏngan Province, accounting for 17.3 percent of the national total.[38] The national average ratio of population to *kyŏl* of cultivated land was 9.3, compared to 15.4 in P'yŏngan Province. The ratio in Chŏlla, the province with the largest area of wet fields, was 6.1. The land and population records of that time do not, however, fully reflect the reality

of the situation.[39] The number of *kyŏl* in P'yŏngan may have been underesti-
mated, though it is also possible that a more thorough population survey was
carried out in P'yŏngan Province than elsewhere, precisely because of the high
demand for military and labor services in the region. Even so, the amount of
arable land at the time seems to have been too little to support P'yŏngan's
population, especially considering the relatively low agricultural productivity
of the province. It is quite plausible to argue that the extra population was
supported by trade and commerce. Indeed, possibilities for profit in both
domestic and international trade opened up in P'yŏngan Province as large-
scale commercial operations in P'yŏngyang, Anju, and Ŭiju expanded in the
late Chosŏn period. The merchants of Ŭiju and their associates were most
active in taking advantage of commercial opportunities in connection with
the Qing trade, as already discussed.

It is difficult to detail precisely how the Ŭiju merchants operated because
there are no extant records kept by them. They seem to have joined the embassies as packhorse drivers, obtained appointments as special commander-
cum-commercial agents for government offices involved in the *p'alp'o* trade,
and participated in the Zhamen and Chunggang after-markets. Experienced
packhorse drivers from northern P'yŏngan were the preferred hires for the
Chosŏn embassies. Of the thirty-five packhorse drivers of the Winter Solstice
Embassy of 1777, twenty-three were from northern P'yŏngan, five from southern P'yŏngan, and seven from Hwanghae.[40] Packhorse drivers were originally
drawn from among post station slaves, but private merchants looking for
ways to participate in the embassy trade also posed as slaves to secure a spot
in the embassy entourage. It is likely that some of these were Ŭiju merchants.

The Ŭiju magistracy held both the largest share of trading rights in the
Shenyang market and the authority to tax the Zhamen after-market. This of
course meant that Ŭiju merchants enjoyed great commercial opportunities in
both places. The Qing trade was carried out on a considerable scale. At this
time, more than 100,000 *yang* were required for a single after-market, and
500,000–600,000 *yang* of silver were transported across the border to the
Qing markets every year.[41] Qing merchandise purchased with this silver was
sold in Chosŏn domestic markets.[42] P'yŏngan was the place where Chinese
goods passed through, and also where they were temporarily stored. All these
commercial movements and transactions must have bolstered spin-off busi-

nesses in the areas of transportation, warehousing, lodging, entertainment, and other related services, creating jobs for local residents and thus contributing to the growth of the regional economy.

In contrast, Kyŏngsang Province played a much less significant role in Chosŏn's diplomatic and commercial relations with Japan in late Chosŏn. Between 1607 and 1811, only twelve Korean embassies were sent to the Edo bakufu while fifty-four much smaller scale and less prestigious envoys were dispatched to the lord of Tsushima, who was the official conduit between the Chosŏn court and the Edo bakufu. Japanese envoys visited Chosŏn more often, 1.1 time per year on average, but they were never permitted beyond Tongnae with one exception throughout late Chosŏn. An official inn called the Japan House (Waegwan) was maintained in Tongnae and a large number of Japanese resided in the walled community in Tongnae. It is apparent that Chosŏn maintained much less frequent official contacts with Japan, which therefore would have incurred less expense. One study of a comparison of the value of gifts that the 1763 Chosŏn mission to China and the 1763 Chosŏn mission to Japan presented to each country also shows that the former was about one third of the latter.[43] Because of irregular contacts between Chosŏn and Japan and the limited scope of contact and trade, the financial burden that Kyŏngsang Province had to bear was significantly less than P'yŏngan Province. Trade through the Japan House was confined to the tiny area of Tongnae and the amount of commercial transactions was considered inconsequential and did not promote any comparable commercial developments as seen in P'yŏngan Province.

It is difficult to estimate how much the economic growth in P'yŏngan Province enhanced the overall living standards in the region. The facts that elite-led cultural activities, such as establishing schools and shrines, visibly increased and that the region produced numerous higher civil service examination graduates from the eighteenth century on seem to support a hypothesis that at least the elites in the region benefited from the commercial growth.[44] The wealthy residents of P'yŏngan Province were, however, subject to arbitrary exploitation in various ways. In their desire to enhance their social status and earn exemption from military and labor services, they paid to become members of the local yangban association (hyangan).[45] Yet they sometimes found that this did not bring them the social prestige and other boons they expected, and consequently became frustrated.[46] They were also targeted to take charge of supervising local finances, and then had to make up for any lost funds.[47] Magistrates also forced wealthy residents to purchase local official appointments in an effort to augment revenues. The sale of appointments was a matter of the vice of the individual magistrate, but this form of corruption was especially commonplace in P'yŏngan and anger with local authorities grew increasingly acute.[48] Merchants involved in the Qing trade, were, in turn, limited by strict controls over illegal trade and by policies granting more favorable commercial privileges to interpreters and Seoul merchants. They naturally harbored much distaste for the central government and also for the merchants of the capital with whom the court colluded.

The accumulated discontent of regional merchants and wealthy residents of the province manifested in their active participation in the early phases of the Hong Kyŏngnae Rebellion of 1812. A number of studies on this regionally confined resistance movement suggest economic causes for the rebellion. The most popular explanation is that overall social economic changes in the late Chosŏn period resulted in the pauperization of the rural population at the bottom layers of society and thus prompted class conflict. Although other studies pay attention to the participation of merchants and local wealthy people, they tend to marginalize the economic aspects of the rebellion and highlight political problems instead.[49] This chapter proposes that the economic links to the rebellion may have been stronger than has been heretofore been thought, because without economic growth neither the rising political and social aspirations of the P'yŏngan people nor their resentment of and discontent with the central government would have emerged. Eventually, the economic development of this region and the ensuing frustration over Chosŏn's conservative social and political system seem to have driven the P'yŏngan people toward modern ideas and cultures, including Christianity in the late nineteenth and early twentieth centuries as Chapters 7 and 9 in the present volume show.

NOTES

1. The Jurchen kingdom of the Later Jin became Qing in 1636.
2. Kwŏn Naehyŏn, *Chosŏn hugi P'yŏngan-do chaejŏng yŏn'gu*, 120–68.
3. *Kwanghaegun ilgi*, 31:615, 1611/3/29.

4. The average number of days that a Qing embassy spent in Chosŏn during the period 1637–1656 was 44.6 days; 15.7 days of this time were spent in P'yŏngan Province. If this figure is multiplied by the average number of embassies per year (2.30) for the period, the result is 36.1 days. The same process was carried out for the remaining regions. These figures were drawn from *Tongmun hwigo, 44 ch'aek, choch'ingnok*.

5. *Kwansŏ chich'ik chŏngnye, hoegam*.

6. This type of diplomatic burden was similar to Tongnae, where the Japan House (Waegwan) was located, and Kyŏngsang Province in the southeast also played a central role in relations with the Japanese. For the study of the Japan House, see Lewis, "The Pusan Japan House (Waegwan) and Chosŏn Korea."

7. Table 2.2 is based on data from the following sources: Yi Yo, *Yŏndo kihaeng*; Kim Chŏngjung, *Yŏnhaengnok*; Yi Ap, *Yŏnhaeng kisa*; and Pak Saho, *Simjŏn'go*.

8. Zhamen was a barrier on the border built for protection of the original Manchu homeland when the Qing Dynasty moved its capital to Beijing. To go from the Chosŏn to the Qing capital, it was necessary to pass through Zhamen south of Fenghuangcheng.

9. For a discussion of the Qing trade and the merchant groups in the late Chosŏn period, see Yu Sŭngju and Yi Ch'ŏlsŏng, *Chosŏn hugi chungguk kwa ŭi muyŏksa*.

10. Kim Chŏngjung, *Yŏnhaengnok*, 1792/3/3.

11. The three channels of the Yalu River during the Chosŏn Dynasty were called Sosŏ-gang, Chung-gang, and Sam-gang, respectively. The Chunggang market was held on Ŏjŏk Island located between Sosŏ-gang and Chung-gang channels.

12. Yi Ch'ŏlsŏng, *Chosŏn hugi taech'ŏng muyŏksa yŏn'gu*, 36.

13. *Taejŏn hoet'ong*, 2:21b–25a, *hojŏn, suse*.

14. Sŏryang was a temporarily added tax imposed to assist military provisioning of Ming troops stationed on Ka Island from the late part of King Kwanghae's reign to the period of King Injo's reign.

15. *Man'gi yoram, chaeyong p'yŏn, suse*.

16. Kyŏl is a constant measure of crop yield produced by an area that varied from 2.2 to 9.0 acres depending on the fertility of the land.

17. *Sok taejŏn, hojŏn, suse*.

18. *Yangyŏk silch'ong*.

19. *Kwansŏ chich'ik chŏngnye, chŏnbae*.

20. *Kyŏngjong sillok*, 41:299, 1723/8/11.

21. For example, a Chosŏn subject crossed the northern boundary in 1662, causing a diplomatic problem. At that time the Chosŏn court paid 2,000 *yang* of silver as a bribe, much more than the usual 500 *yang*, in order to appease the Qing envoy. Because the envoy was not satisfied with the usual amount, additional silver was given as a bribe. *Hyŏnjong sillok*, 36:332, 1662/5/20.

22. *Kwansŏ chich'ik chŏngnye, chŭngsin; Haesŏ chich'ik chŏngnye, chŭngsin;* and *Kyŏnggi chich'ik chŏngnye, chŭnggŭp.*

23. *Kwansŏ chich'ik chŏngnye, chŭngsin;* and *Haesŏ chich'ik chŏngnye, chŭngsin.*

24. *Kwansŏ chich'ik chŏngnye, hoegam.*

25. *Man'gi yoram, chaeyong p'yŏn* 5, *chich'ik.*

26. *Man'gi yoram, chaeyong p'yŏn* 5, *yŏnsa.*

27. *P'yŏngan-do nae kagŭp min'go chŏngnye chŏlmok.*

28. *Pibyŏnsa tŭngnok,* 1714/10/28, 1723/1/9, 1724/10/3, 1725/3/26, and 1726/2/3.

29. The following discussion on Shenyang *p'alp'o* trade is based on Yi Ch'ŏlsŏng, *Chosŏn hugi taech'ŏng muyŏksa yŏn'gu;* and Yu Sŭngju and Yi Ch'ŏlsŏng, *Chosŏn hugi chungguk kwa ŭi muyŏksa.*

30. Zhang Cunwu, *Qing Han zong fan mao yi,* 1637–1894, 97; and Kwŏn Naehyŏn, *Chosŏn hugi P'yŏngan-do chaejŏng yŏn'gu,* 179.

31. For a more detailed discussion of the official hat system, see Yi Ch'ŏlsŏng, *Chosŏn hugi taech'ŏng muyŏksa yŏn'gu;* and Yu Sŭngju and Yi Ch'ŏlsŏng, *Chosŏn hugi chungguk kwa ŭi muyŏksa.*

32. *Pibyŏnsa tŭngnok,* 1816/5/27.

33. *Kwansŏ ŭpchi, Ŭiju, changsi;* and *Man'gi yoram, chaeyong p'yŏn* 5, *chunggang kaesi.*

34. *Pibyŏnsa tŭngnok,* 1718/8/6.

35. *Man'gi yoram, chaeyong p'yŏn* 5, *ch'aengmun husi.*

36. Kwŏn Naehyŏn, *Chosŏn hugi P'yŏngan-do chaejŏng yŏn'gu,* 239–80.

37. Kang Sŏkhwa, *Chosŏn hugi Hamgyŏng-do wa pukpang kyŏnggye ŭisik,* 169–78.

38. *Chŭngbo munhŏn pigo,* 161, *hogugo, yŏktae hogu.*

39. For the study of Chosŏn population data from household registrations, see Son Pyŏnggyu et al., *Tansŏng hojŏk taejang yŏn'gu;* Michell, "Fact and Hypothesis in Yi Dynasty Economic History"; and Kwŏn T'aehwan and Sin Yongha, "Chosŏn wangjo sidae in'gu ch'ujŏng e kwanhan ilsiron."

40. Yi Ap, *Yŏnhaeng kisa,* 1777/11/27.

41. *T'ongmun'gwan chi,* 3, *sadae kaesi.*

42. *Pibyŏnsa tŭngnok,* 1736/6/3.

43. Yi Ch'ŏlsŏng, "T'ongsinsa wa yŏnhaengsa ŭi pigyo yŏn'gu," 103.

44. For the cultural maturity of P'yŏngan elites, see Sun Joo Kim, "Chosŏn hugi P'yŏngan-do Chŏngju ŭi hyangan unyŏng kwa yangban munhwa," 73–87.

45. For the nature and management of the *hyangan* in P'yŏngan Province, see Sun Joo Kim, "Chosŏn hugi P'yŏngan-do Chŏngju ŭi hyangan unyŏng kwa yangban munhwa," 87–100.

46. One extreme example is Yi Hŭijŏ, originally a post station slave, who passed the military examination, and eventually bought *hyangan* membership. He probably engaged in various commercial enterprises to become wealthy. His membership was ultimately

rescinded by the district magistrate, which must have made him resentful. He was one of the financiers of the Hong Kyŏngnae Rebellion in 1812. Pang Ujŏng, *Sŏjŏng ilgi*, 11; and Sun Joo Kim, *Marginality and Subversion in Korea*, Chapter 5.

47. Ko Sŏkkyu, *Sipku segi Chosŏn ŭi hyangch'on sahoe yŏn'gu*, 197–202.

48. Ko Sŏkkyu, *Sipku segi Chosŏn ŭi hyangch'on sahoe yŏn'gu*, 88.

49. The most representative studies of the Hong Kyŏngnae rebellions are: Sun Joo Kim, *Marginality and Subversion in Korea*; Karlsson, "The Hong Kyŏngnae Rebellion 1811–1812"; O Such'ang, *Chosŏn hugi P'yŏngan-do sahoe palchŏn yŏn'gu*; Chŏng Sŏkchong, "Hong Kyŏngnae nan ŭi sŏnggyŏk"; and Hong Hŭiyu, "1811–1812 nyŏn P'yŏngan-do nongmin chŏnjaeng kwa kŭ sŏnggyŏk." Hong Hŭiyu emphasizes poor, exploited peasants as the leading force of the rebellion; O Such'ang highlights the activities of resistant intellectuals that grew outside the dominant system; Sun Joo Kim emphasizes the political and economic growth of local people and discrimination by the central government; and Anders Karlsson stresses confrontation between the local region and the center.

3

Regional Identities of Northern Literati

A Comparative Study of P'yŏngan and Hamgyŏng Provinces

JANG YOO-SEUNG

INTRODUCTION

This chapter examines regional identities of literati from P'yŏngan and Hamgyŏng provinces in the seventeenth and eighteenth centuries. The northern region was politically and culturally alienated during the Chosŏn Dynasty. Although the origins of such alienation are not clearly understood, political discrimination and social prejudice against residents of the northern region was deep-rooted and gravely affected their fate. Northern literati developed their own unique regional identities in response to regional discrimination and made various attempts to attain fair political and cultural space in Chosŏn Korea.[1] Although their efforts to overcome alienation continued from the seventeenth century to the modern period, this study focuses on the seventeenth and eighteenth centuries, when northern literati were most passionately involved in developing a regionally distinct culture and identities. It highlights the different ways that the two northern groups—P'yŏngan and Hamgyŏng literati—perceived themselves and coped with regional discrimination. However, any consideration of cultural diversity within the northern region must be preceded by proper understanding of the cultural characteristics of the northern region in general.

The cultural characteristics and identity of a given region are best displayed in the writings on that particular region, which tend to emphasize unique aspects of the area's culture and history while also recognizing them as a part of the whole dynasty. There were three types of locally produced literature in Chosŏn Korea. First, there were gazetteers (ŭpchi) published for the purpose of local administration. Although a gazetteer was often compiled by the local government, assistance from local literati was essential. Furthermore, local literati themselves compiled and published local gazetteers, and a few chronicles were actually compiled by regional literati.[2] Second, biographies of local people were written for propagating Confucian ideas. Those compiled by the government aimed at teaching Confucian ethics to local people, thereby establishing the Neo-Confucian order of the country, whereas those compiled by the local literati were intended mainly to uphold the stature of a given family by praising the achievement of their ancestors.[3] The third type of locally produced writing consisted of cultural histories of a particular region. Two extant examples are the Sŏgyŏng sihwa (A Talk on Poetry from the Western Capital) and Kwanbuk sisŏn (Selected Poems from Hamgyŏng Province). Two other publications survive only as titles: the Kwansŏ munhŏllok (Literature of P'yŏngan Province) and Kwanbuk munhŏllok (Literature of Hamgyŏng Province).

Gazetteers and biographies were compiled by both the government and local literati, whereas cultural histories were compiled solely by regional literati and were based on a strong consciousness of shared identity. Indeed, locally compiled cultural histories became the most important source for forming regional identity among northerners, because these histories required extensive data collection and investigation that could not be carried out without a clear recognition of regional consciousness.

On a slightly different note, except for local gazetteers, there were relatively few regionally compiled writings in the Chosŏn Dynasty. It is even harder to find examples of regionally compiled literary works. In fact, the Sŏgyŏng sihwa (which is a literary criticism on poetry written by P'yŏngan literati) and the Kwanbuk sisŏn are the only known and extant literati works compiled on a regional level in the Chosŏn period. The fact that these two regional compilations emerged in the northern region suggests that they were the result of an especially strong sense of regional identity and cultural tradition.

These works are two of the main sources of the present chapter. In addition, I used the munjip (collected literary works) of literati from the two northern provinces. I have identified about forty collected works of literati from Hamgyŏng Province who were born before 1700, and double that number born after that year.[4] I have been able to locate only thirteen munjip of literati from P'yŏngan Province. This is partly due to insufficient research but may also be a result of the fact that most collected works of literati in P'yŏngan Province have been lost over time.[5]

THE EMERGENCE OF THE NORTHERN LITERATI

Discussions on appointing people from the northern region at the central court began immediately after King Injo's Restoration (Injo panjŏng) in 1623, on the grounds that "the North is like the home of the Zhou and Han dynasties and the West is the root of restoration."[6] This characterization of the North refers to Hamgyŏng Province's status as the birthplace of the Chosŏn Dynasty, while the description of the West refers to P'yŏngan Province's distinction as the last stronghold during the Japanese invasion of 1592, and hence the place where struggle against the invaders to recover occupied territory took place.[7] Apart from such rhetoric, there were pressing reasons why the policy on hiring northerners was discussed at this particular time in history. King Injo (1623–49), who had come to power through a coup, may have wanted to pay special attention to the dynastic birthplace, Hamgyŏng Province, as a way of securing his legitimacy. He also needed to emphasize that the loyal support of P'yŏngan residents during the Japanese invasions had been critical to the survival of the Chosŏn Dynasty, in order to mobilize the human and material resources of the province for defense against the rising Manchu.[8]

The Chosŏn court considered employing northerners and improving their bureaucratic standing throughout the late Chosŏn period, though northerners seemed to fare the best during Injo's reign in terms of successful bureaucratic advancement. A few prominent northern figures who reached relatively high positions are discussed here to examine the emergence of the northern literati in the late Chosŏn period.

Transplantation

Hamgyŏng Province became a part of Chosŏn only in the fifteenth and sixteenth centuries, and was often considered the most desolate place in the country because of its poor soil and frequent natural disasters. The northern area near the border of Jurchen was especially unstable, and there were frequent battles even after the establishment of six garrisons (yukchin) in the mid-fifteenth century. The government therefore sought to secure the area by having people move from the southern provinces of the Korean peninsula to Hamgyŏng Province.[9]

The activities of literati from Hamgyŏng Province became noticeable in the sixteenth century. These literati were mostly descendants of people who had migrated from the south, mostly through being banished in the previous century as part of a population relocation policy. Mun Tŏkkyo (1551–1611) is the earliest example of a Hamgyŏng literatus who left sizeable writings that were later compiled as a *munjip*. He was also the first to be enshrined in a private academy (*sŏwŏn*). His family had originated in Kaeryŏng, Kyŏngsang Province; they settled in Hamgyŏng Province when his ancestor Mun Ch'ŏnbong, six generations before him, moved to Hamhŭng. According to the *Veritable Record of King T'aejong* (*T'aejong sillok*), Mun Ch'ŏnbong was a military official, though the reason for his moving to Hamhŭng is not clear.[10] Mun Ch'ŏnbong's direct descendants served as military officials; the family began to produce literary men when his great-great-grandson, Mun Tŏkkyo's grandfather, passed the lower civil service examination (*saengwŏnsi*). Mun Tŏkkyo passed this exam in 1573, and the higher civil service examination (*munkwa*) in 1585. The first government office he held was a low-rank position at the Office of Editorial Review (Kyosŏgwan); later he served as a librarian at the Royal Confucian Academy (Sŏnggyun'gwan Chŏnjŏk) and as the assistant section chief at the Ministry of Punishments (Hyŏngjo Chwarang). He retired after serving as the magistrate (Hyŏngam) of Hŭngdŏk in 1604, and returned home after spending twenty years in the government. In 1667, Mun Tŏkkyo was enshrined in Munhoe Private Academy (Munhoe sŏwŏn), a great honor given only to illustrious scholars and officials.[11]

Kim Ni (1540–1621) was one of two literati from Hamgyŏng Province who were promoted to the highest ministerial post. His family, originally from Kyŏngju in Kyŏngsang Province, began to reside in Hamgyŏng when his great-grandfather Kim Chŏm was exiled to that region. Kim Chŏm was a Confucian scholar without a particular government post at the time. Kim Ni's grandfather served as a superintendent of a royal tomb (Ch'ambong). Kim Ni himself passed the lower civil service examination in 1576 and the higher civil service examination in 1582. He began his government career as an instructor (Hundo) of the Yŏnghŭng district in 1585, an unduly low position compared to those given to *munkwa* degree holders from other regions. Later he served as a low-rank officer at the Royal Confucian Academy and the Office of Diplomatic Correspondence (Sŭngmunwŏn), and as the magistrate of various districts. According to the *Veritable Records*, he was recognized several times for his competency as a district magistrate. Later in life he attained a vice minister position (Ch'amp'an) according to various records, including his biography in his *munjip*.[12]

Yi Chion (1603–1671), whose mother was Mun Tŏkkyo's daughter, was the second of the two Hamgyŏng literati who reached the highest ministerial post (the other being Kim Ni). His family had originated in Kongju, Ch'ungch'ŏng Province and had begun to reside in Hamgyŏng Province after his ancestor eight generations before him was exiled to Kyŏngsŏng. Although Yi Chion's great-great-grandfather was said to have excelled in military arts, his great-grandfather focused on literature and studied under Yu Hŭich'un (1513–77), a prominent scholar-official of the time who had also been banished to Kyŏngsŏng. This indicates how a member of a military family could take up a civil career. Yi Chion's grandfather finally passed the higher civil service examination and held some government positions. His father also passed this exam, but his bureaucratic career stopped at the low-rank position of superintendent of a royal tomb.

Yi Chion passed the lower civil service examination in 1630 and the higher civil service examination in 1633. He was assigned a government post for the first time as third proctor at the Royal Confucian Academy (Sŏnggyun'gwan Hagyu). For about forty years, however, he transferred from one position to another, mostly as a local magistrate. Although there were three opportunities for him to be promoted to third inspector of the Office of the Inspector-General (Sahŏnbu Changnyŏng)—one of the reputable and prestigious positions (ch'ŏngyojik)—he did not obtain this appointment because of his regional origin. Nonetheless, he was recognized for his diligent service, was selected as an "honest government officer" (ch'ŏngbaengni), and consequently became third magistrate of the Seoul Magistracy (Hansŏngbu Uyun) in 1668. In 1669 he was promoted to vice minister of the Ministry of Punishments (Hyŏngjo Ch'amp'an).[13] This was an unprecedented accomplishment for a literatus from Hamgyŏng Province.

The high achievements of these three men were not duplicated by Hamgyŏng literati in the late Chosŏn period. Yet the social backgrounds of Hamgyŏng literati of the seventeenth and eighteenth centuries were quite similar to those of the men just discussed. Ch'oe Sin (1642–1709) and Yi Chaehyŏng (1665–1741), who played critical roles in consolidating scholarly tradition in that province, are good examples. Ch'oe Sin's family began to reside in Hamgyŏng Province after three siblings of his ancestor six generations before him were exiled to Kyŏngwŏn, Hoeryŏng, and Kilchu, respectively. His great-great-grandfather and great-grandfather were military officials, and the family was only exempted from military duty when his grandfather finally became engaged in Confucian study.[14] Ch'oe Sin did not know the locations of his ancestors' graves prior to his great-great-grandfather, and he did not know his family origins in detail because he lost his parents when young. Yi Chaehyŏng's history fits a similar mold. Originally a descendant of Prince Tŏkch'ŏn (Tŏkch'ŏn-gun) of the Chŏnju Yi royal family, Yi Chaehyŏng's family began residing in Kyŏngsŏng when his ancestor seven generations before him was exiled there. His grandfather passed the military examination (mugwa), but his father began to engage in Confucian study.[15]

According to various munjip by Hamgyŏng literati, they had a clear understanding of their social origins as descendants of early Chosŏn scholar-officials (sadaebu) who had migrated from the southern regions in the early Chosŏn period. They maintained their pride and stature as scholar-officials even after they moved to Hamgyŏng Province, both by compiling genealogies from the time they came north and by writing biographies of their ancestors. This emergence of literati from Hamgyŏng Province can be considered "transplantation" in this context. Descendants of these migrant families served as military officials or took up local quasi-official positions (hyangim) for several generations, and finally moved into Confucian study and civil careers through achieving success in the civil service examinations.

Interestingly, Hamgyŏng literati in the earlier period came from the southern part of that province, whereas those in the later period were mostly from the northern part. Mun Tŏkkyo and Yi Chion were from Hamhŭng, and Kim Ni was from Chŏngp'yŏng, both located in southern Hamgyŏng Province. The reason for the later shift to the northern Hamgyŏng is that early residents settled in the southern area because exploration of northern Hamgyŏng was not yet complete. From the mid-fifteenth century, when northern Hamgyŏng had stabilized, exiles were sent farther north, near the Tumen River. As a result seventeenth-century leading literati tended to be from northern Hamgyŏng.[16] The fact that northern Hamgyŏng became the center of literati activities proves that transplantation was the major factor in the emergence of literati in this province.

Indigenousness

P'yŏngan Province is the cradle of ancient Korean civilization: it is known to be the place where Tangun, the legendary founder of the first Korean state, built his capital, and the place from which Kija spread Chinese civilization. P'yŏngyang had been the center of the region from very early in Korean history, owing to its strategic and convenient location for trade, and had prospered as the capital of ancient Koguryŏ (37 BCE?–668). Later, Koryŏ (918–1392) kings recognized the strategic military importance and geomantic benefits of P'yŏngyang and designated it the western capital. During the Koryŏ Dynasty, P'yŏngyang was a center of commerce and the gateway for international trade with China, and such economic foundations resulted in high cultural standards.[17]

The history of P'yŏngan Province, however, was not always illustrious and stable. Because it bordered China it was susceptible to frequent invasions from northern tribes. In addition, a number of rebellions led by local elites originated in this region. Production of literary works before the Chosŏn Dynasty was also quite slim. In the *Sŏgyŏng sihwa*, after the introduction of a few ancient songs, such as the "Maeksuga" (Mourning Yin Melody), "Hwangjoga" (Song of the Nightingale), and "Konghuin" (Song of a Husband Not Crossing the River), only the writings of Chŏng Chisang (?–1135) are included.[18] This is not because the old records had been lost, but because literary activities were few and far between.

Only after the Chosŏn Dynasty was established was the northwestern region of the Korean peninsula firmly incorporated into the state administrative system, which eventually brought about territorial as well as social stabilization. P'yŏngyang was still the political, social, and cultural center of the region during the Chosŏn Dynasty, and the diplomatic and trade route between Chosŏn and China ran through the coastal regions of P'yŏngan Province. Although the region was trampled by the Japanese (1592–98) and Manchu invasions (1627 and 1636), its economic and social foundations quickly recovered, and it enjoyed further commercial growth during the late Chosŏn period (as Kwon Naehyun discusses in Chapter 2).

P'yŏngan literati began to emerge around the same time literati appeared in Hamgyŏng Province. In the first phase, P'yŏngyang became the center of literati activities. For example, Hwang Yunhu (1587–1648) obtained the position of third inspector of the Office of the Inspector-General in 1633. This was noted as an encouraging appointment by other P'yŏngan literati who had not been given reputable and prestigious posts because of their regional affiliation.[19] Hwang then served as first tutor of the Crown Prince's Tutorial Office (Sigangwŏn P'ilsŏn) and also held other posts. In 1648, the year Hwang Yunhu died, Sŏnu Hyŏp (1588–1653) was appointed second assistant master at the Royal Confucian Academy (Sŏnggyun'gwan Saŏp) in recognition of his accomplishments in the study of the Confucian classics.[20] And in 1685, Yang Hyŏnmang (1633–?) was also appointed third inspector of the Office of the Inspector-General, like Hwang Yunhu before him.[21] These two appointments were mainly symbolic gestures on the part of the central court, yet they show that the central elite had to acknowledge the P'yŏngan literati group.

Hwang Yunhu, Sŏnu Hyŏp, and Yang Hyŏnmang were all from families of indigenous surname groups (t'och'ak sŏnggwan) that had deep historical roots in P'yŏngan Province. The ancestral seat of Hwang Yunhu's family was Chean in Hwanghae Province, and the Chean Hwang lineage was one of the most prestigious in P'yŏngan Province. The Chean Hwang—a branch of the Ch'angwŏn Hwang of Kyŏngsang Province—was established by Hwang Ŭlgu, who had been appointed the lord of Chean (Chean-baek) during the reign of King Kongmin (r. 1351–1374).[22] Sŏnu Hyŏp's lineage originated from Taiyuan, in Shansi, China, and its members were known as the direct descendants of Kija.[23] For generations, the Sŏnu family maintained the Kija Shrine in P'yŏngyang, and Sŏnu Hyŏp's father also inherited the position of superintendent of the shrine (Sunginjŏn Kam).[24] Yang Hyŏnmang's family was from Tangak in P'yŏngan Province. Members of the Tangak Yang lineage lived in the region for generations after the progenitor Yang Po was appointed lord of Tangak (Tangak-kun) in the Koryŏ period.[25]

In contrast, many literati of P'yŏngan Province after the seventeenth century came from the region north of the Ch'ŏngch'ŏn River (Ch'ŏngbuk), close to the Chinese border. Kim Chŏm, the editor of the *Sŏgyŏng sihwa*, remarks that when Yi Sihang (1682–1736), from Unsan in Ch'ŏngbuk, first made his name known to P'yŏngyang's literati circle, there was no one from that city whose talent was comparable to his. Kim even expresses shame that the number of people who passed the *munkwa* from P'yŏngyang had declined while numbers from the Ch'ŏngbuk Region had continued to rise.[26]

Yi Sihang was a member of the Suan Yi lineage. His family had resided in Suan, Hwanghae Province, for generations, but Yi's ancestor seven generations before him had moved to Unsan following the migration policy of King Sŏngjong (r. 1469–94). Although this appears to be similar to the migration of literati into Hamgyŏng Province, the personal history of Yi Sihang's ancestors clearly shows that the family settled down immediately with their prestige intact.

Kye Tŏkhae (1708–75) from Sŏnch'ŏn, whose ancestral seat was Suan is another example of a successful literatus from the Ch'ŏngbuk Region. The founder of the lineage, Kye Sŏkson, had been from Ming China and had settled in Suan toward the end of Koryŏ. His descendants moved to Sŏnch'ŏn and other places in P'yŏngan Province, probably in search of new wealth and better opportunities.[27] It appears that the Suan Kye lineage soon established itself as one of the renowned lineages, because the Minister of Personnel (Ijo P'ansŏ) Yi Chujin, when recommending Kye Tŏkhae for a government position, emphasized that Kye was from a prominent lineage of P'yŏngan Province (*Kwansŏ taejok*).[28]

A few renowned families of P'yŏngan Province can actually sustain the claim to be indigenous. In his "Song of the Western Capital" (Sŏgyŏngbu), Yi Sihang records twenty-one renowned local lineages in P'yŏngan Province, six of which were called *kwabŏl*—lineages that produced a considerable number of *munkwa* graduates. These six were the Chean Hwang, Koksan Kang, Changyŏn No, Paech'ŏn Cho, Tangak Yang, and Namyang Hong. The first four originated in Hwanghae Province, and the last two in P'yŏngan and Kyŏnggi provinces, respectively.

It is plausible to argue that lineages with a majority of members living in P'yŏngan Province had a firm foundation in the region and a shared sense that their identity was closely tied to that specific location.[29] However, such strong ties between identity and location do not necessarily imply that these indigenous lineages formed an exclusive ruling stratum in the region or led regional society for a long period of time. Many other lineages representative of P'yŏngan Province originated elsewhere, migrated into the region, and subsequently moved within it looking for new land to settle. As in Hamgyŏng Province, there were lineages that had moved to P'yŏngan through exile in the early Chosŏn period. Even then, literati of P'yŏngan Province placed little weight on relationships with the south; rather, they claimed their prominence by emphasizing lineage and tradition within the region. They developed a strong sense that their history was entwined with that of P'yŏngan Province, compared to the Hamgyŏng lineages, which had branched more recently from southern roots.

SCHOLARLY ORIENTATIONS OF NORTHERN LITERATI IN THE SEVENTEENTH AND EIGHTEENTH CENTURIES

Dogmatism

Policies that encouraged Confucian learning in Hamgyŏng Province were adopted in the early Chosŏn period, but do not seem to have been implemented effectively. Cultural development of Hamgyŏng Province in the seventeenth century depended more on the individual efforts of local administrators dispatched by the central government, such as the provincial military inspector (Pyŏngma p'yŏngsa) or provincial governor (Kwanch'alsa), than on institutional support.[30]

Two men are particularly renowned: Yi Tanha (1625–89), a provincial military inspector appointed in 1664, and Min Chŏngjung (1628–92), a provincial governor from 1664/7 to 1667/9. They played a key role in elevating Hamgyŏng's stature by establishing private academies where Confucian scholar-officials who had previously exerted cultural influence over the region were enshrined, and in recognizing people of distinguished service during the Japanese invasions. They also advanced regional education by requesting books and instructors from the central government, and by publishing Confucian classics at the governor's office and distributing them widely. Their influence in Hamgyŏng Province is evident in the rumor that militarism there disappeared after Min Chŏngjung became governor.[31]

Their most important contribution was that, as core members of the Patriarch Faction (Noron), they introduced Hamgyŏng literati to Song Siyŏl (1607–89), the leader of that faction, and helped build the Hamgyŏng Region's scholarly connection to the Patriarch Faction. From then on, Hamgyŏng literati could form a scholarly genealogy with Song Siyŏl as its apical founder. This unified scholarly tradition promoted consolidation and solidarity among

Hamgyŏng literati, which strengthened their stature vis-à-vis other members of the community.

The scholarly tradition of Hamgyŏng Province was subdivided into two lines.[32] The first originated with the aforementioned Ch'oe Sin (1642–1709), who had studied directly under Song Siyŏl and shared Song's political stance. Ch'oe was respected as a founder of Neo-Confucianism in Hamgyŏng Province. He first studied under the provincial military inspector Yi Tanha, who recognized his talent. Subsequently, the provincial governor, Min Chŏngjung, recommended him to study under Song Chun'gil (1606–72), who was distantly related to Song Siyŏl. Ch'oe traveled hundreds of miles to learn from Song Chun'gil in Seoul. Later, he studied under Song Siyŏl for ten years, and put together what he learned from Song Siyŏl as a book, *Records of Things Heard and Seen at Hwayang* (*Hwayang mun'gyŏllok*). When Song Siyŏl was banished after being defeated in political strife, Ch'oe Sin, as Song's ideological "right arm," was likewise exiled to a remote southern region for twelve years. Though his exile ended in 1694, he was not able to return to the political scene and died after years of poverty in Kwangju, Kyŏnggi Province, where Song's grave was located. Ch'oe's life is detailed in the 470 verses he composed. These poems, complete with detailed annotations, were written to inform his nephews about family history and his life, and to request that they preserve the family's tradition. Taken together, these poems can be considered a family chronicle of literati of Hamgyŏng Province.[33]

Ch'oe's scholarly orientation was passed down to literati in the areas of Hoeryŏng and Chongsŏng. Han Seyang (1656–1725) was known as the authoritative successor of Ch'oe Sin's line, and Han's nephew, Han Mongnin (1684–1762), continued the tradition. Han Mongnin passed the lower civil service examination in 1710, but he gave up hope of passing the higher civil service examination after repeated failure. He devoted himself to Neo-Confucian learning and established his name as a scholar of the learning of the Way (*tohak*) by compiling literary works such as the *Reflections on Things at Hand, Continued* (*Sok kŭnsarok*). In a letter to Song Siyŏl's great-great-grandson, Song Nŭngsang, he claimed to be a legitimate disciple of Song Siyŏl, writing, "I fortunately took lessons from the pupil of the master's pupil." This scholarly tradition continued with Han Mongp'il (1699–1782), a brother and pupil of Han Mongnin, and then with his pupil Nam Myŏnghak (1731–98), a nephew on Han Mongp'il's mother's side.[34] Song Hwan'gi (1728–1807), Song

Siyŏl's fifth-generation descendant, publicly recognized Nam as one of the legitimate successors of Song's scholarship.[35]

The second scholarly tradition of Hamgyŏng Province began with Yi Chaehyŏng. Yi Chaehyŏng studied under Kim Ch'anghyŏp (1651–1708), a military inspector, appointed in 1685, who had been one of the best disciples in Song Siyŏl's academic circle. Kim Ch'anghŭp (1653–1722), a younger brother of Kim Ch'anghyŏp, met Yi on a trip to Hamgyŏng and spoke highly of him by saying that "my older brother's Way is in the north." Upon returning to Seoul, Kim Ch'anghŭp also recommended Yi Chaehyŏng to his older brother Kim Ch'angjip (1648–1722), who held ministerial rank at the time. Thus Yi Chaehyŏng's scholarship came to be widely known to the central court owing to its recognition by one of the core families of the Patriarch Faction. Yet Yi's connection to the central power group was limited to the exchange of letters and discussions on learning. He did not enter government service, although the king repeatedly dispatched a royal secret inspector and provincial governor to persuade him to hold office.

Whereas Ch'oe Sin, as a pupil of Song Siyŏl, had been called the founder of Neo-Confucianism in Hamgyŏng Province, Yi Chaehyŏng's scholarly contacts and achievements earned him the honorable title of master of Hamgyŏng Province (Kwanbuk puja). The central court also recognized him, together with Han Mongnin, as a representative literati from Hamgyŏng Province.[36] Yi Chaehyŏng's scholarly achievement was followed by that of literati from Kyŏngsŏng and Kilchu. Yi Wŏnbae (1745–1802) continued Yi Chaehyŏng's scholarly tradition, which was handed down to him through his grand-uncle Yi Yangse and his grandfather, Yi Sŏse, who had been pupils of Yi Chaehyŏng.[37] Yi Wŏnbae earned much fame because he was recognized by King Chŏngjo (r. 1776–1800). Im Chongch'il (1781–1859) studied under Yi Wŏnbae and continued the tradition of legitimacy set forth by Yi Chaehyŏng.[38]

Just as literati who continued Ch'oe Sin's scholarly tradition were recognized by descendants of Song Siyŏl, literati who carried on the tradition of Yi Chaehyŏng were officially recognized by descendants of Kim Ch'anghyŏp. This recognition can be seen in their collected literary works (munjip), because one of the functions of the preface and postscript to a munjip was to certify the academic and literary authority of its author. Kim Wŏnhaeng, a grandson of Kim Ch'anghyŏp, wrote the epilogue to Yi Chaehyŏng's mun-

jip (which was entitled *Songamjip*) and Kim Yigyo of the same Kim family wrote the introduction to Yi Wŏnbae's *munjip* (entitled *Kwiamjip*). Kim Pyŏnghak, Kim Ch'anghyŏp's sixth-generation descendant, wrote the introduction to the collected works of Im Chongch'il (entitled *Tunojip*), who continued Yi Wŏnbae's scholarly tradition. In this way Hamgyŏng literati's connection to the powerful and famous Kims and to the Patriarch Faction at the center was secured, which in turn solidified their stature in their home region.

The most crucial characteristic of Hamgyŏng literati's *munjip* in the seventeenth and eighteenth centuries is their devotion to Neo-Confucian ideology. Most writings in these collections are discussions of Neo-Confucian classics. Their subject matter tends to be their authors' academic experiences and dedication to scholarship. Even the poetry—the most creative form of literature—is filled with messages that encourage Neo-Confucian ideology. Yet it is difficult to conclude that these literary works, though profuse, are based on a true understanding of Neo-Confucianism. The academic achievements of the literati of Hamgyŏng Province seem pale compared to those of literati from the southern regions, who had benefited from a long history of cultural opportunities. To attain a high level of scholarship, it was necessary to appreciate academic trends and communicate with other scholars. It would be unrealistic to expect this of Hamgyŏng Province, where exchange with central literati was difficult and where access to books, mostly circulated through transcription, was extremely limited. Hamgyŏng literati put a higher value on careful and repeated readings of basic texts than on broad knowledge gained through wide-ranging books, and emphasized the practice of Confucian ethics and rituals. Thus they stressed the practice of fundamental Neo-Confucian ethics, the kernel of the *Sohak* (Elementary Learning).

Literati of Hamgyŏng Province tried to establish their identity both by advocating the scholarly tradition built around central literary figures in the capital and by being faithful to Neo-Confucianism. But a scholarly tradition with a central literary figure at the top entails academic subordination, and the blind pursuit of Neo-Confucianism creates academic rigidity. With such constraints, one could hardly expect academic diversity from the literati of Hamgyŏng Province.[39]

Pluralism

The aforementioned Sŏnu Hyŏp (1588–1653) is well known as the founder of Neo-Confucianism in P'yŏngan Province. Since Sŏnu Hyŏp's family was poor and had no books, he had to visit the library at the Kija Shrine, far from his home, to read them. One day, when he was exhausted and fell asleep, Kija appeared in his dream, gave him a poem, and told him to take it to the provincial governor. The poem was about the need to repair Kija's decayed shrine, and it carried a stern message: "As the world is tough, people become thoughtless, lose their gratitude, and forsake virtue."[40] The governor was very surprised at this poem and requested that the central government permit the repair. Sŏnu Hyŏp was twelve years old at the time.

Acquaintances tried to persuade Sŏnu Hyŏp to enter government service, but he declined, citing the excuse of supporting his parents. When he was thirty-eight, suddenly inspired while reading the chapter "Confucius ascended Tai Mountain" (Kongja tŭng T'aesan chang) in *Mencius*, he jumped to his feet, left the house, and headed for Kŭmgang Mountain. He wanted to experience what Confucius had seen before him—that the world looks very small from atop a mountain. Sŏnu Hyŏp came down from Kŭmgang Mountain, headed south, and arrived at Tosan Academy (Tosan sŏwŏn) in Kyŏngsang Province. Over several months there, he finished reading the whole literary collection at the academy. He then went to meet Chang Hyŏn'gwang (1554–1637) in Oksan, Kyŏngsang Province, and took a few days of lessons from him. He subsequently stayed at an abandoned temple on Yongak Mountain in his home region and studied Neo-Confucianism. Pupils gradually began to gather.[41]

Sŏnu Hyŏp's writings were published as the *Tunam chŏnsŏ* (Complete Works of Sŏnu Hyŏp) in 1681. *Chŏnsŏ* (complete works) is a title reserved for the collected works of a widely recognized Confucian sage and is thus not to be used indiscriminately. In this case the title seems to represent an effort by P'yŏngan literati to identify Sŏnu Hyŏp as one of the great Confucian sages, thereby enhancing the reputation of P'yŏngan literati and their scholarship.

It is difficult to find a scholarly genealogy of the literati of P'yŏngan Province, in contrast to Hamgyŏng Province, where such genealogy originates with scholars from Seoul. Sŏnu Hyŏp formed a brief connection with Chang Hyŏn'gwang, a celebrated scholar at the time, but never tried to adorn his scholarship with Chang's authority. Rather, the fact that he studied under a regional literati, Kim T'aejwa (1541–?), was emphasized. In the case of Kye Tŏkhae, a record shows that he studied under exiled central literati such as Yi Chinsu (1684–1732) and Kang Paek (1690–1777). Yet these two were not authoritative scholars and Kye was with them only briefly. More important was the fact that when he was young Kye was a pupil of the regional literatus Kim Hongun (1666–1751).

Our knowledge of scholar-pupil relationships among the literati of P'yŏngan Province is fragmentary. Sŏnu Hyŏp's scholarship was imparted to Chang Seryang, and then inherited by Hwang Minhu in Chang's later years.[42] However, there is no indication that this was recognized as a scholarly succession. In 1800, King Chŏngjo met Kim Tŏkhong and Kim Toyu of P'yŏngan Province, who had been selected for their scholarship, and granted books to them. This is the first known case of P'yŏngan literati recognition by the center of power since Sŏnu Hyŏp, over two hundred years. This record suggests that Sŏnu Hyŏp's scholarly tradition was not, in any clear fashion, handed down among the literati of P'yŏngan Province.[43]

Interestingly, the literati of P'yŏngan, including Sŏnu Hyŏp, focused on the study of the *Book of Changes* (C. *Yi jing*, K. *Yŏkkyŏng*). Most of Sŏnu Hyŏp's *munjip* are discussions and writings on this particular Confucian classic. Chang Seryang, Sŏnu's leading pupil, left writings such as the *Yŏksŏl* (Discussions on the Book of Changes) and the *Yŏngmun yuch'wi* (Collections of Divinatory Writings).[44] Another student of Sŏnu Hyŏp, Cho Kwan'guk, also excelled in the study of the *Book of Changes*.[45] The aforementioned Kye Tŏkhae, a representative literatus of the Ch'ŏngbuk Region, also devoted himself to the study of that book, and had writings from the *Book of Changes* all over the house.[46] According to *Sŏgyŏng sihwa* (A Talk on Poetry from the Western Capital), the *Chuyŏk yŏnŭi* (Explication of the Book of Changes) by Min Kwangbo rivaled Sŏnu Hyŏp's writings on the *Book of Changes*, and Hwang Ching, too, excelled in studies on the book. Both Min and Hwang are from P'yŏngan Province. Hŏ Mok (1595–1682), a leading scholar from the center, commented that Yi Kŏju, a P'yŏngan literatus, focused on the *Book of Changes* and nothing else.[47] Song Siyŏl said that Sŏnu Hyŏp's concentration on the *Book of Changes* embodied the academic tradition of the region, which derived from Kija, who had allegedly composed a chapter of the *Shu jing* (Book of History) entitled "Great principles to order the world" (Hongbŏm). Yi Sihang also confirms this.[48]

P'yŏngan literati were unique in stressing the study of the *Book of Changes*. The main focuses of scholarship among central literati of the time were on rituals and rites (*yehak*) and the learning of the mind and heart (*simsŏngnon*), although they did not disregard the learning of divination (*yŏkhak*). Several inferences as to why the learning of divination was popular in P'yŏngan Province can be made. First, it may have originated from a pedantic desire to show off while hiding academic backwardness. The *Book of Changes* is known to be one of the most puzzling and difficult of the Confucian classics. Some Confucian scholars, mostly local ones, wanted to be recognized for their competency in the *Book of Changes*. Although Sŏnu Hyŏp was known to have excelled in the learning of divination, his academic achievements fell short of deserving the title *chŏnsŏ* (complete works) that was attached to the collection of his literary accomplishments. As Song Siyŏl pointed out, most of the pieces in the *Complete Works of Sŏnu Hyŏp* (*Tunam chŏnsŏ*) are summaries of existing commentaries on the Confucian classics. Song Siyŏl explained that this was a real service to the scholars of P'yŏngan Province, who suffered from an acute shortage of books. But there is no doubt that Sŏnu Hyŏp's achievement was somewhat overstated.[49] The level of textual understanding of Sŏnu Hyŏp and of other P'yŏngan literati was generally not much higher than that of Hamgyŏng literati.

Second, the learning of the *Book of Changes* explains the principle of creation and changes of the universe. It is nondogmatic and value-neutral compared to the learning of nature and principle (*sŏngnihak*), which had become largely orthodox as the governing ideology of Chosŏn. It is also metaphysically pliable in various fields, which suited the relatively flexible academic trends of the P'yŏngan Region. One peculiarity of the *Book of Changes* is its pluralistic dimension as a divinatory document. For this reason, some local intellectuals and religious leaders used it to "delude the world and deceive the people." It was also used as an ideological foundation for rebels against the ruling ideology. Even into the late Chosŏn, Neo-Confucianism was not firmly accepted as an ideological foundation in some areas of the north, which was known as a place of rampant heresy and heterodoxy that tolerated Buddhism, Daoism, and other religions. Within the northern region, P'yŏngan Province was most notorious for such heresies. Royal secret inspectors dispatched to P'yŏngan Province were specifically warned to look out for people carrying mysterious books and spreading false teachings, and places like Paengnyŏng-bang in

Yŏngbyŏn and Sinsŏngul in Sŏngch'ŏn were pointed out as trouble spots. Various prophetic writings were widespread in P'yŏngan Province, and restlessness among the populace was seen as a serious problem.[50] Such trends in pluralistic ideology or religion can also be seen in the Sŏgyŏng sihwa. The editor of the Sŏgyŏng sihwa recorded many anecdotes about ghosts and writings on divination in the appendix, under headings such as "miracles" (sini) and "witchcraft" (panggi).[51]

The ideological flexibility in P'yŏngan Province is also apparent from the emergence of many eminent Buddhist monks there. The relationship between the production of high priests and deep-rooted regional discrimination is yet to be clarified. What is clear is that, despite Chosŏn society's general stigma against Buddhist monks, that stigma was not as severe in P'yŏngan. Sŏsan Hyujŏng (1520–1604), P'yŏnyang Ŏn'gi (1582–1644), Wŏlchŏ Toan (1638–1715), Sŏram Ch'ubung (1651–1706), and Hŏjŏng Pŏpchong (1670–1733) are among the monks from P'yŏngan Province mentioned in the Sŏgyŏng sihwa. Their stature in Korean Buddhist history is much greater than the stature of literati of the same region in Korean literary history.[52]

Further evidence of the flexible ideological orientation of the region is found in the quality of P'yŏngan's attainment in art and literature rather than in study of the Confucian classics per se. It seems that P'yŏngan literati considered it more important to hand down a poetic tradition than a scholarly one. Anecdotes to the effect that Hwang Yunhu designated Kim Uk as his successor after testing Kim's literary skills, and that Yi Sihang did the same with Kim Chŏm—the compiler of the Sŏgyŏng sihwa, whose talent was supposedly on a par with that of Lu You (1125–1210), a renowned Chinese poet—show P'yŏngan literati's pride in their regional literary tradition.[53] Although this type of succession did not continue for many generations, it is striking that such a tradition did not exist among the Hamgyŏng literati.

The literary achievements of P'yŏngan literati were considered far superior to those of Hamgyŏng literati, and they produced celebrated painters and writers from early on. The Sŏgyŏng sihwa is lavish in speaking of their achievements.[54] Whereas Hamgyŏng literati came into contact with central literati only when the latter were appointed as local magistrates or exiled to Hamgyŏng Province, P'yŏngan literati had repeated opportunities to meet scholars and officials from the center when they passed through the region on diplomatic missions to and from China. This explains both the development of Chinese poetry as a means of literary exchange and the growth of Korean poetry for entertainment in the region.[55] Some literati whose talents were recognized were given the opportunity to aid Chosŏn officials in dealing with Chinese envoys. P'yŏngan also had a relatively broad human basis for literature. The *Sŏgyŏng sihwa* contains literary critiques by Confucian literati, Buddhist monks, commoners, and even women, in contrast to the *Selected Poems from Hamgyŏng Province* (*Kwanbuk sisŏn*), which only presents Confucian literati and their works.

One of the reasons P'yŏngan Province came to display relatively high cultural standards and diversity was the development of print culture in Chosŏn, for which P'yŏngyang was an important hub. The P'yŏngyang district office owned its own blocks of type in the early Chosŏn period, and it continued to produce various kinds of metal and wooden types and to publish books throughout the Chosŏn period. Several national publication projects of multivolume works were carried out in P'yŏngyang.[56] In addition, quite a few imported books were circulated there, a benefit of being on the route to China.[57] Such features of P'yŏngyang's book culture surely had a great influence on the expansion and growth of regional literati.

Excellence in literature, however, did not guarantee success at the central court. The regional literati's cultural achievements were mostly byproducts of their devotion to studying for the state examination, success at which exempted them from mandatory labor and military service and enabled them to maintain status as members of the local elite. There are records that Pyŏn Hwan, Yi Chin, Kye Unsik, and others carried on a ghostwriting (*taejak*) business in the examination hall.[58] Generally, ghostwriting was done by those with talent but without social status, who were therefore not eligible to serve in the government. The fact that these highly regarded people, included in the *Sŏgyŏng sihwa*, were in the business of ghostwriting tells us that the pathway of advancement for a literatus of P'yŏngan Province was a very narrow one.

RECOGNITION OF REALITY AND REACTIONS

As the economic and cultural gap between the center and the periphery widened in the late Chosŏn, regional alienation deepened. Nowhere was this felt more acutely than in the northern region. As Yi Ik (1681–1763) put it, "Half of the country is cut off and discarded."[59]

For three hundred years, from the beginning of Chosŏn until the early eighteenth century, when the *Sŏgyŏng sihwa* was compiled, only eleven people from P'yŏngan Province passed all three (preliminary, second, and final) stages of the civil service examination.[60] Although this number increased rapidly in the late Chosŏn, the most successful candidates were assigned to the lower positions, such as district magistrate (Hyŏngam) or superintendent of a royal tomb or shrines (Ch'ambong). The increased number of degree-holders did not mean much in itself because few northerners earned ministerial ranks (*tangsanggwan*), and rarely were they advanced to reputable and prestigious posts (*ch'ŏngyojik*). The situation was no different for Hamgyŏng Province. There were only two civil servants, Yi Chion and Kim Ni, who had advanced to a government post higher than vice minister (Ch'amp'an) until the end of the nineteenth century.[61] There were also only two military officers, Chang Seryang and Chŏn Paengnok, who had advanced to a government post higher than provincial military commander (Pyŏngma chŏltosa). This situation continued during the late Chosŏn, when northern societies experienced dynamic changes.

P'yŏngan and Hamgyŏng provinces were treated similarly by the center, but engaged in no joint effort to systematically overcome the alienation. This was partly due to a lack of mutual exchange and understanding between the two provinces. More importantly, they had fundamentally different regional histories, cultures, and ways of assessing and responding to marginalization. Literati of the two regions knew that both groups were being discriminated against. However, their views of the reasons for the discrimination and ways of reacting to it differed from each other. A sense of belonging in Hamgyŏng versus a confrontational attitude in P'yŏngan explains these differences.

A Sense of Belonging

Most literati of Hamgyŏng Province acknowledged the marginalization of the region as an established fact and did not attempt to look for its cause. They simply accepted that Hamgyŏng Province was a frontier with barren soil, that it was far from the center, and that it could not measure up culturally to the standards represented by the capital.[62] This resignation underwrote a willingness to admire the central literati and to accept the idea that the continued growth of regional society in the north since the beginning of Chosŏn had occurred thanks to the attention and consideration of the central elite as argued earlier.[63]

There are several reasons for this regional lack of self-esteem. First, Hamgyŏng people thought that their regional history began with the Chosŏn Dynasty. As mentioned earlier, Hamgyŏng literati stressed the fact that their home was the place of origin of the dynasty, and they tried to establish their regional cultural tradition from this standpoint. The *Records of Tombs and Shrines in Hamgyŏng Province* (*Pukto nŭngjŏn chi*), compiled in 1747 by Wi Ch'angjo (1703–71), promotes such an idea. It contains detailed records on the achievements of King T'aejo (r. 1392–98), the founder of the Chosŏn Dynasty, and his ancestors. The author apparently collected vast amounts of data that had been scattered throughout Hamgyŏng Province. For this meritorious deed he was awarded a government post. Yet his recognition of regional history before the foundation of Chosŏn remains slim. Other Hamgyŏng literati shared Wi's position, for local gazetteers compiled by them included very little information on the region before the Chosŏn era. This attitude contrasts sharply with that of P'yŏngan literati, who traced their regional history back into ancient times and maintained a clear sense of regional culture and identity.

The perspective adopted by Chu Ch'ŏjŏng (1649–?), the compiler of the *Kwanbuk sisŏn*, seems to have been similar. Chu Ch'ŏjŏng completed editing this anthology in 1710 and received the preface from Hamgyŏng's governor, Chŏng Ho (1648–1736), in 1711. With the help of regional literatus Han Chewŏn (1663–?), the book was printed with woodblocks in 1714.[64] The first section, a "record of families" (*ssimyŏng sajŏk*), includes detailed personal histories of sixty-two selected literati of Hamgyŏng Province. The fact that there is no entry during the pre-Chosŏn era indicates that the book's recognition of regional history begins with the founding of the dynasty. And the fact that Kim Ni is the earliest entry suggests that the literati themselves admitted that the emergence of regional literati as a group occurred fairly late. From the perspective of a central literatus, however, the achievements of Hamgyŏng literati were not so notable. In the preface, Chŏng Ho is enthusiastic only about the unaffected and honest expressions of emotion evident in the collection.

The *Kwanbuk sisŏn* contains 305 poems in literary Chinese (*hansi*) and eleven prose writings by Hamgyŏng literati. This number of poems imitates the structure of the *Shi jing* (Book of Odes). Just as the first section of the *Shi jing* contains songs collected from the birthplace of the Zhu Dynasty, such as the "Zhunan" and "Zhaonan," so the *Kwanbuk sisŏn* clearly claims that Hamgyŏng Province was the source of the Chosŏn royal family, and projects the hope that Hamgyŏng literati will be incorporated into the royal court.[65] In sum, the *Kwanbuk sisŏn* is an important document illustrating that Hamgyŏng literati consciously and collectively identified themselves with the Chosŏn dynasty.

A Confrontational Attitude

P'yŏngan literati tended to be convinced that political discrimination against them originated from ill feelings harbored by members of the central elite, and thus they developed deep-rooted anger and a pervasive confrontational attitude toward this group. Central officials targeted for criticism included Kim Pusik (1075–1151) and So Seyang (1486–1562), who were regarded as the engineers of regional discrimination. P'yŏngan literati thought that Kim Pusik had been jealous of the superior literary talent of Chŏng Chisang of P'yŏngyang and had Chŏng executed on the pretext that he had been behind Myoch'ŏng's rebellion in 1135.[66] It was also widely believed among P'yŏngan people that So Se-Yang, a central literary figure of the early Chosŏn, had initiated political discrimination against them because Hong Sŭngbŏm from P'yŏngyang had composed a poem mocking him.[67]

Not surprisingly, few central figures were respected or worshipped by P'yŏngan people. Rather, their antipathy was acute, and was sometimes expressed in satirical *kasa* (long vernacular verses) that criticized government officials.[68] Periodic damaging statements about the region by the central elite also hurt P'yŏngan literati, causing them to react with rage. As they began to emerge as a power group, P'yŏngan literati did not hide their dissatisfaction over unfair treatment from the center. They even launched organized responses to the injustice and prejudice held by the central court.

For example, in 1694, Yi Chŏng, the magistrate of Sŏngch'ŏn, wrote in a memorial that local officials of P'yŏngan Province were the descendants of slaves, that Confucian scholars (of this region) were a group of vagrants and bandits, and that they were undutiful to their parents. When this memorial became known, furious Confucian scholars of P'yŏngan immediately rebutted it in an appeal. Yet the court supported Yi Chŏng, further incensing residents of the province.[69] Two decades later, as a royal secret inspector to P'yŏngan Province in 1714, one Yŏ P'ilhŭi reported un-Confucian aspects of the province's customs and disparaged its residents as "barbarians and beasts." In response, more than 160 Confucian scholars of P'yŏngan, led by Kil Inhwa, submitted a joint petition, penned by Yi Sihang, to censure Yŏ P'ilhŭi. When Yŏ P'ilhŭi was nevertheless appointed an examiner at the state civil service examinations, all the applicants from P'yŏngan Province refused to enter the examination hall, protesting that they could not relate with him as students to a master.[70] Still later, in 1781, Third Minister of the Ministry of Military Affairs (Pyŏngjo Ch'amŭi) Yun Myŏndong (1728–?) offended P'yŏngan literati in a memorial reporting abuses of military administration in the region. He criticized their tendency to lose themselves in literature and then asked, "What use would this group be even if they do read?"[71] In this case King Chŏngjo issued a royal ordinance to console the P'yŏngan people, but the situation worsened when Confucian scholars of P'yŏngan in the Royal Confucian Academy refused to apply for examination. The king severely punished the instigator of this protest by exiling him and expelling his followers from the academy.[72] These examples show that Confucian scholars of P'yŏngan Province reacted to offense and discrimination as a group and attempted to censure people who made prejudiced statements against the region. Such cases cannot be found in Hamgyŏng Province.

The *Sŏgyŏng sihwa* was compiled to promote the cultural tradition and excellence of the P'yŏngan Region. Its editor, Kim Chŏm from P'yŏngyang, had passed the lower civil service examination in 1721 and been admitted to the Royal Confucian Academy. However, he never passed the higher civil service examination and spent an unrecognized life in P'yŏngyang. In 1774, at the age of eighty, he had a chance to meet Ch'ae Chegong (1720–99), who had been appointed governor of P'yŏngan Province. Ch'ae Chegong read ten of Kim's books, was amazed at their excellence, and at the same time felt sorry for Kim's misfortune, a consequence of his regional origin. Later, when Kim Chŏm died, Ch'ae acted on the request of Kim Chŏm's son and wrote an introduction for Kim's collected literary works.[73]

Kim Chŏm was relatively young when he realized the necessity of collecting and compiling regional literature and embarked on this mission. He stated in the first introduction to the *Sŏgyŏng sihwa*, in 1728, that he was compiling this book because he was concerned that literary achievements by

P'yŏngan people might vanish if they were not made widely known to others. Kim Chŏm always referred to the province as "our P'yŏngan Province" (osŏ) and to P'yŏngyang as "our P'yŏngyang" (ogi), showing his affection and appreciation for regional culture. He clearly developed close solidarity with fellow regional literati. He compiled the first edition in 1728, but was dissatisfied that its contents were limited to the writings of P'yŏngyang literati. Thus he broadened the scope to include writings from all of P'yŏngan Province, and finished the enlarged edition five years later, in 1733. About a hundred literati of P'yŏngan Province are represented and 320 poems were included in this comprehensive anthology of regional literary works.

Whereas the *Kwanbuk sisŏn* limited its scope to works by literati of Hamgyŏng Province during the Chosŏn period, the *Sŏgyŏng sihwa* went beyond Chosŏn and included literature handed down from ancient times. Names are unknown for all but three of the pre-Chosŏn authors whose writings are included in the *Sŏgyŏng sihwa*: Kija, Ŭlchi Mundŏk, and Chŏng Chisang. As the compiler of the *Sŏgyŏng sihwa*, Kim Chŏm made every effort to elevate the long and illustrious literary tradition of the province, even listing the names of authors whose writings were no longer extant.

The *Sŏgyŏng sihwa* was also unusual in that it extended its spatial reach into Manchuria and incorporated Koguryŏ culture as a part of P'yŏngan's cultural history. Koguryŏ territory had not been limited to P'yŏngan Province, and the exact birthplaces of Koguryŏ people were unknown in most cases. Nevertheless, the *Sŏgyŏng sihwa* included the culture of Koguryŏ as a part of regional cultural history and regarded all Koguryŏ people as people of the region.[74] Such historical recognition was not unique to the editor of the *Sŏgyŏng sihwa*. In the *Gazetteer of the Western Capital (Sŏgyŏngji)*, Yi Sihang, Kim Chŏm's teacher, pointed out that previous gazetteers had erred in dropping the historical facts prior to Koguryŏ's transfer of its capital to P'yŏngyang. He claimed that Koguryŏ's entire history should be included in the regional history, just as the genealogy and chronology of the royal family of Silla (57 BCE?–935) were included in the gazetteer of Kyŏngju, capital of Silla. He indicated that the remains of King Tongmyŏng, the founder of Koguryŏ, were still in P'yŏngyang, along with other materials related to Koguryŏ history in the region, because P'yŏngyang had been the capital of Koguryŏ for many years. Thus, he urged that all sources be diligently collected and incorporated into the regional history.[75]

Kim Chŏm, following his teacher's injunction, included in the *Sŏgyŏng sihwa* songs of ancient times that had been handed down in P'yŏngan Province. He pointed out that "the way of our poems and songs all originated from these," and reminded readers that the root of Chosŏn's literature was in P'yŏngan Province.[76] He also stressed that P'yŏngan literati, though not prominent in their official careers, continued the regional cultural tradition through decent literary achievements comparable to those of the literati of earlier times. Many anecdotes in the *Sŏgyŏng sihwa* tell us that P'yŏngan literati defeated the central literati with their poetic talent. This further suggests their confrontational attitude toward the center literati.

Another work that shows this attitude is Yi Sihang's "Song of the Western Capital" (Sŏgyŏngbu), a long poem of about 4,000 Chinese characters that is quoted in the *Sŏgyŏng sihwa*. The "Sŏgyŏngbu" consists of conversations between a host of the western capital (Sŏgyŏng chuin) and a guest from the eastern capital (Tongdo pin). It ends with the song of a master from the central capital (Hando taein) who declares that he will help the civil administration by hiring talented people from P'yŏngan Province. The host of the western capital is from P'yŏngyang and the guest from the eastern capital is from Kyŏngju. Each brags about his regional history, culture, and prominent people, but in the end the host completely defeats the guest. The "Sŏgyŏngbu" describes the humiliated guest "running away senselessly" after losing the debate.[77] It may be difficult to assert that this confrontation originated from a deep-rooted antagonism between northern and southern culture. However, given that the guest represents the former capital of the Silla kingdom in the southern region and is boasting about its long cultural tradition, it is not too much to argue that the poem tries to manifest pride in the northern cultural tradition. As mentioned earlier, its author, Yi Sihang, had also written the memorial censuring Yŏ P'ilhŭi's prejudice against the P'yŏngan's regional culture in 1714.

CONCLUSION

The northern region had been well integrated into the dynastic ruling system ever since being incorporated into the territory of Chosŏn. Residents of the area bore heavier labor and military responsibilities than the rest of the kingdom because the north was a border region as well as the frontier of the dynasty. Although some magistrates with military service backgrounds created problems of mal-administration, administrative rules and Confucian ethics effectively penetrated the region. Thus the general population of the region probably did not receive obvious mistreatment from the central court.

However, members of elite groups in the north, who were theoretically eligible for central bureaucratic positions and had rather frequent contact with literati from other regions, did encounter discrimination in their relations with the central literati. Regional discrimination in terms of bureaucratic advancement clearly distinguished them from literati from other regions, leaving them in unequal and unfavorable partnerships with scholarship and politics. In the late Chosŏn, literati from the two northern provinces of Hamgyŏng and P'yŏngan had therefore invested in distinctive regional identities in a conscious effort to overcome the prejudicial treatment they received from the center.

Many northern elite families had put great emphasis that they originally migrated from the south. Northern literati incessantly tried to forge connections with the central elite and hold offices in the central court, and they pursued Confucian scholarship and culture. These elements could have bound literati from the two provinces together. Yet the literati of each province perceived themselves differently and employed different strategies in response to the discriminatory politics of the center. And such differences originated from diverse regional histories and cultures.

The regional history of Hamgyŏng literati begins only with the founding of Chosŏn. Their records show almost no pre-Chosŏn history, and even when mentioned, the area before Chosŏn times is depicted as a backward region that civilization did not reach. The fact that the founder of Chosŏn had his power base in Hamgyŏng was highlighted whenever possible. The region's elites claimed ancestry from southern literati exiled to the area, not from the indigenous population. By tracing their ancestry to the southern yangban and their scholarship to centrally prominent figures, they were able to distinguish themselves from the general population of the region and strengthen their position as the ruling elite of the province.

In contrast, P'yŏngan literati made full use of the province's long history from ancient times, and of its deep cultural roots. They felt great pride in their cultural heritage, and even those who had migrated from the south took such regional culture as their own. Rather than connecting their scholarly genealogy to the literati in the center, they emphasized their own scholarly origin and tradition. This enabled them to put their culture on a par with that of the central elites. They wanted not only to secure their superior status within their own home region, but also to earn equal treatment from the center.

NOTES

*This chapter is a slightly revised, translated edition of my paper, "Chosŏn hugi sŏbuk chiyŏk munin chiptan ŭi sŏnggyŏk—P'yŏngan-do wa Hamgyŏng-do ŭi chiyŏk chŏngch'esŏng ch'ai rŭl chungsim ŭro" (The Characteristics of Literati in the Northern Region—Focusing on the Regional Identities of P'yŏngan and Hamgyŏng Provinces and Their Differences), *Chindan hakpo* 101 (2006): 391–425.

1. For previous studies on the northern region, regional identity, and the issue of discrimination, see Sun Joo Kim, "Negotiating Cultural Identities in Conflict"; and O Such'ang, *Chosŏn hugi P'yŏngan-do sahoe palchŏn yŏn'gu.*

2. Gazetteers were compiled by local literati from the early Chosŏn period on. In Hamgyŏng Province, Mun Tŏkkyo (1551–1611) compiled the *Hamsanji* (Gazetteer of Hamhŭng) by supplementing the section on Hamhŭng in the *Tongguk yŏji sŭngnam* (Survey of the Geography of Korea). The *Hamsanji t'onggi* (Gazetteer of Hamhŭng, 1699) by Chu Yŏjŏng was published independently and widely circulated. Yi Sihang (1672–1736), with the support of the local government, compiled the *Kwansŏ t'ongji* (Comprehensive Gazetteer of P'yŏngan Province) and *Sŏgyŏngji* (Gazetteer of the Western Capital). There are quite a few gazetteer-type writings included in the collected literary works of local literati.

3. The *Kwansŏ ch'unghyorok* (Records of Men of Loyalty and Filial Piety from P'yŏngan Province, 1732) by Song Inmyŏng (1689–1746) is an example of biographies compiled by the government. *Suyŏl ch'ŏnch'u chŏn* (Biography of Ch'oe Hyoil, 1843) by Ch'oe Chungsik (1772–?) is an example of a biography by a local literatus.

4. Chang Yusŭng (Jang Yoo-seung), "17–18 segi Hamgyŏng-do chiyŏk ŭi munjip p'yŏnch'an kwa sŏjŏk kanhaeng," 65–66.

5. There are works by more than a hundred literati from P'yŏngan Province in the *Sŏgyŏng sihwa*, yet only thirteen collected works of P'yŏngan literati are extant. Kim Chŏm, *Sŏgyŏng sihwa*, 590–91.

6. *Injo sillok*, 34:39, 1625/10/18.

7. O Such'ang, *Chosŏn hugi P'yŏngan-do sahoe palchŏn yŏn'gu*, 65–67.

8. King Injo's court adopted an uncompromising anti-Manchu policy because one of the justifications for the coup had been to restore Chosŏn's "loyalty to the Ming

Dynasty" (*taemyŏng ŭiri*), which had sent military aid to Chosŏn when it was invaded by the Japanese. The previous king, Kwanghae-gun (1608–23), was pictured as having betrayed the Ming because he had pursued a neutral policy when the Manchus were emerging as the new power and the Ming's fate was in danger. For foreign policy by Kwanghae-gun and Injo, see Han Myŏnggi, *Kwanghae-gun*.

9. Yi Sanghyŏp, *Chosŏn chŏn'gi pukpang samin yŏn'gu*, 17–27.

10. The last entry for Mun Ch'ŏnbong in the *T'aejong sillok* concerns his appointment as a garrison commander in the northeast region (Tongbuk-myŏn Ch'ŏmjŏlchesa) on 1409/10/27. Given this, it is probable that he settled in the area after proceeding to Hamgyŏng Province to hold the position. *T'aejong sillok*, 1:516, 1409/10/27.

11. Mun Tŏkkyo, *Tonghojip*, *Tongho sŏnsaeng Mun-gong haengjang* (composed by Han Kibaek), appendix: 8b–9a. There are records of Mun's correspondence with famous central literati such as Kim Sanghŏn (1570–1652) and Ch'a Ch'ŏllo (1556–1615). Mun Tŏkkyo also seemed to have had considerable wealth because Ch'a Ch'ŏllo described Mun Tŏkkyo's manor as being very large. Ch'a Ch'ŏllo, *Osanjip*, *Tongho pyŏrŏpki*, 5:13a–b.

12. Kim Ni, *Yudangjip*, *haengjang* (composed by Yu Kilchun), appendix 2:4b. This biography states that Kim Ni was promoted to vice minister in the Ministry of Military Affairs (Pyŏngjo Ch'amp'an) in 1613, although there is some doubt in his collected works about the records concerning his later life.

13. Yi Chion, *Pin'gyo munjip*, *haengjang* (composed by Han Su), 4:7a.

14. Ch'oe Sin, *Hagamjip*, *haengjang* (composed by Min T'aeho), appendix 2:1a–b.

15. Yi Chaehyŏng, *Songamjip*, *haengjang* (composed by Kim Wŏnhaeng), 6:1a.

16. For claims that the cultural standard was higher in northern Hamgyŏng Province than it was in the south, see Chŏng Wŏnyong, *Pukhaeng surok*; and Han Hoesŏn, *Yujaejip*, *Yujaejip pal* (composed by Mun Sulmo):1b–2a.

17. Yun Tusu, *P'yŏngyangji*, 1:2b–4a and 4:1a–36b.

18. Kim Chŏm, *Sŏgyŏng sihwa*, 572.

19. *Injo sillok*, 34:538, 1633/11/13.

20. *Injo sillok*, 35:337, 1648/10/5.

21. *Sukchong sillok*, 39:35, 1685/6/25.

22. Kwŏn Sangha, *Hansujaejip*, *T'ongjŏng taebu Sŭngjŏngwŏn Tongbusŭngji kyŏm Kyŏngyŏn Ch'amch'an'gwan Hwang-gong Yunhu haengjang*, 34:24a–b.

23. Chung, the apical ancestor of the Sŏnu lineage, was a descendant of Kija. After Kija was enfoeffed in Chosŏn, he was given a land grant in U. Thus Chung created his surname, Sŏn-U, using the second half of the word "Chosŏn" and the word "U," and took Taiyuan as his ancestral seat. His descendants settled in T'aech'ŏn, in the northwestern part of the Korean peninsula, during King Kongmin's reign. Sŏnu Hyŏp, *Tunam chŏnsŏ*, *haengjang* (composed by Yi Tam), appendix:1a.

24. Sŏnu Hyŏp, *Tunam chŏnsŏ, haengjang* (composed by Yi Tam), appendix:1a.

25. Yi Sihang, *Hwaŭnjip, Hoehŏn Yang-gong haengjang*, 7:6b–7a.

26. Kim Chŏm, *Sŏgyŏng sihwa*, 586–87. This is verified by the *Kwansŏ chinsillok* (Civil Service Examination Passers from P'yŏngan Province). P'yŏngyang literati were dominant in the *munkwa* until the mid-Chosŏn period. However, the rise of literati from the Ch'ŏngbuk Region, which had produced no *munkwa* passers in the early Chosŏn, was a phenomenon of the late Chosŏn period. As pointed out in the *T'aengniji* (A Guide to Select Villages), Chŏngju literati's performance was particularly distinguished and eventually surpassed that of P'yŏngyang. Yi Chunghwan, *T'aengniji*, 8–9.

27. Kye Tŏkhae, *Ponggok Kye Ch'albang yujip, Ponggok Kye sŏnsaeng haengjang* (composed by Kim Chemyŏn), 12:17a.

28. Kye Tŏkhae, *Ponggok Kye Ch'albang yujip, yundae*, 10:1a.

29. In Chean Hwang's family, all but one of the thirty-seven people who passed a lower civil service examination resided in P'yŏngan Province. Among the thirty-three members of the Koksan Kang family who passed the exam, twenty-seven resided in P'yŏngan Province (81.8 percent), and in Tangak Yang's family, eight successful exam candidates resided there. There were also many from the Paech'ŏn Cho, Namyang Hong, and other lineages who resided in P'yŏngan Province, but because these were originally large lineages whose members lived all over the country, successful candidates from P'yŏngyang Province represented only a fraction of the whole. Other successful candidates who resided in P'yŏngan Province included nine from the Taiyuan Sŏnu family (that produced Sŏnu Hyŏp) and ten from the Suan Kye family, whose line included Kye Tŏkhae. Looking more broadly at statistics of those passing the lower exam, 118 lineages (about 34 percent of the total) out of 355 lineages of P'yŏngan Province produced successful candidates only in P'yŏngan Province. Ch'oe Chinok, "Chosŏn sidae P'yŏngan-do ŭi saengwŏn chinsasi hapkyŏkcha silt'ae," 228–37. For a similar trend in the higher civil service examination, see Wagner, "The Civil Examination Process as Social Leaven."

30. Military inspectors played an important role in promoting education in Hamgyŏng Province. Only highly renowned and talented literary men were recommended for the position, and those who served in that role from the sixteenth to eighteenth century were from the highest literary circles of the time. Military inspectors resided in the Office of Inspector (Tosach'ŏng) located in Kyŏngsŏng, and since Confucian scholars gathered to learn from them, Kyŏngsŏng became one of the cultural centers of Hamgyŏng Province.

31. *Sukchong sillok*, 38:299, 1675/8/29.

32. O Sanggyu, *Koejŏngjip, Kwanbuk yŏnwŏllok*, 1:99b–101b.

33. Ch'oe Sin, *Hagamjip, Hwajŭng chilson Sanghyo Sangŭi Sangch'ung manin kyŏm sijejok si*, 1:1a–5a.

34. Han Mongp'il, *Yuhŏn yugo*, *Yuhŏn yugo sŏ* (composed by Hwang Sŭngwŏn).

35. Nam Myŏnghak, *Oryongjae yugo*, *Oryongjae yugo sŏ* (composed by Song Hwan'gi).

36. *Yŏngjo sillok*, 42:565, 1737/8/26 and 43:536, 1754/7/17; *Sunjo sillok*, 48:163, 1820/7/23; and *Hŏnjong sillok*, 48:443, 1836/4/5.

37. Yi Wŏnbae, *Kwiamjip*, *Myogalmyŏng* (composed by O Hŭisang), appendix:1b.

38. Im Chongch'il, *Tunojip*, *haengjang* (composed by Cho Pyŏngdŏk), 11:1b.

39. Han Sŏkchi (1709–1791) may exemplify the dogmatic academic tendency of Hamgyŏng Province. Han attained academic "enlightenment" at the age of thirty-five, in 1743, and began to write about his unique philosophical system. What stands out is his claim that Neo-Confucianism had been affected by Daoism and Buddhism and thus distorted the essence of Confucianism, which needed to be recovered from the Confucianism of ancient times. The strength of this condemnation of Neo-Confucianism was unprecedented, and it confronted the central literati by publicly criticizing the ruling ideology of the time. However, Han lacked a deep understanding of Neo-Confucianism; his ideas are mainly a denial of Buddhism and Daoism, and not really an investigation of Neo-Confucianism. His faithful attitude toward Confucianism even renders his ideas dogmatic. Perhaps a similar dogmatism is evident in later literati of Hamgyŏng Province, such as Sŏl T'aehŭi (1875–1940), who was known as a reformist Confucian. Han Sŏkchi, *Myŏngsŏllok*.

40. Sŏnu Hyŏp, *Tuam chŏnsŏ*, *haengjang* (composed by Yi Tam), appendix:1b–2a.

41. Sŏnu Hyŏp, *Tunam chŏnsŏ*, *haengjang* (composed by Yi Tam), appendix:1a.

42. Yi Tŏksu, *Sŏdang sajae*, *Sŏnggyun Chikkang Hwang-gong myogalmyŏng*, 8:31b–32a.

43. *Chŏngjo sillok*, 47:253, 1800/3/28.

44. Yi Tŏksu, *Sŏdang sajae*, *Hwaam Chang-gong myogalmyŏng*, 7:2b.

45. Yi Sihang, *Hwaŭnjip*, *Kamch'al Cho-gong myogalmyŏng*, 8:6b–7a.

46. Kye Tŏkhae, *Ponggok Kye Ch'albang yujip*, *Ponggok Kye sŏnsaeng haengjang* (composed by Kim Chemyŏn), 12: 18b.

47. Hŏ Mok, *Kiŏn*, *Yi-ch'ŏsa myop'yo*, *pyŏlchip* 25:1b.

48. Sŏnu Hyŏp, *Tunam chŏnsŏ*, *Tunam sŏnsaeng chŏnsŏ sŏ* (composed by Song Siyŏl); and Yi Sihang, *Hwaŭnjip*, *Kamch'al Cho-gong myogalmyŏng*, 8:6b–7a.

49. Sŏnu Hyŏp, *Tunam chŏnsŏ*, *Tunam sŏnsaeng chŏnsŏ sŏ* (composed by Song Siyŏl).

50. *P'alto ŏsa chaegŏ samok*.

51. Such a pluralistic tendency is rarely found in the tradition of Hamgyŏng literati, who committed themselves to defying unorthodox ideas as a way of consolidating Neo-Confucian order in the region. Even in long vernacular verses (*kasa*), major themes consisted of defying heterodoxy and encouraging Confucian ideology.

52. Most of these monks left *munjip*. Yet their regional identities are not pronounced in their writings, probably because they were Buddhist monks. The only exception is

Ch'ubung's *History of Myohyang Mountain* (*Myohyangsanji*), which contains detailed information about the remains and the myth of Tan'gun.

53. Kim Chŏm, *Sŏgyŏng sihwa*, 577 and 581.

54. Kim Chŏm, *Sŏgyŏng sihwa*, 592–94.

55. Poems and songs in Korean created in P'yŏngan Province were strongly oriented toward entertainment. In Hamgyŏng Province, by contrast, poems and songs of regional literati mostly describe the lives of noble families or aim to propagate Confucian ethics. Examples of the latter are: "Kwan'gok p'algyŏng" (Eight Scenic Places in Kwan'gok), "Ch'aemiga" (Song of Picking Herbs) and "Nongbusa" (Song of Farmers) by Kim Kihong, and "Kilmongga" (Song of Auspicious Dreams) by Han Sŏkchi.

56. Yun Pyŏngt'ae, "Chosŏn sidae P'yŏngyang ŭi inswae munhwa."

57. According to an anecdote in the *Sŏgyŏng sihwa*, a Chinese merchant came to sell eccentric books of ancient and modern times. When a literatus of Anju, Pyŏn Chiik, recited them from memory, the merchant was startled and gave a shipload of books to Pyŏn. The fact that Kye Tŏkhae had been restrained from possessing a forbidden book, the *Hwangmyŏng t'onggi* (Comprehensive History of the Ming Dynasty), shows that Chinese books circulated in the northern region. Cho Segŏl, a wealthy artist of P'yŏngyang, was known to possess many Chinese paintings and writings. The fact that Cho Hŭiryong, a great writer and artist, came from P'yŏngyang testifies to the heightened cultural standard afforded by its economic prosperity.

58. Ch'ae Chegong, *Pŏnamjip, Hyŏnp'o saninjip sŏ*, 33:15a–16b; Sin Kwangsu, *Sŏkpukchip, Chŭng Sŏngch'ŏn Pak-saeng sŏ*, 15:8a–9a.

59. Yi Ik, *Sŏngho saesŏl*, 300–2.

60. Kim Chŏm, *Sŏgyŏng sihwa*, 614.

61. *Pukchŏng ilgi*, 3:6a.

62. Nam Myŏnghak, a Hamgyŏng literatus, argued that the marginalization of the region resulted from the government policy to ban Hamgyŏng people from taking the civil service examinations after Yi Siae's Rebellion in 1467 in Hamgyŏng Province. Yet there is no corroborating evidence. Nam Myŏnghak, *Oryongjae yugo*, 38b.

63. See also Ch'oe Sin, *Hagamjip, Yŏ Han Sŏngjang*, 1:25b.

64. Chu Ch'ŏjŏng, *Kwanbuk sisŏn*, 89a–90a.

65. Chŏng Ho, *Changamjip, Kwanbuk chosisŏ*, 23:6a–7b.

66. Kim Chŏm, *Sŏgyŏng sihwa*, 573.

67. Kim Chŏm, *Sŏgyŏng sihwa*, 574. Such a claim is difficult to accept, and Yi Pokhyu in the late Chosŏn had already proven this was false. According to O Such'ang, the fact that So Seyang, a central Neo-Confucian scholar-official during King Chungjong's reign, was singled out as the primary culprit in the discrimination against northerners may indicate that the discrimination took shape in the sixteenth century, when Neo-

Confucian literati began to dominate society and politics. O Such'ang, *Chosŏn hugi P'yŏngan-do sahoe palchŏn yŏn'gu*, 21–22.

68. *Sukchong sillok*, 39:273, 1692/12/30.

69. *Sukchong sillok*, 39:294, 1694/3/13.

70. *Sukchong sillok*, 40:543, 1714/10/8. Also see Sun Joo Kim, "In Defense of Regional Elite Identity and Culture."

71. This type of criticism seems to have been universal among central literati of the time. Song Siyŏl commented that Sŏnu Hyŏp "stood out among exiles and nomadic beggars and knew how to learn by himself without a master." On the one hand, this recognizes the meritorious deed of advocating Neo-Confucianism in P'yŏngan Province; on the other, it reveals Song's negative impression of literati there. Sŏnu Hyŏp, *Tunam chŏnsŏ, Tunam sŏnsaeng chŏnsŏ sŏ* (composed by Song Siyŏl).

72. *Chŏngjo sillok*, 45:274, 1781/10/28.

73. Ch'ae Chegong, *Pŏnamjip, Hyŏnp'o saninjip sŏ*, 33:15a–16b.

74. Kim Chŏm, *Sŏgyŏng sihwa*, 610.

75. Yi Sihang, *Hwaŭnjip, Sang Ch'oe Kollyun*, 6:1a–2a.

76. Kim Chŏm, *Sŏgyŏng sihwa*, 594.

77. Yi Sihang, *Hwaŭnjip, Sŏgyŏngbu*, 1:6a–16b.

4

The Shadow of Anonymity

The Depiction of Northerners in Eighteenth-Century "Hearsay Accounts" (kimun)

JUNG MIN

INTRODUCTION

This chapter explores how intellectuals in eighteenth-century Korea perceived the people from the northern region of the Korean peninsula. To do this, I will analyze their biographical accounts. The northerners had continuously experienced social and political discrimination, especially in their pursuit of official careers. By the eighteenth century, such discrimination became increasingly pervasive, to the point where everyone recognized the problem but could do nothing about it; thus, the northerners simply internalized their discontent.[1]

As existing studies and Chapter 2 in the present volume have pointed out, we find some notable changes in the economic activities along the trade route that ran through Seoul, Hwanghae Province, P'yŏngan Province, and all the way to the "palisade settlement" (ch'aengmun) from the mid-seventeenth century. The P'yŏngan Province, in particular, had been known to favor the military and was traditionally referred to as a "military-honoring region" (sangmu chi hyang) or "region of archery and horsemanship" (kungma chi hyang). Yet, the politics of "impartiality" (t'angp'yŏng) during the reigns of King Yŏngjo (r. 1724–1776) and King Chŏngjo (r. 1776–1800) brought about significant changes to the treatment of military personnel from the northwestern region.[2]

With such social economic changes as backgrounds, unprecedented development in Korean literature took place in the eighteenth century. It appears that there was a general trend where authors took greater interest in the daily lives of the people, including those of the northerners. The authors from this period, who lived in a world where the problems and contradictions of the Confucian social structure were becoming more severe, yearned to escape from this world. Given this context, we find that the unshackled lifestyle of the northern people became a source of envy and admiration to these authors. In other words, the literary works by these authors serve as a valuable source through which we can reconstruct the general perception of the northerners by other Koreans at the time as well as the various social problems that were inherent in late Chosŏn Korea.

This chapter is primarily based on the eighteenth-century biographical accounts of people from Hwanghae, P'yŏngan, and Hamgyŏng provinces. The cause of social discrimination in each of these provinces varied slightly, and these minute differences manifested themselves in the protagonists' actions in such stories. I will not delve too much into the historical background or details and will simply rely on the fruits of conventional studies undertaken by historians. Since these biographical records that survive in the private literary collections (munjip) portray a far more lively depiction of this period than any other forms of historical record, I believe that a close analysis of these literary texts will lead us to ascertain a more concrete picture.

This chapter is divided into two parts. It will first begin with a discussion of the discrimination and oppression of the northern region, followed by close analysis of the portrayal of each of the three northern provinces in the biographical accounts. I have made my selection from eight stories that are categorized as "hearsay accounts" (kimun). For Hwanghae Province, I have used Sin Kwangsu's (1712–1775) "Story of Horseman Ma" (Sŏ Ma kisa sa), Pak Chiwŏn's (1737–1805) "An Account of a Monk with Unshaven Head" (Palsŭngam ki), and Yi Yonghyu's (1708–1782) "A Beggar from Hwanghae Province" (Haesŏ kaeja); for P'yŏngan Province I have surveyed Kim Iyang's (1755–1845) "Hearsays from P'yŏngan Province" (Kwansŏ kimun), Im Ch'angt'aek's (1782–1823) "Biography of Hwang Kojip" (Hwang Kojip chŏn), and Chŏng Yagyong's (1762–1836) "Biography of Chang Poksŏn" (Chang Poksŏn chŏn); and for Hamgyŏng Province I have examined Yi Kwangdŏk's (1690–1748) "Biographies of Outstanding Men from Hamgyŏng Province" (Hamgyŏng iin chŏn), and Sin Kyŏng's (1696–?) "Biography of Turyŏn, A Filial Female Entertainer" (Hyogi Turyŏn chŏn).

THE DISCRIMINATION AND OPPRESSION
OF THE NORTHERN REGION

The Chosŏn Dynasty's (1392–1910) discrimination and oppression of the northern region seems to have become prevalent from the mid-dynastic period. Writing at the turn of the twentieth century, Pak Ŭnsik (1859–1925), a native of Hwanghae Province, expressed his frustration in the inaugural issue of the periodical Sŏu (Friends of the West). He stated that the Chosŏn Dynasty had been discriminating against the people from P'yŏngan and Hwanghae provinces to the point where the northern literati were mere underlings of the southern ministers' families, and the commoners were easy prey for the local clerks. Even the most successful of the northern literati, he claimed, was forced to end his career after barely passing the chinsa examination, and even the most determined of such literati wasted their lives away visiting the home of high officials and living in temporary lodging until their hair and beards grew white—all in hopes of gaining an official post.[3]

The discrimination of northerners was frequently discussed by intellectuals of the Chosŏn period as well. Yi Ik (1681–1763) in his literary collection Yi Ik's Trivial Remarks (Sŏngho saesŏl) for example, criticized the discrimination against the northerners especially in chapter 10, "The Sentiment of the Northwestern People" (Sŏbuk minsim), and chapter 11, "The Military Officials from the Northwestern Region" (Sŏbuk musa). He questioned the reason why the state, for more than three hundred years, had barred the people from north of Kaesŏng from having government posts, even though Seoul was located right in the middle of the peninsula and the three northern provinces comprised a full half of the country's territory. He lamented the reality which left an entire half of the dynasty abandoned. Furthermore, the people from the three northern provinces concentrated their skills on military arts, and thus many of them passed the military examinations. However, many northerners who passed the examinations were simply awarded their degrees but were not assigned government posts. Given these circumstances, according to Yi Ik, it was only natural that the northerners resented the state, thus making it nonsensical for the state to expect loyalty from these people in times of trouble.[4]

In the same writing, Yi Ik also goes on to say:

Moreover, the people of Kaesŏng are the descendants of those who had preserved their loyalty to the Wang royal family (of the Koryŏ Dynasty). I often find the influence of this tradition still alive. Kaesŏng is near Seoul, but owing to the notable inequality between these two cities, it looks like the Imjin River became the barrier which divides these two. This problem is caused by the mismanagement of the state. Therefore, I argue that one of the most urgent agendas is to employ talented northerners and assign them into fitting positions.[5]

And in the "Sentiment of the Northwestern People," he called for better treatment of the northerners. He feared that should these martially oriented northerners grow too frustrated, the central government would have no means to bring them under control.[6]

In his "Preface to the Record of the Chinsa Exam Passers from Chŏngju" (Chŏngju chinsa chemyŏngan sŏ), Yi Kahwan (1742–1801), a grandson of Yi Ik, also severely criticizes the state for not recruiting men of talent from the northwestern region.[7] When Yi was serving as the magistrate of Chŏngju in P'yŏngan Province, he found a booklet that recorded the town's chinsa degree holders from 1450 to 1786. He noticed that very few of these chinsa degree holders had actually gained government positions and was even more astonished to find that it had been over one hundred years since the last person from this province was actually assigned an official government position.

How did this happen? Yi Kahwan attempts to provide an explanation. The state passed two hundred people at the regular triennial examinations and gave them the degree of chinsa. Official posts were granted only to the most outstanding of these men. Those who resided in the Seoul area easily gained government positions when they passed this exam. On the contrary, those from the remote places usually hurried back home to celebrate their success, after which they would simply wait, for the rest of their lives, to be assigned government posts. They were never assigned to these posts—no matter how talented they may be. Yi Kahwan then concludes with the following lament:

Alas! Does Heaven impede them from gaining government positions? Why, then, does the state prevent them from being given government positions after awarding the *chinsa* degree to those who pass the exams on the basis of their talent? I went through the legal statutes carefully but could not find a single clause that prohibits the state from employing the northerners. Moreover, the king sincerely suggested the employment of northwesterners every time there were changes in personnel. The reason why I purposely bring attention to this matter is because Heaven is impartial, and thus it is only appropriate that the state is impartial as well. Those who are responsible for the appointment of personnel should understand the weight of their responsibility.[8]

After witnessing the invisible discriminations against the northwesterners, he warned that high officials should abandon their trivial prejudice when appointing personnel.

Such words of concern expressed by Yi Ik and Yi Kahwan became a reality in the form of numerous social unrest and popular rebellions, including the Hong Kyŏngnae rebellion of 1812. One scholar argues that the *Chŏnggamnok* (Book of Chŏng Kam), which prophesied the downfall of the Chosŏn Dynasty and the coming of a new dynasty, first appeared in the northwestern region, and indeed a number of plots to overthrow the Chosŏn ruling house were linked with clairvoyant men from the northwest. Therefore, it is not difficult to understand the basis for the people from this region of Korea's resentful sentiments.[9]

THE DEPICTION OF THE NORTHERNERS IN LITERARY WORKS

In the context of the discriminatory treatment against the northerners, I will examine the portrayal of the northerners in the collected works of the eighteenth-century literati. The northerners, who could not express their presence in Chosŏn society due to the structural restrictions imposed on them, sought other means to define their identity. The economic growth of the northwestern region, especially along the trade route between Seoul and Ŭiju, transformed them into a new intellectual class after the eighteenth century. In lieu of abandoning officialdom at the central court, they instead relied on their economic base to foster a new unique culture.

Hwanghae Province

Out of three selected stories about men from Hwanghae Province, we begin with Sin Kwangsu's "Sŏ Ma kisa sa" (Story of Horseman Ma).[10] Ma is the surname of the protagonist, and *kisa*, literally meaning "horse-riding gentleman," represents his social status. His actual name remains unknown. Sin Kwangsu hears about Horseman Ma from his younger brother Sin Kwangha (1729–?), who claims to have met Horseman Ma on one of his excursions, and records this account.

Horseman Ma is six feet three inches tall; he has bushy eyebrows and a well-kept beard. He wears a pair of ornately patterned leather shoes and a silk waistband, and holds a black whip decorated with silver in his hand. At an inn in Pyŏkche Station, Sin Kwangha encounters Horseman Ma, who is not accompanied by any servants but does have two fine horses. Horseman Ma orders a boiled pig's head and some wine, and eats the pork using a blade on which two characters "*ch'uri*," or "autumn carp," are engraved.

Drawn by his extraordinary appearance and behavior, Sin Kwangha asks who Horseman Ma is and is told that he is a cavalryman who is on his way back from Seoul after completing his garrison duty. They exchange some poems and Sin Kwangha is repeatedly amazed at Horseman Ma's insight into poetry. Horseman Ma then introduces himself as a military official at the Capital Garrison (Kŭmwiyŏng) and the Royal Guards Command (Ŏyŏngch'ŏng), offices that rank below the Three Internal Offices (Naesamch'ŏng) which is in charge of guarding the king.[11] In other words, Horseman Ma is a low-ranking military official solely because he is a native of Hwanghae Province and he is prevented from gaining promotion beyond garrison posts.

As the influence of liquor kicks in, Horseman Ma begins to open up about his past to Sin Kwangha. He is a native of Haesŏ (Hwanghae Province), is enrolled in military service and is very fond of knights-errant. When he was young, he was once crossing over a hill and faced a number of robbers. He killed them all using his "autumn carp" blade. He also had a *kisaeng* entertainer whom he loved, but when he found out that she was unfaithful to him, he killed her as well. Then he went into hiding for a few years, but soon resumed his life. He went on excursions to several famous mountains and traveled all over the country—from Hamhŭng and the six garrisons (*yukchin*) in the north to Chiri Mountain and the shores of Tongnae in the south.

After traveling to every corner of the country, he visited Cheju Island. He went there with an eccentric fellow who was very skilled in cursive calligraphy. During the trip, when Horseman Ma composed poems, the fellow would grind ink and record the poem on rocks but did not do so on paper. At last, they bought a ship, went on a voyage across the sea and climbed up Halla Mountain all the way to the Paengnok Crater Lake.

On the day of autumn equinox, he was ecstatic to find the rising of the Southern Polaris, a star that was unobservable on the mainland. Every time Horseman Ma composed a poem, the calligrapher recorded them in cursive script and threw them into the lake or between the rocks. For four days they had a great time before returning to the mainland. They then traveled north together, but with the calligrapher's sudden death on the road, Horseman Ma decided to use all his money to buy a coffin for his fellow traveler's body before burying him at the side of the road. After that, Horseman Ma no longer went on excursions.

Sin Kwangha is deeply impressed by Horseman Ma's life stories and exchanges another set of poems before parting. Horseman Ma's poem reads: "The sun is setting; let us now part. There is no need to know each other's names. Simply remember me as Horseman Ma; I shall remember you as a scholar. We are bound to meet each other again." He then spurs his horse and parts his way without looking back.

In the end, Horseman Ma remains a nameless figure in Sin Kwangha's memory, and this anonymity makes Horseman Ma ever more mysterious. The calligrapher is also left unnamed. Upon hearing the story from his younger brother, Sin Kwangsu makes inquiries for any information regarding Horseman Ma and finds that he is a native of Haesŏ, had engaged in trade at Kaesŏng, and that he once wrote an indignant poem on the Golden Pavilion in the Hu Market in Chang City in China. (The Golden Pavilion is where King Zhao of Yan, during the Warring States period, placed gold at the top of pavilion in order to attract the attention of men of talent). Sin also learns that Horseman Ma frequently borrows money from others in order to earn several hundred times more than his original investment, only to collect the sum of money that he had originally invested while giving the rest to the lender as gift.

Sin Kwangsu's appraisal of Horseman Ma reads as follows: "His poems are intense and vigorous, like roars of a man filled with indignation. Ah!

Horseman Ma, a man of valiant character, has been confined to lead a life at the bottom stratum of society; he has had no choice but to suppress his ambitions and has often had himself immersed in nature to release some of his frustrations through poetry and wine. How could his poems not be filled with cries of indignation?" And Sin further remarks: "Our country may be small, but surely Horseman Ma is not the only talented recluse who hides himself in the mountains and ponds. When they perish in the wilds, without a trace, the world is not even aware of the existence of such men. How sad!"

Horseman Ma is a man who was not only talented in the military arts but also in poetry. However, the only people whom he kills with his fine blade were petty robbers and a woman he deemed unfaithful. In addition to this, he uses his sword as a steak knife to slice and eat boiled pig's head. The state, however, does not grant him the opportunity to realize his ambitions or to make use of his talent. It is also interesting to note that he, as a garrison officer, engages in trade and visits China. He establishes a solid economic base by such means and is thus able to comfortably travel in and out of Korea.

The next northerner in question is Kim Hongyŏn, a native of Kaesŏng who appears in Pak Chiwŏn's "An Account of a Monk with Unshaven Head." We can also find an alternative story of Kim Hongyŏn in Kim T'aegyŏng's (1850– 1927) *Hagiographies of Kaesŏng's Respected Elders (Sungyang kigu chŏn)*. Here, I will refer to both.[12]

Palsŭngam, which literally means "the cell of a monk with unshaven head," is not a place name; it is the sobriquet of Kim Hongyŏn, a son of a wealthy family in Kaesŏng who lived in a Buddhist temple as a lay person. Kim is a *walcha*, or a chivalrous swordsman or knights-errant known for his unrestrained personality. He holds a military examination degree, which he received at a young age, possesses the strength to defeat a tiger with his bare hands, and can jump a fence several feet high while holding two *kisaeng* entertainers.

He spends his money lavishly; his hobby, in fact, includes collecting antiques and extremely rare flowers and plants. He rides on fine horses, with two fleet hawks perched upon his shoulders. Another hobby of his includes excursions to famous mountains and rivers so much so that there are no mountains in Korea that he has not hiked before, including Halla Mountain and Paektu Mountain. We are told that he hiked Paektu Mountain twice and that on every mountain he climbed, he engraved his name on a boulder.

Kim T'aegyŏng's version of the story gives us a more detailed account of the moment when Kim Hongyŏn was taking his military examination. Kim apparently said: "Ah! I cannot waste my entire life as a rural person. But then, even if I do manage to pass the military examination, who would be willing to appoint me a general?"[13] From this remark, we can discern the frustration of the northerners who were barred from pursuing careers in officialdom. Kim, realizing the hopelessness of his predicament, intentionally wore long sleeves to the archery examination so that the bow would get stuck to his sleeve and the arrow would misfire. He disqualified himself this way several times, infuriating his father. He then had a change of heart and proceeded to the archery examination in short sleeves and passed the military examination with top honors.

Kim's decision to wear long sleeves and intentionally disqualify himself stems from his recalcitrant desire to illustrate the meaninglessness of the examination system. As he predicted, the only position that he was given after passing the military examination was a job as a *walcha* swordsman which led to his frequent visits to *kisaeng* houses and his callous spending habits on antiques and material things that whittled away his family fortune. And yet, he enjoyed going on excursions in the mountains and loved to climb steep cliffs in order to engrave his name in stone. He does so because he "wishes the gentlemen of the later generations to know the name Kim Hongyŏn and grieve for him." Why should we grieve for him? He asks us to grieve with him over the harsh reality that prevented him from making use of his ambition and talent.

Unlike anonymous Horseman Ma, however, Kim Hongyŏn was obsessed with leaving his name to posterity by climbing up dangerous cliffs with a ladder in order to inscribe his name with chisels. Presumably, he must have felt some limitations to this approach, so he visited Pak Chiwŏn with the request that Pak write down his story. In his "An Account of a Monk with Unshaven Head," Pak Chiwŏn indirectly satirizes society by expressing his criticism of Kim's vain attachment to his name. However, in fact, Kim Hongyŏn's behaviors imply the limitations imposed on him as a Kaesŏng native, who could do nothing for his country after passing the exam—a sentiment that Pak Chiwŏn sympathizes with.

The following story is about a beggar in Yi Yonghyu's, "A Beggar from Hwanghae Province."[14] This is a very short story whose original text is composed of less than four hundred characters. It uses the great famine of 1741 (the seventeenth year of King Yŏngjo's reign) as its setting. One day, a certain beggar comes to sit and lean his back against a fence. Finding his appearance unusual, Yi approaches him and asks about the beggar's personal history and whether he had once been a local official. The beggar strongly denies this and replies that he was a mere farmer. His son worked at a government-operated silver mine but because the mine ran out of silver, the taxes got heavier. After exhausting his family fortune to pay off his debt, he became penniless, and due to the famine, he had no option but to become a beggar.

While eating a peach that Yi gave him, the beggar recounts his story as follows: He lived in a village in Hwanghae Province, and his surname was Kim. (At the time when Yi and the beggar met each other, the beggar was almost eighty years old). In his youth, he was taught by a local teacher, whose surname was Ch'oe. According to the beggar, Teacher Ch'oe was a man with honorable behavior and had great talent in writing. Teacher Ch'oe had passed a provincial examination with high seating in his youth but gave up the idea of taking the capital examination, saying, "How can a thousand-li horse (ch'ŏllima), [ch'ŏllima is a horse that can gallop one thousand li in one day, thus implying a highly talented man] be buried here?" He then went into the mountains and built a humble house where he taught his students.

The reason why Teacher Ch'oe refused to take the capital examination after passing the provincial examination was that he clearly understood that there was no use taking it. Although he was sufficiently self-confident to compare himself to a thousand-li horse, he still understood that he could not demonstrate his ability through passing the examinations. Instead, he became determined to devote his life to teaching the future generation in seclusion.

Seeing that the beggar was such an honest man in his speech and behavior and that he did not exaggerate his personal and family background, Yi Yonghyu believes Kim's life story. Simply put, the old beggar Kim is not a mere farmer but an educated yangban. Yi Yonghyu concludes the story like this: "Ah! Teacher Ch'oe is really a literatus with high aim. However, since he hides his virtue, few people recognize him. The beggar is also a good man. Even in old age, he does not lose his integrity and simple-mindedness. We can learn from this that there must be talented men even among those who make a bare living in a desolate plain, a deep valley, or a remote place."[15]

Up to this point, we have seen three men from Hwanghae Province: Horseman Ma, Kim Hongyŏn, and Teacher Ch'oe. Their behaviors share some common characteristics. Let us first analyze Horseman Ma and Kim Hongyŏn. Horseman Ma passes the military examination and is assigned a low-ranking post. Kim Hongyŏn also passes the military examination. They are also both skillful in swordsmanship and archery; in other words, they were born with the qualities of knights-errant. They both established a solid economic base through trade, which would have provided resources for their scholarly or bureaucratic pursuit. Well aware of the discrimination against Hwanghae Province, however, they either gave up the idea of gaining promotion in the government bureaucracy or refused to take the higher-level examinations. Horseman Ma releases his indignation by going on excursions in famous mountains and rivers all over the country, from Hwanghae Province in the north to Cheju Island in the south. Similarly, Kim Hongyŏn gains fame by hiking famous mountains and engraving his name in boulders. Both Horseman Ma and Kim Hongyŏn climbed the Paektu and Halla mountains, which were quite uncommon feats at the time. Teacher Ch'oe was a scholar, thus different from the two military men. Yet, he decided to give up higher-level examinations, knowing that he had no future as a bureaucrat. This frustration was shared by Kim Hongyŏn who intentionally failed the military examination.

These three stories pertaining to figures from Hwanghae Province reflect the general image of northerners at the time. The Hwanghae men are depicted as talented people who are filled with frustration and as romantic figures who sought to release their indignation by going on excursions.

P'yŏngan Province

The next region to investigate is P'yongan Province. We will focus on and analyze the following characters: the P'yŏngyang native Chi Yangnyong and his sister, an anonymous man (whom Pak Sŭnggŏm, a native of Sŏngch'ŏn, claims to have met), Hwang Sunsŭng (who goes by the nickname Obstinate Hwang), and the P'yŏngyang native Chang Poksŏn.

First, we will look at the story of Chi Yangnyong and his sister.[16] Chi Yangnyong, a native of P'yŏngyang, had a brave heart and the features of a knight-errant; he usually wore funeral garments, several layers of shoes, and a square bamboo hat, so very few people, even those of his own village, saw his face. His choice of attire, however, carries significant meaning. The square bamboo hat implies that he felt too ashamed to see heaven, while wearing several layers of shoes implies his refusal to step on earth. Simply put, we can observe from his odd behavior the deeply rooted indignation and resistance against reality.

At the time, a member of the royal family had been dragging private runaway slaves to the Yŏn'gwang Pavilion by Taedong River and punishing them there illegally. Because of his power, the local government did not do anything but turn a blind eye. Hearing this, in order to explicitly denounce the various crimes that the aristocrat was responsible for, Chi Yangnyong immediately breaks into the man's home at midnight. Chi continues by saying: "Because you as a member of the royal family have harmed people with cruel punishments instead of taking care of them, the roads are crowded with runaways. Both Heaven and the people are indignant over what you have done. How can you avoid punishment?"[17] With this, Chi grabs hold of the man's two ankles and drags him out to the bridge railings. Chi pushes him into an area of the river where the ice is so thin that nobody would attempt to cross it. After pushing him, Chi flies away like a bird on his bamboo stick. Believing that the aristocrat was punished by a ghost, the people of P'yŏngyang do not even try to apprehend Chi. In fact, most people deem what he did to be justifiable and noble. It is said that in retribution for what occurred, the member of the royal family nearly died but survived just to become insane. Kim Iyang recorded that this news motivated King Yŏngjo to make a firm resolution to liberate private slaves.[18]

Chi Yangnyong's sister is just as gallant. For example, when she is once on a swing with her friends and notices her brother's approach, she jumps from the swing and directly into the yard of her house a dozen strides away in order to avoid her brother's potential scolding. A couple of days after her marriage, she observes that the entire village is overwhelmed with great anxiety. Inquiring into its origins, she is informed by some villagers that an influential family would bury the body of a deceased person right behind her residence. The villagers tell her that though this is illegal, there is no way for them to stop it. She gives them her word and appears in front of the funeral procession the next day, disguised in men's clothing. She holds up the bier with one hand, so that the procession cannot proceed one step further.

Dumbfounded, the several hundred people who are part of the procession stand in awe as she swiftly pulls down several pennants carried at the front of the procession. Everyone who watches this spectacle by the roadside is astonished. The bier carriers cannot but help turn back the procession. Afterwards, even cruel villains dare not break into her house, and people call her house "the house of a female general."

At the end of the story of Chi Yangnyong and his sister, Kim Iyang attaches his thoughts as follows:

> Nie Zheng was a righteous man. However, when Nie discarded his life to assassinate Xia Lei, Prime Minister of the Han Dynasty, he did so in order to seek revenge for the sake of another person (Yan Zhongzi). Chi Yangnyong is different from Nie Zheng in many regards. He is motivated by his will to save people from their sufferings without telling people who he is, and unlike Nie Zheng, he does not suffer for his actions. His sister, as a young bride, can save her husband's family and pacify the entire village single-handedly without drawing too much attention to herself. There is no doubt that she is also much wiser than Nie Zheng's sister.[19]

Nie Zheng was an assassin who appeared in the "Biographies of Assassin Retainers" (Ci ke lie zhuan) section of Sima Qian's *Records of the Grand Historian* (*Shi ji*). He peeled off the skin of his face in order to conceal his identity and then finally killed himself by disembowelment after taking revenge on Xia Lei on behalf of Yan Zhongzi who had recognized his worth. His elder sister knew that her brother concealed his identity by peeling off his skin in order to protect her but did not want her brother's death to come to nothing, so she disclosed his identity by killing herself in front of her brother's dead body which was being displayed in public. In contrast, Chi Yangnyong solves people's problems rather than being motivated by personal vendettas of revenge, and his identity is never disclosed. Moreover, according to Kim Iyang's judgment, Chi Yangnyong's sister is wiser than Nie Zheng's sister because she uses her strength to stop an unjust deed, unlike Nie Zheng's sister who killed herself for no great purpose.

The subsequent story is about an anonymous man and his brothers whom Pak Sŭnggŏm claims to have met at the T'ong-gu Market outside Pukkwan (northern Hamgyŏng border), a market Pak frequented for business purposes. Pak, a native of Sŏngch'ŏn, P'yongan Province, is the kind of man who regularly boasts about his physical strength. One day, Pak visits T'ong-gu to trade silk but encounters several evil monks who had been controlling the market by arbitrarily setting the price for commodities. He complains that the price for his commodities was ridiculously slashed, but is forced to flee after being threatened by the evil monks. Because he does not even have a chance to retrieve his commodities, he brims with rage at a riverside several miles away from the scene. There, he comes across a man riding a donkey and recounts his story to the stranger. The man responds by explaining that he is also well aware of the evil monks and is, in fact, on his way to kill them. Pak Sŭnggŏm follows the man and witnesses him killing the three monks in a flash. After that, they return to the riverside, but an even more treacherous monk is waiting in ambush. Through cooperative teamwork, they kill that monk, too. Afterwards, the market in Pukkwan returns to peaceful operations.

When the man says good-bye to Pak Sŭnggŏm, Pak begs to follow him. After a one hundred li walk along a rough mountain path, they arrive at the man's place. Pak finds out that the beggar lives with his one-hundred-year-old father and two brothers. The next day is the father's birthday, so the brothers prepare a banquet to which Pak is invited. They consume all the meat piled on the table and ten jars of wine in an instant. The father tells Pak Sŭnggŏm: "My sons possess a little physical strength and talents, but the second is not as good as his brothers. However, I think that the second son was still strong enough to handle the monks, so I sent him on purpose." Pak then observes that the three brothers had caught and played with three tigers inhabiting a cave. After witnessing the strength and talents of these three brothers, he stops boasting about his physical strength and is reborn as a new man. When people are puzzled by his drastic change and asked its cause, he tells them the story of the three brothers in detail.

Kim Iyang concludes the foregoing story which he had heard in P'yŏngan Province as follows:

Long ago, I saw a huge tree fall down between cliffs in Sŏrak Mountain, which reminded me of a dragon or a tiger. That huge tree could have been used as a pillar but was simply decaying among thorny shrubs. I exclaimed, "There must be numerous men who are just born and die in the woods without being recognized by people, because they are born in the wrong time, in the wrong place." Alas, I could not fathom the depth and width of the ambition of those three brothers from the north who could stand out through their courage and physical strength among ten thousand men. If they had been born at the right time, they might have been the head of Three Armies and taken the world by storm. If so, how could we have predicted its consequence?[20]

Hwang Sunsŭng of P'yŏngyang is famous for his obstinacy in acting on the basis of fundamental rules; he is thus better known as Obstinate Hwang.[21] He always acts according to what he believes to be correct, no matter how difficult the situation. For example, he once visits Seoul on personal business and hears the obituary of his friend, but he thinks it is inappropriate to participate in the funeral of a deceased friend because he had come to Seoul for another purpose. Thus, he immediately returns to P'yŏngyang, changes into funeral garments, and heads back to Seoul to pay respects to his deceased friend.

Another time, he encounters a bridge made of limestone that was taken from a tomb. Hwang believes that it is inappropriate to step on something that used to be in a tomb, so he decides to lift up his trousers and crosses the stream on foot. The author of this story continues to introduce other interesting episodes pertaining to Hwang's erratic behavior. His obstinate behavior, based on his radical beliefs, was so widely known at the time that it caused what may be called Obstinate Hwang Syndrome. Many versions of his story can be found in eighteenth-century writings. The fact that Obstinate Hwang's story disseminated far and wide reflects a society in crisis which had lost its moral principles and rules.

Chang Poksŏn of P'yŏngyang is also famous for helping those in need as though they were his own kin.[22] He is a guard who is in charge of looking after the silver storage in Provincial Governor's Office. He takes silver out of this storage and helps people in need. Later Governor Ch'ae Chegong discovers that two thousand yang of silver is missing from the storage area; he imprisons Chang for embezzling government money and orders his execution. The P'yŏngyang people hear of Chang's punishment and readily donate their valuables such as hairpins and rings and ask for Chang's release.

The commonality of these stories of unusual people of P'yŏngan Province collected by Kim Iyang is that these are about figures with extraordinary powers; although they abandoned their social lives, they still put their sense of justice into practice rather than overlooking unrighteousness. Chi Yangnyong and three unnamed brothers that Pak Sŭnggŏm met have Herculean powers. Hwang Sunsŭng obstinately lives according to ritual propriety that nobody else seems to follow. And finally, Chang Poksŏn's story delineates an unusual conflict between a local clerk who works for the people and the central government which is negligent of the northern region. Throughout the text, we can read the author's indignation over the powerholders' abuse over the powerless, as well as his awe toward the persistent determination and bold actions taken by these men and women from the marginalized north in order to realize social justice.

Hamgyŏng Province

The following two characters provide a window through which we can understand the social conditions of Hamgyŏng Province in the eighteenth century: a brave, anonymous hunter living in a remote place (who appears in Yi Kwangdŏk's "Biographies of Outstanding Men from Hamgyŏng Province") and Turyŏn, a female entertainer of Pukch'ŏng (who appears in Sin Kyŏng's "Biography of Turyŏn, a Filial Female Entertainer").

Unlike the writings we have seen so far, in the "Biographies of Outstanding men from Hamgyŏng Province,"[23] the author attaches some rather lengthy comments at the beginning and end of each story. The introductory part of this book, which begins with an allusion to a poem from the Book of Odes (Shi jing), can be paraphrased as follows: During the Zhou Dynasty, King Wen transformed the people and their customs through virtuous instruction, and talented men who lived in the remotest areas of the dynasty were recruited to serve as officials, including those who made their living catching rabbits and pounding stakes. Accordingly, there was no one who wasted their lives away in the woods and hills. Starting from the medieval period, however, the kings became entrapped by personal greed and arrogance and became negligent in their search for talented men. Consequently, talented men were left unused, rather than gaining prestigious government positions, and once the talented men had learned that the kings took no interest in recruiting them, they, in turn, no longer wished to display their talents in public. Most of them simply hid themselves within the masses or deep in the mountains.

This tale of an extraordinary man from Hamgyŏng Province is based on what the writer heard from his friend, Mr. Yi of Namwŏn, who claims to have personally witnessed it. The story goes as follows: Mr. Yi, who passed the military examination, is on his way back from his duty at the frontier defenses with his friend Mr. Pang. Then night falls and the two decide to find lodging at a hunter's home in a remote area. The hunter's wife serves them food until her husband comes back at midnight carrying a tiger, boar, roe-deer, deer, and other game animals on his shoulders. He throws them down onto the yard and sees to the guests. He bows and treats them with utmost respect. Then, he brings out a large kettle of rice into the yard and instantly eats all the animals that he caught that day. Mr. Yi and Mr. Pang are extremely astonished and even suspect that the hunter might be a monster or a ghost.

The next morning, the hunter packs his hunting tools and prepares to leave. As he heads out, he asks Mr. Yi and Mr. Pang to stay until evening. However, he does not return until so late into the evening that his wife begins to wait anxiously for him outside. Just at that moment, a big tiger snatches her and runs away. Shortly after, the hunter returns home and hears what happened. Enraged, he and Mr. Yi set out to catch the tiger. They fight the tiger in pitch dark conditions and eventually manage to kill it and return home with the wife's body. The hunter then asks Mr. Pang and Mr. Yi to guard her at the home; he soon returns with three tiger cubs.

Mr. Yi, as a young military officer, usually boasted of his physical strength, but after witnessing what had just happened, he could not help but feel as small as an insect. He then finds out that the wife was only in shock; once the hunter massages her body and allows her to rest in the warmth of the room, she regains her consciousness. The hunter has an intimidating appearance and rowdily drinks wine and eats meat, but he treats his guests very politely, as though he were a specialist of rituals and ceremonies.

The following epilogue recapitulates the main theme of this story as well as the main points that this chapter presents:

Four hundred years have passed since the establishment of our dynasty. Owing to this, the entire country below the Yalu River is well civilized, so the good customs are carried out, and the entire country is full of strong vital energy. This environment has produced amazingly talented figures, and we can compare this with the reign of King Wen of Zhou which produced lots of virtuous men even among rustics. Thus, it is not surprising that Hamgyŏng Province has also produced extraordinary figures. Due to this long-lasting peace, however, people have come to only esteem civil culture, and have begun to look down on military culture. Thus, men who are talented [in the military arts] would rather hide themselves from the world than display their abilities. Such men do not compete for fame or personal profit; they would rather ease their troubled mind by plowing, gathering firewood, or hunting foxes, rabbits, tigers, and leopards—to please themselves in the deep mountains or by the seashore.[24]

Yi Kwangdŏk concludes his "Biographies of Outstanding Men from Hamgyŏng Province" with his lament that highly talented men have vanished without being used by the world.

Sin Kyŏng's work, "Biography of Turyŏn, a Filial Female Entertainer," is the story of a woman named Turyŏn.[25] Ch'a Tŏkpong, a literatus from Turyŏn village in the Taehŭng district of Ch'ungch'ŏng Province, follows his village friend, Sŏng Im, to Pukch'ŏng, for Sŏng was just assigned a new post there. In Pukch'ŏng, they stayed in the official guest house of the local government where Tŏkpong falls in love with an official female entertainer, Ch'oan, and ends up making her pregnant. Within a couple of months, however, Ch'a Tokpong's friend, Sŏng Im, is dismissed from his post, and the two friends return home together. Before parting with one another, Tŏkpong presents a fan to Ch'oan. He writes on the fan that if she gives birth to a boy, she is to name him Taehŭng; if a girl, Turyŏn. Ch'oan gives birth to a girl and names her Turyŏn as Tŏkpong had suggested. Since the District of Taehŭng was more than several hundred li away from Pukch'ŏng, they soon lost contact.

One day, Tŏkpong was sick in bed with malaria and received a package of clothes, ginseng, and a letter from Turyŏn in which she states her sincere desire to visit him. Tŏkpong was unaware that Ch'oan had given birth to a girl who is now fully grown. Tŏkpong was so moved by her sincerity that he immediately replied with a poem that he had composed from his sickbed. In the autumn of the same year, Turyŏn properly dresses herself and travels one thousand li on horseback to meet her father for the first time. Because of legal restrictions, however, Turyŏn cannot stay with her father for long. After their first meeting, she receives permission to travel and visit her father two or three more times, and when her father is about to die, she stays by his side until his last breath and returns to Pukch'ŏng dressed in mourning garb.

Sin Kyŏng adds his praise of Turyŏn at the end of the story: "Despite her lowly status as a female entertainer, Turyŏn completely fulfills the duty of a daughter. What an extraordinary example she leaves behind!" He sees it highly praiseworthy that she, a lowly female entertainer, visits her father whom she had never met before, and, moreover, fulfills her filial duties.

Despite their difficult situations, both the anonymous hunter in the "Biographies of Outstanding Men from Hamgyŏng Province" and Turyŏn in the "Biography of Turyŏn, a Filial Female Entertainer" fulfill their humane duties. Despite his fearsome appearance, the hunter does not neglect his duty to pay respect to his guests; despite her lowly status as the daughter of a female entertainer, Turyŏn maintains her filial piety toward her estranged father.

CONCLUSION

From the stories discussed above, which are interestingly contained in the collected literary works of each author, we can detect the changes in the view of the north during the late Chosŏn period. Horseman Ma and Kim Hongyŏn from Hwanghae Province love trips and adventures. They both possess excellent martial arts capabilities and pass the military examinations. However, they do not gain government positions after passing the exams, so they soothe their sadness by turning their interests to traveling in the country. Although he lives on alms, the old beggar Kim from Hwanghae Province does not lose his sincerity of mind. Writing down these stories, the authors deplore the circumstances encountered by men who possess great ambition and talent but who are not given the opportunity to use these gifts, and thus vanish in frustration and poverty.

Without concern for their personal welfare, Chi Yangnyong, Chi's sister, and the three brothers whom Pak Sŭnggŏm met are always ready to respond to injustice. Despite their formidable physical strength, they are not employed by the government. Instead, they use their strength to chastise evil persons and capture thieves. Moreover, instead of bragging about their amazing feats, they possess the virtue of modesty. And, even in unfavorable conditions, they never abandon their familial duties of filial piety and brotherly affection. In addition, they rarely disclose their discontent with a world that fails to recognize their worth.

We can also read the stories of the anonymous hunter and Turyŏn in the same vein. Despite his insurmountable courage, the hunter cannot mark his name in history or lead the life of a gentleman. Nonetheless, he practices humane ethics and etiquette. Whereas, Turyŏn, a lowly female entertainer, fulfills to the utmost of her abilities, her filial duties to her father.

What can we learn from the viewpoints of the authors who delivered these stories of the northerners? What kind of values were they looking for from the stories of these extraordinary figures? Most of the authors lament that these people were alienated by the dynastic system so much so that they were unable to find the opportunities to realize their personal ambitions. Kim Hongyŏn criticizes the state of affairs in which passing the examinations could not ensure northerners an official career. Teacher Ch'oe, Beggar Kim's teacher, asserts that an examination hall is no place to bury a thousand-li horse and gives up taking the higher-level examinations. Chi Yangnyong also conceals his identity by disguising himself in strange clothes like bamboo hats and funeral garments. The three brothers from Pukkwan, on the other hand, possess "useless" physical strength, as their father had stated, so they renounce the world and retreat deep into the mountains.

One common feature of these stories is that these writings convey the sorrow of talented people who were neglected by the state. Kim Iyang expresses his disappointment by using the analogy of a mighty tree decaying amidst the shrubs. It seems clear that the authors were confronting this type of world with a single voice. The state discriminates against them and does not grant them the opportunity to succeed, but men with extraordinary abilities live hidden in the northern region. Many authors believed it was time to grant them the opportunity to work for the world. In addition to this, some authors conveyed their voices of protest through the characters they portrayed in their stories.

As pointed out above, the figures in these stories share some common characteristics. First, they never overlook injustice. They kill thieves, punish members of the royal family who abuse their authority, and squarely protest against unjust violence. Second, they never cling to personal fame or profit. They preserve the purity of good motives by concealing their names after carrying out good deeds. Chi Yangnyong conceals himself after helping others;

the brothers from Pukkwan kill the treacherous monks and then disappear without trace; and Horseman Ma makes a profit one hundred times as much as the principal, but returns all the extra profit to those from whom he had originally borrowed the money. Third, they love traveling and possess the spirit of knights-errant. This includes Horseman Ma and Kim Hongyŏn, who traveled to every corner of the country from Paektu Mountain in the north to Halla Mountain in the south, as well as the three brothers who played with tigers. They are never daunted by the corruption that ordinary people are not able to cope with. They are the kind of people who supplied "military misfits" (changsach'ŭng) who later played an important role in the making of the Hong Kyŏngnae rebellion in 1812.[26] Fourth, they always behaved with proper etiquette. The hunter welcomes his guests with unexpected friendliness; the lowly female entertainer fulfills her filial duty to her father better than most people; the walcha passes the examination to relieve his father's worries; and the brothers from Pukkwan possess a great sense of filial piety.

And more importantly, despite their extraordinary abilities, most of them remained anonymous. Kim Hongyŏn and Chi Yangnyong may be exceptions, but even they do not reveal their identity much. Not even Chi Yangnyong's neighbors know what Chi looked like. Horseman Ma and the calligrapher remain anonymous; the three brothers, the extraordinary man from Hamgyŏng Province, and Teacher Ch'oe are no exception. This "anonymity" represents the frustration with the unjust social system. They possess talents as great as a thousand-li horse, but they have no alternative but to waste their lives away in the countryside. This despairing situation drives Kim Hongyŏn to cling onto and inscribe his name in cliffs. In addition, they are liberated from customary constraints and managed their lives in a lively manner, thus further highlighting their ethical awareness. Their deviation from the norm is also expressed in the form of protest against the immoral and unjust. In other words, these actions reaffirm the fact that their personalities were just as refined as their abilities. On the other hand, the elevated ethical awareness in these stories serves as motivation to justify their seemingly erratic behavior.

By introducing the lives of these figures, the authors accused the state of using irrational policies in its selection of talented persons, while at the same time, they highlighted the point that ideal individuals were hiding predominantly in the northern region. Through this, the authors carefully uncovered the reality of discrimination in order to prove its irrationality. However, the fact that a person's talent was kept hidden in the shadow of anonymity increases its tragic beauty. It is interesting to note that it was in the eighteenth century that these types of writings suddenly began appearing in large quantities. The state did not listen to the problems that the authors had pointed out, but, instead, continued their discrimination against the northerners. This accumulated frustration among the northerners manifested in the form of the Hong Kyŏngnae rebellion. Lastly, it is also worth pointing out that the hearsay accounts about people from other regions do not share the unique characters laden in the stories discussed in this chapter.

It is rather ironic that eighteenth-century authors eagerly looked for traces of moral values from the righteous men from the northern region that the state discriminated against. And finally, we should pay more attention to the fact that these authors themselves tended to be marginalized scholars and literati. This tendency flows in the same vein as a saying that is attributed to Confucius: "If ritual propriety is lost, seek it in the countryside."

NOTES

1. The discrimination of the northern provinces in the Chosŏn Dynasty has received much attention in the field of Korean history. The following are some representative works: O Such'ang, *Chosŏn hugi P'yŏngan-do sahoe palchŏn yŏn'gu*; Kwŏn Naehyŏn, *Chosŏn hugi P'yŏngan-do chaejŏng yŏn'gu*; Ko Sŭnghŭi, "18, 19 segi Hamgyŏng-do chiyŏk ŭi yut'ongno paltal kwa sangŏp hwaltong"; and Sun Joo Kim, *Marginality and Subversion in Korea*. For studies of literature, see Chang Yusŭng, "17, 18 segi Hamgyŏng-do chiyŏk ŭi munjip p'yŏnch'an kwa sŏjŏk kanhaeng" and Chang, "Chosŏn sidae Hamgyŏng-do chiyŏk ŭi munin chiptan kwa munhak hwaltong."

2. See O Such'ang, *Chosŏn hugi P'yŏngan-do sahoe palchŏn yŏn'gu* for more details.

3. Pak Ŭnsik, "Nonsŏl," 10.

4. Yi Ik, *Sŏngho saesŏl, Sŏbuk musa*, 11:12a.

5. Ibid.

6. Yi Ik, *Sŏngho saesŏl, Sŏbuk insim*, 10:34a.

7. Yi Kahwan, *Kŭmdae simun ch'o, Chŏngju chinsa chemyŏngan sŏ*, 2:463.

8. Ibid.

9. Paek Sŭngjong. *Han'guk ŭi yŏn munhwasa*, 73–106.

10. Sin Kwangsu, *Sŏkpukchip, Sŏ Ma kisa sa*, 499.

11. For the treatment of military men from P'yŏngan Province, see O Such'ang, *Chosŏn hugi P'yŏngan-do sahoe palchŏn yŏn'gu*, 108–26.

12. Pak Chiwŏn, *Kugyŏk Yŏnamjip, Palsŭngam ki*, 1:78–83; and Kim T'aegyŏng, *Sungyang kigu chŏn*, 184–86.

13. Kim T'aegyŏng, *Sungyang kigu chŏn*, 184.

14. Yi Yonghyu, *Hyehwan chapchŏ, Haesŏ kaeja*, 2:217.

15. Ibid.

16. Kim Iyang, *Kim Iyang munjip, Kwansŏ kimun*.

17. Ibid.

18. Actually, the liberation of private slaves does not take place until the late nineteenth century. We should read this simply as a reference to Yŏngjo's concern with the ills of the institution of slavery.

19. Kim Iyang, *Kim Iyang munjip, Kwansŏ kimun*.

20. Ibid.

21. Hwang Kojip's biography is found in Im Ch'angt'aek, *Sŭngak chip*, 546.

22. Chang Poksŏn's biography is found in Yi Ok, *Yi Ok chŏnjip*, 263.

23. This biography is found in Yi Kwangdŏk, *Kwanyangjip*, 519.

24. Ibid.

25. This biography is found in Sin Kyŏng, *Chigamjip*, 522.

26. O Such'ang, *Chosŏn hugi P'yŏngan-do sahoe palchŏn yŏn'gu*, 291–305.

5

P'yŏngan Dialect and Regional Identity in Chosŏn Korea

PAEK DOO-HYEON

INTRODUCTION

The most characteristic aspect and distinguishing feature of the P'yŏngan dialect (*P'yŏngan pangŏn*) during the Chosŏn Dynasty and into the modern era is the fact that it failed to undergo the t (ㄷ)-palatalization (*tigŭt kugaeŭmhwa*) process experienced by almost all other Korean dialects. Thus, commonly cited examples are the Sino-Korean word for "train station," Modern Standard *chŏnggŏjang* (ʧəŋgəjaŋ), pronounced *tŏnggŏdang* (təŋgədaŋ) (from earlier *tyŏnggŏdyang*), and the Chinese character for "heaven," "天," pronounced *ch'ŏn* (ʧʰən) in Modern Standard, and *t'ŏn* (tʰən) (from earlier *t'yŏn*) in P'yŏngan dialect. This non-realization of the transformation from ㄷ (t), ㅌ (tʰ) sounds to ㅈ (ʧ), ㅊ (ʧʰ) remains the single most characteristic and stereotypical feature of P'yŏngan dialect. The phonological change that produced ㅈ (ʧ) and ㅊ (ʧʰ) from ㄷ (t) and ㅌ (tʰ) before i and y is called t-palatalization. This process took place in almost all other dialects of the Korean peninsula, including the remote southern island of Cheju, as well as areas contiguous to P'yŏngan, namely Hwanghae and Hamgyŏng provinces. The only regions to escape this t-palatalization were the dialects of P'yŏngan and the *yukchin* area, situated in the northern extremity of Hamgyŏng Province.[1] Why did this not occur in the P'yŏngan dialect? The purpose of this chapter is to examine just what the reasons are and to discuss how this exception relates to the formation of identity in the P'yŏngan region.

Scholars have offered phonological explanations as to why t-palatalization did not take place in P'yŏngan Province.[2] While incorporating these scholars' ideas, the present work indicates some shortcomings in the purely phonological interpretations and suggests that we also need to take into account the historical, political, and geographical environments in which speakers of the P'yŏngan dialect were living. This revised approach will deepen our understanding of the peculiar link between language and identity that developed in the P'yŏngan region.

ANALYSIS OF SOURCES ON THE P'YŎNGAN DIALECT

What do documentary records from the late Chosŏn period that were either published in P'yŏngan Province or reflect P'yŏngan dialect tell us about the status of t-palatalization in the region? Let us now analyze the appearance of t-palatalization in Chosŏn-era Korean documents that show evidence of P'yŏngan dialect influence.

Illustrated Conduct of the Two Bonds (Iryun haengsilto 二倫行實圖, 1727), P'yŏngan Provincial Governor's Office Edition

Woodblock-printed editions of the Iryun haengsilto can be found in six different extant editions as listed in Table 5.1.

Table 5.1 Editions of the Iryun haengsilto

Edition	Publication date	Publication information
Oksan sŏwŏn edition (玉山書院本)	circa 1520	Presumed to be the first edition
Hakpong edition (鶴峰本)	circa 1570	Royal gift edition bestowed upon Hakpong Kim Sŏngil
Kiyŏng edition (箕營版)	1727	Published by P'yŏngan Provincial Governor's Office
Wŏnyŏng edition (原營版)	1730	Published by Kangwŏn Provincial Governor's Office
Yŏngyŏng edition (嶺營版)	1730	Published by Kyŏngsang Provincial Governor's Office
Haeyŏng edition (海營版)	1730	Published by Hwanghae Provincial Governor's Office

Subsequent to the publication of this work by the P'yŏngan provincial governor's office in 1727, the last three editions were published in the same year by different provincial governors' offices. The Wŏnyŏng edition is an exact copy of the Kiyŏng edition and thus there are no differences in the linguistic data. However, the Yŏngyŏng and Haeyŏng editions were each carved out from their own original manuscript versions, and therefore there are a number of differences in the linguistic data among the different editions. The most salient source of differences concerns how each edition reflected certain aspects of t-palatalization. In the Kyŏngsang dialect, the t-palatalization process had more or less already run its course by the early eighteenth century, and, thus, examples of t-palatalization appear rather frequently in the Yŏngyŏng edition. On the other hand, t-palatalization had not yet made any inroads into the dialects of P'yŏngan and Hwanghae, and consequently the Kiyŏng and Haeyŏng editions do not show any evidence of t-palatalization. The following chart demonstrates the clear contrast between the Kiyŏng and the Yŏngyŏng editions in terms of t-palatalization. The Haeyŏng edition, which is almost identical to the Kiyŏng edition in terms of non-realization of t-palatalization, is also included here for reference.

In addition to these, more than twenty other examples from the Yŏngyŏng edition reflecting t-palatalization can be found. The Kiyŏng edition, by contrast,

Table 5.2 Word Comparison Among Three Editions

Yŏngyŏng edition	Kiyŏng (P'yŏngan) edition	Haeyŏng edition	Meaning in English
malliji mothăya (1a)	mallidi mothăya	malnidi mothăya	cannot stop (it)
kaji malla (1a)	kadi malla	kadi malna	do not go
ŏjida (4a)	ŏdida	ŏdida	good
tuji anihăndae (4b)	tudi anihăndae	tudi anihăndae	did not consider
chugiji anihănira (6a)	chugidi anihănira	chugidi anihănira	did not kill
p'yŏnanch'i mothăni (8a)	p'yŏnant'i mothăni	p'yŏnant'i mothăni	uncomfortable
chyejă (44a)	tyejă	tyejă	disciple
tyŏnji (30a)	tyŏndi	tyŏndi	land
chăjye (31a)	chădye	chădye	sons and brothers

Table 5.3   Comparison Between the Yŏngyŏng and Haeyŏng Editions

Haeyŏng edition	Yŏngyŏng edition	Meaning in English
hyŏngjyŏ (7a)	hyŏngdye	brothers
hyŏngjye (8a)	hyŏngdye	brothers
naech'il kkŏsiida (8a)	naet'il kŏsiida	drive away
p'yŏnanch'i mothăni (8a)	p'yŏnanch'i mothăni	uncomfortable

does not show any palatalized examples at all; however, there are a few examples from the Haeyŏng edition reflecting t-palatalization (see Table 5.3). The Haeyŏng edition was carved from a new manuscript copy prepared specifically for this publication. Thus, these examples of palatalized words would seem to indicate that t-palatalization had made inroads into Hwanghae Province around 1730. But the evidence from the 1765 Hŭngnyul Temple edition of the *Selected Prayers to Buddha* (Yŏmbul pogwŏnmun, 念佛普勸文) published in Hwanghae Province, testifies otherwise. Although the Hŭngnyul edition was based on the Tonghwa Temple edition of 1764 from Taegu, Kyŏngsang Province, all those words that showed palatalization in the original were corrected back to their pre-palatalization forms. This testifies that Hwanghae residents did not know t-palatalization.[3] A more detailed evaluation of these two conflicting pieces of evidence with regard to whether t-palatalization had taken place in Hwanghae Province in the early- to mid-eighteenth century is presented later in this chapter; for now, it suffices to point out here that the Kiyŏng edition of the *Iryun haengsilto* does not show any evidence of t-palatalization.

The "Old Cathayan" in Vernacular Korean (Nogŏltae ŏnhae 老乞大諺解, 1745), P'yŏngan Provincial Governor's Office Edition

Among the five different editions of the well-known textbook in colloquial Chinese for Korean interpreters, the *Nogŏltae*, shown in Table 5.4, the edition most pertinent to our discussion is the *Nogŏltae ŏnhae* published by the P'yŏngan provincial governor's office in 1745. In this edition, which specifies at the end of the book that it was "republished by the provincial governor's office in P'yŏngan Province" (P'yŏngan Kamyŏng chunggan), forms with t-palatalization begin to appear. Examples are "kŭ chyung e" (1:4a)[4] for expected "kŭ tyung e,"

Table 5.4   Editions of the *Nogŏltae*

Editions	Publication information
Pŏnyŏk nogŏltae (飜譯老乞大)	circa 1510
Nogŏltae ŏnhae (老乞大諺解)	circa 1670
Nogŏltae ŏnhae (老乞大諺解)	1745 by P'yŏngan Provincial Governor's Office
Nogŏltae sinsŏk ŏnhae (老乞大新釋諺解)	1763
Chunggan nogŏltae ŏnhae (重刊老乞大諺解)	1795

"kaji mothăl ka" (1:2a) for expected "kadi . . . ," and "ŏjinira" (1:6b) for expected "ŏdinira." However, we must not rush to assume that the appearance of such t-palatalized forms indicates any prevalence of the t-palatalization phenomenon in P'yŏngan dialects at this time, because the actual business of compiling this book was carried out at the Bureau of Interpretation (Sayŏgwŏn), a central government office. As the publication information proves, eight professional interpreters (*yŏkkwan*) were in charge of compiling and editing this publication. The preface of the book mentions that the actual printing was done in P'yŏngan Province in accordance with the king's order that the book should be printed there because all the interpreters frequently traveled through the province on their diplomatic missions to and from China.[5] The t-palatalization forms appearing in the P'yŏngan provincial office edition of *Nogŏltae ŏnhae*, therefore, reflect that this particular phonological process was active in the central dialects of the period, and not in P'yŏngan dialects.

Selected Prayers to Buddha (Yŏmbul pogwŏnmun 念佛普勸文, 1765), Yongmun Temple (龍門寺) Edition from P'yŏngan Province

This book was re-printed in several temples in different regions, and today we know of six different editions (see Table 5.5). The Hŭngnyul Temple edition is based on the Tonghwa Temple edition, but the palatalized forms from the latter edition were strictly edited to conform to the Hwanghae dialect, as discussed earlier. In contrast, the Yongmun Temple edition of P'yŏngan Province, which was likewise a copy of the Tonghwa Temple edition, did not edit out the palatalized forms and left them as they were. At the same time,

Table 5.5   Editions of the *Yŏmbul pogwŏnmun*

Editions	Publication date	Publication place
Yongmun Temple edition (龍門寺板)	1704	Yech'ŏn, Kyŏngsang Province
Tonghwa Temple edition (桐華寺板)	1764	Taegu, Kyŏngsang Province
Hŭngnyul Temple edition (興律寺板)	1765	Kuwŏl Mountain, Hwanghae Province
Yongmun Temple edition (龍門寺板)	1765	Yŏngbyŏn, P'yŏngan Province
Haein Temple edition (海印寺板)	1776	Hapch'ŏn, Kyŏngsang Province
Sŏn'un Temple edition (禪雲寺板)	1787	Mujang, Chŏlla Province

however, we find that a number of *t*-palatalized words from the Tonghwa Temple edition have been "corrected" and converted back to their pre-palatalization forms, as exemplified in Table 5.6.

In the late eighteenth century, people of Kyŏngsang Province must have already recognized *t*-palatalization as a peculiar marker of their dialect, and such recognition in turn helped to form a certain self-awareness or identity for the people of that region. In contrast, the speakers of P'yŏngan dialect were not only unaware of *t*-palatalization, but also convinced that pronunciation of words *without* this change was both correct and proper. And this belief appears to have led P'yŏngan people to recognize *non-realization* of *t*-palatalization as a characteristic feature of their dialect and thus to revise the

Table 5.6 Word Comparison Between the Tonghwa Temple and Yongmun Temple Editions

Tonghwa Temple edition Kyŏngsang Province	Yongmun Temple edition P'yŏngan Province	Chinese characters / han'gŭl
ch'yŏndigan (5a)	t'yŏndigan (9b)	天地間
chyungsamp'um (6a)	tyungsamp'um (10a)	中三品
ch'yungsin (11b)	t'yungsin (15b)	忠臣
chyŏrina (11b)	tyŏrina (15b)	뎔(寺)이나

P'yŏngan provincial office edition accordingly. In other words, just as t-palatalization came to be recognized as a defining characteristic of Kyŏngsang dialect speakers, non-realization of t-palatalization became the marker of P'yŏngan dialect speakers. The examples from the P'yŏngan edition of the Yŏmbul pogwŏnmun discussed here show clearly such an understanding on the part of P'yŏngan people from this period.

Instructions for the People in Vernacular Korean (Kyŏngminp'yŏn ŏnhae 警民編諺解, publication year unknown), Presumed to be a P'yŏngan Provincial Governor's Office Edition

Six different editions of the Kyŏngminp'yŏn are extant; of interest to us is the sixth, namely the edition whose publication year as well as location have yet to be determined. It has been assumed, however, that this edition was published in P'yŏngan Province, a hypothesis based on the inclusion of the "Eight Admonitions" (p'algye 八戒) composed by Song Inmyŏng (1689–1746). Although there is no record that the "Eight Admonitions" were composed by Song Inmyŏng in this anonymous edition, Yi Chŏngso (1674–1736), who wrote an epilogue for the Wanyŏng edition, mentions that it was written by

Table 5.7 Editions of the Kyŏngminp'yŏn

Editions	Publication date	Publication information
Tokyo Teacher's College edition	1578	Reprint edition, printed in Chinju
Kyujanggak edition	1658	Revised edition by Yi Huwŏn
Ch'ogye edition (草溪板)	1731	Hapch'ŏn, Kyŏngsang Province, first edition
Ŭlch'uk Wanyŏng edition	1745	Chŏlla Province
Mujin Wanyŏng edition[i]	1748	Chŏlla Province
Anonymous edition	Unknown	Chŏlla Province

i. As the same woodblock-printed book, there is a Namwŏn edition, which has a colophon, "first edition, printed in Namwŏn in the seventh month of the mujin year" (戊辰七月日龍城開刊).

Song. Because Song served as the provincial governor of P'yŏngan Province between 1729 and 1730, it is believed that the anonymous edition was published around that time.[6] This edition most certainly reflects the P'yŏngan dialect, because in it we find the quintessentially P'yŏngan form "ădălp" ("eight," from presumed earlier yădălp) in Song's "Eight Admonitions."[7] In addition, this edition contains only forms without t-palatalization, such as "ŏsti" (sŏ:3b), "het'igi" (sŏ:4a), "tyŏ" (sŏ:3b), "tyohwahămi" (sŏ:4b), "adi mothănănda" (sŏ:5a), etc. This illustrates that t-palatalization had not occurred in the P'yŏngan dialect of that particular time period. Although Song was a resident of Kyŏnggi Province, the language of the Eight Admonitions as well as of the rest of the *Kyŏngminp'yŏn* followed the P'yŏngan dialect, as the readers of this edition were people from that region.

Ch(ㅈ)-palatalization in the Corean Primer

The *Corean Primer*, a textbook published by the pastor John Ross in 1877, reflected the language of Yi Ŭngch'an, who was from Ŭiju in P'yŏngan Province.[8] More importantly, the book includes not only vernacular Korean alphabet transcriptions, but also roman script ones as well, thereby affording us a precise look at the phonetic characteristics of the Ŭiju dialect in the latter half of the nineteenth century. In the *Corean Primer*, ㅈ is transcribed with (ds) and (j), the phonetic values of which we can interpret as (ts) and (ʧ), respectively, while ㅊ is transcribed with (ts) and (ch), whose phonetic values are to be interpreted as (tsʰ) and (ʧʰ), respectively. These transcriptions reflect the palatalization of ㅈ from (ts) to (ʧ), and of ㅊ from (tsʰ) to (ʧʰ), in certain phonetic environments in and around 1877. In other words, (ʧ) and (ʧʰ) appear when ㅈ and ㅊ appear in front of /y/ or /i/ and reflect the palatalization of ㅈ and ㅊ in the Ŭiju dialect in the latter half of the nineteenth century. The process by which partial ch(ㅈ)-palatalization emerged in Ŭiju basically followed the same phonological transformation that the other regional dialects had earlier experienced. In other words, there was a time lag in the onset of palatalization in the Ŭiju dialect compared to other regions, and ch (ㅈ)-palatalization in Ŭiju was not complete until the mid-twentieth century.

Ch (ㅈ)-palatalization in Ŭiju dialect was likely promoted by frequent contact with other dialects. Ogura Shimpei (1882–1944) discovered certain changes in the P'yŏngan dialect in its peripheral areas in the early twentieth century and explained these changes as influenced by contacts with other dialects.[9] Ŭiju was an important border town where traffic of people with various regional backgrounds and dialects was heavy. Because of this geopolitical particularity, residents of this town came to learn of other cultures, including dialects, and adopted *ch* (ㅈ)-palatalization earlier than people in the rest of P'yŏngan Province.

APPEARANCE OF T- PALATALIZATION
IN MATERIALS ON THE P'YŎNGAN DIALECT

In order to analyze the development of t-palatalization in P'yŏngan dialects in the twentieth century, I will now examine five sources on the P'yŏngan dialect compiled by dialectologists:

Ogura Shimpei, *Chōsengo hōgen no kenkyū* (Tokyo: Iwanami shoten, 1944)

Kim Pyŏngje, *Pangŏn sajŏn* (P'yŏngyang: Sahoe kwahagwŏn ch'ulp'ansa, 1980)

Kim Ihyŏp, *P'yŏngbuk pangŏn sajŏn* (Seoul: Han'guk chŏngsin munhwa yŏn'guwŏn, 1981)

Li Ungyu, Sim Hoesŏp, and An Un, *Chosŏnŏ pangŏn sajŏn* (Yŏnbyŏn inmin ch'ulp'ansa, 1990)

Kim Yŏngbae, *P'yŏngan pangŏn yŏn'gu, charyo-p'yŏn* (Seoul: T'aehaksa, 1997)

Among the above materials, the first is an investigation of the P'yŏngan dialect in the first half of the twentieth century, while all the others treat the dialect in the latter half of the twentieth century. Kim Yŏngbae's work is a comprehensive collection of P'yŏngan dialect materials that integrates the first three works as well as his own investigations based on work with refugees from P'yŏngan Province before and during the Korean War (1950–1953). Therefore, this section relies on Kim's work and examines the progress and geographical distribution of t-palatalization in the region in the latter part of the twentieth century.

Examples of T-palatalized Words

1. chiju 지주 (地主) and chŏnju 전주 (田主) meaning "landlord" (18)[10]

   tŏnju 던주: South P'yŏngan Province (SP) (Taedong, Kangdong, Maengsan,

Kaech'ŏn, and P'yŏngwŏn) and North P'yŏngan Province (NP) (Chasŏng and Huch'ang)

tenju 뎬주: SP (Sunch'ŏn and Anju) and NP (Pakch'ŏn, Yŏngbyŏn, Hoech'ŏn, Unsan, T'aech'ŏn, Kusŏng, Ch'angsŏng, Wiwŏn, and Kanggye)

tiju 디주: SP (Tŏkch'ŏn) and NP (T'aech'ŏn)

chiju 지주: SP (P'yŏngyang, Yangdŏk, and Yŏngwŏn) and NP (Chasŏng)

2. chip 짚 (straw) (18–19)

tip 딥: SP (all districts except P'yŏngyang, Yangdŏk, and Yŏngwŏn)

tip 딮: SP (Mundŏk and Anju) and NP (Pakch'ŏn, Yŏngbyŏn, Kujang, Unjŏn, Kusŏng, and Hyangsan)

chip 집: SP (P'yŏngyang, Yangdŏk, and Yŏngwŏn)

3. chŏlgu 절구 (mortar) (42)

tŏlgu 덜구: SP (all areas except Yangdŏk) and all districts of NP

chŏlgu 절구: SP (Yangdŏk)[11]

4. chilgŭrŭt 질그릇 (earthenware) (43)

tŭlgŭrŭt 들그릇: SP (P'yŏngyang and three other districts)

tilgŭrŭt 딜그릇: SP (all districts except P'yŏngyang, Yangdŏk, and Maengsan) and NP (all districts except Unsan and Ch'ŏlsan)

chilgŭrŭt 질그릇: SP (Yangdŏk)

5. namp'yŏn 남편 (husband) (109)

namdŏng 남덩: SP (Onch'ŏn and Yonggang) and NP (Yŏngbyŏn, Kujang, and Sŏnch'ŏn)

namjŏng 남정: NP (Kanggye)

6. changga kada 장가가다 (marry) (120)

tanggae kada 당개가다: SP (all districts except Chinnamp'o) and NP all districts

changgae kada 장개가다: SP (Chinnamp'o)

7. chinhŭk 진흙 (mud) (206)

tinhŭk 딘흙: SP (all districts except Yangdŏk, Maengsan, and P'yŏngwŏn)

chinhŭk 진흙: SP (Yangdŏk and Maengsan) and NP (Ch'angsŏng and Chasŏng)

8. chuya 주야 (晝夜 day and night) (205)

tuya 두야: SP (Chunghwa, P'yŏngyang, Sunch'ŏn, and Anju) and NP (9 districts except Pakch'ŏn and Yŏngbyŏn)

chuya 주야: NP (Huch'ang)

9. haejilnyŏk / hae tida 해질녁 / 해 디다 (dusk / sun sets) (208)

hae tida 해디다: SP (Taedong, Chinnamp'o, Sŏngch'ŏn, Kaech'ŏn, and Tŏkch'ŏn) and NP (Sinŭiju, Ŭiju, and Sakchu)

haedilnyŏk 해딜녁: SP (all districts except Chinnamp'o, Sŏngch'ŏn, Yangdŏk, Tŏkch'ŏn, and Sunch'ŏn)

haedilnyŏk 해딜녁: NP (Wiwŏn, T'aech'ŏn, Pakch'ŏn, Yŏmju, Ŭiju, Chŏngju, Yongch'ŏn, Yŏngbyŏn, and Taegwan)

haejilkkol 해질꼴: SP (Yangdŏk and Kaech'ŏn) and NP (Kusŏng, Sinŭiju, Ŭiju, and Huch'ang)

10. chohta 좋다 (good) (225)

tot'a 도타: SP (Chunghwa, P'yŏngyang, Sunch'ŏn, Sukch'ŏn, and Anju) and NP (Pakch'ŏn, Yŏngbyŏn, Hŭich'ŏn, Kusŏng, Chŏngju, Sŏnch'ŏn, Yongam, Ŭiju, Kanggye, Chasŏng, and Huch'ang)

to:t'a 도:타: NP (Ŭiju, Sakchu, P'ihyŏn, Yongch'ŏn, Ch'ŏlsan, Taegwan, Unsan, and Tongnim) tohta 돟다: SP (all districts except Yangdŏk)

chot'a 조타: SP (Chunghwa) and NP (Huch'ang)

chohta 좋다: SP (Yangdŏk)

Examples of Words That Did Not Undergo T-palatalization

1. chŏgi 저기 (over there) (204)

   tŏgi 더기: SP (Yonggang, Onch'ŏn, Sukch'ŏn, and Anju) and NP (P'ihyŏn, Ŭiju, and six other districts)

   tegi 데기: SP (Yonggang and Onch'ŏn) and NP (Yŏngbyŏn, Kujang, Hyangsan, Pakch'ŏn, and Hŭich'ŏn)

2. chŏl 절 (寺 temple) (58)

   tŏl 덜: SP (P'yŏngyang) and NP (Pakch'ŏn and five other districts)

3. Myŏnjang 면장 (面長 subdistrict head) (112)

   Myŏndang 면당: multiple districts

4. chosu 조수 (潮水 tide) (205)

   tosu 도수: SP (Maengsan and Kaech'ŏn)

   toesu 되수: NP (Kusŏng and Ŭiju)

5. chusŏk 주석 (錫 tin) (205)

   tusŏk 두석: NP (Yŏngbyŏn, Hŭich'ŏn, and Kanggye)

   twisŏk 뒤석: SP (P'yŏngyang) and NP (Pakch'ŏn and Kusŏng)

6. chinda 진다 (落 fall) (378)

   tinda 딘다: SP (Chunghwa, P'yŏngyang, Sunch'ŏn, Sukch'ŏn, and Anju) and NP (Pakch'ŏn, Yŏngbyŏn, Kusŏng, Chŏngju, Sŏnch'ŏn, Yongam, and Ŭiju)

7. chipta 짚다 (touch) (260)

   tipta 딮다: NP (Yŏngbyŏn, Kujang, Hyangsan, Pakch'ŏn, Unjŏn, and Kusŏng)

We can glean a few prominent tendencies from these two types—words that show t-palatalization and words that do not. In South P'yŏngan Province, we find frequent examples of t-palatalized words from a few districts such as P'yŏngyang, Yangdŏk, Yŏngwŏn, Maengsan, Chinnamp'o, and Chunghwa. P'yŏngyang and Chinnamp'o were areas of heavy traffic and thus were probably influenced by dialects from other regions. Yangdŏk, Maengsan, and Yŏngwŏn border on South Hamgyŏng Province, an area that underwent t-palatalization earlier. In North P'yŏngan Province, Sinŭiju, Ŭiju, Huch'ang, and Chasŏng were also border towns which experienced heavy traffic and frequent contact with other dialects, resulting in more t-palatalization.

As discussed above in the examples from the *Corean Primer*, *ch* (ㅈ)-palatalization, which is considered to be the first stage of the overall palatalization process, had taken place in Ŭiju around 1877, but the second stage of palatalization, t-palatalization, had not. The evidence from the late twentieth century date proves that t-palatalization had been realized in P'yŏngan Province by that time. Interestingly, there is no evidence that any areas other than Ŭiju experienced *ch* (ㅈ)-palatalization in the late nineteenth century. Moreover, we cannot explain the occurrence of palatalization in P'yŏngan region phonologically. In other words, no phonological environment ideal for palatalization was provided, because in the P'yŏngan dialects the semi-vowel /y/ following /t ㄷ/ and /t' ㅌ/ was either dropped (e.g., t'yŏn 텬 → t'ŏn 턴) or else the vowel was contracted (e.g., tyŏ 뎌 → te 데). In conclusion, palatalization in P'yŏngan Province must have been due to the influence from dialects outside the region, and reflected both diffusion and borrowing from other regional varieties, and it could not have been an internal development within the P'yŏngan dialect.

A SOCIO-HISTORICAL APPROACH TO LINGUISTIC PHENOMENA IN THE P'YŎNGAN DIALECT

Until the present day, linguists of the Korean language have explained the non-realization of ㄷ(t) > ㅈ (ʧ) palatalization in P'yŏngan dialects from a phonological perspective involving specific features of pronunciation in these dialects. Ogura Shimpei in 1944 pointed out that in the northwestern dialects, ㅈ-category sounds were pronounced as dentals rather than as alveolars or alveopalatals, and that therefore palatalization of ㄷ (t) and ㅌ (tʰ) could not occur.[12] Yi Kimun in 1972 also argued that the ㅈ in the northwestern dialects was a dental, and explained this as a conservative retention of the position of the tongue in articulating this consonant series in Middle Korean. Based on the hypothesis that the key prerequisite for t-palatalization is pronunciation of ㅈ as a palatal, Yi asserted that the non-realization of t-palatalization in P'yŏngan dialects was due to the fact that P'yŏngan ㅈ was a dental, not a palatal.[13] This interpretation is important in that it links the development of phonological changes to the phonological system.

According to the *Hunmin chŏngŭm haeryebon* (Correct Sounds for the Instruction of the People: Examples and Explanations), each Korean consonant is categorized as follows in terms of its place of articulation.[14]

Labial—	p ㅂ, p' ㅍ, m ㅁ
Dental—	s ㅅ, ch ㅈ, ch' ㅊ
Alveolar—	t ㄷ, t' ㅌ, n ㄴ
Velar—	k ㄱ, k' ㅋ, -ng ㅇ
Guttural—	h ㆆ, ㅇ

Six consonants are classified as either dental or alveolar sounds, but none were classified as palatals. In all modern Korean dialects except P'yŏngan, ㅈ has developed from dental (ts) to palatal (ʧ). In written form, of course, the ㅈ remains the same, but its sound value has changed. This transformation took place first in southern dialects starting in Chŏlla and Kyŏngsang provinces. For example, the *Chunggan tusi ŏnhae* (Poems of Du Fu in Korean Vernacular, reprint edition) and the letters from the Hyŏnp'ung Kwak family, both of which reflect Taegu (Kyŏngsang Province) dialect from the seventeenth century, show the change ㄷ ➔ ㅈ in front of /i/ and /y/.[15] This phonological change can only take place when ㅈ is already a palatal in its articulation. The fact that changes of ㄷ ➔ ㅈ are attested in written form means that the palatalization of the dental ㅈ (ts) ➔ (ʧ) had already occurred in this area, probably in the late sixteenth or early seventeenth centuries, because logically this *ch* (ㅈ)-palatalization has to precede the change from ㄷ → ㅈ. Thus, there are two stages to the overall palatalization process:

First step: palatalization of the dental ㅈ (ts) → (ʧ)[16]
Second step: palatalization of ㄷ (t) → ㅈ (ʧ)[17]

In contrast to other dialects that had both steps—i.e., both the phonetic-articulatory and phonological changes—P'yŏngan dialect experienced neither the first step (palatalization of ㅈ), nor the second step (ㄷ (t) → ㅈ (ʧ)). So why was it that P'yŏngan dialects uniquely rejected the palatalization of ㅈ? Because phonetics and phonology alone cannot offer a satisfactory answer to this question, I will seek a sociohistorical explanation. Language is not a mechanical structure that self-regulates its own directions of change, but is subject to users affected by certain social and historical contexts. Thus, it is reasonable to take into account users' consciousness in language practice and their social environments when seeking to explain the causes of a particular linguistic phenomenon.

In the dialects of Chŏlla, Kyŏngsang, and Hamgyŏng provinces, the ㄷ → ㅈ palatalization had already begun in the latter half of the sixteenth century or, in some cases, in the early seventeenth century. By the late seventeenth and early eighteenth centuries, the phenomenon had already become quite prominent. In fact, even in the materials published in Seoul, examples of ㄷ → ㅈ palatalization appear quite frequently in texts by the mid-eighteenth century. The P'yŏngan dialect, however, still had not undergone this palatalization process until well into the early part of the twentieth century, leaving a temporal gap of about 400 years between the onset of the process in the southern regions and its attestation in P'yŏngan. This discrepancy between P'yŏngan and other regions was due not only to phonological reasons, but also to other factors involving language use. Because people are the agents of language use, it is reasonable to hypothesize that speakers' understanding of and attitude toward their language can wield considerable influence over their linguistic practice. Here, I would like to examine more closely these other, extra-linguistic reasons for the lack of palatalization in the P'yŏngan dialect by focusing on P'yŏngan speakers' attitudes toward their dialect and on their understanding of its peculiarities.

Self-awareness of Regional Dialect and Regional Identity

Speakers of the P'yŏngan dialect did not accept t-palatalization and understood the absence of this process to be a distinct characteristic of their dialect. Moreover, it seems clear they had already made a sort of value judgment regarding this state of affairs. The essay titled, "An Opinion on the Rights and Wrongs of Our Nation's Dialects" (Adong pangŏn chŏngbyŏn sŏl 我東方言正變說) by Paek Kyŏnghae (1765–1842), a man born in P'yŏngan and a government official, reveals what the people of P'yŏngan thought of t-palatalization.[18]

Our country did not have its own script for writing. Great King Sejong, who was extremely intelligent and benevolent, was not only a monarch but also a teacher. He greatly promoted culture and corrected music. Together with Sŏng Sammun and Sin Sukchu, who were well-versed in old documents, he invented the vernacular script and enabled vernacular writing. He accomplished this after consulting Ming scholars thirteen times to perfect the script. There is nothing that cannot be communicated with this script, and it is indeed a treasure of our country that should be preserved for thousands of years.

In the present day, only in one province, P'yŏngan, has the correct pronunciation been preserved, thereby keeping the old tradition. In the seven other provinces, "t'yŏn 텬" is pronounced "ch'yŏn 쳔" and "ti 디" has become "chi 지." In general, all forms that belong to the rows "ta t'a 다타" have become mixed up and have reverted to the rows "cha ch'a 자차." While among all these places the regional dialects and local customs are not all the same, when it comes to the sounds "t'yŏndi 텬디," the seven provinces make the same error together. This is indeed strange. Those classics translated into vernacular Korean before the mid-Chosŏn period all used these sounds from the time of King Sejong, but recent translations [do not follow the correct sounds] so cannot be regarded as standard.

P'yŏngan Province is the place where our country's history began. Great teacher Kija from the Shang Dynasty moved here and established the standard culture. When King Sejong invented the script, how could he not know that history? He must have pondered on these origins, taken into account the appropriate customs, and incorporated the middle way.

Among those who were born in P'yŏngan Province but have lived in Seoul for a long time there are those who have changed their pronunciation. However, those who have stayed in this region, living from the earth and water here, still speak adhering to tradition and not changing [their pronunciation]. Therefore, the P'yŏngan region truly provides the correct basis for our language.

As I recall, I heard from my teachers and elders that King Sukchong once inquired at a royal lecture, "The speech sounds from the eight [Korean] provinces are all different. Which is to be taken as correct?" One renowned scholar at the lecture replied, "The P'yŏngan dialect is correct." This scholar was then praised for his knowledge of languages. I have not known any similar discussion these days. So I say, "As concerns the speech sounds of the universe, China is to be taken as correct; as concerns the speech sounds of our country, P'yŏngan Province is to be taken as correct. Moreover, it is P'yŏngan Province whence originate our language and writing."

The strongest and most consistent assertion in Paek Kyŏnghae's essay is his understanding that both the correctness and origins of the Korean language lie in the P'yŏngan dialect, which had yet to be exposed to the ㄷ → ㅈ transformation. In other words, Paek was speaking proudly of the idea that the sounds determined during King Sejong's reign had remained unchanged by the people of the P'yŏngan region, unlike those of the seven other provinces. The people of this region were linguistically inclined to hold at bay the ㄷ → ㅈ transformation. In this way, Paek argued that the P'yŏngan dialect was the correct root of the Korean language. This pride was bolstered by tradition and gained historical legitimacy when combined with the belief that Kija founded a state in P'yŏngyang, which was regarded as the seat of Korean civilization.

One question we need to ask concerns chronology; when exactly did P'yŏngan residents come to interpret the lack of t-palatalization as a cultural trait unique to their province? The Yongmun Temple edition of the Yŏmbul pogwŏnmun published in P'yŏngan Province in 1765 provides clear evidence that P'yŏngan people rejected the ㄷ → ㅈ phonological change because this edition actually removed t-palatalized forms from its base copy, the Tonghwa Temple edition of Kyŏngsang Province. From this evidence, we can surmise that a regional consciousness to the effect that non-palatalized forms were somehow unique to the P'yŏngan dialect and, moreover, that this state of affairs represented the "correct sounds," must have come into existence as early as the 1760s. And Paek's essay is as succinct and clear a defense of this new consciousness as one could hope for.

The Impact of Standardized Sino-Korean Pronunciation

Another reason why P'yŏngan people evinced negative attitudes to t-palatalization may have been their consideration of Sino-Korean pronunciation— the vernacular Korean reading of Chinese characters which constitutes a major portion of the Korean vocabulary. Paek Kyŏnghae declared in his essay that the speech sounds of the universe based their correctness on China. Any notion of "correctness" in Sino-Korean must refer to the pronunciation of Chinese characters as recorded in rhyme dictionaries. Paek also argued that King Sejong and his assistants consulted Chinese scholars thirteen times when determining the correct sounds of Chinese characters in vernacular Korean script. In addition, Paek pointed out that the reason why King Sejong took the P'yŏngan dialect as "standard" was because he was aware that this region was the place where Kija, a legendary man from the Chinese Shang Dynasty, had established cultural standards long, long ago. Relying on these pieces of evidence stemming from China, Kija, and later King Sejong, Paek tried to piece together the legitimization of the P'yŏngan dialect as representing the standard, correct sounds for Sino-Korean pronunciation dating back to the time of King Sejong and extending to Paek's own time, while other dialects had deviated from this standard over the years. In other words, the standard Sino-Korean pronunciation recorded in the rhyme books motivated P'yŏngan residents to reject t-palatalization.

P'yŏngan Koreans maintained their conservative standpoint in terms of preserving standard Sino-Korean pronunciations as late as the early twentieth century. According to the *Thousand Character Classic in P'yŏngan Dialect* (*P'yŏngbuk pangŏn ch'ŏnjamun*) compiled by Kim Ihyŏp, who received a traditional education in the Chinese classics in P'yŏngan Province early in the century, non-palatalized words such as "*hanăl t'ŏn*" (vs. Modern Standard *hanŭl ch'ŏn*), "*tta ti*" (vs. Modern Standard *ttang chi*), "*chip tu*" (vs. Modern Standard *chip chu*), etc., were prominent.[19] The lack of palatalization, then, seems to have been derived from the linguistic consciousness of the P'yŏngan people who wished to preserve the "correct" Sino-Korean pronunciation as determined in the fifteenth century (See Chapter 6 for a further detailed discussion of P'yŏngan dialect speakers' language identity and their fights against the Unified Han'gŭl Orthography).

Political Discrimination against the P'yŏngan Region and Linguistic Identity

It is also necessary at this point to examine how the political discrimination directed against the people of P'yŏngan and, in turn, the resistance to this regional discrimination and a victim mentality may have affected the formation of a specifically northwestern identity. O Such'ang in his work in 2002 and Sun Joo Kim in her recent book have shed much light on the reality and historical development of discrimination against the P'yŏngan region during the Chosŏn Dynasty.[20] As Chapters 3 and 4 in the present volume discuss, discrimination against the people of the northwestern region continued from the middle of the Chosŏn Dynasty well into the nineteenth century. The people of this region consequently harbored much despair and a sense of injustice, and subsequently were hindered from developing any pride on the socio-political plane. It is more probable that they lived with a sense of inferiority caused by the deterioration of their social status, a condition which could be accompanied by and/or precipitate a psychological desire for compensation on some other level. The Kija legend provided a perfect cultural resource for such a demand and thus the people of P'yŏngan lived with and expressed a sense of pride in their residing in Kija's provenance, a fact which also came up every time the royal court tried to tame them. However, while P'yŏngan people expressed pride in living in the land of Kija, they could not very well hide the sense that they were less civilized, especially in comparison to the objective cultural superiority of other regions such as Kyŏnggi, Ch'ungch'ŏng, Kyŏngsang, and Chŏlla provinces. One part, then, of the effort to soothe this sense of inferiority and to restore regional pride was to dignify their P'yŏngan dialect as the "correct" root and basis of the Chosŏn language, as expressed so forcefully in the aforementioned opinion of Paek Kyŏnghae. By keeping ㄷ

→ ㅈ palatalization at bay and thereby protecting the old ㄷ-category sounds as determined by King Sejong when he promulgated the *hunmin chŏngŭm*, they preserved the P'yŏngan dialect as distinct from the dialects of the seven other provinces which, in the meantime, had incorporated "incorrect" pronunciation, becoming, in effect, corrupt. In this way, people in the northwest solidified an understanding of the P'yŏngan dialect as the one correct and historically legitimate model for Korean (and Sino-Korean), which, in turn, played a role in the formation of P'yŏngan regional identity.

Regional Isolation and the Problem of Conservatism in the P'yŏngan Dialect

In order to explain the linguistic peculiarities of the P'yŏngan dialect, it is helpful to compare them to those of other Korean dialects. The non-realization of ㄷ → ㅈ palatalization in the P'yŏngan dialect was due to the dialect's retention of older linguistic forms, and one can see similar phenomena in other dialects, albeit with other linguistic features, as in the following:

1. The retention of a distinctive pitch-accent in the Kyŏngsang dialect.

2. The retention of a distinctive pitch-accent in a manner strikingly similar to that of Middle Korean in the *yukchin* dialect of North Hamgyŏng Province.

3. The retention of the "arae a" vowel (ǎ ♀) in Cheju dialect.

Regional isolation has played, and still continues to play, a significant role in the preservation of linguistic archaisms such as these. For example, the *yukchin* region is situated in the northeasternmost corner of the peninsula, while Cheju is an island separated from the rest of Korea by the sea; similarly, Kyŏngsang Province is isolated from Ch'ungch'ŏng and Chŏlla provinces by the Sobaek Mountain range. However, P'yŏngan Province is a different story altogether. There are no insurmountable topographical obstacles between Seoul and P'yŏngan Province. Moreover, because P'yŏngan was on the itinerary for frequent missions and envoys going back and forth to China and was thus also situated along a major trade route (see the discussion by Kwon Naehyun in Chapter 2), there must have been quite extensive contact between the people of P'yŏngan and those of the southern regions, including Seoul. From these considerations, then, it is safe to conclude that the retention of the ㄷ before /i/ and /y/ (with subsequent loss of these conditioning elements, which, on the other hand, gave rise to the change t ➔ ch, etc., in other dialects) in the P'yŏngan dialect is fundamentally different in character from the preservation of archaic features in the yukchin, Cheju, and Kyŏngsang dialects, all of which can be attributed to regional isolation. Therefore, it is necessary to consider not only geographical and topographical causes, but also the complexities of speakers' linguistic attitudes as well as numerous socio-political concerns in order to fully understand the retention of this particular archaism in P'yŏngan dialect.

CONCLUSION

William Labov, who conducted an investigation of local dialects spoken on Martha's Vineyard in the New England region in 1961, reported an interesting phenomenon. Once a quiet fishing village, this beautiful island community had become a popular summer vacation spot for numerous outsiders who flocked to the island, thereby causing unexpected changes in the lives of the residents. The original residents, probably in defense of their identity, transformed the pronunciation of diphthongs in words like "house" by raising the first vowel: from (haus) to (həus). This change was led by male residents in their thirties and forties who felt strong solidarity as fishermen.[21] Labov argues that they initiated this linguistic change in order to differentiate themselves from the summer vacationers. Their attachment to their home island and their desire to express their own, separate identity must have motivated them to create these linguistic distinctions vis-à-vis outsiders. This is a classic example in the sociolinguistic literature of a speaker's consciousness playing a critical role in a linguistic change.

It is very plausible, then, that speakers of the P'yŏngan dialect at some point in time came to understand their dialect's characteristic feature as the non-realization of ch (ㅈ)-palatalization, which in turn took away the environment for the ㄷ ➔ ㅈ phonological change; this consciousness could only have grown increasingly clearer as generations passed. In contrast to the dialects of the seven other provinces of Chosŏn, which had already been exposed to and undergone the ㄷ ➔ ㅈ change, the P'yŏngan dialect, in conjunction with the idea that its speakers were preserving the "correct sounds" established by King Sejong, fueled the P'yŏngan people's determination to protect their dialect from the ㄷ → ㅈ sound change. This linguistic attitude vis-à-vis the P'yŏngan dialect in combination with the political discrimination imposed on the P'yŏngan region, assisted in the formation of regional identity in the P'yŏngan Province. The diagram below provides a visual explanation of the main points of this chapter.

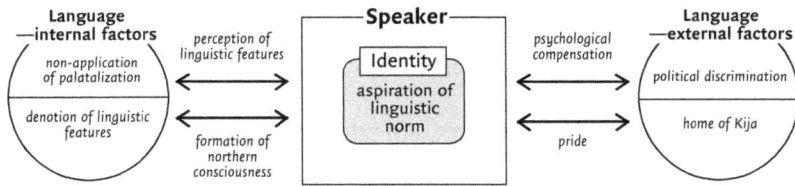

Fig. 5.1 Dialect and Regional Identity

NOTES

1. The *yukchin* area refers to contemporary districts such as Onsŏng, Hoeryŏng, and Chongsŏng in northern Hamgyŏng Province. Just as in the P'yŏngan dialect, t-palatalization is not realized and /y/ is omitted. Examples are: *tot'a* corresponding to Modern Standard *chot'a* (good) and *tŏnggŏdang* corresponding to Modern Standard *chŏnggŏjang* (train station).

2. For examples, see Ogura Shimpei, *Chōsengo hōgen no kenkyū* and Yi Kimun, *Kugŏ ŭmunsa yŏn'gu*.

3. Kim Chuwŏn, "18 segi Hwanghae-do pangŏn ŭi ŭmun hyŏnsang," 29–31.

4. This page reference refers to *sang kwŏn* (first volume), recto (a) of fourth printed sheet. "b" refers to the verso of each printed sheet.

5. Sŏk Chuyŏn, *Nogŏltae wa Pak t'ongsa ŭi ŏnŏ*, 41–42.

6. For Song Inmyŏng's appointment as P'yŏngan provincial governor, see *Ch'ŏngsŏn'go, kwŏn* 15, Kwanch'alsa.

7. *Kyŏngminp'yŏn, sŏ,* 1a–1b.

8. Discussions on the *Corean Primer* and Yi Ŭngch'an are based on Han Sŏngu, "Ŭiju pangŏn ŭi ŭmunnonjŏk yŏn'gu."

9. Ogura Shimpei, *Chōsengo hōgen no kenkyū*, 2: 254–67.

10. The number in parentheses refers to the page number from Kim Yŏngbae's 1997 book, *P'yŏngan pangŏn yŏn'gu, charyo-p'yŏn.*

11. We find "chyŏlgu 졀구" and "chyŏlgo 졀고" in eighteenth-century documents. See *Tongmun yuhae, ha,* 2a and 2b. "tyŏlgo 뎔고" and "tyŏlgu 뎔구" are not found in any premodern documents.

12. Ogura Shimpei, *Chōsengo hōgen no kenkyū*, 2: 254–67.

13. Yi Kimun, *Kugŏ ŭmunsa yŏn'gu,* 64–69.

14. *Hunmin chŏngŭm ŏnhae haerye.*

15. See *Chunggan tusi ŏnhae;* and Paek Tuhyŏn, *Hyŏnp'ung Kwak-ssi ŏn'gan chuhae.*

16. This change was applied to ㅈ first in front of /i/ and /y/ and then spread to other environments.

17. This variation was realized only when ㄷ (t) preceded /i/ or /y/. For example, 뎌 tyŏ → 져 chyŏ, 디 ti → 지 chi.

18. Paek Kyŏnghae, "Adong pangŏn chŏngbyŏn sŏl," in *Suwajip,* 6:27a–28a, published in 1884, *Kuksa p'yŏnch'an wiwŏnhoe* collection D3B 263. I would like to express my gratitude to Professor Sun Joo Kim of Harvard University for kindly introducing me to this source. See also her article for a more detailed discussion of Paek Kyŏnghae's life and thoughts: Sun Joo Kim, "Negotiating Cultural Identities in Conflict, A Reading of Paek Kyŏnghae (1765–1842)'s Writings."

19. Kim Ihyŏp, *P'yŏngbuk pangŏn sajŏn,* 558.

20. O Such'ang, *Chosŏn hugi P'yŏngan-do sahoe palchŏn yŏn'gu;* and Sun Joo Kim, *Marginality and Subversion in Korea.*

21. William Labov, *Sociolinguistic Patterns.*

6

Dialect, Orthography, and Regional Identity

P'yŏngan Christians, Korean Spelling Reform, and Orthographic

Fundamentalism

ROSS KING

INTRODUCTION

In an earlier publication, I attempted a detailed outline of the main tenets of
the South Korean vernacular belief system, one key element of which can be
summarized as follows: "When Korea finally reformed its government in the
1890s, han'gŭl,[1] the indigenous script, was waiting to save the day, and Korean
linguists, led by Chu Sigyŏng (1876–1914) and his students, championed its
revival and reform, achieving a unified, standard Korean language and orthography already in the 1930s in the face of Japanese colonial oppression. Both
the unified orthography of 1933, and the standard language norms of 1936,
based on Seoul speech, were the achievements of the Chosŏnŏ hakhoe
(Korean Language Society) and its scholars."[2] This particular aspect of the
Korean vernacular belief system would be endorsed today in North Korea,
too, with one caveat: North Korean sources never use the word han'gŭl and
replace it instead with chosŏn'gŭl (Korean writing) or urigŭl (our script). This
seemingly innocuous account of the rise of modern Korean standard language and orthography, as well as the apparently minor point about the designation for the Korean writing system, both in fact elide significant debates
and controversy concerning the definition of the standard language in colonial Korea, and about orthographic reform. As we shall see below, the word
han'gŭl itself stood just as much (perhaps even more) for a particular orthography—that of the Chosŏnŏ hakhoe—as it did for the script itself, and the
debates that surrounded Korean language and spelling reveal much about

regional and national identity during the period from the turn of the last century and well into the 1950s. In this chapter, we borrow the notion of a "language ideological debate" to examine these controversies and what they reveal about issues of regional (northwestern) and national identity.

ORTHOGRAPHY, IDENTITY, AND LANGUAGE IDEOLOGY

The notion of a "language ideological debate" comes from Jan Blommaert, who pleads for more research on the "historiography of language ideologies" and "the historical production and reproduction of language ideologies." He complains, quite rightly, that "language history as something that pertains to speakers, to societies, to social and cultural systems, is only rarely the history used in linguistics or adjacent sciences.... It is our ambition to add to the history of language and languages a dimension of human agency, political intervention, power and authority.... The precise discursive mechanisms by means of which linguistic symbolic resources are being produced, distributed or circulated, and the value attached to these resources, are the foci of our attention."[3]

Sally Johnson develops Blommaert's concept of a "language ideological debate" in her study of the recent failed attempt to reform German orthography. For Johnson, language ideological debates occur "in specific times and places where real social actors have collectively disputed the nature and function of language."[4] The "concrete attempts to secure closure in a given debate" are "'bids' for AUTHORITATIVE ENTEXTUALIZATION."[5] Thus, for Johnson, it is important to "try to understand how and why some views of language gradually emerge as dominant while others are suppressed and marginalised."

One key locus or site for the de- or re-construction of histories of particular language ideologies is spelling debates. Johnson notes the "contingent nature of orthographic practices generally" and the "ideological nature of transcription processes more generally in the construction, conscious or otherwise, of social identities."[6] In this connection, and with specific respect to Germany, she notes the "paradox that surrounds orthography generally: Its commonly perceived insignificance, which meant that the question of reform was repeatedly marginalized in favor of more pressing political concerns, coupled with its huge symbolic significance."[7] In another article on the German spelling debate of the late 1990s, Johnson concludes from her analysis of the "discursive drift" of the controversy that "No longer was this a dispute about *orthography*. It was not even a question of the written language. What was clearly at stake here was the German language in all its force as a signifier of cultural and national unity."[8] She cautions: "language planners are unwise to marginalize the cultural, political, and even emotional allegiances which many language users attach to their established orthographic practices."[9]

Another recent work that has exploited spelling debates as a site for the uncovering of language ideologies is Bambi B. Schieffelin and Rachelle Carlier Doucet's paper on Haitian Creole. Citing the importance of studying "contested orthographies," they show how orthographic debates are rich sites for investigating competing nationalist discourses.[10] To draw on Benedict Anderson's evocative notion, orthographic choice is really about "imagining" the past and the future of a community.[11] For Schieffelin and Doucet, orthography is important as "representation: how the language sounds and looks,"[12] and they note that "the recent arguments regarding the implementation of the reform of the French orthography are a good example of how a country can stick to its orthographic icons as symbols of its identity."[13] We shall see ample illustrations of these tendencies from Korea below.

What, then, is "language ideology?" Research on language ideologies has grown in the past fifteen to twenty years out of interdisciplinary work spanning sociolinguistics, linguistic anthropology, sociology, history, education, and other fields. Shirley Brice Heath defines language ideologies as "self-evident ideas and objectives a group holds concerning roles of language in the social experiences of members as they contribute to the expression of the group."[14] Susan Gal notes that "ideologies that appear to be about language, when carefully reread, are revealed to be coded stories about political, religious, or scientific conflicts."[15] And as we shall see, language ideologies often refer to script and orthography. Schieffelin and Doucet write: "Language ideologies are likely places to find images of "self/other" or "us/them," as, for example, in the recent debates about the English Only movement and American language policies."[16] In this chapter, our focus will be on the ideas of Koreans from P'yŏngan Province—especially Protestants—about their dialect and *han'gŭl* orthography as a potentially rich site for a discussion of P'yŏngan regional identity and language ideology.

THE HISTORICAL ORIGINS OF P'YŎNGAN DIALECT IDENTITY

In his fascinating preceding chapter, Paek Doo-hyeon presents evidence of two types that speakers of P'yŏngan dialect in the late eighteenth and early nineteenth centuries had developed a strong dialect-based linguistic identity. The first argument was based on the fact that reprints edited and published in P'yŏngan Province of earlier han'gŭl books "corrected" linguistic forms in line with P'yŏngan dialect phonology, and the second argument was based on Paek Kyŏnghae's (1765–1842) "Adong pangŏn chŏngbyŏn sŏl" (An Opinion on the Rights and Wrongs of Our Nation's Dialects). This P'yŏngan dialect-based linguistic identity hinged on the recognition that lack of t-palatalization was a dialect marker specific to P'yŏngan, and moreover, that this lack of t-palatalization was the "correct pronunciation (chŏngŭm) and ... followed the old sounds of Sejong," and that "the Kwansŏ region is the origin of Korean language and writing."

Citing William Labov's famous 1960s study on Martha's Vineyard, Paek tries to explain the 400-year gap with respect to onset of t-palatalization between P'yŏngan dialect and other Korean dialects in terms of "sociohistorical linguistics," but I would like to extend his observations in two ways. First, I show that the strong sense of dialect pride and dialect-based regional identity in P'yŏngan manifested itself concretely in two different language ideological debates about Korean orthography in the modern period, and that the effects of P'yŏngan attitudes at that time can still be found today. Second, I demonstrate that the P'yŏngan dialect identity facts are better treated from the point of view of "language ideology," the relatively new interdisciplinary field introduced above.

The Earliest Korean Translations of the Bible

As we saw above, by the beginning of the nineteenth century some P'yŏngan speakers had developed pride in their dialect as preserving the "correct sounds" from the time of King Sejong. This pride seems to have been encouraged later in the nineteenth century by the translation of the Bible into Korean. As Na Ch'aeun notes, most of the earliest Bible translators were from the northwest, namely, Sŏ Sangyun, Yi Ŭngch'an, and Paek Hongjun.[17] Ch'oe T'aeyŏng notes that all the translators of the Ross version (1887) were from

P'yŏngan Province.[18] As a result of his analysis of the linguistic forms in the Ross translation, Ch'oe concludes that the obvious efforts on the part of the translators to compensate for or "hypercorrect" northwestern dialect forms to more central forms were by and large unsuccessful, and that "the *Yesu syŏnggyo chyŏnsyŏ* (New Testament) is a P'yŏngan Province dialect version."[19] In their exhaustive history of the Korean Bible Society, Ryu Taeyŏng et al. record the continued demand for the Ross translation that persisted in the 1890s in the Korean Protestant and missionary communities in the Korean-Manchuria border region and in northern Korea.[20] Still, with the advent of the Board of Official Translators and the movement to produce an authoritative new Korean translation of the Bible, criticisms of the Ross version soon surfaced. Thus, Ryu et al. record that on May 6, 1893, Protestant missionary and official Bible translator James Scarth Gale wrote to Kenmure, the agent for the British and Foreign Bible Society (BFBS), concerning some of the shortcomings of the Ross translation; e.g., use of *kwa* after vowels instead of *wa* in phrases like *ahăykwa* (with the child), etc. The next day, George Heber Jones (1867–1919), another missionary and member of the Board of Official Translators, sent a letter criticizing the following three types of "provincialism" in the Ross translation to Kenmure, who preferred the Ross version: (1) cases where the P'yŏngan dialect semantics differ from those in other regions, e.g., *kăygul* means *tonggul* in other regions; (2) too many items that, while understandable, are dialect and/or vulgar, especially in the verbal morphology; and (3) too many words that are impossible to understand, e.g., *chyŏngmil*. Jones also complained about the "disorderly orthography."[21]

Ryu et al. also include discussion of the seven Korean translators working on the revised translations of the scriptures. Most were well educated in literary Chinese (*hanmun*), and most were from Seoul or the central region. As Ryu et al. point out, this was a significant contrast with the Koreans who had worked with Ross on the *Yesu syŏnggyo chyŏnsyŏ*, who also knew *hanmun*, but were ostensibly merchants, probably upper-middle class, and were all from the northwest. Ryu et al. remark: "In choosing as the language of the *Sinyak chyŏnsyŏ* (New Testament) that of the middle and upper classes of Seoul, the *han'gŭl* bible would later contribute greatly to the unification of *han'gŭl* and the propagation of the standard language."[22] But as we shall see below, the eventual triumph of Seoul speech did not come without controversy or challenge.

The Linguistic Details of P'yŏngan Dialect

But what, then, were the precise characteristic features of P'yŏngan dialect? The linguistic details of P'yŏngan dialectology are not the subject of this paper, and can be found elsewhere.[23] Nonetheless, to facilitate the discussions that follow below, we should review and outline some of the basic features of P'yŏngan or northwestern dialects. The earliest and most succinct statement of these features can be found in the 1824 Ŏnmunji 諺文志 (A Study of the Ŏnmun) by Yu Hŭi (1773–1837): "Only people from Kwansŏ say 텬 t'yŏn (天, heaven) differently from 쳔 ch'yŏn (千, thousand), and say 디 ti (地, earth) differently from 지 chi (至, up to). . . . From this, we can see that the confusion between 디 ti and 지 chi is recent."[24] Thus, Yu Hŭi makes it clear that by the time he was writing in 1824, the palatalization and affrication of Middle Korean sequences 디 [ti]—댜 [tya], 뎌 [tyŏ], 됴 [tyo], 듀 [tyu]—to 지 [chi]—쟈 [chya], 져 [chyŏ], 죠 [chyo], 쥬 [chyu]—had taken place everywhere else in the Korean peninsula.[25]

Related to this development (or lack thereof, in the case of P'yŏngan Province), was the historical development of ㅈ [ch] (pronounced as [ts] in P'yŏngan, but palatalized to [č] elsewhere), 니 [ni]—냐 [nya], 녀 [nyŏ], 뇨 [nyo], 뉴 [nyu]—, 시 [si]—샤 [sya], 셔 [syŏ], 쇼 [syo], 슈 [syu]—, and Sino-Korean 리 [ri]—랴 [rya], 려 [ryŏ], 료 [ryo], 류 [ryu], etc.—all preserved in P'yŏngan dialects with the initial ㄹ [r] changed to ㄴ [n]. Whereas P'yŏngan dialects maintained, in one form or another—not necessarily intact—most of the distinctions found in fifteenth-century Korean texts, other Korean dialects collapsed or lost many of these distinctions. Thus, Ch'oe T'aeyŏng assumes that loss of ㄴ [n] before i, y started elsewhere in Korea in the eighteenth century, while palatalization of ㄷ [t] and ㅌ [t'] started in the mid-seventeenth century in the central regions and was finished by the beginning of the eighteenth century. Neither development reached P'yŏngan Province until the twentieth century.[26] What is *less* clear, whether from Yu Hŭi's description or indeed from modern research, is the development and chronology of /y + vowel/ sequences in P'yŏngan dialects. In other words, Yu Hŭi's description implies that P'yŏngan dialect had 텬 t'yŏn (heaven), whereas all modern descriptions of this dialect record 텐 t'en. The modern shibboleth for P'yŏngan dialect is the word for "train station," pronounced *chŏnggŏjang* (정거장 停車場) in standard Korean, but pronounced in

P'yŏngan dialect as *tŏnggŏdang* (덩거당) from the earlier pronunciation of *tyŏnggŏdyang* (뎡거댱).[27]

Here in Table 6.1, then, to give a feeling for the correspondences involved, are some examples of Sino-Korean words in their modern, standard versions, and their P'yŏngan dialect renditions.[28]

Table 6.1   Contemporary Standard Korean and P'yŏngan Dialects

Standard (ROK) Korean	McCune-R	English	P'yŏngan Dialect	McCune-R
경황 (景況)	kyŏnghwang	situation	겡왕	kengwang
내년 (來年)	naenyŏn	next year	내년~내넌	naenen~naenŏn
냉면(冷麵)	naengmyŏn	cold noodles	냉멘	naengmen
영변 (寧邊)	Yŏngbyŏn	Yongbyon	넹벤	Nengben
전년 (前年)	chŏnnyŏn	previous year	젠넌	chennen
여자 (女子)	yŏja	woman	너자~네자	nŏja~neja
염려 (念慮)	yŏmnyŏ	worry	넘너~넴네	nŏmnŏ~nemne
이별 (離別)	ibyŏl	saying farewell	니빌~니벨	nibil~nibel
전주 (田主)	chŏnju	field owner	덴주	tenju
지경 (地境)	chigyŏng	boundary	디경~디겡	tigyŏng~tigeng
선녀 (仙女)	sŏnnyŏ	fairy	선너~센네	sŏnnŏ~senne

THE MISSIONARY SPELLING DEBATE OF 1902–1906 AND AFTER

The first orthography debate began in 1902, when Canadian Presbyterian missionary James Scarth Gale (1863–1937) and Yi Ch'angjik, his Korean assistant on the Bible translation committee, convinced the missionary community to approve a reformed orthography for immediate use in all Protestant publications, including, of course, the Bible. This new spelling, which followed a "one sound - one character principle," had the following features:

1. Abolish the "arae a" (rendered by "ă" in McCune-Reischauer).

2. Change the "arae a" to ŭ in the accusative particle.

3. abolish "silent y" after ㅅ[s], ㅈ[ch], ㅊ[ch'], ㄷ[t], ㅌ[t'] (e.g., 서[sŏ], 셔 [syŏ] → 서 [sŏ]; 차 [ch'a], 챠 [ch'ya], 츠 [ch'ă], 탸 [t'ya] → 차 [ch'a])

This new system was supposed to have the effect of unifying language and writing throughout the entire country, but "because of the severe backlash from church members in the northern region," it was decided at the October meeting to revert to the old spelling. This was because of pressure from the churches in the northwest region who claimed that abolishing the "arae a" would make it impossible to write the northwest dialect properly.[29] It is unfortunate that we do not have any written records from this time detailing the precise objections of P'yŏngan Protestants to the "reformed spelling," but the debate that continued on the pages of the Korean missionary press makes occasional reference to the fact that there were parts of the country where the so-called "silent y" was *not* silent, and that there was indeed opposition from the northwest. Ch'oe Hyŏnbae also remarks of this aborted reform spelling of 1902 that "... it got rid of the 'arae a,' silent ㅑ [ya], ㅕ [yŏ], ㅛ [yo], ㅠ [yu], and simplified spelling into an easy orthography. But the opposition from P'yŏngan Province was extremely severe, and they claimed that it was different from the language in their region, so there was no choice but to destroy what had already been published."[30] Ch'oe was referring to the print run of 5,000 copies of the New Testament in press at the time in Yokohama that had to be destroyed at the last minute.

Other Assertions of P'yŏngan Dialect before 1910

As I have noted elsewhere, explicit statements in print on matters concerning language cultivation are not in abundance for the period preceding 1910, and thus it is not always easy to identify sources relevant to questions of language ideology.[31] However, I have been able to locate two publications that appear to continue the tradition of asserting the authenticity and correctness of P'yŏngan dialect forms (and/or orthography reflecting these). The first is Han Sŭnggon's *Kungmun ch'ŏlcha ch'ŏpkyŏng* (Shortcut to Korean Spelling) of 1908, published in P'yŏngyang. Here are some excerpts from the preface to this work:

> Our national script is not only easy to learn, but *was created on the basis of our nation's dialects (uri nara pangŏn ŭl chotch'a: emphasis mine)*. Hence, there is

nothing that cannot be recorded in the national script, and if one only records things correctly, it is much clearer than writing in *hanmun*. But regrettably, among our compatriots there are those who look down on the national script, clearly have no intention of learning it, and write any which way they please with the result that it has become an unreliable script. This is truly unfortunate.... There are many people who, though capable of writing compositions in *hanmun*, cannot write properly in the national script; it is truly shameful when a person does not know his own nation's script clearly but claims to learn foreign scripts. For example, what use is there in a child learning not the language of his parents first, but only the language of foreigners? If they are concerned not with learning the language of their parents, but just with the learning of foreign languages, what will they do when they have something to say to their parents? In like fashion, the national script is the writing of the nation—the parental writing that our fellow Koreans must learn first. If learned well, it can be used without hindrance throughout the nation; even if one should strive to learn *hanmun*, English and Japanese, one must first learn the national script clearly. Moreover, even when learning foreign scripts, it is only the person who has learned the national script properly who understands quickest. This *Shortcut to Korean spelling* was created on the basis of the spelling in the Korean-English Dictionary of the American, Dr. Gale.[32]

The reference here to James Scarth Gale is interesting, insofar as Han clearly means Gale's 1897 work, written in the same, historical "Bible orthography" that all of the other Protestant missionary publications used. Given that the missionary spelling debate seems to have raged as late as 1906, it is tempting to read Han Sŭnggon's little spelling manual as a reaffirmation, by a P'yŏngan Christian author publishing out of P'yŏngyang, of this historical spelling that allegedly enshrined the "correct sounds" preserved in the northwestern region. In any case, Ha Tongho in 1973, in his introduction to the reproduction of this text published in *Han'gŭl*, the official journal of the Han'gŭl Society (the post-Liberation successor to the Chosŏnŏ hakhoe in South Korea),[33] concludes that, while the spelling in the book is claimed to be based on Gale's 1897 translation, there is "no question that P'yŏngyang speech was the model."[34] This supposition is supported by the fact that Han is especially careful to distinguish all the Sino-Korean historical readings tyŏ ~ chyŏ, *t'yŏn ~ ch'yŏn, su ~ syu,* etc.[35] I would like to read Han's remark that the Korean script (meaning, it would appear, the historical spelling) "was created on the basis of our nation's dialects" as an understated claim that the historical orthography was somehow pan-dialectal, subsuming—thanks to its preservation of old distinctions maintained to the present day in P'yŏngan Province—differences across different regions. Such a view would imply an approach to spelling that was more "semantographic" or "ideographic" (*p'yoŭi*) as opposed to *p'yoŭm* (phonographic), and dictate "spell historically/etymologically, but pronounce locally," with obvious parallels to Chinese writing; we will see a more explicit statement of this line of orthographic thought below.

The second pre-1910 source I have found with a P'yŏngan dialect identity connection is the article "Summary explanation of the consonant and vowel sounds of the national script,"[36] published in 1909 in *Taedo,* (The Korean Evangel), in San Francisco. No author is listed for this article, and instead we read only that it was "reprinted from the *Sinhan minbo,*" the Korean language newspaper published in San Francisco at the time. However, it seems certain that the author of this article was the famous P'yŏngan Methodist, Yang Chusam (1879–?).[37] The evidence comes from Wm. H. Baird, who cites with approval the following lines from this same article, attributed to one "Mr. Yang Choo Sam," in the San Francisco *Korea Evangel:*

> Men of truly enlightened nations declare of our Kookmoon (national script) alphabet that the fine discrimination of its principles, and its accuracy in indicating sound, are such as to constitute a cause for just pride, and to give it a place in the front rank of written languages. If, by the preparation of an unabridged dictionary, and by reducing the rules of grammar and composition to a system, the scope of the Kookmoon should be increased, then Chinese with its bare ideographs, Japanese with its imperfect alphabet, English with its inconsistencies of spelling, and others of like ilk, would be left to blush over their deficiencies.[38]

Yang's article is a rather sophisticated treatment of Korean script and orthography from the point of view of writing system typology, and appears to have escaped the notice of scholars in Korea today. On pages 12–13, Yang distinguishes three kinds of communication—gesture, speech, and writing—and three kinds of writing: phonetic (*p'yoŭm*), ideographic or semantographic (p'yoŭi), and hybrid. Using the word for "one" to exemplify each type, Yang puts Korean hăna in the first category, which is a disadvantage because the meaning does not immediately "enter the eye." Yang writes, "But because there are many people working hard at editing dictionaries now, I aver that the day is not far off when our writing, too, will represent meaning, as well (ditto for Japanese writing)." The second type is represented by the Chinese character 一, "but has the disadvantage that, because it cannot represent sound, it is difficult even for Chinese themselves to learn. The third type is represented by English "one," which represents both sound and meaning." This synopsis of writing system typology is followed by a short summary of the history of writing in Korea, ending with Sejong's creation of the Ŏnmun'guk (Vernacular Script Office) in the palace and the propagation of the kungmun[39] and its twenty-eight letters, "a useful vessel for the people."

The P'yŏngan connection in this article comes on page 15 in Yang's discussion of "silent letters" (mugŭm): "When ㅅ s and ㅊ ch are followed by ㅑ ya, ㅕ yŏ, ㅛ yo and ㅠ yu, the y of the diphthong becomes silent, and when ㄷ t and ㅌ t' combine with ㅑ ya, ㅕ yŏ, ㅛ yo, ㅠ yu, ㅣ i, ㄷ t changes to ㅊ ch and ㅌ t' to ㅊ ch'. *Because only the pronunciation of individuals from P'yŏngan Province is able to preserve the original sounds (wŏn'ŭm) one can say that the proper form (chŏnggyŏk) for pronunciation is in the northwest region* (emphasis mine)."[40] He concludes, on page 16, "Such are the general outlines of an analysis of the consonant and vowel sounds of our national script. In the determination of its principles and the convenience of their application, it is truly worth being proud of as the best writing system in the world among peoples of civilized nations."

And so, to summarize what we have examined so far, there is evidence to suggest that, prior to 1910, some P'yŏngan dialect speakers had formed a notion of their dialect as the unique custodian of the wŏn'ŭm (original sounds) and chŏngŭm (correct sounds). Moreover, some Christians from P'yŏngan had taken this one step further, and come to believe that the historical or etymological spelling in the Bible reflected this state of affairs—any attempt to reform it or to water down the elements seen to be tied to P'yŏngan dialect, were to be opposed. Finally, we see the inklings of a notion of historical (and hence P'yŏngan-related) spelling as "pan-dialectal orthography," coupled with a new typology of writing that saw Korean script as phonographic (rep-

resenting sounds), the Chinese script as semantographic (representing meaning), and English spelling as a happy medium—unique graphic representations
for each word which suggested their pronunciation because of the etymological archaisms in their written representation. The future of orthographic
thought and reform in Korea would be dominated by the question of how,
and to what extent, to "semantographize" (p'yoŭihwa) Korean spelling in the
vernacular script.

HAN'GŬL VS. CHŎNGŬM: OPPOSITION TO THE UNIFIED HAN'GŬL ORTHOGRAPHY OF 1933

The second spelling debate concerned the Han'gŭl mach'umpŏp t'ongir-an
(Unified Han'gŭl Orthography) which was announced on October 29, 1933,
by the Chosŏnŏ hakhoe. Founded in January of 1931, the Chosŏnŏ hakhoe
was the continuation under a new name of the former Chosŏnŏ yŏn'guhoe
(Korean Language Research Society), formed on December 3, 1921 by ten
former students of Korean linguist and language reformer Chu Sigyŏng.[41] The
story of the Chosŏnŏ hakhoe and the struggle of its members and researchers
to establish a modern orthography and to define and codify a standard Korean
language under Japanese colonial domination are well-known. Led by scholars like Ch'oe Hyŏnbae, Yi Yunjae, Yi Kŭngno (Kŭk-ro), Yi Hŭisŭng, Sin
Myŏnggyun, and many others, the Chosŏnŏ hakhoe also promulgated the
Sajŏnghan chosŏnŏ p'yojunmal moŭm (Revised Compendium of Standard Korean)
on October 28, 1936, and was hard at work on a comprehensive dictionary of
the language until its leading members were imprisoned by the Japanese
colonial authorities in October of 1942. What is less known or remembered
is the vociferous opposition to the Unified Spelling put forth by a scholar
name Pak Sŭngbin (1880–1943) and his associates.[42]

Pak Sŭngbin and the Chosŏn Ŏhak Yŏn'guhoe

As both Pak Pyŏngch'ae and Sin Ch'angsun (2003) point out, the linguistic
ideas of Pak Sŭngbin, the activities of his Chosŏn ŏhak yŏn'guhoe (Research
Society for Korean Linguistics), and the articles published in the society's
journal, Chŏngŭm (Correct Sounds), the name of which harked back to the
Hunmin chŏngŭm that promulgated the indigenous Korean script in 1446,

have remained underappreciated to this day.⁴³ If anything, they are brought up in order to scorn them as heretical, and it is difficult to find research publications after 1945 that make reference to them. Pak Sŭngbin launched the Chosŏn ŏhak yŏn'guhoe on December 12 of 1931 with the purpose of conducting research into Korean grammar, in order to rationalize the orthography. But the debate had already broken out into the open by the late 1920s, as can be seen from the work of Sin Myŏnggyun, an ardent member of the Chosŏnŏ hakhoe. According to Sin, the *Chōsen shisō tsūshin* ran a series of articles in 1929 debating the pros and cons of the spelling ideas of the Chosŏnŏ hakhoe; of some twenty prominent names surveyed, only seven were opposed.

Sin summarizes their opposition as follows: (1) Korean spelling is already simplified enough—why simplify more? (2) Why go against the times and be classicist? (3) The proposed new spelling is not popular or populist (*minjungjŏk*) enough.⁴⁴ In this article, Sin also makes it clear that one of those seven names was Pak Sŭngbin, and attacks Pak Sŭngbin's early critique of the Chosŏnŏ hakhoe titled "Muŏs-ŭl wihan kaejŏng inya?" (Reform for What?) Thus, Sin cites Pak as opposing the changing of 댜 [tya], 뎌 [tyŏ], 탸 [t'ya], 텨 [t'yŏ] in line with pronunciation to 자 [cha], 저 [chŏ], 차 [ch'a], 처 [ch'ŏ] for the following reason: "Pronouncing 天 (heaven) as 천 [ch'yŏn] (rather than as the historical 텬 [t'yŏn]) is just a mistake owing to pronunciation habits; not maintaining the historical Chinese character readings is a fundamental destruction of the Korean language, and a flouting (*musi*) of the historical principles behind the *chŏngŭm* (correct sounds)." Indeed, according to Sin, Pak Sŭngbin is overly insistent on the problem of the historical Chinese character readings, and considers it a good thing if the Chinese character readings for Chinese, Japanese, and Korean resemble each other more (as they would do, if left in their historical spellings).⁴⁵

Thus, Pak Sŭngbin's ideas on Korean grammar and spelling were at the center of the society's activities, and were diametrically opposed to those of the Chosŏnŏ hakhoe and Chu Sigyŏng's disciples. After the Chosŏnŏ hakhoe officially announced its unified orthography in 1933, the Chosŏn ŏhak yŏn'guhoe stepped up its opposition on the pages of its new journal *Chŏngŭm*, published every other month beginning on February 15, 1934, right up until April 26, 1941, totaling over thirty-seven issues. Moreover, on July 2, 1935, Pak published his own grammar of Korean, *Chosŏn ŏhak* (Korean Linguistics), in which he laid out his own views on Korean grammatical structure and orthography in opposition to those of the Chosŏnŏ hakhoe.

Because Pak Sŭngbin's grammatical views are summarized well and sympathetically in the aforementioned works by Pak Pyŏngch'ae and Sin Ch'angsun, I will not dwell on them here. The key point for our purposes is that Pak's analysis of Korean verbal morphology led him to espouse a completely different orthography from Chu Sigyŏng or the Chosŏnŏ hakhoe. In orthography, Pak Sŭngbin and his society professed to follow three principles: (1) observe rules based on academic truth, and reject fantastic, forced views; (2) respect the historical system, and reject idiosyncratic and baseless claims; and (3) value popular practicality (*minjungjŏk siryongsŏng*), adopt easy, concise analyses, and reject confusing and abstruse (*nansaphan*) treatments.[46]

Thus, Pak and his associates favored writing s-clusters (rather than geminates) for the tense, unaspirated consonants, opposed the use of ㅎ [h] as a *patch'im* or syllable-final consonant (too abstract), rejected the use of any "double-*patch'im*" that could not actually be pronounced (in other words, allowing only ㄺ [lk] ㄼ [lp] ㄻ [lm]), and rejected morphophonemic spelling, which strives to write verb bases and noun stems in one consistent and unchanging shape.[47] In effect, Pak Sŭngbin and his associates were championing the historical (especially with regards to Sino-Korean words), *phonemic* spelling found in the Bible, with new idiosyncrasies introduced into the verbal morphology, while the Chosŏnŏ hakhoe was advocating a radically new system that abandoned the historical spellings and introduced *morphophonemic* spelling.

The enmity between the Chosŏnŏ hakhoe and Pak Sŭngbin's Chosŏn ŏhak yŏn'guhoe was quite public—the *Tonga ilbo* (East Asia Daily) even hosted a series of three public debates from November 7–9, 1932 between the two societies. The Chosŏn ŏhak yŏn'guhoe was represented at these debates by Pak Sŭngbin, Chŏng Kyuch'ang, and Paek Namgyu (1891–1956).[48] Unfortunately, it is rather difficult to locate detailed information about the other leading members of the Chosŏn ŏhak yŏn'guhoe and many of the contributors to the journal *Chŏngŭm*. Other key members of the "*Chŏngŭm* faction" appear to have been Kim Chindong, Pak Sŭngdo, Song Chusŏng, Ko Chaehyu, Ko Chaesŏp, Ch'ae Chŏngmin, etc. Kwŏn Yŏnghŭi and Kwŏn Yŏngjung served as editor and publisher, respectively, of the journal.

In any case, the journal was by no means a crank publication printing nonsense by total unknowns. For example, issue no. 28 (1938) has an article by P'yŏngan poet Ansŏ Kim Ŏk (1893–?) titled "On Embracing Dialect" (and written with archaic, P'yŏngan-like forms) in which he makes reference to the "tasteless standard language" and notes, with respect to the English word "castle," that "nobody pronounces the 't.'" He likens this to the way in which, in "our Chinese character dictionary, where for 天堂 (standard *ch'ŏndang*, meaning heaven or paradise) it tells you to pronounce *t'yŏndang*, but in actual pronunciation people in Seoul say *ch'ŏndang* while in P'yŏngan Province they say *t'ŏndang*."[49] Other prominent names that could be found writing on the pages of *Chŏngŭm* were Yang Chudong (1903–1977), An Chasan (original name An Hwak, 1886–1946), Kanazawa Shōzaburō, and Yun Ch'iho (1865–1945). For example, Yun Ch'iho (1934a) has a short piece complaining about the new syllable-final *patch'im* and the use of geminates (ㄲ [kk], ㅃ [pp], etc.,) for the tense, unaspirated consonants in the new Unified Orthography.[50]

Han'gŭl vs. Chŏngŭm: The Spelling Debate Intensifies

Once the Chosŏnŏ hakhoe's Unified Orthography was announced in 1933, both linguistic societies intensified the defense of their positions and their attacks on their rivals. Pak Sŭngdo, in his article on "The Bible in the newly adjusted spelling," continued the Chosŏn ŏhak yŏn'guhoe's defense of historical spellings, including, of course, retention of the "arae a." Thus, he argues in favor of keeping this vowel, and says that just reading "arae a" as "a" and writing 邪 朝 秋 as 사 [sa] 조 [cho], 추 [ch'u]) (rather than as the historical 샤 [sya], 됴 [tyo], 츄 [ch'yu]) cannot be tolerated on the basis of respecting history. He declares, "It is nothing other than trying to force their own pronunciation onto the masses."[51]

It should be clear by now that the advocacy by Pak Sŭngbin and the Chosŏn ŏhak yŏn'guhoe on behalf of historical spellings, especially for Sino-Korean words, and its insistence on "correct sounds," jibed with the P'yŏngan dialect sensibilities examined above. Thus, it should come as no surprise that the Chosŏn ŏhak yŏn'guhoe attracted to its cause discontented P'yŏngan Christians, or more deviously perhaps, that it actually sought to win over such elements to its side. Let us examine the latter case first. The Chosŏnŏ hakhoe's "Open Letter Concerning the Plot in Opposition to the Han'gŭl Unification Movement" in 1935 is an exasperated exposé by the Chosŏnŏ hakhoe of the Chosŏn ŏhak yŏn'guhoe's clumsy attempts to win over allies to their anti-*han'gŭl* campaign on two different occasions. The first was an incident whereby members of the Chosŏn ŏhak yŏn'guhoe toured a few middle schools and conducted "experiments" involving dictation with the two rival spellings.[52] The second involved dispatching a society member on "provincial speaking tours" to none other than P'yŏngan Province. This "open letter" reveals that a certain Kim Myŏngjin was dispatched no less than three times to (1) Sŏnch'ŏn in North P'yŏngan, (2) Yŏngbyŏn in North P'yŏngan, and (3) Sukch'ŏn in South P'yŏngan. During his tour of Sŏnch'ŏn, Kim was reported to have made remarks about the alleged "Seoul bias" of the new spelling, and in Yŏngbyŏn he "urged local citizens of repute to join the opposition movement." Even worse, in Sukch'ŏn, the speaker was quoted as having claimed that the Goverment-General (Ch'ongdokpu) had promised to repeal the new spelling if the Chosŏn ŏhak yŏn'guhoe could secure enough signatures (*tojang*) in support of the opposition movement, a claim that the Chosŏnŏ hakhoe took pains to discredit.[53]

Ch'oe Hyŏnbae launched another spirited counterattack, and was more specific about the role of dialect. Ch'oe first characterizes Pak Sŭngbin's group as conservative reactionaries, then writes: "they take some person with nothing better to do as their stooge, and get him to collect signatures in opposition to *han'gŭl* in a certain unnamed province (*mo chibang*), and to bewilder people of standing in said province (*chibang insa*), whether by social tactics or unreliable fast talking." For Ch'oe, the idea of a petition campaign against the new spelling is ludicrous, and he likens this tactic to trying to approve Newton's or Einstein's ideas on physics on the basis of a popular vote. More to the point concerning dialect, Ch'oe characterizes the speaker as having said: "'The Unified Orthography is too based on Seoul speech, and flouts (*musi*) your regional speech—don't just take it sitting down!' The key region where you began your speaking tour this time seems to have been P'yŏngan Province."[54]

Ch'oe then moves on the question of standard language and the (by then) obvious fact that the standard language would be based on Seoul speech: "This will perhaps evoke a certain amount of dissatisfaction with respect to the language feelings (*ŏgam*) of individuals in P'yŏngan Province and their dialect . . . it is universal that other dialects must be sacrificed to a certain extent." Ch'oe then goes on to accuse the Chosŏn ŏhak yŏn'guhoe of willfully exploiting the apparent resemblance between their insistence on historical spellings with P'yŏngan dialect facts:

But this faction, for whom the fundamental goal is opposing our *han'gŭl* movement, noticed such, and from the very beginning has chosen as part of their twisted theory spellings like *t'yŏndi* (天地, heaven and earth), *tyŏnch'a* (電車, tram), and *kadi malla* (don't go!) and has flirted (*ch'up'a*) with people in P'yŏngan Province, the home ground (*ponbadak*) of such speech; and now they seek signatures in recompense for this flirtation.... But I am certain of this: it is patently clear that no educated individuals from P'yŏngan Province will ever agree to such foolishly manipulative words and actions.[55]

But it seems clear that those P'yŏngan elements that opposed the new Unified Orthography were not confined to discontented elements suckered in by the Chosŏn ŏhak yŏn'guhoe. Cho Hŏnyŏng, in defense of the new Unified Orthography, divides those opposing the new spelling into eight different groups, one of which includes those who "claim it is different from their own opinions and claims." He divides this group into two subtypes, one of which "is a bias owing to regional dialect, and the other of which is a difference in grammatical claims." The regional dialect in question was obviously P'yŏngan.[56]

The Chosŏnŏ hakhoe was so incensed with Kim Myŏngjin and his speaking tour in P'yŏngan Province, that Yi Sŏngnin (Sŏk-rin) published an article attacking him personally.[57] Yi Sŏngnin characterizes the *Chŏngŭm* group as opportunists and ridicules Kim's appeal to dialect pronunciation as follows: "If one has as one's goal the unification of a language, it is universally the case that one takes as standard the language of the central region for politics, culture and communications, and sacrifices to a certain extent other dialects."[58]

As the years passed and the Unified Orthography gained ever wider acceptance, the attacks on the pages took on an even shriller tone. The title of Kim Myŏngsik's 1938 article says it all: "The Han'gŭl Movement and Fascist Consciousness." But the attacks also moved beyond just orthography. For Kim, the Chosŏnŏ hakhoe is ultranationalist, classicizing, and exclusivist, and he criticizes the movement to get rid of Chinese character-based vocabulary and replace these with pure Korean neologisms as fundamentally destroying the internationalism inherent in Korean.[59] Another article in a similar vein is Kim Chunsik ("In P'yŏngyang," 1938), who characterizes the Chosŏnŏ hakhoe as a "*han'gŭl* dictatorship." For him, the new spelling is simply too difficult— "the *hanmun* pains of old have been replaced with today's *han'gŭl* pains."[60]

The New Spelling and the Korean Bible

By the time the Chosŏnŏ hakhoe officially promulgated its Han'gŭl Unified Orthography in 1933, it had garnered enthusiastic support for the new spelling in virtually every corner of Korean society. But besides Pak Sŭngbin and his associates in the Chosŏn ŏhak yŏn'guhoe, there was one other holdout, and a most significant one at that—the Korean Bible. The two key organizations here were the Korean Bible Society (and above it, its umbrella organization, the British and Foreign Bible Society) and the Presbyterian Council (Chosŏn yasogyo changnohoe ch'onghoe). Because neither of these hugely influential societies agreed to switch their publications over to the new spelling once it was announced in 1933, the Chosŏnŏ hakhoe set about pressuring them to adopt the han'gŭl spelling. On December 20, 1933, a letter signed by Chosŏnŏ hakhoe representatives Paek Nakchun, Kim Yun'gyŏng, Ch'oe Hyŏnbae, Yi Hŭisŭng, Yi Yunjae, Yi Mangyu, Chŏng Insŏp, and Kim Sŏn'gi, was sent to the Korean Bible Society. Here are some excerpts:

> In this new spelling, we have reduced the unnecessary, chaotic and corrupt practice of representing a unitary language (irŏn) in multiple forms of writing. . . . Already numerous publications, starting with the *Kidok sinbo* (New Journal of Christianity) are using this new spelling. . . . It is our wish that, ultimately, all your Society's numerous publications be published on the basis of the new spelling; but in the first instance, we hope you will publish new editions of the Bible according to the conditions below: We are not demanding that all older editions be destroyed; rather, we demand that you issue a special edition in the new spelling and sell it simultaneously with the older editions. We will take responsibility, at no cost to you, for amending and copy-editing the spelling.[61]

This letter was received by Hugh Miller of the Korean Bible Society, and in March of 1934, he shared the letter with the Bible Committee. With the assistance of Namgung Hyŏk, Kim Kwansik, Ch'ae P'ilgŭn, and Charles Allen Clark (1878–1961), Miller struck a Reformed Spelling Subcommittee, and decided to study the various proposals concerning reformed spelling and report back at the next meeting.[62]

Then, on September 5, 1934, another letter went out, this time to the Korean Presbyterian Council, and was signed by Yi Hŭisŭng on behalf of the Chosŏnŏ hakhoe. In his letter to the Korean Presbytery, Yi Hŭisŭng emphasized that the new Unified Orthography represented three years of labor and twenty-five meetings lasting more than four hundred hours, and urged the Presbytery to approve the publication of new editions of both the Bible and the hymnal using the new orthography:

The defects of the orthography used in the Bible can be summarized as follows:

1. The spelling in the Bible, as an historical, classicized spelling, is not only unsuitable for practical purposes, it also cannot be treated as a standard norm from either the phonological or grammatical perspective.

2. The spelling in the Bible is completely incompatible with that of modern people (*hyŏndaein*), and is a distorted, crank (*p'yŏn'gokhan*) spelling that cannot be found anywhere in the various books, journals and newspapers circulating in general society. Thus, it is extremely difficult for it to gain widespread usage among the general public.

3. The spelling in the Bible is significantly incompatible with that used in textbooks in all the schools now, and because there is a concern that it will confuse the pure brains of children, it has become a huge stumbling block with respect to education.

To sum up, the contributions of the Protestant Church (Yesu kyohoe) to our society in the fields of cultural work and propagating script have been immense; if now you claim that you cannot carry through something like the reform of this Bible spelling, I fear that it will be difficult for the church to avoid criticisms on the part of lay persons of insufficient understanding that the church has fallen behind the times.[63]

But the Korean Presbyterian Council's reaction was not positive, and stopped simply at accepting Namgung's report on behalf of the subcommittee on reformed spelling struck earlier. Meanwhile, on November 20, 1934, the Chosŏn kidokkyo kyoyuk yŏnmaeng (Korean Protestant Education League) decided to launch a movement to promote publication of the Bible according to the Han'gŭl Unified Orthography, and approached Hugh Miller of the Bible Society in writing with this request.[64]

At the 1935 spring meeting of the Bible Society, it was decided to postpone discussion of the new spelling problem until the next meeting, and to "defer to and take under reference the decisions of the Methodist Conference (Kamnigyo yŏnhoe) and the Presbyterian Council."[65] At the fall 1935 meeting of the Bible Society, with J. R. Temple of the BFBS present, there was a long discussion of the Chosŏnŏ hakhoe's demand, and it was decided to suggest to the London editorial subcommittee that they allow the publishing of a new version of the New Testament according to the new spelling used in Government-General textbooks. When in April of 1936 the BFBS editorial committee received the report on the results of Temple's visit to Korea, they decided: "We are interested in the new han'gŭl spelling, and give permission for publication of the New Testament in the new spelling." In October of that year, the Bible Society back in Korea then decided to use the Ch'ongdokpu spelling, in effect, saying they would adopt the Unified Han'gŭl Orthography (the two orthographies were quite similar). But, in opposition to the efforts on the part of the Bible Society and general Protestant institutions to adopt the new spelling, the Presbyterian Council and Presbyterian Church, where the majority of members were from P'yŏngan Province, held fast in their opposition to the new spelling.[66]

When it became clear that the Korean Protestant community was dragging its feet, more polemics erupted on the pages of both Han'gŭl, the journal of the Chosŏnŏ hakhoe, and Chŏngŭm, the organ of the Chosŏn ŏhak yŏn'guhoe. Thus, Hwang Kyujŏng in his 1936 essay urged reform of the Bible spelling,[67] and Yi Yunjae, in the same issue of Han'gŭl, repeated many of the arguments found in Yi Hŭisŭng's letter above (e.g., "completely incompatible with the spelling of modern people") and gave an example of what the reformed spelling would look like with an excerpt from Psalms 23 in both the old and new spellings. In the same article, Yi Yunjae acknowledges that there is still lingering opposition to the new spelling, but dismisses the opponents as non-specialists, saying, "there is indeed some opposition from a minority with different views and absolutely no connection to research on matters linguistic."[68]

Yi Sŏngju's piece is written with specific reference to the new edition of the hymnal, published in the wake of the Bible Society's minor concession to abolish just the "arae a." Recalling the public pronouncement of seventy-seven leading literary figures in support of the new spelling published on July 9, 1934, Yi Sŏngju finds that one of the most serious defects in the new hymnal is its "mixture of regional and Seoul speech. . . . In other words, sometimes they write in Seoul speech, and other times they write in regional speech (especially P'yŏngan dialect)." He alludes to the "scaremongering" of "a few individuals on the Presbytery" and notes that the Presbytery had already voted in principle to approve the Unified Orthography. That the new hymnal failed to go far enough with spelling reform was "simply either the unnecessary scaremongering of those in charge, or an exposure of their ignorance about han'gŭl."[69] Chŏn Yŏngt'aek is rather more harsh in his criticism of the Protestants. Admitting Protestantism's many contributions to the propagation of the Korean script, and especially to han'gŭl-only usage, Chŏn nevertheless laments the way that spelling has fallen into chaos, and emphasizes that the Bible spelling can no longer function as a standard. For Chŏn, whereas earlier the Protestants were "pioneers" in promoting Korean language and script, now they had not only fallen behind, but were actually becoming a hindrance.[70]

Reverend Ch'ae Chŏngmin and the P'yŏngan Dialect Factor

It was at this juncture, in 1935, that Reverend Ch'ae Chŏngmin (1872–1953),[71] a Protestant pastor from P'yŏngan Province, published an essay in the journal Han'gŭl. This particular piece does not (yet) make explicit reference to P'yŏngan dialect, but Ch'ae's concerns share a common thread with other P'yŏngan-related themes we have already seen, and he would soon publish a long stream of attacks on the new spelling that invoked P'yŏngan dialect. Here he writes:

> I have never read the Bible in either the pure hanmun version or in the mixed script version, and have already been in the habit for the past thirty-five or thirty-six years of only ever reading the Bible as it is written in pure han'gŭl. Now, it is no easy task to find quickly where such-and-such a passage is, and sometimes after you read it the meaning does not immediately appear, making it somewhat difficult to grasp the gist. This is one defect of our script. Thus, I enthusiastically commend the new spelling for its amazing syllable forms and its marvelous combinations of sounds. But nonetheless I consider points like the following to be defects:

1. the elimination of ㅑ *ya*, ㅕ *yŏ*, ㅛ *yo*, ㅠ *yu* in the rows 사 *sa*, 자 *cha*, 차 *ch'a*, 다 *ta*, 타 *t'a*

2. the mixed usage of ㅑ *ya*, ㅕ *yŏ*, ㅛ *yo*, ㅠ *yu* and ㅣ *i* in the rows 나 *na*, 라 *ra*, 아 *a*, and

3. the abolition of 디 *ti*, 긔 *kŭi*, 킈 *k'ŭi*, 싀 *sŭi*.

> Our script is already poor in diacritic marks and differentiating marks (*p'yoho*), and it is not right to eliminate even more symbols as if to add insult to injury.... Moreover, it is my understanding that the ideals of the Chosŏnŏ hakhoe in distinguishing stems from endings, and original sounds (*wŏn'ŭm*) from changed sounds (變音 *pyŏnŭm*) are most lofty. And yet, what about (. . .): *yŏnjŏn* (年前), *yŏnmal* (年末) but *kŭmnyŏn* (今年), *myŏngnyŏn* (明年). This appears to me to be nothing more than making lots of changes and taking away the differentiating marks (*p'yoho*). Besides these, it is possible to distinguish 사기 *sagi* (詐欺) and 샤긔 *syagŭi* (邪氣), 툐인 *t'yoin* (超人), 쵸인 *ch'yoin* (抄人) and 초인 *ch'oin* (楚人), and 텬디 *t'yŏndi* (天地) and 쳔디 *ch'yŏndi* (賤地). Also, 저 *chŏ* (己) is reflexive, but 더 *tyŏ* (彼) is about others. If, in the Bible where it says "*tarŭn saram ŭn tyŏ rŭl punbyŏlch'i mothanda*," we were to write this as *chŏ*, who would be able to tell "self" from "other?"[72]

The overriding concern with homonymy and "keeping words apart" is also clear at the end of Ch'ae's article, where he writes: "In Greek, *pneuma* is both 'God' [actually, "spirit; breath"] and 'wind,' and as a result of this defect, much heresy arises to the present day. . . . The most rational way is to distinguish in writing words that have different meanings. But how can we differentiate all the many words with only a few differentiating symbols (*p'yoho*)? It is my fervent request that han'gŭl be made so as to surpass mixed script orthography, even if it means inventing new graphic shapes."[73]

The P'yŏngan dialect connection with respect to opposition to the Unified Orthography appears in *Chŏngŭm* at approximately the same time. Thus, Pak Sanghŭi[74] in 1935 claims P'yŏngyang as his hometown, and harks back to articles in *Chōsen shisō tsūshin*, where Koreans Yi Wanŭng,[75] Yu Ilsŏn, Im Kyu, and Chi Hŏnyŏng came out in opposition to the new spelling, as well as the Japanese Itō, president of the journal.[76] Ch'ae Chŏngmin, in his article in reaction to the news that the Presbyterian Council had actually voted in favor of revising and publishing the Bible and hymns according to the new orthography (and signed with a tagline from Kaech'ŏn in South P'yŏngan), was now much more candid with respect to P'yŏngan dialect, and much more provocative in his tone. Thus, he claimed that, among the churchgoers in P'yŏngan, "The ignorant fear it (the new orthography) like they would a fierce tiger emerging from the forest," that the new orthography is "difficult to learn," and that "even if they publish the Bible in the new spelling, nobody will buy it and the Bible Society will lose money."[77] Ch'ae argues:

> Sino-Korean readings should be rendered in their historical spellings, and the eighteen members of the Unified Orthography Committee should have their heads chopped off for ignoring P'yŏngan dialect. Why create eighteen *patch'im* and increase one hundred-fold the illiteracy pains of the uneducated when we can get along fine with just eight *patch'im*? ... In terms of numbers, church members who live north of the Taedong River account for more than half of Korean churchgoers, and many church members in the other eleven provinces are South P'yŏngan people who have scattered from their homes.[78]

This outburst from Ch'ae Chŏngmin called forth a response from Yi Sŏngnin, whose 1937 work titled "Does the Treatment of Chinese-Character Readings in the Unified Orthography Really Flout (*musi*) P'yŏngan Province Dialect?" Yi tried to assert the inevitability of Seoul speech as the basis for standard Korean, and to show that the notion that P'yŏngan dialect preserved intact the oldest, most correct readings of the Chinese characters was erroneous. He points out:

> People often claim that in P'yŏngan Province today the Chinese character readings have not changed at all and are the historical readings, and that it is not right to abandon the historical spelling.... At the time of promulgation of the *Hunmin chŏngŭm*, too, they must have adopted the readings of Hanyang (Seoul), the center of Korean civilization; and at that time, too, just as now, the readings in P'yŏngan Province and in Hanyang were likely not the same. One cannot deny the fact that, in advocating the adjustment and unification of speech and writing today, we do so on the basis of Kyŏngsŏng (Seoul) speech, just as it was done on the basis of Hanyang then.[79]

Yi Sŏngnin then lists a number of Sino-Korean compounds in their historical spellings and P'yŏngan vs. Kyŏngsŏng readings, and concludes: "I repeat: even if one were to admit that the historical readings are produced in P'yŏngan Province today, we must do this (create a standard spelling) on the basis of Kyŏngsŏng speech sounds ... neither P'yŏngan Province people nor any Koreans pronounce according to the original sounds."[80]

In a pointed message to Ch'ae Chŏngmin and other P'yŏngan Christians on the pages of the journal Han'gŭl, Yi Pongsu refers to the P'yŏngan pastor as "Old Reverend Ch'ae Chŏngmin" and claims: "Moreover, in conjunction with a certain wealthy P'yŏngan Province elder (changno), he circulated a petition in opposition to the spelling to each of the newspapers ... you are an outsider (munoehan) to linguistics." Yi Pongsu continues:

> According to what we hear, the fact that the revision of Bible spelling has come down to us today as an unresolved issue is because of the problem of how the P'yŏngan dialect is flouted in the treatment of Chinese character readings.... Is it not the case that it has remained unresolved to this day because of the opposition of its members, the majority of whom are from P'yŏngan?... Stop this "my dialect this and my dialect that," rise above it, and stop claiming that more than two-thirds of churchgoers are from P'yŏngan; have you not the faith to carry the cross in order to offer them a weapon and sustenance suitable to obtain for the people of all eight provinces God's salvation on account of spelling reform?[81]

Ch'ae Chŏngmin published a number of other contributions in Chŏngŭm between 1937 and 1940. It is precisely Ch'ae's status as a non-linguist (munoehan) that makes his articles potentially rich loci for insights into questions of language, ideology, script, and identity. Ch'ae in his piece in 1938 attacks the use of the new han'gŭl spelling in the Bible, and contains some remarkable assertions about the role of P'yŏngan residents in the history of the traditional Bible spelling:

> But the Bible spelling is based on the spelling in the Korean-English dictionary (i.e., either Underwood et al. 1890 or Gale 1897), the Korean-English dictionary relied greatly on the Korean-French dictionary, and they say that more than one hundred years ago, the Korean-French dictionary was created

by P'yŏngyang resident To Hayŏng for the French missionaries' Korean language studies after he came back after visiting France. From what I hear, the half-burned remaining volumes came into Reverend Underwood's hands, and Reverend Underwood felt the need for a Korean-English dictionary, and so, with the assistance of Ŭiju resident Sŏ Sangyun the work took on the general shape of a dictionary, and, with the editorial cooperation of sixteen scholars from north and south Korea, the dictionary in question was completed.[82]

Therefore, Ch'ae argues, the Bible spelling is both historical, popular *and* "universal" for northerners and southerners alike, whereas the new *han'gŭl* orthography is "heretical" (*idan*). "Not only does the so-called *han'gŭl* ignore the sounds of P'yŏngan Province, it is nothing if it does not also ignore the sounds of Kyŏngsŏng, the *hunmin chŏngŭm* created by King Sejong the great, the documents of the sages over the centuries, the 23 million masses and the 400,000 Protestant Christians."[83]

Ch'ae Chŏngmin, in a piece written in opposition to the new edition of the hymnal in the reformed spelling, claims that parishioners are bothered by the new complex syllable-final *patch'im*; "to add insult to injury, the double letters (i.e., ㅑ *ya*, ㅕ *yŏ*, ㅛ *yo*, ㅠ *yu*) after *sa*, *cha*, *ch'a*, *ta*, *t'a* and *ti*, *t'i*, which are still on people's tongues and where in the western province they have not lost one letter or one sound . . . these are being forcibly wiped out (*tot'ae*) . . . the nerves of north and south Koreans will be paralyzed and half of our sounds will be wiped out."[84] Ch'ae introduces examples of unacceptable homonymy introduced by the new spelling, e.g., (new spelling) 저 좋은 낙원 (*chŏ chohŭn nagwŏn*) vs. (old spelling) 뎌 됴흔 락원 (*tyŏ tyohŭn ragwŏn*)—the former is multiply ambiguous between the interpretations 渠의樂園 (his/her paradise), 自己의樂園 (one's own paradise), and 彼樂園 (that paradise over there). Another example: (old spelling) 뎌 텬사 (*tyŏ t'yŏnsa*) vs. (new spelling) 저 천 사 (*chŏ ch'ŏnsa*) for 渠天使 (his angel), 己天使 (one's own angel), and 彼天使 (that angel over there), not to mention the problem of yet other homonyms reduced to *ch'ŏnsa* in the new spelling: 賤事 (despicable affair), 淺思 (shallow thoughts), 千思 (a thousand thoughts). Says Ch'ae: "The Chinese say *t'yŏn*, the old books say *t'yŏn*, and westerners (i.e., residents of P'yŏngan) of old and today say *t'yŏn*, so shouldn't we continue to spell this way?"[85]

Back to the Question of Reform Spelling in the Bible

Now let us finish the story of the new Unified Orthography and the struggle to get it approved for use in the Korean Bible. It was not until 1937, some four years after the rest of Korea had already welcomed the new spelling[86] that the Presbyterian Council finally voted unanimously to adopt the Unified Orthography. But in 1938, something else came up to block actual publication of the scriptures in the "*han'gŭl*" spelling, namely—the inability to decide on *kyŏngŏbŏp* or honorific usage, because the Japanese Government-General had not yet created policy on this and the Bible Society did not wish to preempt it. Thus, the 1938 edition of the New Testament was actually published in the old "historical spelling." In 1938, the Presbyterian Council once again discussed the issue of publishing the Bible in the Unified Orthography, and discussed a letter sent to them from Chŏng T'aeŭng representing the Bible Society, in which he reminded the Presbytery of the disastrous consequences of the P'yŏngan-inspired opposition to reform spelling nearly forty years ago: "In 1902, the Bible Committee ... (changed the orthography) and issued 5000 copies of the New Testament, but while this method was easiest and unified things ... at the time, because of opposition from a certain region that claimed it was not in line with the dialect there, [the Bible Committee] was forced to destroy all 5,000 volumes."[87]

Yet again, in 1939, the 28th Presbyterian Council decided to publish (finally) in the new orthography, but there was still "stiff resistance on the part of a few individuals"[88] and with the advent of the Pacific War, liberation, and the division of Korea, actual publication of the Korean Bible in the Han'gŭl Unified Orthography did not come to fruition until 1952. Thus, Na Ch'aeun (1985) is fully justified when he comments that "whereas Bible translation in its early stages played a pioneering role in the development of Korean language studies (*kugŏhak*) (and especially exclusive *han'gŭl* usage), starting from the time of the revised translations, it actually reveals retrograde phenomena."[89] In another study of Bible translation, Pak Ch'anuk concludes: "the 'arae a' was replaced with ㅏ only in revised translation editions published after 1937. . . . For one thousand years of Korean linguistic history, the language of the central regions was concerned standard, but with respect to the language of the Bible, the shadow of the northwestern dialect seems thick."[90]

P'yŏngan Literary Figures in the 1920s and 1930s
and Orthographic Experimentation

Based solely on the examination above of the views and debates on matters orthographic as they developed in the two main journals dedicated to linguistics in the 1920s and 1930s, it would be tempting to assume that a matter so seemingly trivial as spelling reform wielded little influence or attracted little attention beyond the narrow confines of a few grammarians and their cohorts. However, questions of language and writing generally, and of orthographic reform, in particular, enjoyed a palpable resonance throughout the Japanese colonial period, and many of the ideas and concerns covered in the sections above were echoed in the literary sphere. More interestingly, many of the P'yŏngan-related notions also found expression during this period in the writings of some of P'yŏngan Province's leading literary figures.

Standard accounts of modern Korean literary history name Yi Kwangsu (1892–1950) and Kim Tongin (1900–1951) as the two pioneering giants of modern literary thought and fiction in Korea. Both men were natives of P'yŏngan Province; Yi Kwangsu was from Chŏngju in North P'yŏngan, and Kim Tongin was born to a wealthy family in P'yŏngyang. Both men began their literary careers at a time when Korea had no standard language or standardized orthography; indeed, Korean had never been the object of sustained cultivation efforts at all. And as writers from a dialect-speaking region struggling to fashion a new, modern Korean literary idiom, they could not help but be sensitive to matters of language, dialect, and orthography. Because I shall have occasion to comment on Yi Kwangsu further below in the next section, I will confine my remarks here to Kim Tongin.[91]

With regard to dialect in general, Kim Tongin enjoys the distinction of being one of the first modern Korean writers to use dialect to good literary effect in his short stories. The stories "Paettaragi" (The Boatman's Song) and "Kamja" (Sweet Potatoes), in particular, are famous for the way in which Kim Tongin placed P'yŏngan dialect in the mouths of his protagonists to create effective characterizations. Indeed, the title "Kamja" itself is in some ways a subtle assertion of the dialect, as it is clear from the story that it designates not plain "potatoes," the meaning of this word in central and hence, "standard" dialects, but "sweet potatoes," which is the normal designation of the word *kamja* in P'yŏngan dialects.

It is obvious from Kim Tongin's 1934 essay, a surprisingly long and detailed discussion of Korean orthography, that Kim was not entirely happy with the new spelling. Here I summarize only the key elements relevant to P'yŏngan dialect identity. Kim takes issue with a number of quite detailed points, most of which ultimately go back to differences between Seoul/central speech and P'yŏngan dialect. For example, Kim notes the confusion and inconsistency with the writing of ㅣ [i] and ㅡ [ŭ] after ㅅ [s], ㅈ [ch], and ㅊ [ch'] in words like 아츰 ach'ŭm ~ 아침 ach'im (morning), 오즉 ojŭk ~ 오직 ojik (only) and 마츰 mach'ŭm ~ 마침 mach'im (just when). He says that the only place that maintains this distinction clearly is south P'yŏngan Province. Likewise for ㅇ (vocalic onset), ㄴ [n], ㄹ [r], ㄷ [t], ㅈ [ch], ㅊ [ch'] + ㅕ [yŏ], ㅑ [ya], ㅛ [yo], ㅠ [yu], ㅣ [i], "only P'yŏngan Province pronounces according to the 'original sounds' (wŏn'ŭm). It is only natural that they should make reference to the dialect in P'yŏngan Province before making their final decisions; to propose to write, without any standard, mach'im, kasum, kacin (all types), ach'im is laughable."[92]

Kim then returns to the problem of too many exceptions to the new spelling's alleged principle of "unchanging word stems" (ŏgŭn pulbyŏn). For verbs like kilda (be long) that were treated as "r-irregular verbs" in Chosŏnŏ hakhoe grammar, Kim proposes to write the "r" in forms where, in pronunciation, it drops: thus, either 길니 kirni or 길으니 kirŭni for what is written and pronounced 기니 kini, and 길나 kirna or 길으나 kirŭna for what is written and pronounced 기나 kina. Here again, we find an overriding concern with homonymy and finding whatever way possible to reduce it. Kim laments: "There is nothing much we can do about cases like pae (which can mean "stomach," "pear," or "boat"), but in cases where we can avoid homonymy (we should)."[93]

In a discussion of the treatment of Sino-Korean readings, Kim finds "grave errors," singling out examples like the new spelling 여객 yŏgaek (旅客, traveler) for what "should be" written 려객 ryŏgaek with the underlying initial r-intact. "When it comes to re-writing /뎌 tyŏ, 됴 tyo, 듀 tyu, 뎨 tyel and /져 chyŏ, 죠 chyo, 쥬 chyu, 졔 chyel as /저 chŏ, 조 cho, 주 chu, 졔 chel and changing /ㅌ t'-/ to /ㅊ ch'-/, and /샤 sya, 셔 syŏ, 쇼 syo, 슈 syul to /사 sa, 서 sŏ, 소 so, 수 sul, this needs a bit more thought." Kim would prefer to keep all these separate in writing, as this "is the only way to keep apart Sino-Korean and pure Korean."[94]

In his concluding remarks, Kim finds that the new spelling "destroys the unity, confuses the system, ignores words stems. . . . moreover, they forget P'yŏngan dialect, which has preserved intact the most exact sounds in Korea (*Chosŏn esŏ kajang chŏnghwakhan ŭm ŭl kŭnyang chŏnhayŏ*), confusing the distinctions of 기 ki ~ 지 chi, 규 kyu ~ 쥬 chyu, 슈 syu ~ 휴 hyu, 시 si ~ 스 sŭ, 치 ch'i ~ 츠 ch'ŭ, 지 chi ~ 즈 chŭ, 오 o ~ 우 u, etc."[95] Kim Tongin's points were taken up one by one and refuted shortly thereafter by Kim Pyŏngje, but it should be clear that Reverend Ch'ae Chŏngmin's concerns were not merely the ravings of a lone lunatic.[96]

ORTHOGRAPHIC FUNDAMENTALISM: LEGACIES OF P'YŎNGAN DIALECT-BASED RESISTANCE TO ORTHOGRAPHIC REFORM

I have already mooted the term "orthographic fundamentalism" in the title to this chapter, so let me now try to define this term further with respect to the P'yŏngan affinities that I believe it encapsulates. The P'yŏngan dialect speakers' position on *han'gŭl* orthography is best summed up as follows: (1) the P'yŏngan dialect uniquely preserves consonant distinctions that go back to the time of invention of the Korean script; (2) therefore, the P'yŏngan dialect is more "correct" than other dialects of Korean; (3) the "historical" (pre-reform) *han'gŭl* spellings honored those distinctions, no matter whether P'yŏngan dialect speakers pronounced them exactly as written or not; (4) indeed, the key is not so much in how one actually pronounces spellings, but in how faithful the spellings are to early, "correct sounds," and in how successful they are at keeping apart graphemically, speech forms that otherwise are homonymous in spoken language, and in maintaining a sufficiently abundant richness of orthographic forms to accommodate the various differences and distinctions encountered across the gamut of Korean dialects, including, first and foremost P'yŏngan dialect; (5) the ideal type of orthography recognizes as many distinctions as possible, but also strives for ruthless consistency: one and the same morpheme—whether it consists of just one morpheme or subsumes multiple allomorphs—should be written the same, always; (6) reformed spellings—especially in the case of Sino-Korean—dishonor P'yŏngan dialect (and hence "correct language" and the "original sounds") and destroy distinctions useful in a reader-friendly orthography.

I would be remiss here if I did not admit that certain aspects of these ideas—the notion of writing morphemes with ruthless consistency, in particular—go back to the ideas of Chu Sigyŏng. Thus, Chu Sigyŏng, in addition to following the historical Sino-Korean spellings, supported spellings like 돕아 *toba* (help), 어둡어 *ŏdubŏ* (dark), 무겁음 *mugŏbŭm* (heaviness), 딸아 *ttar.a* (in accordance with), etc., which are in the same spirit as those mooted by Kim Tongin above.[97] The point is rather that this type of hardline morphophonemic spelling resonated with the language ideological sensibilities of P'yŏngan dialect speakers. Indeed, I would argue that hardline morphophonemic spelling—the urge to spell all morphemes the same, all the time—is one particular natural consequence (perhaps even an inevitable one) of "orthographic fundamentalism" as I have tried to define it here. Thus, it should come as no surprise that the legacies of this type of orthographic thinking can be found in no less than three different spelling systems from northern regions from the period spanning the 1910s to the present.

Orthography in the Taehanin Chyŏnggyobo

The first example comes from the orthography that was experimented with in Chita (Russian Siberia) in the 1910s in the journal *Taehanin chyŏnggyobo* (Journal of the Korean Russian Orthodox Church), the editorial leaders of which (Yi Kwangsu, in particular) were mainly from P'yŏngan Province.[98] I previously examined the experiments with *karo* (p'urŏ) *ssŭgi* (de-syllabified, horizontalized) Korean writing in issues 9, 10, and 11 (1913–1914) of this journal, and noted spellings like the following: retention of orthographic -*b*- and -*s*- in so-called "*s*-irregular" and "*p*-irregular verbs"; retention of the vowel ㅡ *ŭ* in *ŭ*-dropping verbs like *orŭa* for *olla* (go up), *ssŭŏ* for *ssŏ* (write), maintenance of *sV*, *chV* vs. *syV*, *chyV* distinctions and *ni*, *ny*-; historical Sino-Korean spellings like *chadyŏn* (dictionary), and retention of initial Sino-Korean *r*-; spelling of the question morpheme as *ka* rather than *kka*; and retention of the ㄹ [r] in "*r*-irregular verb" forms like *mandŭrn* (modifier form of *mandŭlda* (make).[99] When I first published this article, I stupidly supposed that the word "Oebae" at the top of the page beginning the experimental orthography section was a neologism for "dictionary," when in fact this is pure Korean for

"Koju" (孤舟), literally a lone boat, but a pen name for Yi Kwangsu, who was also editor-in-chief of this particular issue.[100]

1920s and 1930s in the Soviet Far East

In my study of dialect elements in Soviet Korean publications from the Russian Far East in the 1920s, I noted retention of initial *ni*, *ny*- and the *sV* vs. *syV*- distinction in some publications, the lack of *p*-lenition in *p*-irregular verbs, and the retention of *ŭ* after coronals where standard Korean orthography from the 1930s would write *i*.[101] And in another study dealing with Soviet materials published before O Ch'anghwan's normative grammar text of 1930, I noted the retention of Sino-Korean initial ㄹ [r]- and *kŭi*; retention of *ni*, *ny*-; spellings like *mor.ŭnŭn* (not know); uniform spelling of *t*-irregular verbs with ㄹ [r] as in *tarnŭnda* (runs), *sirnŭnda* (loads), etc., retention of *ch(')y*, *t(')y*, *s(y)* in some texts; lack of *p*-lenition; retention of *ŭ* after coronals; isolation of the infinitive vowel in cases like *oll.a kao* (goes up), *nonh.a mŏk-* (shares food), *sŭlp'ŭ.ŏ* (is sad); and various pseudo-etymological spellings.[102]

Similarly, in my 1991 study of O Ch'anghwan's *Koryŏ munjŏn* (A Grammar of Korean) published in 1930,[103] the Korean grammar meant to define orthographic norms for Korean writing in the Soviet Far East, I showed that O Ch'anghwan insisted that verbal bases must be written the same under all circumstances:[104]

Incorrect	Correct	English Translation
nŭr.ŏjyŏsta	nŭr.ŏjiŏsta	drooped
wasta	oasta	came
chwŏsta	chuŏsta	gave
ollyŏsta	olliŏsta	raised up
humch'yŏra	humch'iŏra	wipe it!

Moreover, O Ch'anghwan insists on writing the -*b*- of *p*-irregular verbs even before vowel endings, but says "pronounce as *u*." He waffles on *s* in *s*-irregular verbs, which are a tiny minority in any case, and writes the *t*-irregular verbs as they sound, but with orthographic −*s* rather than −*t* before consonant endings (this class of verbs is tiny, too). In a similar vein, he instructs speakers to drop the ŭ of ŭ-dropping verbs, but often writes it (e.g., k'ŭŏsta (was big)). He retains ni, ny-, but abolishes the y after s, ch, ch', t, t'; he wants initial ㄹ [r] written and pronounced as such in Sino-Korean; and he rejects any and all sai s or "intercalary s" in compounds: kŭybal for "flag" (pronounced kippal), ch'odae for "candlestick" (pronounced ch'ottae), etc. In other words, O Ch'anghwan defined for the 180,000 or so Koreans in the Soviet Far East an orthography that was, in nearly every way, diametrically opposed to the one that the Chosŏnŏ hakhoe would approve three years later, and which bore most of the features pleaded for by P'yŏngan dialect speakers in Korea itself.[105] At the time I wrote my articles on the Russian and Soviet materials, I was uncertain as to whether to attribute these various orthographic features to dialect facts (for example, the Hamgyŏng dialects spoken by the vast majority of Soviet Koreans did not have p- or s-lenition, and also had some other features that accorded well with "fundamentalist orthography") or to a certain ideological approach to spelling, but now I am persuaded that the latter was more important, and that the dialect facts simply aided and abetted.

North Korean Orthography (and Attempts at Reform)

In her survey history of North Korean orthography, Kim Wŏn'gyŏng notes that both the ROK and the DPRK have based their official orthographies on the Han'gŭl Unified Orthography of 1933, but that each country has modified it in different ways and at different times.[106] The Unified Orthography underwent three sets of revisions in March 1937, June 1940, and September 1946; all were minor revisions that were followed by the ROK until the more substantial revisions of January 1988. The DPRK, on the other hand, used the 1940 versions until September 1954, when it promulgated the Chosŏnŏ ch'ŏlchabŏp (Korean Orthography). Subsequent revisions were approved in July 1966 with the Chosŏnmal kyubŏmjip (Compendium of Korean Language Norms), and again in May 1987.

However, an aborted attempt at quite radical orthographic reform was launched in January 1948, with a document called the Chosŏnŏ sinch'ŏlchabŏp (New Korean Orthography), a spelling system that was also enshrined in the 1949 Chosŏnŏ munbŏp (Korean Grammar). This attempt at radical spelling reform was spearheaded by Kim Tubong (1890–?), an accomplished grammarian and faithful follower of the ideas of Chu Sigyŏng (his teacher) who had managed to rise to the number two political position in North Korea.[107] Discussion about and research on the "New Korean Orthography" continued until 1954, when Kim Tubong was purged and the *Chosŏnŏ ch'ŏlchabŏp* went into effect; the "New Korean Orthography" was never made official policy.

Kim Tubong's "New Korean Orthography" was an example of hard-line morphophonemic spelling—rigid one-form-one-spelling—gone mad, and the crux of his system were the "six new letters" designed to represent with one consistent grapheme cases of morphophonemic alternation like *p~w* in the p-irregular verbs, s-irregular verbs, etc. In addition, this new spelling strove to avoid homonyms and to unify meaning (*ŭimi*) and orthographic representation (*p'yogi*). Thus, in the case of Sino-Korean vocabulary, it abandoned the Han'gŭl Unified Orthography practice of observing the *tuŭm pŏpch'ik* or "head-sound rule" whereby the Sino-Korean initials *r-* and *n-* were dropped when spelling those cases where they dropped in actual pronunciation, and insisted on writing *ponŭm* or "original sounds."[108]

With the demise of the failed "New Korean Orthography" and the promulgation in 1954 of the *Chosŏnŏ ch'ŏlchabŏp* (Korean Orthography), the more extreme morphophonemic treatments were thrown out, but a number of other hard-line, "fundamentalist orthographic" innovations nonetheless became policy. Thus, as of 1954, Sino-Korean *nya, nyŏ, nyo, nyu, ni, nye; rya, ryŏ, ryo, ryu, ri, rye;* and *ra, ro, ru, rŭ, rae, roe* came to be written as such in all positions; moreover, it was stipulated that they were to be *pronounced* as such.[109] The Sino-Korean spellings *kye, rye, hye* were retained, while *p'ye* was abolished in favor of *p'e*, and the question morpheme was defined as *–lka*, etc., with just *ka* rather than *kka*.[110] The revisions of 1966 did away with the earlier *saip'yo* or "intercalary sign" (equivalent in function to the South Korean *saisios* or "intercalary *s*" and written as an apostrophe), leaving more abstract spellings like 바다가 *padaga* (seashore) (= South Korean *padaska*, pronounced *padakka*), 기발 *kibal* (flag) (= South Korean *kispal*, pronounced *kippal*), 내물 *naemul* (stream) (= South Korean *naesmul*, pronounced *naenmul*), etc.

In sum, once one adopts the notion of "orthographic fundamentalism" and/or hard-line morphophonemic spelling, one finds oneself on a slippery slope, reaching towards evermore abstract graphic representations as the phonetic ground slips away beneath one's feet. The orthographic fundamentalist faces two uncomfortable choices: (a) spell abstractly (supra-dialectally) but let people pronounce locally, or (b) spell abstractly and force people to pronounce the way they spell. Option (a) is the view that emerges from my reconstruction of the many P'yŏngan opponents of the Han'gŭl Unified Orthography, while permutations of option (b) became actual policy in both the USSR and the DPRK.

CONCLUSION: SCRIPT NATIONALISM IN KOREA

In his insightful analysis of recent, failed attempts at orthographic reform in France and Germany, Rodney Ball describes how plans to abandon initial capitalization for nouns and the "s-Zett" letter in German "were withdrawn in the face of public hostility" and attributes this to a widespread belief on the part of citizens that "orthographic changes should result from democratic legislation, not from administrative decree," insofar as such changes are perceived as "affecting something 'owned' by the whole community."[111] He muses: "In our century, wide-ranging spelling reforms need perhaps to be accompanied by other socio-cultural upheavals if they are to be successful."[112] The Han'gŭl Unified Orthography of 1933 almost certainly qualifies as a "wide-ranging spelling reform," but resulted from neither democratic legislation nor administrative decree. The apparent lack of democratic process (among other factors) certainly seems to have stirred many P'yŏngan denizens (and others) into opposition to the Unified Orthography, but one cannot help wondering if the new spelling would have been so successful so soon if Korea at the time were not experiencing the socio-cultural upheaval of Japanese colonialism.

In a fascinating study of the politics of spelling reform in Bulgaria, Rossitza Guentcheva finds that the study of orthography debates can help to "expose the politics behind the process of linguistic homogenization of the population within a nation-state ... (and) the culturally constructed nature of the organic connection between nation and language."[113] Bulgarian spelling schemes also swung between those with a more phonetic bias and others with a historicizing, etymological bias. This latter bias, replete with "unifying letters" like the jat designed to "transcend in writing the differences in speech ... sacrificed orthographic simplicity for the sake of a contrasting set of values: tradition, culture, authenticity, identity."[114] The P'yŏngan opponents of the Unified Orthography also found tradition (including appeals, both overt and covert, to the Sino-graphic heritage), authenticity, correctness, and identity in the old Bible spelling, but ultimately it was the "modern," alphabetico-graphic (and not Sino-logographic) cachet and (no doubt) anti-Japanese credentials of the new spelling that won the day for *han'gŭl* rather than *chŏngŭm* spelling.

To return to the notion of a "language ideological debate" with which we began this chapter, we must agree with Blommaert that "language is *being changed* by debates.... The tropes, associations, symbolizations used in discussing languages, their qualities or disadvantages, and the way in which they ought to be used in society, all reveal a magnificent amount of insights into available ideological sources or traditions, their (lack of) power, their intertextuality with other cases, sources or traditions and so on. This is why inconsequential or marginal debates can be very informative."[115]

Moreover, the fact that the orthographic controversies and language ideological debates outlined in this chapter are all but forgotten in Korea today serves as a poignant reminder of the way in which the language standardization process involves discursive practices that "may result—willingly or not—in normalization, i.e., a hegemonic pattern in which the ideological claims are perceived as "normal" ways of thinking and acting (thus, Pierre Bourdieu qualified standard language as *un produit normalisé*)."[116]

Ultimately, the P'yŏngan dialect-based opposition to Han'gŭl Unified Orthography confirms both the utility of major episodes of language reform for the study of Korean cultural history[117] and the centrality of writing—both scripts themselves as well as orthographic praxis—to modern Korean linguistic identity. In his study of language and identity in East Asia, Florian Coulmas remarks on the "common confusion between language and script" in this region, and notes that "script reform discussions are invariably politically charged" as a result.[118] Building on this and similar observations, I argue that "script nationalism" is one of the defining characteristics of modern Korean identity—both regional and national: the case of the P'yŏngan Protestants and their opposition to reformed orthography demonstrate yet again that linguistic nationalism and linguistic national identity in modern Korea are, more than anything else and perhaps more than *anywhere* else, a matter of writing system—including, above all, orthography.

NOTES

1. Note that the "arae a" vowel of pre-1933 orthography is rendered in the McCune-Reischauer system as "ă."

2. King, "Nationalism and Language Reform in Korea," 33.

3. Blommaert, "The Debate is Open," 1–7.

4. Johnson, "On the Origin of Linguistic Norms," 551.

5. Citing Silverstein and Urban, *Natural Histories of Discourse*, 11.

6. Johnson, "On the Origin of Linguistic Norms," 552.

7. Ibid., 554.

8. Johnson, "The Cultural Politics of the 1998 Reform of German Orthography," 120.

9. Ibid., 125.

10. Schieffelin and Doucet, "The 'Real' Haitian Creole," 311.

11. Ibid., 285; Anderson, *Imagined Communities*.

12. Ibid., 299.

13. Ibid., 306.

14. Heath, "Language Ideology," 53.

15. Gal, "Multiplicity and Contention among Language Ideologies," 323.

16. Schieffelin and Doucet, "The 'Real' Haitian Creole," 285–86.

17. Na Ch'aeun, "Kaeyŏk sŏngsŏ e issŏsŏ ŭi kugŏhakchŏgin munjechŏm," 30.

18. Ch'oe T'aeyŏng, "Ch'ogi pŏnyŏk sŏngsŏ yŏn'gu II," 271–83.

19. Ibid., 283.

20. Ryu Taeyŏng et al., *Taehan sŏngsŏ konghoesa II*, 30.

21. Ibid., 30.

22. Ibid., 47.

23. For a standard treatment, see Kim Yŏngbae, *Chŭngbo P'yŏngan pangŏn yŏn'gu*.

24. Ibid., 271–83.

25. The exception, of course, was the *yukchin* region in northernmost Hamgyŏng Province, a fact that eluded (South) Korean linguists well into the 1980s.

26. Kim Yŏngbae, *Chŭngbo P'yŏngan pangŏn yŏn'gu*, 271–83.

27. The issue is especially thorny with the sequence /y + vowel/ after ㅅ [s]; Ch'oe T'aeyŏng, based on his examination of the Ross translation of the Bible (one of the few pieces of evidence we have for P'yŏngan dialect before the twentieth century), claimed that P'yŏngan dialects maintained y after s, but this is controversial. Ch'oe T'aeyŏng, "Ch'ogi pŏnyŏk sŏngsŏ yŏn'gu II," 278.

28. Cited from Kim Yŏngbae, *Chŭngbo P'yŏngan pangŏn yŏn'gu*, 273–74.

29. Ryu Taeyŏng et al., *Taehan sŏngsŏ konghoesa II*, 59–60 and 117. For more details on this debate, see King, "Western Missionaries and the Origins of Korean Language

Modernization."

30. Ch'oe Hyŏnbae, "Chibang yuse ŭi u," 60.

31. See King, "Nationalism and Language Reform in Korea."

32. Han Sŭnggon, *Kugŏ ch'ŏlcha ch'ŏpkyŏng*, 1–2.

33. Note how the name itself indicates the extent to which this society identified itself with the new orthography.

34. Ha Tongho, "Kugŏ ch'ŏlcha ch'ŏpkyŏng, haeje," 55.

35. As for Han Sŭnggon himself, he was closely associated with the famous P'yŏngyang Sanjŏnghyŏn Church, where he was selected as an assistant in 1906 and became an elder (*changno*) in 1908; he graduated as a member of the fifth class of the P'yŏngyang Theological Seminary in 1912. See http://www.1907revival.com/news/quick-ViewArticleView.html?idxno=1340 (accessed May 3, 2009).

36. The Korean title is "Kungmun chamoŭm yakhae."

37. Yang (aka J. S. Ryang) was a major figure in the Korean Methodist Church. Born on January 25, 1879 in Hongmun-ri, Sannam-myŏn, Yonggang-gun, South P'yŏngan Province, he appears to have joined the church through his association with W. M. Baird and W. A. Noble. In January 1906, he traveled to the USA; after a few months in New York, he moved to San Francisco, where he established the San Francisco Korean Church (December 15, 1906). In March of 1907, he was officially designated an evangelist (*chŏndosa*), and in 1908 he launched the journal *Taedo*. Later, he graduated from Vanderbilt Theological Seminary in June 1913, and had already been ordained as a minister in October of 1912. Yang entered Yale Theological Seminary in September 1913, but after one year, in January 1915, he returned to Korea after an absence of fifteen years. He was arrested by North Korean forces on August 23, 1950, and was never heard from again.

38. Baird, "The Future of Unmoon," 205.

39. *Kungmun* (i.e., 國文, "national script") is a term for the indigenous Korean script that came into use after the Kabo Reforms of 1894–1895.

40. Yang goes on to complain that vowel length is not observed in writing, and that "it is regrettable that the dots originally determined by Sejong are not used," referring to the *pangchŏm* or "side-dots" used to designate pitch accent in Late Middle Korean. The question of whether or not to indicate distinctive vowel length in modern Korean orthography was another hotly debated issue, but is not relevant to the P'yŏngan dialect facts.

41. Members included Im Kyŏnghae, Ch'oe Tusŏn, Yi Kyubang, Kwŏn Tŏkkyu, Chang Chiyŏng, Sin Myŏnggyun, and others.

42. One contemporary account of the controversy surrounding the new *han'gŭl* orthography that came to my attention in the final stages of preparing this chapter is George Paik's work titled, "What is Han Keul?" published in 1935. His title suggests

that "Han Keul" was still an unknown term for Western missionaries in Korea, and Paik outlines no less than four different "schools" in the "Han Keul movement": the Chosŏnŏ hakhoe, the Chung Eum school, the Government plan, and those who support the spelling in the Korean Bible. His discussion of the latter "school" does not delve into regional affiliations.

43. Pak Pyŏngch'ae, "'Chŏngŭm' haeje"; and Sin Ch'angsun, *Kugŏ kŭndae p'yogibŏp ŭi chŏn'gae.*

44. Sin Myŏnggyun, "*Han'gŭl* chŏngni rŭl pandaehanŭn kokhaeja ege," 87.

45. Ibid., 89–91. Sin does not give the publication details of Pak's critique.

46. Pak Pyŏngch'ae, "'Chŏngŭm' haeje," 10.

47. Ibid., 11.

48. A poet, grammarian, mathematician and educator, Paek was also an Esperantist. Some sources imply that he was originally a student of Chu Sigyŏng, but if so, it is not clear why he changed sides.

49. See Kim Ŏk, "Sat'uri onghoron," 1768 and 1755.

50. Yun Ch'iho, "Sinch'ŏlchabŏp e taehaya."

51. Pak Sŭngdo, "Chŏngnidoen ch'ŏlchabŏp e ŭihan sŏnggyŏng," 556.

52. Yi Yunjae discusses and debunks these experiments in 1935 in his "P'ilgyŏng haksaeng kkaji sŏndong hanŭnya?"

53. Chosŏnŏ hakhoe, "Han'gŭl t'ongil undong e taehan pandae ŭmmo kong-gaejang."

54. Ch'oe Hyŏnbae, "Chibang yuse ŭi u," 25.

55. Ibid., 25–26.

56. Cho Hŏnyŏng, "Soi rŭl pŏrigo 'Han'gŭl t'ongir-an' ŭl chijihaja."

57. A longtime and long-lived member of the Chosŏnŏ hakhoe, Yi Sŏngnin (1914–1999) was born in Seoul, and published an article at the time advocating a new letter for the long /ŏ/ (see Yi Sŏngnin, "Tokcha ŭi sori: 'ㅡㅓ' rŭl tŏ ssŏssŭmyŏn …"). He also wrote an attack against P'yŏngan Presbyterian pastor Ch'ae Chŏngmin.

58. See Yi Sŏngnin, "Tokcha ŭi sori: Kim Myŏngjin ssi ŭi pansŏng ŭl ch'okham," 14. From Yi Sŏngnin's discussion, it is clear that Kim is a middle school teacher and a member of the Chosŏn ŏmun chŏngni kisŏnghoe (Action Committee for the Rationalization of Writing in Korean Script), yet another organization founded under Pak Sŭngbin's auspices in June 1934 (see Pak Pyŏngch'ae, "'Chŏngŭm' haeje," 2).

59. See Kim Myŏngsik, "Han'gŭl undong kwa p'asyo ŭisik." Kim Myŏngsik's identification of fascist elements in the thought of the Chosŏnŏ hakhoe and in Korean literary trends of the time is prescient, especially in light of the recent upsurge of interest in this topic in South Korean literary research. Thus, Kim complains that Korean literature "of late" is fascist-leaning—"soft literature," based on "classical thought." But his sharpest criticisms are of the purism of the Chosŏnŏ hakhoe: "not even the Nazis

try to make their language pure (just their race); replacing Sino-Korean words with pure Korean ones will turn the language into a regional dialect, since the dialects are where all the pure Korean resides."

60. Kim Chunsik, "Han'gŭl kyojŏngbu nŭn han'gŭl tokchae kigwan," 1657.

61. See "Chosŏnŏ hakhoe ŭi kongham i'gŏn."

62. See Ryu Taeyŏng et al., *Taehan sŏngsŏ konghoesa II*, 175.

63. See "Chosŏnŏ hakhoe ŭi kongham i'gŏn," 9.

64. Ryu Taeyŏng et al., *Taehan sŏngsŏ konghoesa II*, 176. See also "Kidokkyo kyoyuk yŏnmaeng kyŏrŭi."

65. Ryu Taeyŏng et al., *Taehan sŏngsŏ konghoesa II*, 177.

66. Ibid., 178.

67. Hwang Kyujŏng, "Sŏnggyŏng ŭi ch'ŏlcha kaejŏng ŭl ch'okham."

68. Yi Yunjae, "Sŏnggyŏng ch'ŏlcha rŭl kaejŏnghara," 5.

69. Yi Sŏngju, "Sinp'yŏn ch'ansongga ŭi munhwajŏk ŭiŭi," 11–13.

70. Chŏn Yŏngt'aek, "Kidokkyo wa Chosŏn muntcha," 4.

71. Ch'ae Chŏngmin appears to have been a rather prominent pastor in the P'yŏngan Protestant community. According to a website, http://koreandb.nate.com/history/people/detail?sn=12552 (accessed May 3, 2009), Ch'ae came to the Protestant faith through Yi Sŏngha and Ch'oe Irhyŏng, two of the very first Protestants to be baptized. His own proselytizing efforts in his local community led to the founding of the Sŏlmae-dong Church, and he became an assistant (*chosa*) in 1900. A leader of the revival in 1907, he later participated in the March First movement, and was a central figure in (and jailed twice for) the movement opposing participation in Shinto worship (see also http://sanjunghyun.co.kr/main/sub.html?Menu_Code=1, which connects him in this regard to the same Sanjŏnghyŏn Church in which Han Sŭnggon was active, and http:wwwi-seomoon.or.kr/his_1939_ser/his4-2-3.htm; both sites accessed May 3, 2009).

72. Ch'ae Chŏngmin, "Tokcha ŭi sori: han'gŭl sinch'ŏlcha ŭi yangchŏm kwa kyŏlchŏm," 17.

73. Ibid., 17.

74. Pak Sanghŭi renders his name in Chinese characters as 伊藤軒堂, but in other sources it appears as 伊藤韓堂, while the 1929 issues of *Chōsen shisō tsūshin* list 伊藤卯三郎 as the publisher.

75. Yi Wanŭng was a grammarian who worked closely with Japanese researchers and published grammar texts in both Japanese and Korean. See Yi Wanŭng, *Chōsengo hatsuon oyobi bunpō*; and idem, *Chungdŭng kyogwa Chosŏnŏ munjŏn*.

76. Pak Sanghŭi, "Han'gŭlsik ch'ŏlchabŏp pandae undong pogosŏ."

77. These notions were cited and attacked in Kang Taehŭi, "Ch'ae Chŏngmin ssi ŭi kŭl ŭl ilkko," 7.

78. Ch'ae Chŏngmin, "Uri ch'onghoe ka sinch'ŏlcha ch'aeyongham ŭl tŭtko," *Chŏngŭm*, 21 (1937), but cited in Ryu et al. as 'Feb. 1936 issue of *Chŏngŭm*', and quoted in Sŏnggyŏng ch'ŏlcha kaejŏng ŭi kyŏrŭi (1937).

79. Yi Sŏngnin, "T'ongir-an ŭi hanchaŭm ch'ŏri nŭn kwayŏn P'yŏngan-do pangŏn ŭl musihan kŏsin'ga?" 10.

80. Ibid.

81. Yi Pongsu, "Ch'ae Chŏngmin ssi ege irŏnham," 36.

82. Ch'ae Chŏngmin, "Chosŏnŏ t'ongil kwa sŏnggyŏng ch'ŏlcha ŭi han'gŭlsik kaejŏng pulga-ron," 1607.

83. Ibid., 1607–1608.

84. Ch'ae Chŏngmin, "Ch'ansongga ch'ulp'an ŭl pandaeham,"1892.

85. Ibid., 1892.

86. Ko Chaesŏp (1937), in another provocative piece published in *Chŏngŭm* and titled "I refute the decision to change for the worse the Bible spelling, a reform that ignores the principles of the *Hunmin chŏngŭm*," goes so far as to suggest that this decision, which coincided with the retirement of Min Hyu (Hugh Miller) of the Korean Bible Society at age sixty-five and his departure from Korea, actually precipitated his resignation, and implies that Miller left in disgust at the advent of the new spelling.

87. See Ryu Taeyŏng et al., *Taehan sŏngsŏ konghoesa II*, 179 and footnote 85 on the same page, citing *Chosŏn yesugyo changnohoe ch'ongyo che 27hoe hoerok*, 1938, 38.

88. Ryu Taeyŏng et al., *Taehan sŏngsŏ konghoesa II*, 179.

89. Na Ch'aeun, "Kaeyŏk sŏngsŏ e issŏsŏ ŭi kugŏhakchŏgin munjechŏm," 31.

90. Pak Ch'anuk, "Han'gugŏ sinmyŏng ko: chŏngsŏbŏp esŏ pon hanŭnim," 104–105.

91. Here we confine our remarks to just Kim Tongin, but a full discussion would include the poets Kim Sowŏl (1902–1934) and Paek Sŏk (1912–1995), the latter of whom continued his career in North Korea after liberation in 1945.

92. Kim Tongin, "Han'gŭl ŭi chiji wa sujŏng: Chosŏnŏ hakhoe ŭi Han'gŭl mach'umbŏp t'ongir-an e taehayŏ," 489.

93. Ibid., 492.

94. Ibid., 498–99.

95. Ibid., 501–502.

96. For Kim Pyŏngje's work, see "Han'gŭl t'ongir-an pip'an e taehan yakkan ŭi kŏmt'o wa tappyŏn."

97. Chu Sigyŏng, "Han nara mal."

98. Yi Kang (1878–?), the editor-in-chief, was born in Yonggang, P'yŏngan Province, and Yi Kap was born in P'yŏngwŏn, P'yŏngan Province.

99. King, "Experimentation with Han'gŭl in Russia and the USSR." Other features were: use of geminates rather than sC to indicate the tense, unaspirated consonants; no

"arae a"; one dot to indicate vowel length, etc.

100. These publications from 1913–1914 serve as antecedents for the spelling practices of the P'yŏngan poets Kim Sowŏl and Paek Sŏk in the 1920s and 1930s, a discussion that I must defer to another occasion.

101. King, "Dialect Elements in Soviet Korean Publications from the 1920s."

102. King, "Experimentation with Han'gŭl in Russia and the USSR."

103. Imagine my shock and disappointment when I discovered one day in Kyobo Bookstore in downtown Seoul a reproduction of my own personal copy of this grammar in Ko Yŏnggŭn ed., *Pukhan mit chaeoe kyomin ŭi ch'ŏlchabŏp chipsŏng*, 411–518, with the following note to the reader in the editor's introduction on page 7: "The (unacknowledged and uninformed!) owner of the original has added marginalia in many places, but it seems these will cause no hindrance in reading, so we have decided to reproduce it as is."

104. O Ch'anghwan, *Koryŏ munjŏn*, 159.

105. See King, "A Soviet Korean Grammar from 1930."

106. Kim Wŏn'gyŏng, "Pukhan ŭi ch'ŏlchabŏpsa."

107. Kim Tubong was from Kyŏngsang Province.

108. For the longest time, the details of the North Korean *Sinch'ŏlchabŏp* were known only from the blistering critique of it by Russian Koreanist A. A. Kholodovich in 1958, "O proekte reformy Koreiskoi orfografii 1949 g." and from the equally critical articles attacking it in the wake of Kim Tubong's fall from political power. Kholodovich notes the theoretical similarities between the North Koreans' "six new letters" and Trubetskoi's concept of "archiphoneme," and Manaster-Ramer in an illuminating analysis concludes that the North Korean linguists behind this reform were either brilliant generative phonologists ahead of their time, or incompetent phonemic analysts (Manaster-Ramer, "The Korean Precursors of Generative Phonology"). In this latter regard he shows that the analysis of Korean phonology in Seung-bog Cho in his 1967 book, *A Phonological Study of Korean, With an Historical Analysis*, is remarkably similar to (and in fact cites) the North Korean sources, but actually goes beyond the linguistic pale in claiming to identify phonetic correlations to the completely abstract units represented by the "six new letters." Ko Yŏnggŭn includes a reproduction of the *Sinch'ŏlchabŏp* (without identifying its provenance), but nobody save Kholodovich outside of North Korea seems to have laid eyes on the 1949 *Chosŏnŏ munbŏp* that one presumes to contain the detailed linguistic argumentation that would resolve the many unsolved mysteries about this abortive orthographic reform. See Ko Yŏnggŭn, ed., *Pukhan mit chaeoe kyomin ŭi ch'ŏlchabŏp chipsŏng*, 57–115.

109. Thus, it is incorrect to claim, as so many English language sources blithely do, that the North Korean spelling and pronunciation of, for example, *nyŏja* for "woman" (as opposed to south Korean *yŏja*) is "because of P'yŏngan dialect"—these are spelling

pronunciations based on orthographic choices dictated by a specific ideological orientation in graphic representation of speech.

110. Kim Wŏn'gyŏng, "Pukhan ŭi ch'ŏlchabŏpsa," 101–108.

111. Ball, "Spelling Reform in France and Germany," 277 and 279.

112. Ibid., 280.

113. Guentcheva, "Symbolic Geography of Language," 355.

114. Ibid., 358 and 360.

115. Blommaert, "The Debate is Closed," 435.

116. Blommaert, "The Debate is Open," 10–11. For Bourdieu's work, see Bourdieu, "Le Fétichisme de la Langue," 28.

117. This is the main point of Sasse, "Sprachreform und Koreanische Kulturgeschichte."

118. Coulmas, "The Far East," 407.

7

From Periphery to a Transnational Frontier

Popular Movements in the Northwestern Provinces, 1896–1904

YUMI MOON

An Chunggŭn (1879–1910), a patriotic Korean youth, assassinated Itō Hirobumi (1841–1909) in 1909 and became an icon of Korean nationalism. He wrote in his memoir that he had killed Itō for "the peace of East Asia" (*tong-yang p'yŏnghwa*) because Itō had betrayed his promise to protect Korean independence after Japan waged war against Russia. Describing his dramatic transition from a "pro-Japanese" Pan-Asianist to a nationalist, An recalled his jubilation upon seeing Japan prevail in the Russo-Japanese War (1904–1905) and his bitter sense of deception when Itō proclaimed protectorate rule over Korea.[1] An's life is emblematic of other Korean reformers who turned to Western knowledge, embraced Pan-Asianist ideologies, yet ended their political careers as militant nationalists.[2] His political shift was an outcome of the ideological fluidity that surrounded Korean reformers of the old regime during the post-Kabo period, the nine years between the fall of the Kabo cabinet and the outbreak of Russo-Japanese War (1896–1904).

Such political fluidity was found, not only among the Korean elites but also in the popular movements of the time. Reckless concession policies and Western ascendancy after the Triple Intervention of Russia, France, and Germany in 1895 caused social unrest and more tightly integrated the Korean peninsula with the rest of the world. In the northwestern provinces of Korea—P'yŏngan and Hwanghae provinces—social restlessness was more dramatic, as abundant resources including gold and timber became, especially in P'yŏngan, the target of imperialist concessions. Besides, the northern location of the provinces and increased trade due to the thriving Chinese migration along the border areas exposed people to change and disorder that originated from China.[3] The Chinese withdrawal from domestic politics in

Korea exacerbated rather than reduced the interactions between Koreans and Chinese. Overall, people's encounters with foreigners increased markedly in these provinces and "unprecedented" popular orientations were observed there during this period.

In order to understand popular sentiments during this period, it is crucial to trace the reshuffling of the defeated peasants and leaders of the Tonghak (Eastern Learning) Rebellion of 1894. Tonghak remnants irritated government officials and continued to surface on and off. They interwove with various types of popular movements. The Tonghak sought a new geographical and political arrangement after their defeat and found a safe haven in the north, which was mountainous, distant from the capital, and open to new ideas. Meanwhile, the circulation of Pan-Asianist discourses across the Korean peninsula paralleled this resettlement of the Tonghak in the north. The Japanese propagated their own version of Pan-Asianism in Korea—a discourse which asserted a Western threat, Chinese backwardness, and Japan's new leadership to "save" Asia. This Pan-Asianist discourse critically impacted the Tonghak exploring a new direction of their movement.

The popular movements in the northwestern provinces during the post–Kabo period were fluid and divergent. These movements were not necessarily nationalistic or due purely to local discontent with central domination. Rather, they were "transnational" to a considerable degree because they were mainly responses and reactions to forces that had been integrating the region with areas beyond the Korean monarchy. The participants in these movements demonstrated complex connections to the ideas, interests, and power relations that foreigners and border-crossing movements brought to the region. Although similar phenomena were found outside the provinces, the larger scope and greater intensity of popular responses were peculiar to the northwestern provinces.

The purpose of this chapter is, above all, to delineate the orientations of these popular movements to the increase in encounters with foreigners. It discusses (1) the political reorientation and resettlement of Tonghak to the northwestern provinces, (2) the Catholic rioters in Hwanghae Province, and (3) the miners' protests in P'yŏngan Province. In conjunction with this, I introduce the changing East Asian regional order observed in the northwestern provinces and argue that the participants in the popular movements during this period distanced themselves from the central monarchy. For example, the Catholic rioters accommodated the enhanced power of Western missionaries to counter the central government, whereas the miners resisted the immediate economic encroachment of the British endorsed by the monarch. Meanwhile, more militant nationalist ideas did not establish a hegemonic or dominant position in the region, at least prior to the Russo-Japanese War.

As noted in the introduction to this volume, the study of region and regional diversity has been obscured due to nation- or class-centered narratives in Korean historiography. Simultaneously, the transnational or global dimension of regional history remains unexplored. How did regionality play out when a region was rapidly integrated with areas broader than the nation itself?[4] Perhaps the peripheral status of the northwestern region in the Chosŏn Dynasty gave the common people and elites of this region more room to pursue power and ideas that could decenter the Korean court, which had long privileged the aristocracy of the central and southern provinces. Although this chapter does not definitively answer the question of how regionality affected the generation of these connections, it does show how the northwest region's integration with outside forces became central to the life of its inhabitants, thus transforming the region from a peripheral part of the Chosŏn kingdom into the dynasty's social and political frontier.[5]

NEW TONGHAK IN A NEW PLACE

One of the most significant political changes in the post-Kabo period was the geographical and political relocation of the Tonghak to the northwestern provinces. The Tonghak leaders fled government persecution in the south during and after the Tonghak rebellions of 1894–95 and moved their base to the northern region of Korea. Beginning around 1900, the Tonghak leaders of the northern section (pukchŏp), who directed the movement—which had religious aspects, though its primary aims were national and economic stability—absorbed reformist ideas that transformed the beliefs of their followers. In 1904, after the outbreak of the Russo-Japanese War, the Tonghak reconvened their uprisings under a new political direction and named their organization Chinbohoe (Progressive Society), which soon merged with the Ilchinhoe (Advance in Unity Society), a pro-Japanese organization during the Japanese protectorate in Korea (1905–1910). Chinbohoe held a conspicuously strong presence in the northwestern provinces. According to the studies of Hayashi Yūsuke and Kim Chongjun, 59 percent of the Chinbohoe members (approximately 70,000) in November 1904, lived in the northern and southern P'yŏngan provinces and more than 80 percent of the districts in Hwanghae and P'yŏngan provinces established Chinbohoe branches. In the rest of Korea, 54.1 percent of the districts had Chinbohoe branches.[6] This strength of the "new" Tonghak represented the rapid expansion of underground Tonghak organizations and their political transformation in the northwestern provinces.

The government knew of the existence of secret Tonghak organizations in the northwestern region but could not entirely root them out.[7] Its investigation immediately after the outbreak of the Russo-Japanese War revealed how the Tonghak organizations had expanded into P'yŏngan Province. According to the report made by Ŭiju Magistrate Ku Wanhŭi in June 4, 1904, it had been many years since the Tonghak had set up several sections (chŏp) and subsections (p'o) in the province. Their leaders, called "Great Masters" (Taesŏnsaeng), came mainly from the northern section of the Tonghak religion. Ku wrote that the religious doctrines of the Tonghak in P'yŏngan Province were identical to those of the Tonghak rebels in 1894, yet their organizational origin differed from that of the southern section (namjŏp) of the Tonghak from which more rebellious leaders such as Chŏn Pongjun (1855–1895) originated.

Ku arrested the Tonghak section leaders (chŏpchu) in the region and investigated them. According to his report, the Tonghak organizations began in Samsu and Kapsan, in the far west of Hamgyŏng Province, adjacent to North P'yŏngan Province, followed by more branches (munp'a) in Sŏnch'ŏn, Kaech'ŏn, Anju, Changjin, Kanggye, and Chunghwa in P'yŏngan Province. They also thrived in Ŭiju and neighboring districts, such as Ch'ŏlsan and Yongch'ŏn. Ku estimated that the members in a large section and subsection of the Tonghak religion amounted to several tens of thousands. Even in the small sections, the members per section numbered no fewer than three or four thousand. Interestingly, Ku blamed local clerks (kwanye) for the government's failure to restrain the growth of the Tonghak. He suspected that the clerks had connections with the Tonghak and secretly supported them. Ku came to this conclusion because the reports that the clerks circulated among the districts stated that there were no Tonghak in the province. Comparing the Tonghak forces to "fires on a prairie," Ku warned that if the Tonghak captured the telegraph wires, this would have catastrophic results for the Korean state.[8]

This northern expansion was not a mere extension of the religious aspects of the Tonghak movement, however. Son Pyŏnghŭi, the supreme patriarch of the Tonghak, initiated this expansion and imposed new ideas on the Tonghak believers,[9] placing reformism and pro-Japanese diplomacy at the forefront. The *History of Our Religion* (*Pongyo yŏksa*), an official history of the movement, describes how Son became interested in the discourse on "civilization and enlightenment" in the late 1890s while fleeing the government's manhunt under the escort of Yi Yonggu, one of the crucial leaders of the Tonghak Rebellion and later chair of the Ilchinhoe.[10] According to the *History*, Son considered it necessary to learn about the genuine characteristics of civilization and thus decided to go abroad in the spring of 1901.

> "Hoping to display our Way brightly in this world, we can accomplish our aims only after we understand civilization sufficiently and become the champions of civilization. I think that after I travel and see foreign countries, which I expect to accomplish in ten years, and understand the characteristics of civilization and the circumstances of the world, there won't be any obstacles to spreading our Way widely." Our holy teacher [Son Pyŏnghŭi] said this and asked what others thought. They all agreed that his words were right.[11]

This anecdote reveals that Son Pyŏnghŭi and other Tonghak leaders attempted to reconcile the purpose of their movement with the progress of "civilization." Son recast the Tonghak "Way" as the "champion of civilization" rather than its enemy. Imbued with ideas of progress and a pro-Japanese orientation, Son believed that the Tonghak should acquire new foreign knowledge and sounded out the feelings of other Tonghak leaders on this issue. Finding that they agreed with him, Son selected students from among the children of Tonghak followers and brought them from Wŏnsan in Hamgyŏng Province to Nara, Japan, where he had the students learn the Japanese language. In March 1901 Son himself, his brother Son Pyŏnghŭm, and Yi Yonggu traveled from Wŏnsan to Pusan, the port on the southern coast closest to Japan. Son and his followers then went to Nagasaki and up to Ōsaka. Son returned to Wŏnsan later in 1901 and embarked again for Japan in early 1902 with twenty-four more students. He moved to Kyōto in June 1902 and admitted the students to middle schools established by the Japanese government.[12] He then stayed for four years in Japan before returning to Korea in January 1906.[13]

The positive attitudes of the "new" Tonghak toward Western knowledge and the Japanese differed from those of the "old" ones who sought a more "indigenous" solution to the problems with tax administration and the social status system of the Chosŏn Dynasty. More investigation is needed to find who, among the participants of the Tonghak Rebellion, admitted this pro-reformist and pro-Japanese position. It was hardly a linear trajectory from the rebellious Tonghak to the patriotic righteous armies and their participation in nationalist resistance movements during the colonial period, as nationalist historians have assumed. Kim Ku, one of the most respected nationalist leaders in Korea, fits this trajectory, but his case was isolated from the general direction of Tonghak leadership who, during the post-Kabo period, accommodated rather than confronted Japan's expansionism in East Asia. According to Kim Ku's autobiography, strong Confucian influence drove him from a commoner Tonghak to a militant and anti-Japanese nationalist.

Kim Ku, a famous Tonghak leader (chŏpchu) of Hwanghae and P'yŏngan provinces, commanded several thousand Tonghak believers. He wrote that the egalitarian culture among the Tonghak believers that paid respect to each other regardless of their social status or wealth strongly attracted him. In 1893, as one of the fifteen Tonghak leaders of Hwanghae Province, Kim Ku met with the Tonghak patriarch, Ch'oe Haewŏl, in Poŭn, Ch'ungch'ŏng Province. Kim recalled this as the national meeting of Tonghak leaders that prepared them for the 1894 rebellion. According to his autobiography, Kim participated in the rebellion and, due to his youth and fame, commanded the attack of the Haeju mountain wall.[14]

Interestingly, during the rebellion, An T'aehun, the father of An Chunggŭn, who organized the voluntary troops to subdue the Tonghak in his home district of Sinch'ŏn, approached Kim. An T'aehun successfully defeated the Tonghak in the Ch'ŏnggye subdistrict in Sinch'ŏn, located only twenty miles from where Kim's troops had set up camp. Subsequently, An sent his secret envoy to Kim and warned him that An would be unable to keep Kim alive and safe if the Tonghak attacked the Ch'ŏnggye subdistrict. Kim Ku wrote that An knew of Kim's talent and courage and did not want to kill a youthful and promising leader, who had originated from the same province as An. Kim appreciated An's approach and made an agreement with him that they would not attack each other. After government forces defeated the rebellion, Kim fled to An's residence to escape from government persecution. [15]

The influence of a Confucian scholar named Ko Nŭngsŏn, whom Kim met in the Ch'ŏnggye subdistrict reinforced and mediated Kim's subsequent anti-Japanese position. Kim wrote that Ko Nŭngsŏn was a highly regarded scholar in Hwanghae Province and belonged to the same school as Yu Insŏk, the prominent leader who organized the righteous army after the Japanese assassination of Queen Min. Because of his prominence, Ko was invited to the Ch'ŏnggye subdistrict to educate An's family and the young people that An gathered there. Ko had close relations with Kim Ku and taught Kim Confucian classics and other political matters. Kim's earlier Confucian education for the civil service examinations might have facilitated their connectedness.[16]

Ko asked Kim to visit his place daily instead of going to An's *sarang* (the room for receiving male guests), saying it would help Kim's spiritual growth.[17] Ko at the time developed tensions with An because An proclaimed to believe in Catholicism. Ko's conflict with An escalated when An did not oppose the decree of the pro-Japanese cabinet that ordered male adults to cut off their topknots. Kim Ku was more sympathetic with Ko's position because he disliked An's persecution of the Tonhgak, his inclination to Westerners, and his approval of the pro-Japanese cabinet. Kim left An's residence after consultation with Ko and killed a Japanese soldier as an act of revenge for Queen Min and the Japanese invasion of Korea.[18]

This rather long introduction of Kim's career is to highlight that two competing ideological cores existed among Korean elites during the time, and a more open attitude toward Westerners and the Japanese expanded in the northwestern provinces during the post-Kabo period. To replace the prominent Confucian scholar Ko, An invited the French missionary Nicolas J. M. Wilhelm[19] to this district. This decision might not have been an isolated case because the advancement of modern education in the northwestern provinces was later nationally acknowledged. For instance, the elites from the provinces themselves claimed the northern region's advancement in terms of its educational progress when they organized the regional academy for "enlightenment" in 1906. They argued that the region had been much more forward-thinking than the other regions of the country by absorbing new ideas, sending the talented abroad for study, and educating youth with the knowledge needed for "progress and enlightenment." Chang Chiyŏn, the prominent reformist intellectual of the time, endorsed such regional self-identification and compared this promising situation with the "bigoted" Kyŏngsang Province in which Chang was born.[20] This acknowledged "advancement" in the northwestern provinces reverberated in the popular movements. The aforementioned emergence of the "new" Tonghak after the outbreak of the Russo-Japanese War demonstrated this transition. Prior to this disclosure, new political orientations toward foreigners were found in the popular movements of the provinces.

COLLABORATIVE RIOTERS: THE CATHOLIC PROTESTS IN HWANGHAE PROVINCE

Catholic churches saw popular growth after the Triple Intervention. The increase in the number of Catholics in Hwanghae was the greatest in the country. Various factors may have facilitated this. To a great degree the connection between An Chunggŭn's family and the French priest Nicolas J. M. Wilhelm was responsible for the spread of Catholicism in Hwanghae. The number of Catholics in Hwanghae rose from 555 in 1896 to approximately 7,000 in 1902, at which time the total Catholic population in Korea was 52,539.[21] What was unique was that this growth accompanied Catholic protests over secular issues, such as taxation and local administration. The Korean government attributed this secular involvement to the Tonghak remnants, whom the government suspected had converted to Christianity after the defeat of the 1894 rebellion.[22] Many government reports indicated that former Tonghak disguised themselves as Christians and disobeyed government directives for tax collection. The Hwanghae provincial government called these disguised Tonghak "church exploiters" (kyohoe chŏkt'akcha) and considered them "phony Christians."[23]

On December 7, 1896, Hwanghae Provincial Governor Min Yŏngch'ŏl (1864–?) reported to Foreign Minister Yi Wanyong (1858–1926) about the growing Catholic forces in the province and resulting troubles in tax administration. According to Min, of villages composed of ten households, half of them said they were Catholic.[24] These households pretended to preach the gospel and forced the non-Catholic villagers to pay tribute (kongnap) to them by coercing villagers to buy Catholic texts. The Catholics would then collect cash and grain from villages as payment for the books. Min believed that these Catholics were former Tonghak, writing that "The rebels in the previous revolt entered Catholic churches and assembled their old crowds (*kudang*)." He was convinced that the rebels had resumed their activities in disguise because the "new system" of the Korean government and its reform policies prohibited rebellious elements in society. The erstwhile rebels therefore took advantage of the Catholic churches and continued "plundering" the people as they had during the rebellion itself.[25]

Min worried that these "Catholic riots" would foster disobedience toward the government, yet he could not easily punish the so-called Catholics because this might lead to diplomatic trouble. To suppress the rioters and circumvent complaints from Western missionaries at the same time, he therefore tried to portray the suppression as something other than the religious persecution of Christians. Min insisted that the behavior of the "church exploiters" deviated from Christian doctrines, which could be reconciled with the rule of the Korean government. Min also asked Foreign Minister Yi Wanyong to persuade the Western diplomats in Korea that these "rebels disguised as Christians" should be punished if they violated government laws. Min Yŏngch'ŏl notes:

> The religion of Western Learning [Christianity] is originally good and [holds] fine beliefs for the beautiful and flowering world (*hwahwa chi se*). The belief respects cultivation of agricultural production and improvement of lives as well as purification of minds and behaviors. The old Christians in Hwanghae Province followed these doctrines and minded offending people and kept to their proper places—farmers in agriculture and merchants in commerce. In contrast, the new kinds of Christians imitated Tonghak commotions with Tonghak hearts.[26]

Some Protestants in the province tried to take advantage of the power of the Western missionaries and became involved in illegal conduct.[27] On March 28, 1897, the minister of the Legation of the United States (Chuhan Miguk Kongsa) in Korea sent a letter to the Korean government citing the report of an American doctor and missionary, known in Korean as Wŏnduu, about the unlawful behavior of two "people affiliated with Christian churches" (*yaso kyoin*) in P'yŏngsan, Hwanghae Province. This American missionary must have been Horace G. Underwood (1859–1916), who had been requested to investigate the situation in Hwanghae Province because the Legation of the United States in Korea had received many reports of Christian troubles there.[28] Underwood accused the two Koreans of pretending to be Christians and of using his name to legitimize their illegal behavior. They had put on Western clothes, which they pretended to have received from him, in an effort to exploit the authority implied by the clothing and steal from the people. Underwood reported that the two Korean imposters had lodged a false accusation against another Korean man in the area and had made the local government arrest him. Although Underwood opposed the arrest, the local government had refused to release the man unless Underwood himself explained the situation in a letter. Hence Underwood wrote about the arrest to the Legation of the United States in Korea, censuring the two "Christians" for creating trouble.[29]

In his own letter, the minister of the Legation of the United States in Korea explained his position on this incident. Although he did not wish to intervene in the relationship between the Korean government and its people, he had to forbid the two "Christians" from usurping the authority of Western missionaries and offending the rights of Koreans. The minister requested that these "phony" Christians be punished without harming ordinary Christians.[30] Governor Min viewed this American request as an opportunity to punish the Catholics. He ordered the local magistrates to introduce the letter from the minister of the Legation of the United States if Westerners tried to interrupt the government's punishment of "phony" Christians.[31]

The central figure in the Catholic riots in Hwanghae was An Chunggŭn's uncle, An T'aegŏn. He and his associates kidnapped Yu Manhyŏn, the director of the local elite bureau (hyangjang) in April 1897. They entered town and tricked Yu with a fake letter from the government. They loosened Yu's topknot, tied Yu on the back of a horse, and fled. Since it was raining when they captured him outside the district government hall, the incident was not known until a witness at the market informed the district government. Yu's grandson visited An T'aegŏn's residence two days later and heard that An and his companions had abducted his grandfather to intimidate the magistrate, who had arrested "innocent" Catholics.[32]

The local magistrate rejected An T'aegŏn's argument and blamed Catholic intervention in tax collection as the original cause of this incident. According to the magistrate, An lived in the Turabang subdistrict of Sinch'ŏn. He had been the commander of local expedition troops (p'ogun) against Tonghak rebels and had promoted the spread of Catholicism in the region after the rebellion. He had imported several bundles of books on Catholicism during the winter of 1896 and had forced people to buy them. Then he began to defy the local tax administration. When the regulations of 1895 reduced the tax rates, An ordered his associates, Ch'oe Wŏnsŏk and Yu Ŭnsŏk, to circulate letters in the area explaining that they would collect 3 yang per kyŏl in addition to the fixed tax rate defined in the regulations.

The regulations of 1895 were reformist tax policies devised by the Kabo Cabinet. Recognizing the widespread regional practice of submitting taxes in cash, the Kabo government decided to collect taxes in cash on a national scale. It also tried to unify various tax items into a single land tax and to establish more reasonable tax rates. In Kyŏnggi Province, the government decided on the rate of approximately 30 yang per kyŏl for coastal plain districts and 25 yang for mountainous districts. Other than these fixed rates, the government banned additional tax collection and miscellaneous fees for tax-collecting officials or agents.[33] This resulted in an actual tax reduction for taxpayers, whereas the magistrate accused An T'aegŏn of having imposed additional taxes of 3 yang per kyŏl beyond the regulations.

The magistrate's report is confusing because it indicates that some complied with An's demands. Although the magistrate punished the unit heads of households (t'ongsu) who had paid money to An, this did not stop the people from disobeying the government. The magistrate therefore arrested An's money-collecting agents (sujŏn yusa), Ch'oe and Yu, flogged them, and put them in jail. However, he acknowledged that this did not prevent disobedient Catholics from helping the arrested agents escape from the jail at midnight. He argued that the Catholics later kidnapped the director of the local elite bureau and falsely claimed that their deeds were revenge for the government repression of Catholics.

The magistrate included in his report more details on An T'aegŏn's "illegal" involvement in tax collection. An's "crime" was that he collected more money from his tenants than the amount of the reduced tax rates instituted by the Kabo regulations. In spring 1894 the tax was 82 yang, 8 chŏn, and 8 pun in Tangojŏn currency. In the winter of the same year, the government reduced the tax to 30 yang per kyŏl because the new regulations prohibited "additional taxes" above this rate. The magistrate argued that An and his associates had petitioned the Ministry of Finance to collect taxes at a higher rate than what had been stipulated in the regulations. When the Ministry ordered the local government to investigate the situation, the government found that the 1895 spring tax that An had collected still included items that the Kabo regulations had removed. The government ordered An and his fellows to remove 16 *yang* 5 *chŏn* in copper cash from what they had collected for the spring of 1895. Despite this government order, An selected tax-collecting agents and pressed the people to pay the amount as though it were all for the government.[34]

The compliance of the people seems to indicate that An T'aegŏn and his companions were collecting money to fund their religious activities. From the magistrate's viewpoint, An T'aegŏn was not authorized to collect money; the problem referred to the Catholics' violation of tax collection regulations rather than religious beliefs. Thus the magistrate portrayed An T'aegŏn and his companions' actions as a threat to both the central government and local security. He also reported to the government the rumor circulated among the people that Catholics had assembled in the Ch'ŏnggye subdistrict in order to attack the district seat. According to this rumor, the Catholics planned to eliminate their enemies in the district seat after murdering the abducted director of the local elite bureau. The magistrate also accused An T'aegŏn of misappropriating government revenues, organizing a private army, and deceiving Western missionaries for his own objectives.

An Chunggŭn mentions this case in the memoir he wrote before his execution. He argues that the government suppression of his family and fellow Catholics originated from a conflict between his father An T'aehun (An T'aegŏn's brother) and Min Yŏngjun (1852–1935), a leading figure of the Min clan. According to the memoir, An T'aehun organized the local expedition troop against the Tonghak and confiscated a thousand cloth bags of rice from the rebels.[35] Min Yŏngjun demanded the return of this rice to the government, but An T'aehun refused and did not resolve this dispute over the confiscated rice until he joined the Chonghyŏn Catholic Church (the present Myŏngdong Church) and received protection from the French missionaries.[36]

An Chunggŭn portrays this conflict as an attack by the "reactionary" (*sugu*) official, Min Yŏngjun, on the An family, who supported leaders of the enlightenment school. His memoir partially explains why Hwanghae Provincial Governor Min Yŏngch'ŏl, one of the Min clan, was determined to punish the Catholic protestors.[37] Min Yŏngjun had invalidated An T'aehun's possession of the grain confiscated from the Tonghak rebels and ordered the An family to return it to the government. But the grain may well have been consumed by An T'aehun's troops during the campaign or by his family afterward. In any case An Chunggŭn considers this order unfair, given his family's subjugation of the Tonghak.[38]

Returning to the Catholic riots, An T'aegŏn and his Catholic associates sought the protection of Westerners to resolve this case. An T'aegŏn visited the capital with French missionary Nicolas J. M. Wilhelm and lobbied the central government in opposition to the accusation of embezzlement.[39] This apparently had a beneficial result for the Catholics. Foreign Minister Yi Wanyong sent the local government a reply questioning the credibility of the magistrate's accusations. Yi ordered the magistrate to provide further evidence of An T'aegŏn's violation of the land tax law and his organization of private troops.[40]

An T'aegŏn and the Catholics continued their protests against the penal administration of the Korean government. When the Anak magistrate arrested four Catholics in February 1899, several hundred of An's followers rescued them with weapons and wounded the constabulary officers. Afterward, An T'aegŏn, Wilhelm, and about a hundred Catholics stormed the government hall of the Anak district. They accused the magistrate of failing to train the constables properly and of forcing them to arrest innocent people. An T'aegŏn produced three men who had been "falsely" labeled as "bandits." According to the magistrate, An threatened to "gouge out" the constables' eyes unless the government proved its case that the three "suspects" were criminals. The three suspects, the wounded constables, and a fourth "bandit" who had already been in custody were all brought into the hall of the district government and made to face one another for cross-examination. The arrested man, Yi Chunch'il, correctly identified the three suspects by name and challenged them, "Didn't we commit the crime together?" The faces of the three turned pale, according to the magistrate's report. They dropped their heads and did not say a word. Yi Chunch'il also confirmed that he had confessed his crime without being flogged. An T'aegŏn immediately took off Yi's clothes and hat and inspected his body. Since there was no trace of physical punishment, An opened the gate of the district hall and left the building. Afterward, the father of one of the suspects, who was one of An's troops, took a knife and tried to stab Yi Chunch'il.

An T'aegŏn later returned to the hall and concluded, "Although the three suspects were not able to prove their innocence, they could not be called 'bandits' unless the victims of the bandits confirmed their crimes through a face-to-face examination." He then left the government hall with his fellow Catholics. The Anak magistrate described this case in detail to explain how the Catholics' claims were "unjustifiable." Yet the episode shows that the Catholics challenged government authority by questioning whether the government had clear evidence of the crimes for which it arrested people, and whether or not the arrested were tortured. They also collectively forced the government to release the suspects if the government could not prove their crimes. To the magistrate, this Catholic involvement in the penal administration was offensive to the national laws.[41]

This confrontation continued in other Catholic disturbances in the province as well.[42] In December 1902, Han Ch'isun of Sinch'ŏn, who had a connection with the *Hwangsŏng sinmun* (Capital Gazette) according to the minister of the French Legation, accused two Catholics, Kim Sunmyŏng and Kim Pyŏngho, of abusing people. Han argued that the Catholics antagonized their fellow Koreans and violated the laws of the Korean government. According to Han, a contagious disease killed the cow of a resident named Yi in Han's neighborhood. Yi's neighbor's cow later died of the same disease. The leader of the Catholics and others in the area blamed Yi for having brought a sick cow into the "pure land" of their villages. They gathered together and beat Yi to coerce him into paying for his neighbor's dead cow. They also forced Yi to pay 100 *yang* for the price of a gold ornamental hairpin (*kŭmjam*) that one of their female followers claimed to have lost in the commotion. Han also insisted that the Catholics in Sinch'ŏn forced people to work for the construction of their church in August 1902. If people disobeyed, the followers brought them to the church and privately punished them. When the local government sent constabulary officers to arrest the Catholics, the officers were attacked and expelled. The local magistrate charged a Catholic priest with having sent his followers to assault the constabulary officers.

In another episode, Catholics assaulted local officials and the directors of local elite bureaus in protest of tax collection. This case differed from An

T'aegŏn and his company's claims that Catholics had the right to collect money for religious purposes. The Changyŏn magistrate reported in January 1903 that Catholics in Sinch'ŏn illegally obstructed the constables and interrupted the government's tax collection. When the magistrate arrested the Catholics, tens of their fellows attacked the constables and freed the detainees. The Catholics also demanded that the magistrate pay them 30,000 *yang* as reimbursement for money expended on legal suits for what they considered falsely imposed taxes. The magistrate refused this demand and attached to his report to the central government a petition by Kim Tŏngnyong, whose father, the former director of the local elite bureau in the district, had been seriously injured in a Catholic assault in 1902.

At that time, the bureaus of the local government requested that, as the director of the local elite bureau, Kim's father "cover various official travel expenses" (*ch'ŏng yŏbi*). Kim's father deliberated with the ward chiefs (*pangjang*) and leaders of villages (*tumin*) on how to make up the shortfall. They then distributed the burden across the households in the district and collected the money. A Catholic, Cho Pyŏnggil, filed suit in the capital and obtained a verdict that the local government should return the money to the households. Subsequently, in January 1903, the Catholics rushed into Kim's father's house and accused him of having stolen the wealth of the people. The leader of the Catholic organization ordered his followers to capture Kim's father, who had consequently been beaten by long clubs. Kim Tŏngnyong maintained that the Catholics hit his father so severely that they injured his head and left his body bleeding. In his appeal, Kim Tŏngnyong stated that the vigilante justice by the Catholics seriously violated national law.[43]

Tellingly, Hwanghae Provincial Governor Min Yŏngch'ŏl identified these Catholic rioters as Tonghak. The two groups did resemble each other in their distrust of government authority, discontent over tax administration, and reliance on organizational power for resolving grievances. Yet, the position of the Catholics toward Westerners differed from that of the Tonghak rebels, who considered the West a threat in 1894. The Catholics thrived under the protection of the French Legation in Korea. The legation supported the viewpoint of French missionaries and intervened to prohibit the Korean government from repressing the Catholics.[44] In short, the Catholic protestors were neither nationalistic nor xenophobic during this post-Kabo period. Their discontent with the Korean monarchy preoccupied them.

THE ANTI-WESTERN PROTESTS: MINERS IN P'YŎNGAN PROVINCE

In contrast to the Catholics in Hwanghae Province, some miners and other laborers in P'yŏngan Province waged multiple anti-Western protests. This did not mean that the people in P'yŏngan were backward-looking or more nationalistic than people in other regions. P'yŏngan Province adjoins China and Manchuria across the Yalu River. This geographical location had exposed residents to new ideas and merchandise from China and had also been a benefit for their commercial development. The province emerged as a new social frontier in the late nineteenth century, concomitant with the lifting of commercial restrictions and demographic changes in Manchuria. Two occurrences during this period are indicative of this transition: (1) the travel of wealthy men from Ŭiju to Australia, and (2) the slight response to Yu Insŏk's regiment, one of the most famous volunteer "righteous armies" (ŭibyŏng) that formed after the Japanese assassination of Queen Min in 1895.

In April 1901, the Japanese consul in Seoul informed the Korean government of the deaths of three Korean travelers from Ŭiju in P'yŏngan Province. In December 1900, the travelers had boarded a Japanese steamboat, the Hachimanmaru, bound for Australia. They had died of disease in Manila. The Japanese captain had held a funeral for them and sent their money and personal effects to Korea via the Japanese Consulate in Manila. These travelers were Kim Sanggyŏng, who was forty-years-old; Yu Chaep'ung, who was twenty-six; and Kim Sŏngp'al, who was thirty-six. Kim Sŏngp'al left behind 80 pounds in British gold, equivalent to 750 yen and 91 sen in Japanese gold at the time. Their other possessions included leather shoes, clothes, ginseng products, a Western umbrella, and a silver watch.[45] These travelers may have been merchants, since they carried ginseng and their destination was not a place usually associated with "studies of civilization," such as Japan or one of the Western countries. Their travels indicate that Ŭiju was not a mere border town on the isolated periphery of the Korean peninsula in this period. Rather, some wealthy merchants there were open to the world, consumed Western products, and traveled across the Pacific Ocean via the modern Japanese transportation system. A picture taken during this period shows that Ŭiju was full of tile-roofed houses and comparable to the prosperous parts of contemporaneous Seoul.[46]

Moreover, the tepid regional response to the detachment of Yu Insŏk's "righteous army" shows that the ideological climate of P'yŏngan ran the gamut from Confucian conservatism to conversion to Western ideas, including Christianity, at this time.[47] The leaders of the regiment tried to set up bases of support in the province because northerners were famous for their martial talent and bravery. There was also a strong base there for the Hwasŏ School, an orthodox Confucian academy that some leaders of Yu's regiment had attended. Yet one leader of the Yu Insŏk regiment wrote of his frustration over the lack of a favorable response from this province. He complained that P'yŏngan residents only sought official positions after the "enlightenment party" (*Kaehwa-dang*) abolished discrimination against northerners in the recruitment of state officials during the Kabo reform.[48]

The case of Yi Ch'iyŏng, another leader of the Yu Insŏk regiment, is also illuminating.[49] Familiar with conditions of the northern region as well as in Manchuria, Yi attempted to establish a regional base in the area beyond the Yalu River for the Yu Insŏk regiment in 1897. He advocated people to rise for the purpose of protecting their country and taking revenge for Queen Min. According to Kim Chaesŏng, Yi's personal servant (*sahwan*) for a number of years, Yi even invoked King Kojong's imperial order to persuade residents of the area to fight for the cause. But Yi became involved in a power struggle among the militia leaders and killed at least two of them who were critical of his actions. Later, some residents of his base accused Yi of having plundered the people. They assassinated him and delivered his head to the local magistrate of the Korean government.[50] This dire fate suggests a substantial shift in the ideological climate away from Confucian conservatism and toward local support of the Kabo Cabinet in the province.[51]

Despite this nonconservative atmosphere, fear of the West loomed large after Westerners obtained important economic concessions in the province.[52] Anticipating favorable American commitments on the Korean peninsula, King Kojong had granted James R. Morse, an American businessman, a gold mining concession at Unsan in P'yŏngan Province in July 1895, the first Korean mining concession to a foreign country. The concession did not fulfill Kojong's original diplomatic goals; rather, it triggered competition among other imperialist countries for equivalent privileges in the mining industry.[53] Its immediate consequence was the infiltration of Westerners into the resource-rich northern provinces.

The Korean government had originally tried to limit the inland settlement of foreigners. Local officials regularly investigated and compiled lists of illegal foreign land and real estate purchases outside the boundary of 10 li (about 4.5 km) from the treaty ports.[54] However, there was a lapse in enforcement as Westerners expanded their businesses and demanded that the central government force local assistance to foreign companies. Westerners increasingly frequented P'yŏngan Province as their economic involvement there became active. U.S. Consul General Horace N. Allen asked Korean Foreign Minister Yi Wanyong to open special lodges in the countryside for American travelers, many of whom had difficulty finding food and accommodations on their way to P'yŏngyang and other inland locations.[55]

Despite the fact that Westerners acquired privileges through direct or secret bargaining with the central government, they faced adverse local reactions from those who had previously engaged in mining or other lucrative activities in the province. Yi Wanyong instructed local officials to arrest those who offended foreigners in order to avoid diplomatic incidents.[56] Nevertheless, there were recurrent attacks on foreign businessmen and vendors in the province. The American gold mining company in Unsan was one of the main sites that provoked such anti-Western protests.

When the American businessman Leigh S. J. Hunt arrived at Unsan and opened a mine in July 1896,[57] Koreans in the company's neighborhood lodged a complaint about their losses to the Unsan magistrate. The petitioners argued that the company had cut down tens of thousands of pine trees and never compensated their owners. Furthermore, Korean brokers in charge of employing miners for the company had not paid local merchants for the food and goods that miners consumed. The brokers were accused of counting on the power of the foreigners and of using violence against local merchants to avoid their responsibility to pay the outstanding bills. Local magistrates in the province also stuck to the original directive of the Korean government to limit the inland settlement of foreigners and refused to cooperate with the company. According to this directive, all construction by the company was illegal since foreigners could not buy land or build warehouses in Unsan, which was located outside the specified circumference from the treaty ports. The Unsan magistrate ordered the American company to pay 1 yang per tree and to forbid brokers to cause a public nuisance. The company argued that local residents had cut down and sold most of the trees in dispute. It also insisted that it was the Korean local government that should handle the problems caused by the brokers. This shirking of responsibility was not in the company's best interests, however, because it pushed the local government into punishing the company for illegal lumbering, which was necessary for gold mining. The Unsan magistrate reported to the central government that he would expel the troublesome brokers and order those who had illegally felled the trees to pay those who owned the timber.[58]

The company later complained to the central government that the provincial governor had dispatched police officials who threatened to shoot foreigners who illegally cut down trees. The company also grumbled that the governor had refused to meet with its supervisor. The Korean foreign minister notified the provincial governor that the company had signed contracts with the Bureau of the Royal Household and had permission from the Ministry of Agriculture to cut trees. He then ordered the governor to let the company continue its lumbering operations.[59] Thus the mining company relied on the involvement of the central government to resolve protests from local officials and residents in the province.[60]

When the company tried to open a road from Pakch'ŏn to Unsan on which to move mining machines and other equipment, it faced wage disputes from Korean laborers. The company criticized the Pak'chŏn magistrate for being obstinate and even hostile because he was neutral to the claims of the laborers. The company even suggested in its report to the Korean government that the magistrate himself had promoted the wage disputes, ordering the Koreans not to accept work unless the company paid them 200 *mun* (2 *yang*) per day. The company insisted that it had paid the laborers 175 *mun* per day even though it could have hired Chinese "coolies" for 150 *mun* per day. The acting foreign minister, Yu Kihwan, severely reprimanded the provincial governor with respect to this accusation. Exasperated, the Pakch'ŏn magistrate defended himself and explained the situation differently. According to him, the Americans arrived in Pakch'ŏn in March 1898 and tried to transport machines by river, since road transportation was inconvenient. The company asked the magistrate to send workers to repair the road, and he mobilized laborers to do so. The company did not provide a single penny in the beginning. After the workers completed the construction, the company said that if the magistrate sent workers again, it would hire them immediately. Hence the magistrate ordered people to respond to the company's offer. Since the local government was not in charge of wage increases, the magistrate argued, it was the workers who had demanded that the company pay 2 *yang* a day.

Moreover, he argued that it was not true that the company could hire Chinese laborers at lower wages. The Chinese at the port were unwilling to accept the company's offer because most of them were engaged in trade and commerce. Thus the magistrate criticized the company for falsely accusing him when it was the company that had caused the conflict. He concluded that the company neither paid fair wages to the Korean workers nor properly addressed their protests.[61]

The Unsan gold mine not only provoked economic conflict but also engendered social unrest in the province. The judge of the Provincial Court in North P'yŏngan Province (P'yŏnganbuk-to Chaep'anso P'ansa), Cho Minhŭi, sent a letter to the Korean foreign minister stating that three Americans from the Unsan mining company had mistaken a Korean peasant for a gold thief and shot him to death on May 28, 1899. The judge wrote that even if it was valid to punish the thief, it was unlawful to shoot and kill someone for such a crime. The Korean government could neither arrest Americans nor investigate their crime due to the extraterritoriality clause in their "unequal treaty," though the Korean government did produce meticulous reports of this incident according to the traditional investigation process for murder cases.[62] These reports addressed the shock, fear, and anger that villagers felt toward the Americans responsible for the shooting. The dead peasant, Kim Pongmun from Unsan, and two other villagers had been plowing the fields adjacent to a village house when they heard loud roars from the entrance to the village. Frightened, they looked back and saw three Americans approaching. Kim was extremely scared by the Americans, who were dressed in black clothes (hŭgŭi) and firing their guns at will (nanbang). He tried to run away, but the three Americans chased him. Kim was found dead soon afterward, a bullet in his chest.[63]

In the government reports the villagers repeatedly stated how afraid they had been when they saw the Americans dressed in black and behaving wildly. Female witnesses in the village testified that they could not identify exactly who shot Kim to death. They had hidden in their kitchens and been afraid to come out of their houses after they had seen the Americans in their black clothes.[64] All the witnesses agreed it was not guilt but fear that had made Kim run away. They were frustrated that he had been killed for no reason while simply working in his neighbor's field. Considering the loud roars and gunshots, the Americans may have been drunk when they entered the village. They reportedly returned to the village at midnight and took a bundle of reeds from a village house. They covered the dead peasant with reeds and a pine wood plank and moved the body to the middle of a villager's field. The local government reported the murder to the company and asked it to supply the names of the Americans. The company replied that the gunshots had been due to the stolen gold and did not give the local government any further information.[65]

The British mine in Ŭnsan was another site of conflict in the province. According to the Ŭnsan magistrate's report to the governor of the South P'yŏngan Province, a British citizen called Sŏl P'illim in Korean, three other Englishmen, and fifty Japanese employees had occupied the Ŭnsan mine on February 7, 1900. They started mining without providing the magistrate with a government directive. The magistrate regarded this as a violation of the international treaty and dispatched police officers to the mine. He tried to prohibit the British from capturing the mine and told the Korean miners to continue working there. According to a report by a dispatched police officer, the British raised the Union Jack and inspected those who entered the mine. They also displayed small flags on two guard posts located on high mountain roads. They intimidated people by carrying swords and pistols. At night, they hung lamps and checked the passersby. The police officer reported that those who came to the mine were three Westerners, one black person (hŭgin), fifty-eight Japanese workers and their Japanese supervisor, and one Chinese person. In addition, there were about a hundred Korean employees in the mine. Faced with the local magistrate's ban on the mine, the British protested that they started mining in Ŭnsan because in July 1899 the Korean government allowed them to select one mine in addition to those in P'yŏngyang, Chaeryŏng, Sinch'ŏn, Hamhŭng, Kilch'ŏn, Tanch'ŏn, and Suan.[66]

The British company soon encountered the riots of Korean miners who had previously developed the mine there. Several hundred miners from Yŏngbyŏn and three or four hundred from Sŏngch'ŏn and Sunan came together and camped on the mountains near the British mine. The British put up a notice to explain that the Korean emperor had given them the mine. They warned that the Japanese would protect the company's employees and punish those who hurt them. They wrote in Korean vernacular:

The miners who are making a commotion at the Rohobang gold mine should go back. You should not injure or capture those who are involved with our

company. The Japanese police officers that our company employs will protect
those who are related to our company. Since the people living in this village
are friendly to our company, they are our people. If there are any problems,
they should be reported to Master Sŏl (Sŏl taein), our company's clerk.[67]

This notice did not prevent several hundred miners from joining the
encamped rioters on February 19, 1900, and occupying the east valley of
Yonghwa subdistrict near the mine. The Japanese employees of the company
carried its equipment to the western valley of the subdistrict. The battle line
between the miners and the company employees extended for 3 li (nearly one
mile). This confrontation escalated when the company's Japanese interpreter,
together with several other temporary laborers (kogong), came to Sunch'ŏn on
market day, February 21, where rioting miners confiscated the interpreter's
possessions and confined him in a private house. The British heard of this
and dispatched twenty Japanese and several laborers to the market. They carried weapons and fired many shots in succession. The miners dispersed but
reconvened the next day, destroying the houses of two Korean chief miners
(sipchang) employed by the company. The British and twenty Japanese came to
town again, captured one miner, struck him on the head, and battered him
until he was unconscious. They also injured another miner with their swords.
This bloody showdown further incited the miners and led other miners from
nearby to gather in town. The local magistrate, gravely concerned that the
miners would turn into rebels and attack townspeople, dispatched one hundred soldiers from the local defense army and ended the riots.[68]

These miners' protests coincided with repeated assaults on Westerners in
mining districts. A British technician from the Ŭnsan mine was beaten to
death on August 19, 1900, after he went to a tavern to stop miners from drinking.[69] An unidentified man in Anju shot at a Western-style house where an
American lived.[70] Two hundred Koreans attacked Americans and their clerks
in the Unsan gold mine because they had sexually harassed a Korean woman.[71]
And American diplomats complained in December 1903 that residents of the
Unsan area had thrown stones at foreigners. [72]

When the Russians expanded their influence in the province, they became
another source of conflict. Russians began to buy land and real estate at
Yongam Port in Yongch'ŏn in 1903. The Korean government recorded that the
Russian actions violated their treaty obligations and offended local custom.[73]

The worst thing the Russians did was to destroy local ancestral graves during their construction projects in Yongch'ŏn. The resentment of the residents was fierce. Local village heads in Yongch'ŏn district submitted a petition containing the signatures of the village residents. The subdistrict head (Chonwi), An Ch'igyŏm, complained that the Russians had dug tunnels into the mountain and had removed the soil by train. Several tombs on the mountain had caved in because of these tunnels. The government investigator reported that "cries of the dead echoed along the stream and the wrath of the living filled the grounds."[74] When the Korean government gathered the village leaders to find out how many graves in Yongam Port had been damaged, it found that bones of the dead were exposed in 362 out of 462 graves in the area. The government compiled a list of the victims and offered partial compensation for reburial expenses.[75]

THE CHANGING EAST ASIAN ORDER AND SPREAD OF PAN-ASIANISM

Popular response to the Western ascendance of the post-Kabo period ranged from collaboration to hostility. Western countries competed for economic concessions but showed little interest in mollifying Korean feelings. France found indigenous collaborators in Catholic converts yet did not attempt to expand its power on the Korean peninsula in deference to its ally, Russia. And although Russia increased its control over the Korean court after Kojong's flight to the Russian Legation in 1896, it was indifferent to developing a favorable opinion among Koreans toward Russian expansion. Thus it was Japan that most carefully monitored Korean response toward the changing regional order in East Asia, working to shape that response in favor of Japan's own ambitions there. This Japanese effort may well have been critical in tipping the balance in favor of Japan, given the variety and fluidity of Korean reactions toward foreigners.

Pan-Asianism refers to a set of discourses that imagine an East Asian or Asian community in opposition to the West. Some early Pan-Asianist discourse promoted an East Asian alliance, or federation, in which each of the nations or peoples would enjoy political equality.[76] Yet a cultural hierarchy that denounced traditional Chinese and Korean civilization and highlighted the new "enlightened leadership" of Meiji Japan was still emphasized. This discourse was effective in portraying Japanese expansion in Korea or in Asia as the route for building a new regional order to replace the collapsing Chinese order. The local circumstances in P'yŏngan Province were congruent with some elements of the Japanese Pan-Asianist discourse, especially the discourse's critique of the West and of China's leadership.

As China became unable to control the situation in its northeastern regions, the people in P'yŏngan Province experienced the detrimental effects of China's collapse. Illegal Chinese traders and Chinese bandit raids frequently irritated the province. The magistrate of Samhwa in South P'yŏngan Province complained that Chinese commercial craft swarmed the coastal areas of the region. He wrote in April 1896 that twenty to thirty Chinese boats a day sailed with favorable wind to inland areas such as Chŭngnam Port and laid anchor for trade.[77] According to his report, these merchants, most of whom lived in the Dengzhou area of China, came to exchange Western cotton textiles or iron goods for Korean soybeans or rice. Many did not possess passports yet traveled into the interior, close to P'yŏngyang, and to various coastal districts in Hwanghae Province. The local magistrate did not have any legal right to limit the activities of Chinese merchants before the Korean government signed a new Korean-Chinese Agreement on Commerce and Trade (Han-Ch'ŏng t'ongsang choyak) in 1899.[78]

Chinese timber smuggling was also a serious problem in the province. Korean Prime Minister Pak Chesun (1858–1916) worried that the Chinese loggers had evaded taxes and damaged the finances of the Korean government. He sent regulations to the provincial governor on how to constrain the timber smugglers. If Korean officials found illegal timber piled in the mountains or along the river, the regulations wrote, they had to estimate its market price and levy penalties to compensate for the revenue losses of the Korean government that the illegal lumbering and smuggling caused. To fight illegal lumbering, the Korean government also permitted local officials to hire gunmen (p'osu) should loggers not observe the prohibition. If local officials received bribes from Chinese merchants in return for allowing illegal lumbering, then local magistrates could imprison the corrupt officials.[79]

However, these regulations did not stop the tens, if not hundreds, of Chinese "timber bandits" (mokpi) from continuing their raids in the border areas along the Yalu River. The explosive growth of Chinese migration to Manchuria exacerbated this banditry.[80] As railways were built and population centers developed, the demand for wood increased in Manchuria, and the bandits crossed Korea's northern border to a region rich in forests. In August and September 1900, the Boxer rebels fled Beijing and arrived in the area across the Yalu River. The rebels massacred several Korean Christians and displayed their corpses on the riverbank.[81] In addition, there were numerous incidents of robbery, murder, kidnapping, and other miscellaneous crimes caused by various groups of Chinese.[82]

These Chinese incursions and the recurrent anti-Western protests may well have helped the Japanese make their case to Koreans for an enhanced role in Korea and Asia. This was especially so in P'yŏngan Province, where the Japanese temporarily restrained their aggressive activities before Japan's conflict with Russia escalated into the outbreak of war in 1904.[83] Japan moved quietly yet steadily into the province. Japanese Acting Consul Shinjō Junketsu opened an office in the Yungdŏk subdistrict, inside the Taedong Gate in P'yŏngyang, in August 1899.[84] The Tōa dōbunkai (East Asia Common Culture Society) also extended its reach to the province. This Japanese association, founded by Prince Konoe Atsumaro in June 1898, actively spread a right-wing version of Japanese Pan-Asianism against Russia.[85] The association dispatched one of its members, Shintō Yoshio, to establish schools in Korea. In June 1899, Shintō petitioned the Korean Ministry of Education (Hakpu) to open a school in P'yŏngyang, which subsequently forwarded the petition to the provincial government of South P'yŏngan Province. Shintō received the permission with the following comment:

> The petitioner, Shintō Yoshio, took on the task of educating the younger generation and did not hesitate to make an effort.... Japan recently established the Tonga tongmunhoe (Tōa dōbunkai), selected talented and knowledgeable scholars, and dispatched them to many countries. This person (Shintō) took up the duty.... In the old days of Paekche, Wang In arrived in Japan and transmitted the *Analects of Confucius* (Nonŏ) and the *Thousand-Character Classic* (Ch'ŏnjamun). ... Now, as the Heavenly Way circulates, the time arrives that this person guides our people and transmits the knowledge of enlightenment. How fortuitous could this be?[86]

Shinjō Junketsu, the acting Japanese consul in P'yŏngyang, and Shintō worked together to open a school that would teach new knowledge, including English. They requested that the Korean government allow them to use a government building under the jurisdiction of the Ministry of Finance. Although this request was unusual, the local magistrate granted it because Shintō's school was affiliated with the Ministry of Education. Since the magistrate did not want to allow the school to use the building for free, he received approval of the Ministry of Finance to lease it for a period of two years.[87] Further research is needed to understand how Shintō's ideological orientation influenced his management of the school and the spread of Pan-Asianist ideas in the province. His school was not the only channel through which the Japanese propagated their Pan-Asianist discourse: intellectuals in the province had access to daily newspapers and pamphlets permeated with Pan-Asianist narratives, which circulated broadly in Korea at the time.[88]

The spread of Pan-Asianist discourse in Korea was closely connected to growing Pan-Asianist movements within Japan in the 1890s. The writings of Tarui Tōkichi (1850–1922), one of the earliest Japanese Pan-Asianists, influenced the Tonghak leaders, especially Yi Yonggu, who later took charge of leading the Ilchinhoe (Advance in Unity Society).[89] Tarui wrote the first draft of his book, *Daitō gappōron* (Theory of the Great East Federation), in 1885, while he was involved in the popular rights movement. The draft was lost when Tarui was imprisoned. He rewrote the work and published it in the journal *Jiyu byōdō keiron* (World of Liberty and Equality) in 1890. He then published it as a book in 1893. Its second edition was in print, with the author's new preface, in 1910, the year of Japanese annexation of Korea.[90] The book was written in plain classical Chinese to gain a wider readership among Koreans and Chinese. According to Tarui, Liang Qichao (1873–1929), a Chinese progressive intellectual, praised Tarui's federation theory in the preface of the Chinese edition of Tarui's book. Tarui's book was not successful in Japan. However, Tarui claimed that the 1893 Shanghai edition sold up to a hundred thousand copies. He stated that a thousand copies were distributed in Korea, where both hand-copied and printed versions were widely circulated.[91]

Although Tarui's book made derogatory remarks about Chinese and Korean civilization, his political propositions were bold and radical in comparison with those of the more reactionary Japanese Pan-Asianists of later periods. He envisioned an Eastern federation and emphasized equality within that federation. He argued that the federation should adopt a new title, "the Great East," to avoid discrimination against any one side. Tarui thought it crucial that the federation be founded on a formal agreement based on the equality of each member. He also insisted that the federation guarantee the political participation of the people from all federated countries, arguing that:

> The vital point lies in making it equal and fair for each country to use its right to autonomy and self-governance. If one country monopolizes this right, the others could not claim their rights sufficiently. It would not be different from destroying the other countries.[92]

However, Tarui gave up this vision when he faced Japanese criticism that his argument ruled out the prospect of Japanese rule in Korea. In the author's notes to the second edition of his book, printed in 1910, he denied the radical implications of his earlier federation theory, abandoned the principle of equality in his conception of the federation, and did not mention the need for equal political participation of the people from all three Eastern countries. Instead, he exalted the central importance of the Japanese emperor in the federation.[93]

The circulation of Pan-Asianist discourses and some of their progressive versions influenced the leaders of the Tonghak religion to envision a new political framework in alliance with Japan. Son Pyŏnghŭi, the then Tonghak patriarch, saw an opportunity to overturn the domestic situation in Korea through the outbreak of the Russo-Japanese War. Ch'oe Kiyŏng, who studied Son Pyŏnghŭi's life in Japan, argues that, beginning in 1903, Son attempted to overthrow the Korean government through an alliance with Korean refugees in Japan.[94] One of these attempts involved Tamura Iyojo, the vice chief of staff of the Japanese army. According to the *History of Our Religion*, Son discussed the situation in the East with Tamura in 1903.[95] Both agreed that the pro-Russian faction in Korea must be removed, and Russia isolated, to achieve peace in the East. Son then ordered his brother, Son Pyŏnghŭm, to accompany Tamura to Korea in order to remove Russian influences. This plot was not realized, the *History* continues, because Son Pyŏnghŭm and Tamura both died of a sudden illness as soon as they arrived in Pusan. When Son Pyŏnghŭi received the telegram about their untimely deaths, he grieved bitterly over the failure of the plot and fasted for three days.

Ch'oe doubts the credibility of this narrative in the *History of Our Religion* because Tamura did not actually go to Pusan but died of a chronic disease in the Red Cross Hospital in Tokyo. However, Ch'oe acknowledges the possibility that Son was acquainted with Tamura and discussed with him and Korean refugees in Japan the plot that Son was considering. Son also sought to persuade the Japanese military to help him in his attempt to overthrow the Korean government.[96] The death of Tamura did apparently frustrate Son, who had expected Tamura to help him obtain this military support. When the Russo-Japanese War broke out, Son contributed 10,000 *wŏn* to the Japanese government's war effort. The *History* adds that this money was a token of "his support for the yellow race fighting to expel the white race."[97]

CONCLUSION

The years between the fall of the Kabo cabinet and the Russo-Japanese War were a "transnational" moment in Korean history. The features of this moment were most evident in the popular movements of the northwestern provinces. The conjuncture of often diverging ideological, political, and cultural elements and multiple political possibilities characterized the moment. During this period, the Korean monarch Kojong tried to transform the kingdom into a modern nation-state by declaring the foundation of the Great Korean Empire and monopolizing the country's power and resources. However, in the northwestern provinces, popular attitudes toward the central monarchy were more confrontational than cordial. Catholic rioters used the presence of Western churches to dispute issues ranging from religious repression, penal justice, and corrupt tax collection to government authority and economic benefits at both local and central administrative levels. The protestors of American and British mines resented the fact that the king's concessions expelled them from worksites they had long cultivated. Their neighborhoods also suffered from the cultural and economic transgressions of these Westerners.

It is important to note that the varied popular movements in the northwestern provinces did not immediately transfer to a rise of nationalism there. Rather, the episode about the encounter between An Chunggŭn's family and Kim Ku during and after the Tonghak Rebellion shows that Kim Ku's transition from Tonghak to militant nationalism was mediated by the influence of Confucian orthodoxy. However, this Confucian orthodoxy suffered from isolation rather than prosperousness in the northwestern provinces, at least during this post-Kabo period. When the Confucian scholar Ko Nŭngsŏn left An's residence, the French missionary Willem replaced Ko as An's spiritual guide. The commanders of the "righteous armies" organized by the Hwasŏ school were dismayed by their lukewarm reception in the region. They also detested the northwesterners' approval of Western ideas and of the reform regulations of the "pro-Japanese" Kabo Cabinet. Accordingly, Chang Chiyŏn praised the region's "advanced" status in modern education and contrasted it to that of the southern regions dominated by "bigoted" Confucians.

At this juncture, Pan-Asianism found space for broadening its audience in the northwestern provinces. Japan aggressively disseminated its own version of Pan-Asianism in Korea, and a member of the Tō-A dōbunkai (East Asia Common Culture Society) opened a school in P'yŏngyang. Until the eve of the Russo-Japanese War, Pan-Asianism was influential enough to persuade An Chunggŭn, whose family had been pro-Western when leading the Catholic protests in Hwanghae Province. The spread of Pan-Asianism coincided with the expansion of underground Tonghak organizations in the northwestern provinces and their conversion to Pan-Asianism. It is unclear what exactly facilitated the expansion of the Tonghak and their new position in the northwestern provinces. The popular movements described here can only hint at what the people in the region faced during the time. Clearly, however, the new Tonghak's Pan-Asianism and its reformist solution to Korea's problems resonated with the concerns of the northwesterners, who were coping with the aggressive intrusion of Western forces, Chinese movements and violence across the Yalu River, and the region's complex relations to the Korean court. In short, the multiple orientations of the popular movements discussed in this chapter were not necessarily susceptible to the nationalist solution articulated during Japan's protectorate period. These movements also disapproved Kojong's ambition for a stronger monarchy. From the observation of what happened in this region, caution may be required to argue that the hegemony of nationalist discourses in Korea was established during this period.

NOTES

1. An Chunggŭn, "Tongyang p'yŏnghwaron," 119–23; and An Chunggŭn, "An Ŭngch'il yŏksa," 95–97, 116–17, and 122–23.

2. An Chunggŭn came from a wealthy family who had connections with the "enlight-enment school leaders." His father, An T'aehun, seemed to support Pak Yŏnghyo (1861–1939) during the palace coup in 1884. Pak selected An T'aehun as one of the seventy students to be sent abroad for study. After the failure of the coup, An T'aehun left Haeju and settled in the secluded Ch'ŏnggye subdistrict of Sinch'ŏn district to avoid govern-ment persecution. An T'aehun was a central figure in spreading Catholicism in Hwanghae Province, and his brother, An T'aegŏn, led the "Catholic riots" discussed later in this chapter. When An Chunggŭn was sentenced to death for his assassination of Itō on February 14, 1910, his family moved to the maritime province of Siberia (Yŏnhaeju) to escape Japanese repression. Many of An's brothers and cousins participated in Korean independence movements after his death. An Chunggŭn, "An Ŭngch'il yŏksa," 20–21; and Cho Kwang, "An Chunggŭn yŏn'gu ŭi hyŏnhwang kwa kwaje," 187–93.

3. The provincial administrative structure increased from eight to thirteen provinces in 1897. This was done by dividing five provinces—Hamgyŏng, P'yŏngan, Ch'ungch'ŏng, Chŏlla, and Kyŏngsang—into separate northern and southern provinces.

4. About the importance of bridging the subnational with the transnational or the "larger frameworks" in the studies of region, see Wigen, "Culture, Power, and Region," 1198–99; and Bayly et al., "AHR Conversation," 1463–64.

5. The records in the *Kaksa tŭngnok* (hereafter KSTN) show several differences in the social atmosphere between Hwanghae Province and P'yŏngan Province. In Hwanghae, Korean disputes with Japanese merchants were more serious than in P'yŏngan and frequently escalated into diplomatic problems. This chapter does not give a full account of the difficult economic interactions between the Japanese and Koreans in Hwanghae Province. And although the conflicts between Korean and Chinese merchants were numerous in both provinces, the threat from Chinese banditry was not a problem in Hwanghae.

6. Hayashi Yūsuke, "Isshinkai no zenhanki ni kansuru kisoteki kenkyū," 506–9; Kim Chongjun, "Ilchinhoe chihoe ŭi hwaltong kwa hyangch'on sahoe ŭi tonghyang," 26.

7. Ch'oe Kiyŏng, *Han'guk kŭndae kyemong sasang yŏn'gu*, 225.

8. KSTN 36: 262–63.

9. Ch'oe Kiyŏng and Pak Maengsin, eds., *Hanmal Ch'ŏndogyo charyojip*, "Pon'gyo yŏksa," 2: 270.

10. Ch'oe Kiyong, *Han'guk kŭndae kyemong sasangŏn'gu*, 227.

11. Ch'oe Kiyŏng and Pak Maengsin, eds., *Hanmal Ch'ŏndogyo charyojip*, "Pon'gyo yŏksa," 2: 272.

12. The Tonghak leaders continued to dispatch students to Japan even after they had joined the Ilchinhoe. Yi Kwangsu, the famous Korean novelist, was one such student sent to Japan by the Ilchinhoe. Nagashima Hiroki, "Isshinkai no katsudō to sono tenkai," 66.

13. Ch'oe Kiyŏng, *Han'guk kŭndae kyemong sasang ŏn'gu*, 227.

14. Kim Ku, *Paekpŏm ilchi*, 30–38.

15. Ibid., 38–39.

16. Ibid., 44–45.

17. Ibid., 45.

18. Ibid., 48 and 62–63.

19. Nicolas J. M. Wilhelm (1860–1938) was a French Catholic priest affiliated with La Société des Missions Étrangères de Paris. He stayed in Korea between July 1889 and April 1914 and took charge of the mission in Hwanghae Province. He was known as Hong Sŏkku.

20. Chang Chiyŏn, "Ch'uksa," 5.

21. Yun Sŏnja, "Hanil happyŏng chŏnhu Hwanghae-do ch'ŏnju kyohoe wa Wilhelm sinbu," 111–15.

22. The conversion of Tonghak remnants to Christianity also occurred in other regions. For example, the Tonghak in Chŏlla Province organized the party for English learning (Yŏnghaktang). Yi Yŏngho, "Taehan cheguk sigi Yŏnghaktang undong ŭi sŏnggyŏk."

23. For example, see KSTN 25: 271–73.

24. The original term, *kyoin* (literally, "Christian believers"), does not differentiate Catholics from Protestants in Korean. Yet the religious background of the protestors concerned was Catholicism.

25. KSTN 25: 272. The governor's opinion reveals the political position of the Min clan, one of the most prominent aristocratic families in this period, which constituted a reformist segment of the Kwangmu government. The clan was conciliatory with Westerners yet intolerant of the topsy-turvy domestic situation.

26. KSTN 25: 270–71.

27. Yun Sŏnja, "Hanil happyŏng chŏnhu Hwanghae-do ch'ŏnju kyohoe wa Wilhelm sinbu," 114; and Yi Kwangnin, "Kaehwagi Kwansŏ chibang kwa kaesin'gyo." Compared to Catholic priests in Korea, American Protestant missionaries avoided engaging in Korean domestic affairs due to orders from the American government after what is called the Incident of the Ch'unsaeng Gate (*Ch'unsaengmun sagŏn*) in November 1895. This refers to a failed attempt of pro-American and pro-Russian officials to overthrow the pro-Japanese cabinet after the murder of Queen Min. The officials tried to kidnap King Kojong from the palace and establish a new government. Horace G. Underwood, Homer B. Hulbert, and Horace N. Allen were involved in this incident. This incident prompted the American government to prohibit American missionaries from interfering in Korean domestic politics.

28. Underwood, *Fifteen Years among the Top-Knots*, 273–302.

29. KSTN 25: 271–73.

30. KSTN 25: 271–72.

31. Since Min Yŏngch'ŏl uses the term *kyoin* (Christian believer), it is often unclear whether he is referring to Christians in general or only to Catholics. KSTN 36: 262–63. Yet the specific cases that Min mentions in KSTN are mostly related to Catholics in Hwanghae Province who were connected to French missionaries.

32. For this incident in Sinch'ŏn, see KSTN 25: 273–78.

33. On Kabo regulations on land tax, see Yi Yŏngho, *Han'guk kŭndae chise chedo wa nongmin undong*, 75–118.

34. KSTN 25: 273–76 and Yi Yŏngho, "Taehan cheguk sigi Yŏnghaktang undong ŭi sŏnggyŏk."

35. The local magistrate reported that An T'aegŏn was also the leader of the expedition troops. It seemed that An's family in the Ch'ŏnggye subdistrict collectively took charge of organizing the troops in the region.

36. Yun Sŏnja, "Hanil happyŏng chŏnhu Hwanghae-do ch'ŏnju kyohoe wa Wilhelm sinbu," 113; and An Chunggŭn, "An Ŭngch'il yŏksa," 32–35.

37. Min Yŏngch'ŏl was the adopted son of Min Sŏnho, who was the son of Min Ch'isŏ, a high official of the government. Min Yŏngch'ŏl passed the civil examination and held high official positions as a member of Min clan. He is thought to have been a remote cousin of Min Yŏngjun. Their grandfathers had the same name—Min Ch'isŏ—but with two different classical Chinese characters for the syllable "sŏ."

38. The magistrate's report does not clearly describe the real situation because he simply regarded An T'aegŏn's money collection as illegal. An may have collected some money from his fellow Catholics for the expenses of their church after the Kabo regulations reduced tax burdens. Or he may have imposed additional taxes on the tenants of his land. The magistrate noticed that the taxpayers consented to the extra charge by An. This may indicate that An's involvement in tax administration supported the interests of some taxpayers—at least those who consented to his money collection.

39. KSTN 25: 273–76.

40. KSTN 25: 278.

41. KSTN 25: 338–39.

42. See KSTN 25: 282–83. These Catholic disturbances are called *Haesŏ kyoan* (Catholic persecutions) in Korean Catholic history. See Ch'oe Sŏg'u, "Haesŏ kyoan ŭi yŏn'gu."

43. Similar conflicts between Catholics and the government were observed in other Korean provinces during this period. On Cheju Island, Catholic forces grew large enough to infringe on the interests of the local elites. This caused a "rebellion" of the officials of local elite bureaus (*hyangim*) and residents who were infuriated with the Catholic involvement in tax administration. Pak Ch'ansik, "Hanmal Cheju chiyŏk ŭi ch'ŏnju kyohoe wa Cheju kyoan," 62–106.

44. For example, see KSTN 25: 370–71. The French Legation was silent about Catholic crimes yet demanded that the constabulary officer known as Pak Chŏngmo be punished for his persecution of Christians.

45. KSTN 36: 144, 146–47. Kim Sŏngp'al's brother went to Seoul to retrieve the money. The other travelers' effects were sent to the local governments of their home-towns because their relatives could not afford the cost of travel to Seoul.

46. Yi Kyuhŏn, *Sajin ŭro ponŭn kŭndae Han'guk*, 2: 78–79.

47. Sin Sŏnggwŏn, "Roil ŭi hanbando punhal hoekch'aek," 95–96. After the assassination of Queen Min, Yu Insŏk organized the "righteous armies" under the slogans of "Revenge for the mother of our country" and "Opposing the ordinance-prohibiting topknots." The righteous armies fanned out through the country, killing the "pro-Japanese" provincial governors and local magistrates who supported the Kim Hongjip cabinet.

48. Ku Wanhoe, *Hanmal ŭi Chech'ŏn ŭibyŏng*, 207–19.

49. KSTN 36: 36; and Ku Wanhoe, *Hanmal ŭi Chech'ŏn ŭibyŏng*, 564.

50. KSTN 36: 22–25, 36.

51. Chang Chiyŏn, "Ch'uksa," 5.

52. Yu Sŭngju, *Chosŏn sidae kwangŏpsa yŏn'gu*, 371.

53. Yi Paeyong, "Kuhanmal Miguk ŭi Unsan kŭmgwang ch'aegulkwŏn hoektŭk e taehayŏ," 93–94.

54. KSTN 36: 26.

55. KSTN 36: 28.

56. KSTN 36: 26.

57. Hunt was a businessman from Seattle who was acquainted with Allen and bought the rights to the Unsan mine from James R. Morse, who had originally received the concession at the Unsan gold mine. Yi Paeyong, "Kuhanmal Miguk ŭi Unsan kŭmgwang ch'aegulkwŏn hoektŭk e taehayŏ," 107–17.

58. KSTN 36: 31–32.

59. Ibid., 36: 35.

60. Ibid., 36: 39, 42–43, and 47.

61. Ibid., 36: 44–45.

62. Ibid., 36: 67–83.

63. Ibid., 36: 78.

64. In their reports for the government investigation, the villagers reiterated their fear of the Americans' black clothing. An African American may have been included among the group of Americans since the report includes the term *hŭgin* (black people); we know that a "black person" was hired in the British mining company in Ŭnsan. However, the government reports did not specifically identify any of the three Americans as an African-American.

65. KSTN 36: 81.

66. Ibid., 36: 105–106.

67. Ibid., 36: 106–107.

68. Ibid., 36: 108–109, 112–13.

69. Ibid., 36: 127.

70. Ibid., 36: 100–101.

71. Yi Paeyong, "Kuhanmal Miguk ŭi Unsan kŭmgwang ch'aegulkwŏn hoektŭk e taehayŏ," 182–83.

72. KSTN 36: 229.

73. Ibid., 36: 182. For example, in 1903, Russians cut down trees in the forests of the Paengma Mountain fortress (Paengma sansŏng), which was beyond the areas where they had acquired a logging concession. The Korean government had protected the trees in this forest from being cut down for more than one hundred years.

74. KSTN 36: 203.

75. Ibid., 36: 218, 221.

76. See Tarui Tōkichi, Daitō gappōron (hereafter DTGR).

77. KSTN 36: 2.

78. KSTN 36: 28. The Chinese merchants could expand their commercial activities because the regulations on commerce signed in 1882 guaranteed Chinese merchants privileges in their trade in Korea. After China's defeat in the Sino-Japanese War in 1895, the Korean government renegotiated with China and concluded the new Korean-Chinese Agreement on Commerce and Trade (Han-Ch'ŏng t'ongsang choyak) in 1899. Kwŏn Sŏkpong, "Ch'ŏngIl chŏnjaeng ihu ŭi HanCh'ŏng kwan'gye ŭi yŏn'gu (1894–1899)," 37; and Larsen, "From Suzerainty to Commerce," 106 and 132–33.

79. KSTN 36: 57.

80. Gottschang and Lary, Swallows and Settlers, 2–3, 36–37, and 64.

81. Yi Hun'gu, Manju wa Chosŏnin, 45–55.

82. See KSTN, Vol. 36 for detailed reports on these incidents.

83. The Korean government could punish Japanese illegal trade or smuggling and regulate Japanese merchants according to international treaties. When Korean merchants accused the Japanese of extending their reach to coastal shipping in 1900, the local government defended the interests of the Korean merchants. See KSTN 36: 47–49 and 104.

84. KSTN 36: 89.

85. The Tōa dōbunkai (East Asia Common Culture Society) was one of the main constituents of the Kokumin dōmeikai (Anti-Russian National League) formed in September 24, 1901. In January 1901 the Kokuryūkai (Amur River Society) convened.

86. KSTN 36: 97–98.

87. Ibid., 36: 102–103.

88. Schmid, *Korea between Empires*; and Yi Chema, *Tongmu yugo*, 35, and 235–51.

89. Tarui Tōkichi's political career as a Pan-Asianist began when he went to China during the outbreak of the Sino-French War in 1884. Considering the war to be a crisis of the East, Tarui joined other Japanese to establish the first educational institute (Tōyō gakkan) in China. His interest shifted to the Korean issue when he returned to Japan later that year. Tarui frequently visited the Korean refugee Kim Okkyun and communicated with Genyosha leaders about the Korea issue. See Tarui, DTGR, the first preface; Takeuchi Yoshimi, *Ajia shugi*, 33–34; and Chandra, "An Outline Study of the Ilchin-hoe of Korea," 50–51.

90. Tarui, DTGR, the second preface of the first edition, 7 and 189–91.

91. Ibid., 203.

92. Ibid., 126.

93. Ibid., 189–90; and Hatada Takashi, *Ilbonin ŭi Han'gukkwan*, 54–59.

94. Ch'oe Kiyŏng, *Han'guk kŭndae kyemong sasang yŏn'gu*, 232–38.

95. Weems, *Reform, Rebellion, and the Heavenly Way*, 54.

96. Ch'oe Kiyŏng, *Han'guk kŭndae kyemong sasang yŏn'gu*, 233.

97. Wŏn was the Korean monetary unit at the time. I quoted this record from Korean sources which did not indicate if the money was of Korean or Japanese origin. Since Son was in Japan in 1904, however, it is possible that the money was paid in yen. Ch'oe Kiyŏng and Pak Maengsin, eds., *Hanmal Ch'ŏndogyo charyojip*, "Pon'gyo yŏksa," 2: 274–75.

8

Subversive Narratives

Hwang Sunwŏn's P'yŏngan Stories

BRUCE FULTON

The subversive nature of several of Hwang Sunwŏn's (1915–2000) stories belies the conventional understanding of this major writer as a producer of pure literature and an author who was less engaged than his peers with contemporary social, political, and historical realities. By *subversive* I mean "tending to undermine or overturn established ideological or political structures." Nowhere is this subversive tendency more apparent than in the stories set in the author's native P'yŏngan Province. Far from avoiding historical and political issues, Hwang displays from his earliest stories a sophisticated grasp of contemporary Korean history, society, and culture. But, unwilling to compromise his craft even while foregrounding issues of contemporary importance, Hwang invested several of his most important stories with a subversive subtext that challenges traditional gender-role expectations, Korea's anomalous position as a colony, and post-Liberation Korea's status as an occupied land. I wish to examine six stories that incorporate such subtext in various ways. First, in stories such as "Nun" (1944, trans. "Snow" 2001) and "Nae kohyang saram tŭl" (1961, The People of My Ancestral Home),[1] which I term *kohyang* stories, Hwang uses the setting of his ancestral home (*kohyang*) as a basis for making veiled allusions to Japanese policies such as the grain requisition (*kongch'ul*) system. Second, in stories such as "Nosae" (1943, trans. "The Mule" 1998) and "Mongnŏmi maŭl ŭi kae" (1947, trans. "The Dog of Crossover Village" 2009) Hwang writes ostensibly about the difficulties of Koreans during the colonial and post-Liberation periods, respectively, but the narratives can be read—again, respectively—as allegories of a colonized land and subsequently a land occupied by outsiders; I term such stories *anti-colonial allegories*. Finally, Hwang populates seemingly apolitical stories such as

"Tume" (1952, trans. "A Backcountry Village" 1993) and "Pulgasari" (1955, trans. "Deathless" 2009) with characters who are memorable for their deception and their subversion of social mores; these stories I refer to as *stories of rebellious souls*. Taken collectively, these six stories reveal a writer who in his work was able to subvert the intellectual control apparatus of a colonial regime (by concealing his stories from public view at a time when publication in Korean was strongly discouraged), challenge the expectations of readers (a hidden first-person narrator surfaces at the end of "Mongnŏmi maŭl ŭi kae"), and undermine conventional Neo-Confucian values in, for example, his portrayal of a woman who connives in the murder of her husband, in "Tume," and in the account of a duplicitous salt-peddler and an eloping couple in "Pulgasari." What all of these stories have in common is their P'yŏngan setting. This is not to say that Hwang's stories set outside of P'yŏngan are devoid of subversive tendencies; rather, these tendencies are both more marked and more political in the P'yŏngan stories. My hypothesis is that the setting of these subversive narratives in the author's ancestral home province invests them with a legitimacy and authority deriving from the centuries of tradition and continuity associated with the concept of *kohyang* and with the distinctive social, political, economic, and class milieu of P'yŏngan Province in late Chosŏn. I argue also that the subversion and resistance that inform these stories are consistent with Hwang's background as a native of a province formerly at the center of Koryŏ society but subsequently marginalized by late Chosŏn times. That is to say, subversion and resistance are useful strategies for individuals and societies that find themselves outside the political or cultural center. And just as P'yŏngan was distinct from the center in its economic and religious practices, Hwang Sunwŏn can be said to have chosen a path distinct from the didactic inclinations of Korean literati past and present—a path that is posted throughout his career with subversive narratives.

HWANG'S P'YŎNGAN BACKGROUND

Hwang Sunwŏn was born March 26, 1915, in Taedong County, South P'yŏngan.[2] In 1921 his family moved to P'yŏngyang, "the center of northern (Korean) civilization," where he attended grammar school.[3] Hwang was the son of a schoolteacher and activist and an eighth-generation descendant of Hwang Sunsŭng, a man exemplified as a filial son during the reign of King

Yŏngjo.[4] Scholars and Hwang himself have taken noticeable interest in this eminent ancestor.[5] One of Hwang's most unusual stories, "Harabŏji ka innŭn tessang" (1959, "A Sketch of My Grandfather"), focuses on this man, whose brush name was Chibam but who was known familiarly as Kojip (meaning obstinate). In his uprightness this man seems to have been as unbending as his nickname suggests. In this story the author attempts to re-create the life and character of his illustrious ancestor, and in doing so he notes inconsistencies between the historical record and real life. It is tempting to conclude from this that Hwang was suggesting that real-life events may resist and subvert the intentions of those who compile historical records. In any event the selection of Kojip as the focus of the story is significant if we are to argue that the ancestor of this famously stubborn man produced narratives of resistance set in the Hwang family's native P'yŏngan.

HWANG AS A POLITICAL WRITER

In the ongoing debate in the Korean literary world between advocates of pure literature and advocates of a literature of social engagement, Hwang is usually relegated to the pure literature school.[6] And yet there is ample evidence in Hwang's life and works that he had a highly developed social and political consciousness. Hwang began his writing career at a time when Korean writers were being increasingly pressured by the Japanese, and Japanese sympathizers, to write and publish in Japanese. According to O Saenggŭn, appraisals of Hwang must start from the fact that Hwang continued to write in Korean while many of his contemporaries succumbed to the pressure to write in Japanese.[7] For Hwang it was a matter of principle to write in his native language. He recalls, for example, that when he sent Yi Kwangsu, a fellow P'yŏngan native and author of the work commonly considered to be the first modern Korean novel (Mujŏng [Heartless], 1917), a copy of his first story collection Yi replied in a letter that Hwang should rewrite it in Japanese and compose subsequent works in Japanese; to do so would be better for an unknown (mumyŏng) writer like Hwang.[8] Hwang refused this suggestion and continued to write in Korean even during the amhŭk sidae, the dismal final years of the colonial period, when it was difficult for Koreans to publish in their own language.[9]

That Hwang held steadfastly to his native language should not be surprising in view of the example set for him by his father, Hwang Ch'anyŏng, who was jailed for his role in the March First Independence movement. Hwang Sunwŏn's story "Abŏji" (1947, trans. "My Father" 2009) indicates that the son was sensitive to the importance of his father's political activism. Previously, in 1935, Hwang himself had been jailed for twenty-nine days because he would not submit his poetry collection *Pangga* (Wayward Songs) for the required inspection by the censors at the Japanese governor general's office.[10]

Upon Liberation, Hwang joined the P'yŏngyang yesul munhwa hyŏphoe (P'yŏngyang Association for Arts and Culture), the first literary arts organization to be established in the P'yŏngyang area after August 15.[11] The president of this group was Ch'oe Myŏngik (1903–46), a pioneer of socialist literature in the north and a writer who, from the late 1980s on, has attracted an unusual amount of scholarly attention in the Republic of Korea considering that only a dozen or so stories and half as many personal essays by him are available to us today.[12] The ideologically charged atmosphere of the immediate post-Liberation period was evident in a variety of organizations, among them literary and cultural groups and presumably the P'yŏngyang group of which Hwang was a member. Although Hwang much later in life would intimate anti-communist leanings—not surprising in view of his family's landed background, Christian faith, and their departure from their ancestral home in the north for a new life in the south—it is reasonable to suppose that his membership in 1945 in a cultural organization chaired by Ch'oe Myŏngik reflected at least a tolerance for socialist ideology.

Hwang's awareness of social and political realities is reflected not only in his own life but in his stories. Consider, in addition to the stories on which I focus in this essay, his 1943 story "Mul han mogŭm" (A Drink of Water). The story is set in late autumn amid capricious showery weather, suggesting the uncertainty of life during the late stages of the colonial period. This feeling of uncertainty is reinforced by an old woman's hesitancy to leave for the train station to catch the train to P'yŏngyang. She is bound for an address near a prison, which leads us to wonder if one of her family members is in jail. The mood of uncertainty is heightened by anomalies: Clear skies turn quickly to storm clouds; a Chinese man intimidates Koreans. The powerlessness of Koreans at this time is suggested by the illiteracy of older people in a shed. Modernity, on the other hand, is represented by a young man who can read and who wears a wristwatch, but his potential authority as a representative of progress is undercut by his difficulty in crossing a stream on a log bridge. In these subtle ways the author skillfully sketches the mood of a subjugated people.

Similar anti-colonial subtext appears in other Hwang stories as well. In "Ch'ŏngsan kari" (1948, Potassium Cyanide), for example, the vulnerability of chicks to weasels seems a veiled comment on Korea's susceptibility to foreign predation. The helplessness of colonial Korea is suggested by a character's hemiplegia in "Paeyŏk tŭl" (late 1930s, trans. "The Players" 2009). And the ending of "Iri to" (1948, trans. "Even Wolves" 1990), in which a Japanese hunter is devoured by wolves, is a not-so-subtle critique of militarism. It is tempting, furthermore, to interpret the subversions depicted in Hwang's earliest stories—those written in the 1930s—as a subtle critique of Korea's subordination to Japanese imperial rule. Just as motherhood and various other roles are subverted and twisted in "Samagwi" (late 1930s, trans. "Mantis" 2009) so is a people's collective sovereignty when they are occupied by a foreign power. This reading of Hwang in terms of colonial relationships is buttressed by the author's frequent portrayal of subverted gender roles, in which women display attributes traditionally associated with men, and vice versa. That is, females in Hwang's stories often represent civilization, knowledge, maturity, health, and common sense, and sometimes symbolize the excesses of those characteristics as well: artificiality, corruption, and cynicism. These characteristics are more commonly associated with men than with women. Males in Hwang's stories, on the other hand, are often associated with innocence, purity, frailty, powerlessness, timidity, and indecision—characteristics often associated with women.[13]

Let us see how these various subversive tendencies are manifested in six stories that in their setting and their use of P'yŏngan dialect are strongly associated with the author's home province.

KOHYANG STORIES

"Nun"

The difficulties that the Japanese, and as a consequence Koreans, faced toward the end of the Pacific War are hinted at in the beginning of this short piece. The somber mood of the story reflects the national mood in colonial Korea during the late stages of the Pacific War. The story takes place in the workroom of one of the homes in the narrator's ancestral village, a place where the village men gather nightly to talk and smoke. The men make their living from the land, and the concerns voiced in their conversation are ostensibly about the weather and its effects on crops. But just as importantly the men are concerned about the portion of the crop they must deliver to the authorities in accordance with the *kongch'ul* policy, and about the young men of the village who have been conscripted for labor in Japan under the *chingyong* policy (because this means less hands available for work in the fields). The story takes place in winter, and a heavy snowfall has just begun. One of the men, a native of Hamgyŏng, relates several anecdotes about the heavy snowfall for which that region is known. Heaviness is a central image in the story, reflected in the weighty atmosphere of the men's gathering and in the tales of a heavy snowpack, and is an unmistakable indicator of the onerous nature of the Japanese presence in Korea during the last years of the colonial period.

The Hamgyŏng man relates a brief account of the chance encounter of two snowbound men at an inn. One has been separated by the snow from his wife for the winter while the other was snowbound at the home of the very same woman. Here is an allegorical representation of Korea's status as a colony, the two men stranded by the winter storms symbolizing Koreans abandoned by Western powers and stranded beneath Japanese colonialism. But just as the wife survives a hard winter in the absence of her snowbound husband, Korea can survive quite handily without a colonial overlord.

Nun is a homonym meaning "eyes" as well as "snow." In its former sense it is an apt title in view of the narrator's role in this story, which is that of an observer, silently watching the gathering of the men. More ominously it reflects the awareness of Koreans, albeit oblique, to the omnipresent control apparatus of imperial Japan. On the other hand, *nun* as snow is perhaps as anomalous as the colonial experience itself—salutary in some ways (a good snowpack means plenty of water in spring and summer for the crops) and onerous in many others (numbing and dislocating).

"Nae kohyang saram tŭl"

This autobiographical story takes place in 1943–44 in Changt'ae-dong (or Hwang-ch'on), the common name for Hwang's home village of Pingjang-ni (as it is referred to in the Hwang clan register).[14] Like "Nun," it describes the privations of Koreans in the latter years of the Pacific War. Hwang, as the first-person narrator, deprecates himself as a "pale intellectual onlooker" and provides a detailed description of his own feelings of helplessness bordering on despair. He relates the cat-and-mouse game he plays with a resident Japanese official, who inquires after the author's health (the reason he has moved out of P'yŏngyang) and "borrows" a book of Hwang's written by a subversive Japanese and doesn't return it. This story is also associated with the well-known anecdote that Hwang secreted his three published books as well as his work in progress in a wall closet so that they would not bring upon Hwang or his family undue attention from any colonial officials who might happen to visit.

Hwang then quickly shifts attention away from himself and toward a man named Kim Kujang and the spareness of Kim's life. Kim lives by the law: he loans grain to destitute tenants as a means of adhering to the kongch'ul policy, and he arranges for his only son to become a student-soldier rather than trying to hide him from the draft (those trying to escape the draft face forced labor instead). In this scene Kim is hunting (out of season), having just lost his son on Yuhwang Island (near Kagoshima), which Hwang knew the Americans had bombed. The death notice informs Kim that the authorities will send him his son's fingernails and hair, instead of the usual post-cremation remains, which indicates to Hwang the urgency of the war effort. Hwang, as narrator, notices a razor nick on Kim's face, and realizes that Kim's "airtight" life has developed a chink.

Hwang in this story tells us almost as much through omission as he does through description—a method utilized by all accomplished writers for imparting information. Consider what we can infer from what Hwang does not tell us, rather than from what he does tell us. For example, there are Koreans who, unlike Kim Kujang, did not live according to imperial law. There are young Korean men of age who did not volunteer as student-soldiers for the imperial army. If otherwise law-abiding colonial subjects are hunting out of season, then perhaps Koreans are going hungry. There were Koreans who evaded the kongch'ul policy.

One might ask why Hwang in this story does not offer a more forthright critique of Japanese colonial policy. After all he composed it in 1961, long after the allegorical "Nosae," "Nun," and "Mongnŏmi maŭl ŭi kae," all of which were written during the arguably more dangerous political climate of the last years of the colonial period and the early years of the post-Liberation period. An answer to this question requires broad knowledge of Hwang's fictional world—a world in which political, ideological, aesthetic, and ethical issues were rarely outlined in black and white, but typically appeared in shades of gray. It is a world in which story and character take precedence over theme and issue. By titling the present story as he does, Hwang is asking us to consider a group of people, of whom Kim Kujang and the narrator are representatives. Each in his own way is a transgressor—Kim a poacher and the narrator an able-bodied male who has managed to avoid being drafted for labor or military service—and although the transgression is not on the scale of the subversive actions of the characters in the "rebellious souls" stories, if multiplied by the number of individuals who constitute "nae kohyang saram tŭl," then we see the potential for subversion on a large, potentially nation-wide scale and not just at the level of the individual.

ANTI-COLONIAL ALLEGORIES

"Nosae"

Like many stories of commoners in colonial Korea, "Nosae" has been interpreted as a reflection of the poverty-stricken lives of Koreans.[15] Such analysis is too narrow. From the central image of the mule as a beast of burden, to the conniving of two men who compete for its ownership, to a story-within-a-story about a horse that runs wild, there ranges in this story a subtext of subversion that in the context of Hwang's other P'yŏngan stories demands to be interpreted as a challenge to the status quo.

Mediating the negotiations between young Yu and the mule owner is an elderly man who professes embarrassment at the blandishments (tobacco and alcoholic beverages) of the two men, but who in fact takes pleasure in these treats. The calculating propensities of these three foreshadow the character of Lucky Nose in "Pulgasari," to be discussed shortly. Young Yu's purchase of the mule is made possible by the sale of his sister to a drinking house in P'yŏngyang. It is tempting to interpret this part of the story in light of the acquiescence of the Chosŏn officialdom in 1910, and of the international community five years earlier in the Treaty of Portsmouth at the conclusion of the Russo-Japanese War, in the selling out of Korea to the Japanese. But if Yu's young sister represents the lost motherland, and the mule, the Koreans, who assume the various burdens of life in the Great East Asia Co-prosperity Sphere, then it is equally evident that colonial Koreans are represented as far-from-docile subjects. For once the bargaining over its ownership is finally concluded, the mule ultimately proves a refractory animal and one that is worn down by harsh usage.

Reinforcing this analysis of the story is a short story-within-a-story of another beast of burden. Interjected in the part of the story where Yu begins to put his newly obtained mule to work is an account of a cart-horse that has escaped its master and run free, cart and all, until it breaks its legs and finally drops dead in downtown P'yŏngyang.

The story ends with young Yu and the other man fighting over the former's mistreatment of the mule. Here Hwang is echoing stories ranging back to Hyŏn Chin'gŏn's "Sul kwŏnhanŭn sahoe" (1921, trans. "A Society that Drives You to Drink" 1998); stories that implicitly deplore divisions among Koreans that weaken colonial Korea's attempts to empower itself.

This story, written late in the colonial period (1943), seems a not-so-subtle allegory of resistance. As such it must have reminded readers of the very end of the Chosŏn period, a time when the ŭibyŏng (righteous armies) resisted Japanese soldiers and patriotic Koreans committed suicide at the news of the signing of the annexation treaty in 1910.

"Mongnŏmi maŭl ŭi kae"

"Mongnŏmi maŭl ŭi kae" can be read on at least three levels. At first glance it would seem to be an account of village life colored by superstition and affected by population movements both within Korea and from Korea to Manchuria. A second reading would uncover an allegory of the Japanese occupation, with the dogs in the story representing Koreans, and the two brothers who serve as village headmen, the Japanese overlords. The dog Whitey, like the Koreans, ultimately survives after undergoing much persecution, her irrepressible life force representing the future of the Korean people.[16] Additional analysis of the story, though, leads us to ponder the meaning of the ostracization of Whitey and the role of Pak Ch'osi at the feast of the two brothers' slaughtered dogs.

Whitey appears one day in Mongnŏmi Village,[17] apparently having strayed or been abandoned by one of the many travelers who pass through this bottleneck settlement. Whitey's arrival immediately causes problems in the village. She is starving and constantly scavenging for food; she consorts with the village headmen's dogs; and she is an outsider, and one that lacks a master. The village headmen react by stigmatizing Whitey as rabid, attempting to capture and kill her, and slaughtering their own dogs when it becomes apparent that the animals are keeping company with Whitey and thus are presumably contaminated by her. It is tempting to link this scapegoating of Whitey with the outcast motif that appears in the stories of Hwang's *Irŏbŏrin saram tŭl* (1958, trans. *Lost Souls* 2009) collection.[18] But whereas outcast status in those stories is the result of societal transgression, here it seems to be applied to Whitey primarily because she is an outsider. Whitey's color is also significant in this respect. White is a symbol of Koreans, the "white-clothed people," but it is also the skin color of those who in 1947 were exercising a military occupation of South Korea. This story, then, might be read as a narrative of resistance not only towards the Japanese imperialists but also to the 1945–48 American military government of what would become the Republic of Korea.

The feast of dog meat hosted by the two village headman is equally significant in terms of its political subtext. It would be difficult to improve upon Hyuk-Chan Kwon's analysis of this scene, and I quote from him at length:

> Whitey is chased and persecuted by all the village residents, who are easily influenced and manipulated by the propaganda-like argument of the headmen. The village is organized like a totalitarian state; Blackie and Spotty (the headmen's dogs) are stigmatized as mad dogs and butchered just because they warmly accepted Whitey. Likewise, Kannan's grandfather, the only villager who does not believe in the headmen's stigmatization of Whitey, is publicly ostracized by the headmen, which reminds readers of how traitors and collaborators are punished in a totalitarian society. Village people connive in the wrongful accusation and slaughter of the two dogs to grasp a rare chance for meat. As an illegitimate tyrant would often try to buy political support by dispensing patronage to people of rank and intellectuals, the headmen invite the headman of the neighboring village as well as Pak Ch'osi, the only intellectual appearing in the story, to the dinner of dog meat. Pak, unlike the three village headmen, does not feel comfortable attending this bloody banquet, apparently seeing himself as an accomplice to the unnecessary slaughter of the dogs. Pak is a satirical figure who illuminates the short-

comings of timid intellectuals in times of political turmoil: his self-esteem
... prevents him from cooling off on a hot day by removing his jacket, and
from engaging in singing, and yet he dares not offend the others and instead
simply maintains a sweaty silence.[19]

Scrupulously evenhanded in the ideological subtext of his narrative,
Hwang, in this story, is implicitly commenting on the abuse of power in a
variety of forms—colonization, military occupation, totalitarianism—each of
which he had direct experience with. Moreover—and this is perhaps the most
salient point of Kwon's analysis—he is implicitly criticizing those, such as
Pak Ch'osi, whose silence enables this abuse.

Seen in this way, "Mongnŏmi maŭl ŭi kae" would seem to have been a provocative story, even in the freewheeling years of the *haebang konggan* (post-
Liberation "space"), with its welter of political and ideological activity. Was the
author heedless of how this story might have been interpreted in the increasingly right-wing, anti-Communist climate of South Korea? Herein may lie one
answer to a question that continues to exercise Western readers of Hwang: Why
the profusion of embedded narratives in his stories, and especially the emergence in a few stories, as here, of a first- person narrator in an ostensibly third-
person narrative?[20] In "Mongnŏmi maŭl ŭi kae" a first-person narrator of
middle-school age emerges at the very end of the story to relate that the events
of the story were told to him by Kannan's Grandfather. What purpose could this
narrative device serve other than to distance the author from the political subtext of the narrative? In Hyuk-Chan Kwon's words, Hwang has elected to divulge
the political subtext of this work only to those with "discerning eyes."[21]

STORIES OF REBELLIOUS SOULS

"Tume"

"Tume" is one of Hwang's more unusual stories, an account of sexual intrigue
and murder that echoes both Western-style mysteries and premodern accounts
of Chinese magistrates at work on similarly lurid cases. The setting of the
story is worthy of note. *Tume* means "hinterlands," or colloquially "the boon-
docks," or "the sticks." This setting in the remote countryside is outside the
watchful eye of the Japanese. The nearest constable is in the town over the hill,

which is given access by the aptly named Tiger Pass. The characters in the story make and sell charcoal for a living. They call one another "soot devils," referring to the omnipresent soot resulting from the burning of wood for charcoal and from the charcoal itself. It is tempting to see these black-complexioned people as the opposite of traditional Koreans, "the people in white clothing"— that is, as examples of a people degraded by colonial occupation.

The subversive nature of this story is immediately apparent. The young wife of a forty-year-old charcoal maker, nicknamed Old Beanpole, becomes enamored of a visiting hunter from P'yŏngyang. On her husband's fortieth birthday she slaughters their only chicken—a rooster, appropriately enough— then murders her husband, and finally sets out with the hunter for P'yŏngyang, only to lose her way in a snowstorm and return home alone.

Also significant is the cause of death of the murdered man. It is finally discovered that a nail has been driven through the crown of his skull and then removed, the fatal wound concealed by the victim's hair.[22] If subversion is more effective the more invisible its means, then this particular transgression is effective indeed—at least initially.

The story contains a second subterfuge, one that leads to the exposure of the wife's crime. Learning of the death of Old Beanpole, a childhood friend from a neighboring village journeys through the same snowstorm that trapped the couple, only to collapse at night at the entrance to Old Beanpole's home. He is discovered by the men keeping vigil over Old Beanpole, and is assumed to be dead and is brought inside. Late at night, and while the constable is en route to investigate this second death, the "corpse" awakens from his coma and slips out unnoticed. When the men keeping vigil discover that the body has vanished, they substitute Old Beanpole's body in desperation. It is during the constable's examination of Old Beanpole that the fatal nail puncture in Old Beanpole is discovered. The wife is confronted and immediately confesses.

Here is a story in which things are not as they seem: "the white-clothed people" become black "soot devils," a man dies violently on the date of his birth, a woman seeks the life force of a man whose pastime is to deal death to living creatures, a man presumed dead comes back to life, and a blizzard blurs the landscape until all sense of direction is lost, paralleling the loss of the woman's moral compass. There is little political subtext in "Tume," but subversion and transgression abound.

"Pulgasari"

The title of this story is a dialect variant of *pulgasaŭi*, which has at least two meanings: (1) a mythical creature that has come to symbolize indestructibility; and (2) something mystical and inscrutable. What is indestructible or inscrutable in this story? There are at least three possibilities. The first is Komi and Koptani's desire for each other, which leads them to elope at the end of the story. Elopement is an act of resistance against societal conventions such as marriages arranged by parents and elders. The second possibility is the calculating personality of Lucky Nose. In the context of subversion and resistance narratives, a character's proclivity for deception and self-aggrandizement may be viewed as a kind of survival skill. A related possibility is that the will of Koreans to survive foreign depredations is indestructible.

There is ample evidence in Hwang's stories to support an argument that Hwang in "Pulgasari" is challenging the convention of arranged marriages.[23] On the other hand Hwang, ever the creator of open-ended narratives and never the provider of neat solutions, offers in other stories of the collection, *Irŏbŏrin saram tŭl*, in which "Pulgasari" appears, harrowing accounts of the potential consequences of transgressing social mores.[24] In this story, as in "Tume," subterfuge is the pivot about which transgression revolves. For one thing, Lucky Nose seeks a wife in the person of Koptani, a consequence of his having sold his previous wife, who like Koptani was an innocent back-country girl, into a house of prostitution in P'yŏngyang—unbeknownst to the unfortunate girl's mother, who remains a salt customer of Lucky Nose. But in an ironic twist, Lucky Nose's underhanded attempt to intimidate Koptani into accepting a marriage proposal—he must use intimidation because he is twice the age of his would-be bride—and his subsequent attempt to thwart Komi's plan to elope with Koptani, leads to his own failure and humiliation. In this sense, "Pulgasari" involves a double subversion.

As to the possibility of interpreting calculation as a survival skill, it is significant that Lucky Nose is a peddler of salt. Salt is a subsistence item, one that not only imparts flavor to food but is also a necessary ingredient in some foods as well as a preservative agent. The salt that Lucky Nose peddles is a scarce and much-desired commodity in the remote regions of P'yŏngan. Thus Lucky Nose's ability to survive, and perhaps thrive, is made possible by an ingredient that is perhaps valued as much as money. That Lucky Nose seems to have been thwarted by Komi and Koptani at the end of the story is not to negate the importance of his own survival instincts but is rather an indication that they are subordinate to the indestructibility of the couple's desire to break free of societal restraints. Moreover, if we think of survival instincts as existing on a societal as well as an individual level, then we might argue that they are vital to the inhabitants of an occupied land. Understood in such terms, "Pulgasari" is no less subversive than the stories previously discussed.

CONCLUSION

Recent research has portrayed Hwang Sunwŏn's home province of P'yŏngan as a stronghold of political nonconformists and a place that by late Chosŏn had achieved a degree of economic freedom unrivaled by other provinces.[25] It was also a province in which Christian nationalism prevailed by the time of annexation by Japan.[26] Already by then, and consistent with the tenets of Christianity, there was in P'yŏngan a strong sense of community, one that further strengthened that province's regional identity. Hwang Sunwŏn was a third-generation Christian—albeit in a family renowned in the P'yŏngyang area as a Neo-Confucian yangban descent group—and the son of a patriot imprisoned for his role in the March First Independence movement.[27] It was in this sociocultural milieu—a region marked by an unusual degree of political, economic, and spiritual independence, and a family distinguished by political activism and Christian beliefs—that Hwang began to shape his artistic world-view. As a writer of fiction he was first and foremost a storyteller, and in virtually none of his fictional works does he subordinate story, character, and craft to history, incident, or ideology. The variety of his stories, moreover, defies easy categorization.[28] And yet there is ample evidence in his 100-plus published stories that Hwang did not shy away from commentary on contemporary issues, whether cultural, social, political, or historical. Taken together, his P'yŏngan stories reveal a sensitivity to the realities of life in an occupied land and a proclivity to resist and subvert those realities. The tools he used to this end were the ones traditionally and necessarily used by dissident writers: image, symbol, and allegory.

Studies of subversion in literature have tended to focus on the transgressive nature of subversive narratives.[29] That is, whereas subversion may be understood in the more general sense of opposition to established power and ideological structures, transgression involves a crossing of boundaries, a breaking of limits, and by extension an infringement or violation of laws or moral codes. I have written elsewhere of transgression in Hwang Sunwŏn's story collection Irŏbŏrin saram tŭl,[30] and we can see in the subversive narratives analyzed in the present essay several examples of transgression. The significance of subversion and transgression in literature, however, is not limited to an author's use of these devices in his or her works. Rather, as Keith Booker reminds us, "in cases of literary transgression, much of the transgressive energy must come from the reader."[31] Here is where we see the most potentially important aspect of Hwang's subversive narratives, and at the same time some of the strongest evidence that Hwang can be legitimately read as an engaged and politically sophisticated writer. That is, to the discerning reader, Hwang's subversive narratives may represent a call to action, an attempt to increase our awareness of the capacity of literary artists in an occupied land to resist colonial hegemony, to challenge ossified socio-cultural norms, and to confront ideological tyranny.

It should be emphasized that writers from areas other than the northern provinces have written subversive, even revisionist, fictional narratives. One need only mention such authors as Yi Ch'ŏngjun, Im Ch'ŏru, and Cho Chŏng-nae from Chŏlla, Cho Sŏnggi from Kyŏngsang, and the most subversive of modern Korean writers, Yi Sang, from Seoul. And although there is always risk in attempting to understand a writer's work on the basis of his or her life, it is instructive in the case of Hwang Sunwŏn to know that it is no easier to categorize Hwang, the individual, than it is to categorize his fictional works. While Hwang's reputation in literary circles as a "humanist" writer might accurately describe the man himself, he was politically conservative.[32] Although he received a university education in Japan, he was reluctant to speak Japanese. On the other hand, his coffee table at home always bore a recent issue of a Japanese literary journal. Although his autobiographical story "Abŏji," mentioned earlier, speaks in glowing terms of his activist father, another story that may be autobiographical, "P'ungsok" (1936, trans. "Custom" 2009), features a young male protagonist who has a conflicted relationship both with his wife and with his father. Hwang was at once a gracious man and, where literary critics were concerned, a prickly man.[33] He was both Christian and yet cognizant that Christians can be as hypocritical as non-Christians. The point here is that both Hwang, the individual, and his fictional oeuvre seem as elusive of mainstream status as his home province of

P'yŏngan. In the same way that P'yŏngan exists both on the geographic frontier of the Korean peninsula and perhaps on the margins of Neo-Confucian
late-Chosŏn Korea, Hwang Sunwŏn has, in spite of his acknowledged prow-
ess as a short-story writer, tended to be marginalized by the Korean literature
establishment, which until very recently has privileged those writers who
display "historical consciousness" and a sensitivity to contemporary socio-
political issues. And just as the northern regions of Korea are subject to
increasing research that seeks to broaden our understanding of their role in
the transition of Korea from a traditional to a modern society, future scholarship on Hwang can be expected to situate his fictional oeuvre in a more
central place in modern Korean literary history.

The six stories I have focused on here are not the only stories that reveal
Hwang Sunwŏn's P'yŏngan roots. Approximately 10 percent of his short sto-
ries are autobiographical to some extent and several of these are set in
P'yŏngan. Hwang took pride and pleasure in his P'yŏngan stories, autobiographical or not.[34] Four of the six stories analyzed here were written after
Hwang and his family migrated to southern Korea in 1946—clear evidence that
Hwang continued to take inspiration from his ancestral province. Analysis of
Hwang's later stories, particularly those in the under-researched *Nŏ wa na man
ŭi sigan* (1964, Time for You and Me Alone) and *T'al* (1976, Masks) collections
will reinforce Hwang's significance as a frontier province writer who throughout his career produced narratives of resistance and subversion.

NOTES

1. The first date in parentheses is the year in which Hwang composed the story; for
the year of first publication see the bibliography.

2. For details of Hwang's life in P'yŏngan, see Song Hyŏnho, *Hwang Sunwŏn: Sŏnbi
chŏngsin kwa in'gan kuwŏn ŭi kil*, 20–40; Kim Chonghoe, "Munhak ŭi sunsusŏng kwa
wan'gyŏlsŏng, ttonŭn munhakchŏk sam ŭi k'ŭn mobŏm"; and Kim Tongsŏn, "Hwang
Kojip ŭi mihak, Hwang Sunwŏn kamun." For a chronology of the author's life, current
to 1992, see *Hwang Sunwŏn chŏnjip*, 344–59.

3. Kim Chonghoe, "Munhak ŭi sunsusŏng kwa wan'gyŏlsŏng," 18. In this cradle of
culture, Hwang learned to ice skate and play soccer and took violin lessons. Among his
grammar school classmates was a boy destined to become one of modern Korea's most
distinctive painters, Yi Chungsŏp. Ibid., 20.

4. Song Hyŏnho, *Hwang Sunwŏn*, 20.

5. See Kim Tongsŏn, "Hwang Kojip ŭi mihak," 266–70. Hwang Sunsŭng is mentioned in O Such'ang, *Chosŏn hugi P'yŏngan-do sahoe palchŏn yŏn'gu*, 61 and 198. I am indebted to Sun Joo Kim for bringing to my attention an additional source on Hwang Sunsŭng in *P'yŏngyang sokchi*, 117. See also Chapter 4 where he is referred to as Obstinate Hwang.

6. See, for example, Kim Chonghoe, "Munhak ŭi sunsusŏng kwa wan'gyŏlsŏng"; and Kim Pyŏngik, "Sunsu munhak kwa kŭ yŏksasŏng."

7. O Saenggŭn, "Chŏnbanjŏk kŏmt'o," 11. See also Kim Tongsŏn, "Hwang Kojip ŭi mihak," 272–74.

8. Hwang Sunwŏn, interview by the author, May 20, 1997. Hwang no longer has this letter, having left it in his ancestral home when he migrated to present-day South Korea with his family in 1946.

9. Hwang managed to publish two stories during this time—"Pyŏl" (1941, Stars) and "Kŭnŭl" (1942, Grandfather's Shadow).

10. Kim Chonghoe, "Munhak ŭi sunsusŏng kwa wan'gyŏlsŏng," 22.

11. Kwŏn Yŏngmin, *Haebang chikhu ŭi minjok munhak undong yŏn'gu*, 30.

12. On Ch'oe Myŏngik, see Yi Tongha, "Ch'oe Myŏngik: Segye ŭi p'ongnyŏk kwa chishigin ŭi sooe"; Bruce Fulton, "The *Wŏlbuk* Writers"; and Sin Hyŏnggi and O Sŏngho, *Pukhan munhak sa*, 92, 95, 96, and 205.

13. For examples of stories featuring strong female characters and weak or irresolute male characters see "Sanai" (1954, trans. "A Man" 2003), "Pibari" (1956, trans. "Pibari" 2009), and the 1954 novel, *K'ain ŭi huye* (trans. *The Descendants of Cain* 1997). Among the most precocious of Hwang's female characters is the girl in "Sonagi" (1954, trans. "The Cloudburst" 1980), his best-known story.

14. Hwang Sunwŏn, interview by the author, May 26, 1998.

15. See, for example, Chang Hyŏnsuk, "Hwang Sunwŏn, 'Minjok hyŏnsil kwa isang kwa ŭi koeri'"; Chang Hyŏnsuk, *Hwang Sunwŏn munhak yŏn'gu*, 64 and 75–77; and Song Hyŏnho, *Hwang Sunwŏn*, 60.

16. See, for example, Chang Hyŏnsuk, *Hwang Sunwŏn yŏn'gu*, 136–37.

17. Mongnŏmi Village was an actual locale, where Hwang's wife's family lived and where Hwang spent summer vacations after his family moved to P'yŏngyang. Hwang Sunwŏn, interviews by the author, March 26, 1997; April 3, 1997; and May 12, 1998.

18. Bruce Fulton, "Hwang Sunwŏn tanp'yŏn sosŏl yŏn'gu," 62–73.

19. Hyuk-Chan Kwon, "Hwang Sunwŏn as a Political Writer," 6–7.

20. See, for example, Stephen Epstein, "Elusive Narrators in Hwang Sunwŏn," 104–11.

21. Hyuk-Chan Kwon, 9. Judging from the activism of the students described in Hwang's story "Abŏji," mentioned earlier, one might also argue that Hwang, in using a middle-school-aged boy as an embedded narrator, wished to speak directly to middle-school readers. My thanks to Tracy Stober for suggesting this interpretation.

22. This means of murder was known in premodern China. See, for example, Robert van Gulik, *The Chinese Nail Murders*. Van Gulik wrote several mysteries based on a historical magistrate of the Tang period. In terms of subversion of traditional gender roles, it is significant that the perpetrator of murder in *The Chinese Nail Murders* is a woman, as is the case in "Tume."

23. See Heinz Insu Fenkl, "Buried in a Stained Sweater: The Politics of Misogyny in Hwang Sunwŏn's 'Sonagi'," 18-19.

24. Fulton, "Hwang Sunwŏn tanp'yŏn sosŏl yŏn'gu," 62–73.

25. O Such'ang, *Chosŏn hugi P'yŏngan-do sahoe palchŏn yŏn'gu*, 99–108, 135–50, and 205–209.

26. Chang Kyusik, *Ilcheha Han'guk kidokkyo minjokchuŭi yŏn'gu*, 29–41. Among other issues Chang in this work discusses why northerners were more receptive than other Koreans to Christianity.

27. I thank Sun Joo Kim for reminding me that Hwang's family history might itself be regarded as subversive. It is tempting to see in P'yŏngan's status as a frontier region, one less resistant to outside cultural influences, at least a partial explanation for the apparent anomaly of a well-known yangban family adopting a Western religion whose tenets are in many ways antithetical to Neo-Confucian orthodoxy. See Chang Kyusik, *Ilcheha Han'guk kidokkyo minjokchuŭi yŏn'gu*, 29–41.

28. Much to the dismay of translators eager to grasp the "meaning" of his works; scholars who wish to compartmentalize him as a writer of pure literature or as a practitioner of lyricism, romanticism, or aestheticism; and critics who challenge the logic of his fictional world. For an example of the latter, see Bruce Fulton, "Analysis of a Debate: Kim Yunsik, Hwang Sunwŏn, and 'Hak'." Hwang was a proud man who did not tolerate what he considered to be editorial or critical negligence in reviews of his works. Among the sources used for this essay we may note that Kim Chonghoe miswrites Hwang's 1974 story "Majimak chan" as "Majimak kil," in Kim Chonghoe, "Munhak ŭi sunsusŏng kwa wan'gyŏlsŏng," 24; and Kim Tongsŏn misspells "Haraboji ka innŭn tessang" as ". . .tesaeng," Kim Tongsŏn, "Hwang Kojip ŭi mihak," 268.

29. See, for example, Keith Booker, *Techniques of Subversion in Modern Literature*, 1–19; and Peter Stallybrass and Allon White, *The Politics and Poetics of Transgression*.

30. Fulton, "Hwang Sunwŏn tanp'yŏn sosŏl yŏn'gu," 62–73.

31. Booker, *Techniques of Subversion in Modern Literature*, 15.

32. Before the 1996 presidential elections Hwang confided that he and his wife feared that Bill Clinton was "soft" on North Korea; Hwang Sunwŏn, interview by the author, October 28, 1996.

33. See Fulton "Analysis of a Debate."

34. This became evident to me during my meetings with the author in the course of my dissertation research, and especially during the interview of May 26, 1999.

9

The Missionary Presence
in Northern Korea before WWII:

Human Investment, Social Significance, and Historical Legacy

DONALD N. CLARK

The prevalence of Christianity in Korea, going back to the early twentieth century when the country was becoming known as a comparatively successful Christian mission field, is a much-discussed phenomenon. Today, Christianity has been established as a Korean religion, having adapted to the country's spiritual environment. Although estimates vary, the percentage of Protestant and Catholic Christians in South Korea is at least 25 percent of the population.

In North Korea, though the state tolerates carefully controlled religious organizations, the number of Christians is unknown but assumed to be just a small fraction of what it once was. Before World War II, the northern part of Korea, especially the western provinces of P'yŏngan and Hwanghae, was the heartland of Korean Christianity, with numbers far greater than any other part of the country. The history of Korean Christianity points to the northern region as the area of greatest gain for early missionaries. During World War II there was considerable attrition. During the early years of the Kim Il Sung regime, the government discouraged Christianity and then suppressed it during the Korean War. Many Christians from the northern regions moved south during that time, reestablished their churches, and invigorated the southern church. Their presence and fervor had much to do with the shape and growth of Christianity in South Korea during the period from 1960 to 1990.

The strong presence of Christianity and the number of Christians in northern Korea before 1945 is a remarkable feature of modern Korean history. The question is obvious: What was it about the northern regions, particularly the northwest that made people there so receptive to Christianity? The commonest answers have to do with the relative openness and social fluidity of the region and draw on: (1) the geography of the northwest acting as a corridor for communication between Korea and Manchuria, Liaodong, and China proper and as an area for the positioning of military personnel in connection with border defense; (2) the commercial traffic through the corridor and the high level of merchant activity on both sides of the Sino-Korean border crossing making for a certain tolerance for diversity; (3) the difficulty of agriculture in much of the region above the coastal plain, the small size of farms, and the corollary reliance on economic activity other than agriculture, namely mining, lumbering, handcrafting, and trading; (4) the isolation of the northwest from the political center of Korea in Seoul; and together with this (5) a simmering sense of discrimination borne out by the inability of northern literati, despite rapidly rising rates of examination passage, to gain significant membership among the nation's aristocratic elite.[1] At the turn of the twentieth century, the Sino-Japanese War (1894–1895), the Russo-Japanese War (1904–1905), and the construction of the railroad that connected Seoul with Sinŭiju contributed even more to the social and economic climate that was ripe for change.

In the 1890s, northwestern Korea "opened" for missionary work and teams of American Presbyterians and Methodists founded "stations," first in P'yŏngyang and then in Sŏnch'ŏn, Yŏngbyŏn, Chaeryŏng, Haeju, and Kaesŏng (Songdo). Between 1905 and 1909, the main Protestant missions, seeking to avoid duplication of effort, assigned themselves various territories on the Korean peninsula within which to concentrate their work. The northeast coast north of Wŏnsan went to the Canadian Presbyterians, with the Southern Methodists getting Kangwŏn and all of Kyŏnggi north of Seoul. The Northern Methodists and Northern Presbyterians shared Hwanghae Province and South P'yŏngan up to the city of P'yŏngyang, and the remainder of the northwest was assigned to the Northern Presbyterians as far as the Chinese border.[2] In these territories, the missionaries worked to spread Christianity through the typical "triad" of evangelism, education, and medical work. A good example of the "triad" at work was the Canadian Presbyterian Mission in the Hamgyŏng provinces, where it established in each of its stations—Wŏnsan, Hamhŭng, Sŏngjin, Hoeryŏng, and Lungchingtsun (K. Yongjŏng) in Manchuria—a church, at least one school, and a clinic or hospital. The American Northern Presbyterians did likewise in locations like Sŏnch'ŏn. P'yŏngyang, naturally, was a special case, with multiple schools and institutions alongside major churches, the country's one Presbyterian seminary, and schools at several levels for boys, girls, and adults. In P'yŏngyang, the Christian Hospital, a major institution, was the "union" effort of the Presbyterians and Methodists.

These installations were significant in northern Korea, both visually and culturally. Thousands of people pursued their curiosity about these institutions and responded to the opportunities presented by the missionary "triad." Indeed, while hearing of the resistance presented to their colleagues in other areas of the country, the missionaries in P'yŏngyang and environs were amazed and gratified by their region's enthusiastic response. Elaborating on the reasons for this phenomenon in the region where he grew up, Paek Nakchun (L. George Paik, 1895–1985), later president of Yonsei University, wrote:

> The common people in northern Korea are comparatively free from stubborn conservatism. They have been hard workers, fighting against the mountainous environment in which they till the ground. Not many of the northerners held high offices in the government, but were rather subject to the oppression and extortion of the officials sent from Seoul. Their social customs were also somewhat different from those of the capital. There were no strict class distinctions, as in Seoul and the southern provinces, neither was there rigid separation of the sexes—a custom that was typical of the more conservative areas of the country. People espoused Confucian social norms but these were less formal, and less religious, than in southern Korea. In spiritual matters, Shamanism was the prevailing belief. When the country was opened to the West, the energetic people of the north soon caught the spirit of the times. Thus the character of the people, the political vicissitudes, the social background, and the religious conditions, made possible the success of Christianity in the north.[3]

In his study of class and status at the turn of the twentieth century, Kyung Moon Hwang paints a similar picture, noting that the region was primed to embrace new ideas and institutions such as mass education, capitalism, and inclusive religion:

> Through their cultivation of the Korean vernacular, their construction of churches and schools, and their unshakable aura of progress, missionaries

offered an inviting ideological and ethical alternative to the Korean masses. Intellectuals and other social elites came to equate Protestantism with Western advances, and many of them adopted the religion as a springboard for their participation in the growing educational efforts spreading around the country. To what extent their newfound faith informed their activities remains debatable, but clearly the history of Korean nationalism, in particular, would fall short if it failed to account for the overwhelming presence of Protestants among the prominent figures.[4]

THE DEVELOPMENT OF P'YŎNGYANG AS A MISSIONARY STATION

The city of P'yŏngyang sits on a majestic S-curve in the course of the Taedong River as it makes its way southwestward to the Yellow Sea. In traditional times, P'yŏngyang was a seaport, though the tides made the passage up from Namp'o (then called Chinnamp'o) dangerous to larger craft. In 1866, this fact led to the death of the missionary Robert Thomas and many other Westerners aboard the American ship *General Sherman*, who violated Korean instructions and attempted to travel up the river as far as P'yŏngyang in an effort to open trade and missionary work. The burning of the *Sherman* is remembered in the Democratic People's Republic of Korea (DPRK) with a monument to the "heroic" victory over the American "pirate ship." Cannons and other ship paraphernalia are on display in the Korean Revolution Museum and the Korean Central History Museum.

Modern P'yŏngyang sprawls in all directions, but in the 1890s it was a muddy provincial town surrounded by walls on a boat-shaped piece of land defined on the east by the Taedong River and on the west by the smaller Pot'ong-gang Stream. Early Western visitors described the city itself as unworthy of its superb natural surroundings. The British writer Isabella Bird Bishop, described P'yŏngyang in 1896, just after the Sino-Japanese War, as follows:

> ... a prosperous city of 80,000 inhabitants reduced to decay and 15,000—four-fifths of its houses destroyed, streets and alleys choked with ruins, hill slopes and vales once thick with Korean crowded homesteads, covered with gaunt hideous remains—fragments of broken walls, *kang* floors, *kang* chimneys, indefinite heaps in which roofs and walls lay in unpicturesque confusion— and still worse, roofs and walls standing, but doors and windows all gone,

suggesting the horror of human faces with their eyes put out. Everywhere there were the same scenes, miles of them, and very much of the desolation was charred and blackened, shapeless, hideous, hopeless, under the mocking sunlight.[5]

It was in this unpromising environment that the Presbyterian pioneer missionary Samuel A. Moffett, started a mission that was to become the center of Christianity in prewar Korea. The story of P'yŏngyang as a missionary station began in 1890, when Moffett paid a two-week visit there to investigate the possibilities.[6] The following spring, Moffett and his colleague, James Scarth Gale, visited P'yŏngyang again while on a three-month exploratory journey by foot and horseback.[7] "We spent two weeks among the mountains of China and North Korea," wrote Moffett, finding the region sparsely settled, poor, and so nearly destitute of food that, he continued, "We have given it the name of Starvation Camp as we lived on boiled oats and millet most of that time."[8]

The Moffett-Gale trek through the north quickly entered Korea missionary lore as a kind of legend. From February to April 1891, Moffett and Gale, accompanied by the early convert Sŏ Sangyun, explored the Korean north, held meetings where Sŏ spoke, and cultivated local officials wherever possible in hopes of furthering mission work. They practiced their language skills constantly, made contact with the Scottish missionaries in southern Manchuria, and returned via mountain roads across the peninsula to Hamhŭng and Wŏnsan before returning to Seoul. The fact that they survived the trip at all was remarkable in itself.

However, on their journey Moffett and Gale saw signs that the area might be open to Christianity. On Moffett's earlier trip to P'yŏngyang in 1890, he had found a handful of Methodists and Catholics, and only six actual and potential members of his own Presbyterian denomination, all influenced by protégés of John Ross, the Scottish Presbyterian missionary in "Moukden," or Shenyang, in Manchuria.[9] The government officials and many ordinary people were still "suspicious of foreigners and afraid of Christian books"[10] because the government had recently lifted the prohibition against Christianity. But by the time of his second visit in 1891, when Moffett and James Scarth Gale began their exploratory trek together through northern Korea, the number of Presbyterians had grown spontaneously to thirty, comprised of various social classes. Moffett wrote in more optimistic tones, "The people here are not afraid of the gospel as they are so near China that they have heard of it for 20 years.... A number of the lower officials here are professing Christians and also a number of merchants so that all classes are favorably disposed."[11]

The Northern Presbyterian Mission assigned Samuel Moffett to P'yŏngyang as a full-time missionary in November 1893.[12] The project had a rocky beginning marked by occasional death threats and opposition by officials. He wrote, "The opposition of the governor most probably arose from two causes: first, the interference of a petty official, one of his personal attendants, who was enraged because the Methodist helper refused to buy his house at a high price; and second, the fact that the governor is a rabid Confucianist, ready to prevent us from getting even a clean and respectful place to stay in while in the city."[13] But Moffett managed to buy some property and founded a resident missionary station by January 1895. Over time he added parcels to the original purchase as they came up for sale, and eventually he accumulated more than 120 acres of contiguous land. There, beginning with the Union Christian College (Sungsil College) and the Presbyterian Theological Seminary, and with the help of a number of Protestant pioneer missionaries and their Korean language teachers and assistants, he created a cluster of schools, training institutes, adult education centers, clinics, and even a school for foreign children. From other parts of the city these institutions appeared to be a ridgeline of modern buildings which by all accounts represented a proud display of progress to the citizens of P'yŏngyang. In 1905, Easurk Emsen Charr (Ch'a Ŭisŏk, 1895–1986), whose family members were among the earliest converts to Christianity, emigrated to the United States at the age of ten. He later recalled a childhood visit to the missionary compound ("yangwan" or "barbarian village") as follows:

Pointing at the opposite hillside, my uncle said, "Ah, there's the Yanggwan! Do you see those big beautiful houses over there with glass windows dazzling in the morning sun?" Yes, we saw them. They were in full view now as we were getting closer to those elegant looking big houses located far apart, some on the lower level, some on the top of the hill.... Although we did not see any missionaries, we saw their homes, and we all agreed that they were like fairyland palaces looking so grand and elegant, peacefully quiet and comfortable, except that they looked too cold in winter from the winds on the hilltop and too hot in the summer because it was close to the sun, I thought.[14]

Table 9.1 Korean Christian Mission Statistics (As of June 30, 1908)

	Seoul	Ch'ŏngju	Taegu	Pusan
Churches (Self-supporting)	111	38	105	73
Members	5,820	1,500	7,871	3,370
Children in Presbyterian schools	993	60	939	272
Contributions (US$)	$7,906	$434	$3,648	$1,682

STATISTICAL SNAPSHOT FOR 1908

The enthusiastic response of northwest Koreans to the Christian message was clear from statistics marking the first fifteen years of missionary work that were published in 1908 in the *Korea Mission Field*, a prewar monthly magazine that is an invaluable source for Korean Christian history.[15] The numbers are for the largest and most active denomination, the Presbyterians, reported by Northern Presbyterian mission stations across the country.

These simple numbers point to several significant features of Christian propagation in Korea. It is important to note that all four measures reflect the efforts of Korean Christians as well as missionaries. The relative prevalence of Christianity in northern Korea is indicated not only by numbers of churches and members but also by the members' enrolling their children in Christian schools and depositing dramatically more money in the offering plate. P'yongyang and Sŏnch'ŏn led the nation, with Chaeryŏng in Hwanghae Province not far behind. Kanggye, located in the difficult territory near the Manchurian border, was a poorer area and a tougher mission station throughout its history—and the statistics show it. Similarly, the Canadian mission across the mountains, along the coastal strip between Wŏnsan and the Tumen River, did not report the same kind of success. The statistics point us back to the idea that the roadway to China and the social, agricultural, and commercial characteristics of the northwest helped make the northern area the country's most fertile field for Christianity.

Table 9.1 Continued

	P'yŏngyang	Sŏnch'ŏn	Kanggye	Chaeryŏng
Churches (Self-supporting)	201	108	21	140
Members	22,298	17,996	2,096	12,893
Children in Presbyterian schools	4,253	3,444	280	2,023
Contributions (US$)	$17,622	$19,923	$1,358	$9,157

THE GREAT REVIVAL OF 1907

The 1908 statistics also reflect a surge in the admission of new members to the churches of P'yŏngyang and Sŏnch'ŏn during 1907–1908.[16] This phenomenon was part of the continuing effect of one of the most discussed growth experiences in the history of Korean Protestantism, namely, the Great Revival of 1907. The revival set the tone for much of what followed in the history of Korean Protestantism. A hundred years later, in 2007, centennial commemorations of the revival reminded the Christian community to focus on the persecution of Christianity in the DPRK, and challenged church members to pray and act to restore the church in the northern regions.

The 1907 Revival coincided with a nationwide spiritual crisis related to the collapse of the old order and the coming of the Japanese. The emotional turmoil of the time contributed greatly to the manifestation of a series of church meetings for men across northern Korea, beginning in the east coast city of Wŏnsan. There, an American Methodist doctor, James Hardie, stood up in his local church and stunned his fellow parishioners with a personal confession of sins and shortcomings that he said was necessary in order for him to cleanse his soul and continue his life and work among them.

Hardie's confession, something of a public spectacle, elicited a wave of similar confessions from other parishioners. Before long the church had been swept by a storm of emotional outpouring and appeals for mutual forgiveness. The healing effect was regarded as something positive, and word got around. Before long, the movement had spread across the peninsula to P'yŏngyang, where it created a great stir in the city's Central Presbyterian Church (Changdaehyŏn kyohoe).

Here is an eyewitness account of one such meeting in P'yongyang, after the leader, a missionary named Graham Lee, had called for confessional prayers out loud:

> The effect was indescribable. Not confusion, but a vast harmony of sound and spirit, a mingling together of souls moved by an irresistible impulse to prayer. It sounded to me like the falling of many waters, an ocean of prayer beating against God's throne.... As the prayer continued, a spirit of heaviness and sorrow came upon the audience. Over on one side, someone began to weep and, in a moment, the whole congregation was weeping.... Man after man would rise, confess his sin, break down and weep, and then throw himself to the floor and beat the floor with his fists in a perfect agony of conviction.... Sometimes after a confession, the whole audience would break out in audible prayer and the effect ... was something indescribable.... And so the meeting went on until two o'clock a.m., with confession and weeping and praying.[17]

The Revival of 1907 soon spread to the churches of Seoul and other parts of the peninsula. As Paek Nakchun wrote, "The religious experience of the people gave to the Christian church in Korea a character which is its own.... Korean Christians of today look back on the movement as the source of their spiritual life."[18] The Revival left its mark in the mode of worship that still defines the Korean church: an emphasis on fervent prayer, often before dawn or at retreats in the mountains, confessional prayer, prayer for healing and wholeness, and prayer for deliverance (as from political oppression). Conversion to Christianity represented a renunciation—of ancestor worship, concubinage, gambling, alcohol, and tobacco, and it was a commitment to live a "redeemed life" through participation in symbolic things like strict Sunday observance.

The success of the 1907 Revival was due in great measure to the charismatic leadership of Korean pastors who set the tone for much of what happened in the meetings. These included Kil Sŏnju (1869–1935) and Kim Iktu (1874–1950), both northerners and known for their passionate preaching. Their relationships with the foreign missionary contingent and their role in the revival meetings have often been cited as formative of the Korean church leadership and its style of pastoring. Vestiges of this style are readily seen in Korea's churches today.[19]

Foreign and Korean leaders of Protestant churches at that time thought that they might be able to build a million-member movement by 1910. Though this did not happen, reasonable estimates concluded that there were somewhere between 100,000 and 200,000 Christians of all denominations in Korea by the time of colonial annexation, depending on whether one counted confirmed members or included estimates of family members as well, many of whom identified with Christianity once their elders had converted.

SPECIFIC FACTORS INFLUENCING THE EXPANSION OF CHRISTIANITY IN NORTHERN KOREA

It is often said that the spread of the Presbyterian form of Protestant Christianity was due in large measure to lessons presented during a missionary conference in 1895 by a visiting China missionary named John L. Nevius. The Northern Presbyterian Mission invited Nevius from his base in Shandong Province to talk about the reasons for missionary success there. Nevius explained the principles of what later came to be called the "Three Self Movement," namely, self-support, self-government, and self-propagation. Nevius argued for the fastest possible devolution of control over Korean churches and institutions from missionary to Korean hands, for the soonest possible ordination of Korean pastors, and for self financing and governing of Korean churches through elected elders and deacons. Taking this to heart, the Presbyterian Mission, with the P'yŏngyang seminary at its center, pushed for the training of Korean church leaders. This culminated in the ordination of the first group of Korean seminary graduates as fully qualified pastors in 1907. Included in this number were some of Korea's most famous Christian leaders, including Kil Sŏnju, Sŏ Kyŏngjo, and Yi Kibung. In the same year, the newly ordained Korean clergymen and the foreign missionaries organized the Presbyterian Church of Korea, a formal Protestant denomination.

The creation of self-governing organizations (i.e., churches) concentrated in northern Korea, with the notable exception of 1907 seminary graduate Yi Kibung, who was immediately sent as the denomination's first "missionary" to Cheju Island. Self-government was a major step forward in the birth of civil societies—self-governing organizations whose members joined and associated with each other freely and without [much] interference from the state. Every congregation, no matter how small its numbers or humble its village building, offered members the satisfactions of ritual, belonging, and the opportunity to "be somebody" by getting elected to the leadership. All churches welcomed women along with men, creating new social opportunities and outlets for expression and fulfillment. Many churches used their buildings as schools, with pastors or other educated members serving as teachers of village children, and offered basic literacy education to their communities, often for the very first time.

Missionaries continued to visit, and sometimes supervise, churches in their assigned districts. The P'yŏngyang missionaries thus retained contact with the seminary graduates who pastored the churches, notified them of opportunities for further training, invited their members, both men and women, to adult education programs in P'yŏngyang and the other mission stations, and knit the Christian community together through news and organization. Children who excelled at studies in church schools often were admitted to academies (e.g., the Sinsŏng Academy in Sŏnch'ŏn, and the Sungsil and Sungŭi Academies for boys and girls respectively, in P'yŏngyang). It is hard to exaggerate the attraction exerted by the chance to get an education under the auspices of the Presbyterian Church. For a fortunate few this included the path to higher education at P'yŏngyang's Sungsil College (Union Christian College).

THE APPEAL TO WOMEN IN NORTHERN KOREA

Women missionaries were a major part of the Western presence in early twentieth-century Korea. Though they were far from having equal rights in their own homelands, they made significant gains for Korean women and for themselves through their work in Korea. Missionary women, though never ordained themselves, were important in "women's evangelism"—the contacting and teaching of Korean girls and women in homes, schools, and churches throughout the country. In education and medicine also, where they served as doctors, nurses, and teachers, female missionaries were a main ingredient of the success of Christianity in Korea. There is no better proof of the old adage that "the hand that rocks the cradle rules the world" than the resulting role of Korean Christian women in the building of their church.

The need for women missionaries in Korea derived from the fact that men, and especially foreign men, were barred from contact with respectable Korean women. Horace Allen, the first Protestant missionary doctor, found that under no circumstances could he treat female patients. When he founded his clinic in 1885, he had to borrow palace women, kisaeng entertainers actually, to be "nurses" to assist him in the treatment of women. Lillias Horton, MD, the first woman doctor in Korea, volunteered to work with women explicitly because of this cultural taboo. In the United States, the women of the Methodist church, seeking outlets for their particular concerns for women in mission lands, organized a hospital (now the Ewha Women's Hospital in Seoul), and a school (Ewha haktang, now Ewha Girls High School and Ewha Womans University, also in Seoul).

In the Korean northwest, the Presbyterians and Methodists opened schools for girls which evolved into major academies. The Presbyterians ran "Bible Institutes" to teach church women to be lay leaders and Sunday school teachers. They organized seasonal institutes for farm women to come in to the city, their bedrolls balanced on their heads, to live and attend classes together under the direction of Korean pastors and foreign missionaries. At these institutes the women were taught to read simple han'gŭl scriptures, how to pray, and how to teach. Many of them went home to promote Christianity in their home villages.

It was through these institutes that the idea of "biblewomen" (yŏjŏndosa, or chŏndo pu'in)[20] developed. These women were church ladies who carried Christianity into the inner rooms of homes in Korea's cities, towns, and villages. "Biblewomen" started out as the female counterparts of "colporteuers," male assistants to missionaries who acted as go-betweens on village visits and made their living selling Christian literature that emanated from Christian publishers such as the Korean Bible Society and the Korean Christian Literature Society, in Seoul. Biblewomen likewise often started out as go-betweens for female missionaries, acting as language teachers and protectors (because it was dangerous for any woman to wander around by herself), and as social and cultural interlocutors. Where colporteurs tended to do "public work" dealing with men and selling books on market days, "biblewomen" met and talked with women in their quarters, learned intimate things about them, shared sympathies, and coaxed them to participate in the local church. Their work had everything to do with the formation of Christian families whose generations became the backbone of the Korean church in the northwest, and as elsewhere in Korea.

THE JERUSALEM OF THE EAST

By the mid-1930s, the Presbyterian compound in P'yŏngyang had become the most conspicuous Western installation on the Korean peninsula. P'yŏngyang itself, forty years after having been called "pagan" and "filthy" by the earliest Western travelers, had become the queen city of Korean Christianity, affectionately known as the "Jerusalem of the East."[21] Decades of cultivation had created a skyline of mission buildings and institutions that served as the center of the Korean "Jerusalem." The compound's academies drew students from all over the region. P'yŏngyang's Christians took pride in their city's Sungsil College and Presbyterian Theological Seminary. Students seeking vocational training came to study at the Anna Davis Industrial Shops, where they were joined by Sungsil College students who worked at jobs to help pay their tuition.[22] Girls came from all over the region to learn skills at the Lula Wells Industrial School for Girls. All year long, P'yŏngyang station teemed with life and energy. And each year the entire Northern Presbyterian Mission converged on P'yŏngyang from the faraway stations of Taegu, Andong, Ch'ŏngju, and Seoul, and the nearby stations of Chaeryŏng, Sŏnch'on, and Kanggye, to have their annual mission meeting and, incidentally, to admire the accomplishments of their P'yŏngyang colleagues. The P'yŏngyang missionaries were proud enough of their own success to have their letterhead printed with a sketch of the compound on the reverse side of every sheet (Figure 9.1).

THE MARYKNOLL MISSION AND THE CATHOLICS OF P'YŎNGYANG

The emphasis on Presbyterianism in P'yŏngyang was due in large part to the denomination's prominence in the entire mission effort, but this should not be allowed to obscure comparably enthusiastic responses to missionary work by American Methodists, Seventh Day Adventists, and the American Catholic Missionary Society (the Maryknolls), who made P'yŏngyang their Korean center in 1923.

Catholic missionaries had been in Korea since Zhou Wenmu (1752–1801) a Chinese priest, arrived in 1794. Zhou's martyrdom in 1801 was part of the tragic history of Catholicism in Korea under the monarchy, which culminated in the great persecution of 1866 in which thousands of Korean Catholics and nine French missionaries were killed. It was not until 1890 that Catholic

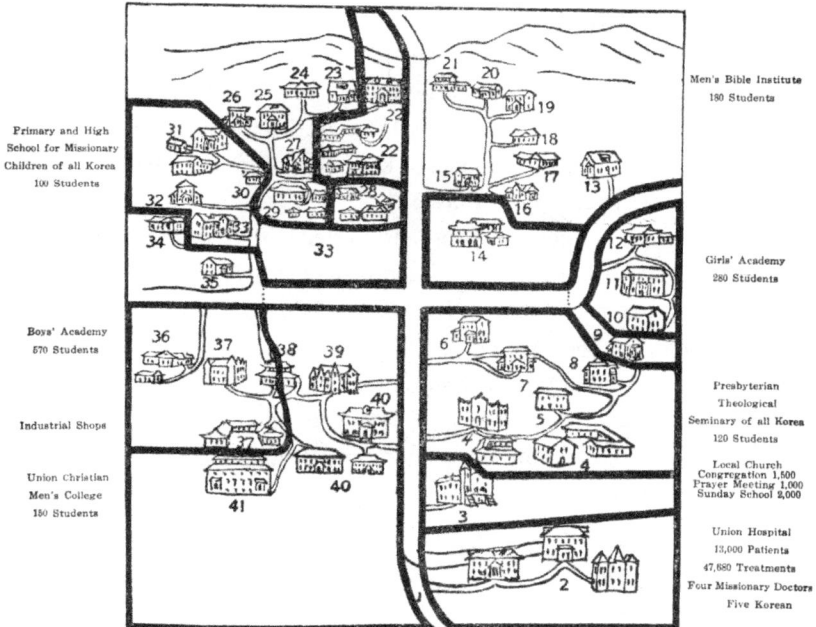

One Sixth of a Square Mile of Missionary Activity (120 Acres)

WOMEN'S HIGHER BIBLE SCHOOL 50 STUDENTS.

WOMEN'S STATION BIBLE INSTITUTE 150 STUDENTS

WOMEN'S INDUSTRIAL SCHOOL 100 STUDENTS.

Men's Bible Institute
150 Students

Primary and High
School for Missionary
Children of all Korea
100 Students

Girls' Academy
280 Students

Boys' Academy
570 Students

Presbyterian
Theological
Seminary of all Korea
120 Students

Industrial Shops

Local Church
Congregation 1,500
Prayer Meeting 1,000
Sunday School 2,000

Union Christian
Men's College
150 Students

Union Hospital
13,000 Patients
47,680 Treatments
Four Missionary Doctors
Five Korean

Pyengyang Presbyterian Compound

15 City Churches
15,000 Christians

$18 Country Churches
in Province
32,789 Christians

1. Entrance to compound
2. Union Christian Hospital Buildings
3. West Gate Church
4. Seminary Administration Building
   and Dormitories
5. Dr. Engel's Home
6. Dr. Clark's Home
7. Dr. Robb's Home
8. Dr. Reynold's Home
9. Dr. Parker's Home
10. Domestic Science Building of Girls' Academy
11. Administration Building of Girls' Academy
12. Miss Snook's Home and
    Girls' Academy Dormitory
13. Y. M. C. A. Residence
14. Men's Bible Institute Buildings
15. Mr. Hamilton's Home
16. Mr. Lutz's Home
17. Dr. Swallen's Home
18. Dr. Blair's Home
19. Dr. Robert's Home
20. Mr. Hill's Home
21. Dr. Bernheisel's Home

22. Women's Bible Institute & Bible School
23. Mr. Philip's Home
24. Mr. Mowry's Home
25. Lady-Workers' Home
26. Dr. Bigger's Home
27. Dr. McCune's Home
28. Miss Doriss' Home & Lula Wells Institute
29. Dr. Moffett's Home
30. Foreign School Teachers' Home
31. Foreign School Dormitories & Infirmary
32. Mr. Reiner's Home
33. Foreign School & Athletic Field
34. Dr. Baird's Home
35. Mr. McMurtrie's Home
36. Anna Davis Industrial Shops
37. Boys' Academy Building & Dormitory
38. Union Christian College Library
39. Union Christian College Science Hall
40. Union Christian College
    Main Building & Dormitory
41. U. C. C. Auditorium-Gymnasium

697 Sunday Schools
in the Province
45,537 Pupils

59 Primary Schools
3,782 Pupils

Fig. 9.1 Missionary Compound in P'yŏngyang

missionary work resumed under the notable leadership of Archbishop Gustav Charles-Marie Mutel, Vicar Apostolic of Seoul from 1890 to 1933, representing the Société des Missions Étrangères de Paris. During his time in Korea, Archbishop Mutel welcomed additional French missions as well as missions from Germany and Ireland. In 1911, he divided the southern half of the country into two vicariates, Seoul and Taegu, and in 1920 he divided northern Korea into the vicariates of Wŏnsan and P'yŏngyang. To develop the P'yŏngyang region, he invited the American church to send a mission, and in May 1923, the first missionaries arrived from the Catholic Foreign Mission Society of America (the "Maryknollers") to start their work. At the time there were approximately 90,000 Catholics in Korea, 4,800 from the P'yŏngan provinces, but no ordained Korean priests.[23]

The Maryknoll Mission in P'yŏngyang started in the existing church compound and consisted of one acre of land with: a gray-brick place of worship seating 300; a two-room, mud-walled convent housing three Korean nuns of the order of St. Paul de Chartres together with their Singer sewing machine, kitchen utensils, and all of their worldly possessions; a brick boys' school built for eighty but accommodating 185 students; and two girls' schools, one mud and one brick, built for 120 but accommodating 240.[24] It was a spartan operation compared with the Presbyterian compound a mile across the valley.[25] The material disparity of the Catholics was part of the difference between Protestantism and Catholicism in the eyes of the Koreans. While in China and Japan these two institutions were distinguished as different religions altogether. In P'yŏngyang, the newly arrived Maryknollers were astonished by the rich resources of their "separated brethren." "Pyeng Yang [P'yŏngyang] is the most Protestant city I was ever in, in America or elsewhere," wrote one Maryknoller.[26] Old-time Catholic missionaries in Korea had explanations for the scale of Protestant success: "unlimited funds—a million dollars a year versus $15,000 for the Catholics; more missionaries—542 Protestants versus sixty Catholics; more paid Korean clergy and catechists; indeed more of everything "in the service of error, [and] on the other [side] a scant budget and a scarcity of apostolic workers in the service of Truth."[27]

The comments of Catholic missionaries in P'yŏngyang are interesting for their suggestions about how the "Jerusalem of the East" was seen from outside the Protestant community. They thought the attraction had something to do with the wealth of the Presbyterians and their missionary budgets. The

Presbyterians, in embracing the "Nevius Method," had expressly meant to escape the trap of "rice Christians," those who claimed to be converting to Christianity but were only going through the motions in order to seek an advantage. Nor was the much-touted discipline that changed converts' lives really making much difference. According to the Maryknollers, local Koreans were drawn to the Presbyterian mission by the appearance of wealth and advantage, and many of the "conversions" were phony. The Presbyterians did not ask much of their converts: "It is not unusual to meet with Koreans, who are active and zealous Protestants but who still have concubines or engage in ancestor worship. They hobnobbed with the upper and middle classes, taking advantage of the Korean thirst for education and putting schools above all else. [T]heir fundamental aim is to educate the people, to instill into them their own mentality and thus to acquire an influence over them.... It is easy to guess what advantages will be in the hands of those who are guiding this evolution at the present time. These advantages will be not only religious but also political and economic."[28]

There was little love lost between the Catholic and Protestant communities of P'yŏngyang. The "separated brethren" were reported to have actually refused medical attention to Catholics at the Protestant Union Christian Hospital on the Presbyterian compound. "Father Kim and I have both tried to obtain treatment for minor sicknesses and have been repulsed," wrote one Maryknoller in 1927. "Perhaps it is better to say that the attitude is not general; without a doubt it depends upon the individual person with which one comes in contact. Dr. Anderson practically threw out Fr. Kim and me when we went there for eye treatment; we went to the Government Hospital and received most courteous treatment, thorough, satisfactory, and efficient"[29]

Working separately, the Catholic Church in northwestern Korea developed its own methods and lines of work under the leadership of Patrick Byrne, dean of the Maryknolls. Byrne opened a chain of missions from P'yŏngyang, which remained the headquarters, to Yŏngyu (also called Op'a), near the Ch'ŏngch'ŏn River, where the Catholic Church and convent were the largest structures in town. In Yŏngyu, the missionaries set up a home for disabled adults, a kindergarten, an "industrial school" to teach sewing, and a home for the elderly that included a number of "blind grannies." Maryknoll nuns founded a dispensary and established sodalities for young married women.

The nuns taught the women singing, sewing, and recreational sports such as volleyball, and coaxed them into leadership roles as deaconesses for the congregation.[30] In this way the Catholics replicated many of the appeals that the Protestants had used earlier to win converts and spread the Christian message throughout the northwest, by using social work, education, and the cultivation of women to build strong communities.

CONCLUSION

As historian Chung Shin Park has pointed out, the influence of the P'yŏngyang area and the Korean northwest in the story of Protestantism began to fade partway through the Japanese colonial period. Although the Presbyterians remained united as a single denomination until the late 1930s, ancient regional frictions arose much earlier between the Christians of the northwest and Christians in the south. The Japanese order to worship at Shintō shrines split the Presbyterian church, beginning with the P'yŏngyang-led conservative faction's refusal to obey and the national Presbyterian General Assembly's decision to go along with the order on the understanding that Shintō worship was a civil and not a religious rite.[31] This prewar schism was immensely complicated by the national division in 1945, which laid additional layers of conflict upon the underlying question of colonial "collaboration." Refugee Christians from North Korea started new congregations in Seoul and elsewhere in the south. Instead of assimilating into the southern church, they formed a faction that stimulated reactions among other groups, as a result the Presbyterian Church of Korea splintered over issues relating to the former colonial period, communism, regionalism, and the experience of wartime suffering and sacrifice. These issues added to the Confucian-based patterns of loyalty to individual ministers, and eventuated in the founding of the four major Presbyterian denominations and more than fifty smaller ones, a few of which consisted of single congregations.

What remains of the missionary effort in North Korea? In January 1951, the United States Air Force undertook a bombing campaign over P'yŏngyang and throughout North Korea that was intended, under orders from General Douglas MacArthur, to destroy the country's economy pending surrender. The Presbyterian mission compound and its buildings were destroyed in the bombing along with churches, clinics, and schools across the country. The bombers did not spare churches, on the suspicion that they might be used by the North Koreans to shelter military equipment. It may therefore be said that if the American missionaries built, or helped build, physical churches in North Korea, Americans also destroyed them with no less zeal and purpose. This fact has always been a favorite talking point when DPRK officials are asked about the remnants of Christianity in North Korea today.

A second favorite talking point is the story of the American missionary doctor who, in 1925, caught a Korean boy stealing apples from his hospital orchard. The doctor hauled the boy into the lab and branded his face with caustic soda spelling the word "thief" in Korean. When the case became known, it became a major embarrassment—a public relations disaster, actually. The doctor, C.A. Haysmeir, was arrested, fined, and deported. However, the story thereafter took on a life of its own and versions of it are told repeatedly in both South and North Korea, as if the doctor's rash act was typical of missionaries in Korea. The notorious Haysmeir unfortunately did hurt the boy, and thus the story is true.[32] The tragedy is that so much else that was good, seems to pale beside the telling of it.

Today, faint echoes of Christianity in northern Korea may still be discerned in the modes of Chuch'e ideology and the cognate concepts of divinity and even the suggestions of the Holy Trinity in the cult of Kim Il Sung whose mother, after all, was a Presbyterian deaconess. The missionary presence has left a legacy that is visible today in the humanitarian work of the Eugene Bell Foundation and the Christian Friends of Korea, two NGOs devoted to medical care, food aid, and technical assistance. These organizations are run by former members of the missionary community, including a handful, very old now, who knew P'yŏngyang as children before World War II. Ironies abound in the contacts these NGOs have with today's DPRK and the relationships they have formed with North Korean officials. As the Koreans gradually find ways to make their broken country whole again, the story of Christianity in northern Korea will be not only reexamined, but also may provide a means to better understand Korean history.

NOTES

1. See Hwang, *Beyond Birth*, Chapter VI, 262–63.

2. Allen D. Clark, A History of the Church in Korea, 168–70. For a map of the territorial division see Harry A. Rhodes, History of the Korea Mission, Presbyterian Church U.S.A., 1884–1934, frontispiece.

3. Paik, The History of Protestant Missions in Korea, 272–73.

4. Hwang, Beyond Birth, 280.

5. Bishop, Korea and her Neighbours, 312–13.

6. For Samuel A. Moffett, see Jong Hyeong Lee, "Samuel Austin Moffett: His Life and Work in the Development of the Presbyterian Church of Korea, 1890–1936."

7. The standard account of the journey is by James Scarth Gale in his book Korean Sketches, 72–103.

8. Moffett, First Letters from Korea, 45.

9. See Grayson, Early Buddhism and Christianity in Korea, 102–104.

10. Moffett, First Letters from Korea, 41.

11. Ibid., 42.

12. Moffett was the leader of a team of three P'yŏngyang pioneers, the other two being Graham Lee and William L. Swallen.

13. Moffett, "A New Mission Station at Pyeng Yang," 107, quoted in Paik, The History of Protestant Missions in Korea, 211.

14. Charr, The Golden Mountain, 63–65.

15. Table of statistics for the year ending June 30, 1908, from "Korea Mission of the Presbyterian Church in the U.S.A." The Korea Mission Field, III, 141.

16. Ibid., 141. Between mid-1907 and mid-1908, the Presbyterian churches of P'yŏngyang and Sŏnch'ŏn admitted 2,206 and 1,287 members respectively, compared with 508 in Seoul, 343 in Taegu, and 317 in Pusan.

17. Blair, Gold in Korea, 66–67.

18. Paik, The History of Protestant Missions in Korea, 374.

19. The influence of Kil Sŏnju and Kim Iktu on the Korean church is a theme of Chong Bum Kim's dissertation, Christianity in Colonial Korea.

20. The English term "Biblewoman" also covered female kwŏnsa, a slightly higher level category of church worker invented after World War II for women church leaders, who could not be elders because they were female. Nowadays, however, women hold many important positions in churches, some of them salaried, and they do everything except administer the sacraments and preach formally from the pulpit. For formal sources on Biblewomen in the prewar era see Eleventh Annual Report of the Korea Woman's Conference of the Methodist Episcopal Church; Pollard, "The History of the Missionary Enterprise of the Presbyterian Church, USA," 70–72; and Hayes, "The Korean Bible Woman and Her Work," The Korea Mission Field, XXX:7 (July 1935), 151–53 and special issues devoted to women's work, such as XVIII:11 (November 1922) and XIX:11 (November 1923).

21. Richard H. Baird wrote that "When the history of the Great Century of modern missionary activity is complete it may well be that Pyongyang Station in Korea will be found to have been the greatest mission station of that period." In *William M. Baird of Korea: A Profile*, 208.

22. Sungsil College founder William M. Baird believed in the character-building value of labor. "As an Indiana farm boy," wrote his son Richard, "he was opposed to the Oriental idea of the long-robed scholar who could not be degraded by manual labor, who grew long fingernails to show that his hands had never been used for work." Baird, *William M. Baird of Korea: A Profile*, 141. The work-study plan was modeled on Park College, in Parkville, Missouri, which required that all students learn self-reliance and a respect for labor by doing fieldwork, janitorial work, or cooking and cleaning for several hours each day. A key difference was that roughly half of all Union Christian College students simply paid the fees, while at Park College in Missouri the labor was a requirement, in effect part of the school's curriculum.

23. Ch'ŏnjugyo P'yŏngyang kyogusa p'yŏnch'an wiwŏnhoe, *Ch'ŏnjugyo P'yŏngyang kyogusa*, 73–74.

24. "Diary from Fr. Byrne," dated May 8, 1923.

25. One Maryknoller described the Presbyterian compound as "a vast oasis of green in a desert of tile roofs, with splendid churches, schools, and colleges." Some Catholics complained that the land had once been owned by a French priest but had been won by the Protestants through legal manipulation. "Now the two challenge comparison in the pagan mind, which can hardly be expected to hesitate in making a choice." "Diary of Maryknoll in Peng Yang, August 1925 to March 1927."

26. Ibid.

27. *The Catholic Church in Korea*, 97.

28. Ibid., 97.

29. Both comments in this paragraph are from "Diary of Maryknoll in Peng Yang, August 1925 to March 1927."

30. The various stations and installations of the P'yŏngyang diocese is discussed in detail in Ch'ŏnjugyo P'yŏngyang kyogusa p'yŏnch'an wiwŏnhoe, *Ch'ŏnjugyo P'yŏngyang kyogusa*, 284–528.

31. Chung-shin Park, *Protestantism and Politics in Korea*, 100–101.

32. *The Seoul Press*, July 1, 13, 18, 20, and 29, 1926.

10

The Northern Region of Korea as Portrayed in Russian Sources, 1860s–1913

GERMAN KIM AND ROSS KING

There is an old Korean proverb that goes "*Namnam, pungnyŏ,*" meaning literally "In the south—men, and in the north—women," hence "Korean men are more handsome in the southern provinces while women are more beautiful in the north." This particular proverb resonated in the South Korean popular imagination during the 2002 World Cup soccer championships hosted by Japan and South Korea that year. The South Korean media devoted an inordinate amount of attention to the charm and beauty of the 300 North Korean cheerleaders who, in effect, often garnered more attention from South Korean fans than what was happening on the soccer field.

So are there really physical differences in appearance and/or differences in character between "northern" and "southern" Koreans? Certainly the Korean traditional sources contain well-known discussions of the issue, and claims of this nature were frequently made by western European observers in the late nineteenth and early twentieth centuries—some on a merely impressionistic basis, and others on more pseudo-scientific (phrenological or eugenistic) grounds. But neither the Russian observations of an ethnographic and pseudo-scientific, racist nature, nor the specific features of Russian "Orientalist" discourse as revealed in Russian-language narratives about Korea from this period, have been collected and analyzed in a comprehensive manner. Thus, this chapter attempts to survey the Russian sources on northern Korea from the 1860s to approximately 1913, and to demonstrate how Russian observers during this period described the northern region of Korea and the Koreans living there. Our presentation begins with a short introduction to some of the theoretical and methodological problems in any examination of Russian narratives of exploration and discovery in Korea. Then we proceed with an overview of the Russian materials on the Russo-Korean "contact zone," which we define as northeastern Korea, the Korean border along the Yalu and Tumen Rivers where many of the early Russian expeditions conducted their work, and the South Ussuri *krai* (region) in the Russian Far East with its new communities of recently arrived Korean settlers, predominantly from the northeastern Korean province of Hamgyŏng.

THE RUSSO-KOREAN "CONTACT ZONE" AND RUSSIAN NARRATIVES OF TRAVEL IN KOREA

In her classic work on western European travel literature, Mary Louise Pratt defines the notion of "contact zone" as follows: "the space in which peoples geographically and historically separated come into contact with each other and establish ongoing relations, usually involving conditions of coercion, radical inequality and intractable conflict."[1]

In this chapter we borrow this notion of contact zone and apply it to those regions in the Russian "Dal'nyi Vostok" or Russian Far East, in northeastern Korea, and along the Sino-Korean and Russo-Korean borders where Russians and Koreans first came into regular contact beginning in the 1860s. The narratives of contact and encounter explored in this paper were rendered by a wide variety of Russians: travelers and explorers, merchants, regional government officials, administrators and their representatives, military officers, scholars and representatives of Russian learned societies, missionaries, students from the Oriental Institute in Vladivostok, writers, ethnographers, and anthropologists. In some cases, the authors and their backgrounds are well-known, while in others, as G. D. Tiagai notes, we know almost nothing (e.g., K. N. Dadeshkaliani, P. M. Delotkovich, F. M. Vebel', V. P. Karneev, V. A. Al'ftan).[2]

There are, to be sure, Russian sources from this period on the central and southern regions of Korea, but for obvious geographical reasons, there is a large and important body of Russian work devoted to the description and study of the northern region of Korea—in particular, the Korean northeast, which we treat here as extending beyond the Russo-Korean border and into the South Ussuri *krai* in the Russian Far East. This fact alone—the abundance of Russian-language materials on northern Korea from the 1860s until the Japanese takeover of Korea in 1910—suggests the necessity to go back to these little-known materials and examine them. As V. T. Zaichikov, the noted Russian geographer of Korea, notes: "If, during all this period, Korea was studied geographically quite weakly in general, then the northern region bordering Manchuria was completely inaccessible for investigations of any sort."[3] A decade later, another Soviet researcher, writing in a rather Cold War vein, adds more context to the potential value of the Russian materials when compared to sources in other European languages: "In pursuit of their goals of colonization, the western 'researchers' never went outside the boundaries of the more populated southern and central Korea. Anything that did not yield immediate gain in the form of capital failed to attract their interest. This is the only reason that mountainous North Korea remained as a complete 'terra incognita' for the world for a long time."[4]

Russian authors writing about the Korean migrants living north of the Russo-Korean border in the South Ussuri *krai* fall into two main groups: those who opposed the "yellow colonization" of the Maritime Region and campaigned for limitation or outright banning of Korean immigration, and those who, to the contrary, sympathized with the immigrants and championed their rights. Among the most colorful representatives of the former group of authors, Pavel Fedorovich Unterberger (1842–?) must rank first and foremost. Unterberger held the post of Maritime Region governor, and from 1905–1910 served as the region's governor general. The contents of his first book published in 1900 reflect, on the whole, the kind of discretion and tact, vis-à-vis the Korean population, befitting a governor of the Maritime Region.[5] His second book published in 1912, on the other hand, was completed in the context of Russia's defeat in the Russo-Japanese war of 1904–1905, the annexation of Korea by a Japan hungry for hegemony in the Far East, and the second wave of Korean migration to the region.[6] In this second book, Unterberger opposes the idea of Korean migration and proposes the introduction of a number of restrictive and prohibitive measures designed to staunch the flow of Korean immigrants and limit their access to employment in the mining and building industries, etc. Among other authors in the opposition camp deserving mention is I. P. Nadarov, whose article from 1889 includes extensive statistical information concerning the Maritime Region population.[7]

Russian authors who were more sympathetic to the Korean migrants in the Russian Far East are more conspicuous, at least as far as published sources are concerned. A. Ragoza and F. Vebel', through their official government posts, had the benefit of direct contact with the Korean migrants upon which to base the personal observations which complement the official materials in their work.[8] The same may be said of another official on assignment from the Immigration Department of the Russian Ministry of Internal Affairs, A. Rittikh, who made a trip to the Maritime Region, where he became acquainted with the social, economic and legal conditions of the Korean immigrants, and subsequently incorporated these descriptions into his book.[9]

One of the great researchers of Russia's Far Eastern Koreans was N. Nasekin, who held the post of chief official on special assignment attached to the Maritime Region governor general in the 1890s, even though Nasekin had never once actually visited the Korean settlements. Included in a long, general article by him is a short historical essay concerning Korean migration, the administrative divisions of the Korean settlements, a geographical and economic survey of the Korean villages, and information about schools, churches, and missions. The article contains a highly professional ethnographic description of the dwellings, household utensils, food, clothing, religion, and wedding and funeral ceremonies, as well as a description of the Korean "national character."[10] In his analysis, Nasekin reviews other authors' observations of the immigrant Koreans' local circumstances, and goes on to draw his own conclusions, worth citing in full:

> So a proper mission and a Russian school are necessary as institutions to bring the Russian spirit into the Korean midst and eliminate differences between the Koreans and the aboriginal Russian population, and to lead its pupils from a very early age in the true Russian direction; and lastly, military service, during which young Koreans will be implanted with the embryo of patriotism and imbued with a sense of faithful devotion to His Majesty. These are the three elements which will make from the Koreans just as loyal men for the Tsar as are dozens of other nationalities, scattered all over the outlying districts of our vast fatherland.[11]

The so-called "Korean problem" in the Russian Far East was one of the objects of research of the Amur Expedition, dispatched in 1911 by order of the Tsar himself. V. Pesotskii's work on the Koreans was an important outcome of this expedition.[12] In the chapter entitled "The Role of the Koreans in the Region," Pesotskii recorded both favorable and unfavorable opinions regarding the Korean population. In his view, among the cons of the Korean population's presence in the Maritime Region were the following: treasury deprivation due to the cost of producing proper papers for the majority of the Korean population; the financial burden caused by periodic deportations of Koreans back to Korea; the challenge to the development of Russian agriculture; the fall in crop yields due to soil degradation; the danger of corruption and threat, posed by alien elements, to the civic order and morality of the lowest administrative ranks; and the possibility of political infraction or subversion. On the other hand, Pesotskii also enumerated the pluses of Korean settlement in the Maritime Region: benefits to the treasury arising from the issue of Russian official documents and passports; agricultural growth in the region; the placement of cheap Korean labor at the disposal of Russian employers; and the stabilizing effect of industrious, unpretentious and law-abiding citizens in the region.

S. Nedachin's 1913 study furnishes more detailed information and discussion worthy of our attention concerning the Korean immigrants. Nedachin contends that, from the point of view of Russian imperialist ambitions, "History hardly ever gave any better material [than the Koreans] to finish its forthcoming mission—to become firmly established in the Far East."[13] Nedachin is also known for his work on the history of the Orthodox mission in Korea and the conversion of the Maritime Koreans to Christianity. In common with many other authors, he considers the Koreans a God-fearing people susceptible to Christian teaching, and is optimistic about the potential for the Orthodox church to attract new believers into its fold.[14]

Among the representatives of the more "democratic" school of writers were some high-ranking officials. F. Busse, an immigration director in the South Ussuri Region between 1882 and 1892, was one of them.[15] Another such official was M. Putsillo, on special assignment and attached to the Amur *oblast'* governor, who left not only the first Korean dictionary in a Western language, but also fond memories in the hearts of Korean immigrants.[16] In the spring of 1870, he was sent to establish Korean refugee settlements near the Suifun River and lived there for a year and a half, during which time he worked selflessly to assist newly arrived Koreans. The Koreans were so grateful to him that they erected two monuments in his honor bearing the words: "Captain Mikhailo Ivanych Putsillo. For the love and justice he showed to the Korean people." Subsequently, one of the villages on the Suifun River was given the name "Putsillovka" in his honor. Putsillo is known to have not enjoyed the favor of the authorities. Essential finances were denied; this undermined his plans to assist the Koreans, and forced him to use his own salary instead.[17]

The famous Russian traveler, explorer, and zoologist, N. Przheval'skii, was sent in 1868 by the governor general of Eastern Siberia to the Ussuri Region. With instructions from the Siberian Department of Natural and Historical Research, he proved himself to be not only a brilliant zoologist, but also a master ethnographic observer. The following oft-quoted words of Przheval'skii describing his impressions of the first stage of Korean migration to the Far East were often cited in support of a positive view of Korean colonization there: "Korean immigration to Russia and settlement there in new dwellings should be regarded as a remarkable phenomenon of late."[18] The Siberian historian and publicist, V. Vagin, was also in the vanguard of open criticism of misguided Tsarist policies toward the Korean problem and at the forefront of efforts to protect the Koreans from the scourges of official tyranny, embezzlement of state resources designated for the benefit of Koreans, and from forced Russification and Christianization.[19]

The various authors share a sense of sympathy toward the Korean population on Russian lands. Admittedly, these writers are not devoid of weaknesses, inaccuracies, or even outright mistakes. Furthermore, the authors themselves, due to their divergent social classes and official and professional backgrounds, are sometimes inconsistent in their opinions on the same issues. Interesting ethnographic materials can also be found in articles and reports about the Korean village of Blagoslovennoe on the upper reaches of the Amur River; in particular, the fifteen-year lapse between studies allows for some longitudinal tracking of ethnographical features and agricultural data.[20]

We find, then, a wealth of data and opinions concerning the Russo-Korean "contact zone" extending from northeast Korea into the Russian Maritime Region from the 1860s to approximately 1913. Apart from the factual, statistical, and other more valuable "objective" data the Russian sources most assuredly afford us, how did these Russian narratives of exploration and discovery depict Korea and Koreans? In other words, can we speak of Russian "Orientalist" discourse, and if so, how does it differ from the (primarily French and British) "Orientalist" narrative strategies first outlined by Edward

Said? Questions of Russia's role in and representations of Asia during the imperial period have been poorly studied, and as Nathaniel Knight notes, "Said's model of Orientalism and the rich discussions it has stimulated have evoked surprisingly little response in studies of the Russian empire."[21]

Such research as exists to date tends to focus on Muslim (Central) Asia rather than East Asia, and studies of the latter almost always concentrate on either China or Japan. With respect to Russian Orientalist discourse vis-à-vis Muslim Asia, David Brower and Edward J. Lazzerini note some "parallels between French and British images of Muslim lands and Russian cultural representations of the peoples in the empire's southern and eastern territories" before cautioning that "the Russian empire occupied a unique place among Western states."[22] The problem with applying Said's notion of Orientalism to Russia is that Russia itself, both in its history and geography, incorporates much that is Asian or Oriental: "As is often pointed out, in Russia the oriental "other" was not necessarily an unknown creature set apart by thousands of miles and vast oceans. In Russia, the "other" was all around."[23]

Brower and Lazzerini lament the marginalization of Russia's legacy in Asia by "the dominant Euro-American academic discourse," and are surely right to attribute it to "both the linguistic handicaps of non-Russianists ... and, contrarily, the indifference of Russianists, though with important exceptions."[24] One of those exceptions is David L. Wells' recent study of Russian travel narratives, in which he shows that the "Russian gaze on Tokugawa Japan was necessarily limited ... the 'contact zone' between the European subject and the Asian focus of observation is extremely narrow."[25] Russian travelers in Japan were often hampered by the inadequacy of available interpreters, something Wells takes as a "metaphor for a more general failure of cultural communication." But as we shall see below, Russians traveling in northern Korea from the 1860s through the first decade of the twentieth century had much better access, better interpreters (some even spoke some Korean themselves), and a generally broader contact zone within which to fashion their narratives of discovery. Thus, we offer this chapter not only as a study of the northern region of Korea, but also as one more contribution to coming to grips with Russian Orientalist discourse on East Asia. To conclude this introductory section, we emphasize that the pre-revolutionary Russian literature on Korea and Koreans—particularly when one includes those works devoted to the study of the Korean immigrant population in the Russian Far East—is significant both in quantity and quality. In terms of quantity, there are a great many general and specialized texts about the Koreans, and in terms of quality, the depth and breadth of the questions considered and the heterogeneity of views expressed on various important aspects are impressive. Thus, the examples discussed below represent only a selection from a broad range of relevant sources.

Russians and the Korean Settlements in the South Ussuri Krai

When the South Ussuri krai was annexed to Russia as a result of the Aigun (1858) and Peking (1860) treaties, Russia and Korea came to share a common border of just sixteen kilometers (9.9 miles) along the lower reaches of the Tumen River. Thus, after 1860 more intensive contact between these two countries began. The immigration of Koreans from northern provinces (overwhelmingly northern Hamgyŏng Province) began in the mid-1860s and continued in several waves through the mid-1920s. Famines, natural disasters, exploitation by Korean government officials, lack of land ownership, and (later) oppression at the hands of the Japanese colonizers pressured many people to emigrate from Korea to Russia. Other "pull" factors included geographical proximity, tolerance by Russian authorities of Korean immigration, ready availability of rich farmland, and the opportunity to start anew.

A number of works by Russian authors appeared during the first migration of Koreans to the Russian Far East. In some of these works, the authors paid attention to the factors underlying the mass immigration, and also to the social, economic, and legal conditions of the new arrivals to the Maritime Region. Since interest in the Korean influx was dictated primarily by pragmatic rather than purely academic considerations, it comes as no surprise that many of the early authors were dignitaries in the Tsar's administration, as well as officials, military men, writers, and journalists.[26]

As the overwhelming majority of Korean settlers were originally from the northern provinces, and considering the short period of residence in the Russian Maritime Region of the Koreans concerned, the descriptions rendered by the Russian authors of the Korean immigrants serve as valuable source materials for our task here. As mentioned above, we propose to view the South Ussuri krai as an extension of the Korean northeastern region, and

to define as the Russo-Korean contact zone the Korean northeast, the Sino-
and Russo-Korean border along the Yalu and Tumen Rivers, and the South
Ussuri Region from the short Russo-Korean border all the way up to
Vladivostok, which began to develop a significant Korean population, both
transient and more permanent, by the 1870s. Now let us turn to a more
detailed examination of some of the more interesting travelogues of the
Russo-Korean contact zone.

PHYSICAL APPEARANCE OF NORTHERN KOREANS AS DESCRIBED BY RUSSIAN AUTHORS

For most Europeans, including Russians, "all Koreans look alike"; indeed,
many will claim that they cannot tell them apart from the Chinese or Japanese.
In their turn, South Koreans visiting Kazakhstan today for the first time will
confess that they cannot distinguish Kazakhs from Koreans. What did northern Koreans look like to the first Russians in Korea—travelers, writers, military personnel, diplomats, and missionaries? Korean faces were perceived by
Russians differently: impressions ranged from the "pure Mongolian" to
"European" types, and the authors compared them with different Asian and
European peoples.

For instance, M. Zuber writes, "Koreans represent a separate branch of the
Mongolian tribe, and look like Tatars; they have the same flat nose, same high
cheekbones, slightly squinting eyes, yellowish skin and very black hair."[27] P.
Delotkevich notes that the faces of Koreans in Seoul are paler and that their
appearance is generally better than that of the Koreans living in the South
Ussuri Region. In one village near Puryŏng (South Hamgyŏng Province) he
saw a 26-year-old Korean who was demonstrated to the people as a rarity
because the hair on his head, eyebrows, and moustache was very light brown,
his face was "white with freckles," and his eyes were slanted. His father and
mother were "normal" Koreans with black hair.[28]

Selivanovskii managed to discern the facial likeness between Koreans and
Kyrgyz:

In their appearance Koreans do not look like either the Chinese or Japanese.
They resemble most of all the Kyrgyz. However, there are some differences
between southern and northern Koreans. In the north of the peninsula

Koreans are taller, white-skinned, attractive, well-mannered and in appearance are to a certain extent close to Europeans. Their cheekbones are not so high, and the eye cut is nearly direct; they have straight beards and slightly aquiline noses. Southern Koreans are closer to the Mongolian type. They have faces with high cheekbones, squinted eyes and thin beards. As a rule Koreans have dark brown eyes, black teeth, coarse hair, and yellowish skin. The men are rather tall, strong, adroit, and smart at work. The women on the contrary, are small, and age very early; when young, they are not beautiful and when old they are ugly."[29]

The most detailed physical description of the Koreans from the northern provinces of Hamgyŏng and P'yŏngan can be found in Lubentsov's work *Khamkenskaia i pkhienanskaia provintsii Korei* (The Hamgyŏng and P'yŏngan Provinces of Korea) published in 1897. As regards the face, skin, and hair, he writes:

The color of the face is slightly yellowish, with a touch of bronze color in P'yŏngan Province. The eyes are dark brown. The hair on the head is black and coarse. They never shave their beards and moustaches, which in general are very sparse. The eyebrows are thin and sharply contoured. The form of the head is partly Caucasian, partly Mongolian. One can meet, especially in the northeastern part of Korea and among the upper class, some persons remarkably resembling Europeans: they are given away only by a unique fold on their eyelids, which forms directly above the eyelashes when they raise their upper eyelids. This fold is a characteristic feature of the Mongolian race. The cheekbones sometimes protrude sharply, but their eyes for the most part are not slanted. Their facial expression is good-natured, lazy, and very rarely energetic.[30]

During his trip to northern Korea, Lubentsov for the first time took measurements of the heights and some other aspects of Korean bodies. Measurements were made according to the method of the well-known English scholar Francis Galton, which was described in his book, *Hints to Travelers*, published by the London Royal Geographical Society in 1878. A stick with two marks was used for taking the measurements. When measurements were taken, only the information as to whether a person was taller or shorter than the marks was recorded. According to Galton, this method helped avoid mistrust or unwillingness on the part of subjects to undergo the measurement procedure.

Lubentsov measured 249 Korean men from Hamgyŏng Province between the ages of twenty and sixty-two. The results of his measurements allowed him to come to the following conclusion: "A Korean is taller than a Japanese and has a rather slender, proportional body. Women, as compared to men, are of very small height." Lubentsov gave as the average man's height 65.3 inches, and as the average length of a Korean man's outstretched arms, 76.25 inches; the average arm length was 28.2 inches; average leg length was 38.1 inches; average hand length was 7.03 inches and average foot length was 9.36 inches.[31]

Another important—indeed, monumental—Russian source from this period is the *Opisanie Korei* (Description of Korea), published in 1900 by the Ministry of Finance.[32] The chapter on "Population" has two sections of interest for our purposes here, namely "Physical Description of Koreans" and "Character of Koreans." The section on "Physical Description of Koreans" cites excerpts from the works of non-Korean authors describing the appearance of Koreans. According to the data cited in this work, the different types of Koreans were not evenly distributed throughout the country but could be linked with specific regions. Thus, according to the opinion presented in the *Korean Repository*, people living in the northern provinces of P'yŏngan, Hamgyŏng, and Kangwŏn were physically much stronger than those who live in Ch'ungch'ŏng, Kyŏngsang, and Chŏlla; they could carry on their shoulders a weight of sixteen *poods* (1 *pood* = 36.11 pounds). On average, it was alleged that northern Koreans differed greatly in appearance from southern Koreans.[33] In the north, Koreans were taller, more attractive, and well-mannered; there was something Caucasian in their faces, the cheekbones were not as high, and the eyes were more oval in form compared to other peoples in the Far East. In the northern parts of the country, women were supposedly more beautiful, especially in the province of Kangwŏn, whence (it was alleged) in olden times girls were chosen for the harem of the Chinese emperor.

Japanese physician Mazanao Koike examined and measured seventy-five healthy Koreans from Pusan between the ages of twenty-five and fifty in 1883 and 1884. The *Opisanie Korei* lists the results of his observations in a table, which for comparison purposes shows similar figures received after observation of a considerable number of Japanese subjects. The comparison revealed that, on average, the height of Koreans ages twenty-one through twenty-five was 5 feet 10 inches, whereas for the Japanese (2,499 persons were measured) it was only 5 feet 2 inches (and for the 919 Japanese soldiers – 5 feet 4 inches). Even taller were the Koreans from the age group between twenty-six and fifty, where the average height was 5 feet 11 inches. Though the difference in height was significant, the weight and chest measurements for the Korean and Japanese people were nearly the same.[34]

To return to Russian sources, one neglected and extremely rare publication is N. V. Kirillov's *Medico-Anthropological Study of Korea*, published in 1913. We have been unable to unearth much information on Kirillov himself, but he appears to have made somewhat of a hobby of traveling around the Russian Far East and taking phrenological measurements from Koreans he could find. Thus, he found that prisons on south Sakhalin included so many Koreans and Chinese as to be a "living anthropological museum."[35] In support of his eugenistic approach, he cites Deniker, Reclus, then Griffis and Ross, the latter of whom sharply divided southern and northern Koreans.[36] Kirillov was aware of and cited both Lubentsov's northern Korean measurements and Koike's Pusan measurements, and was convinced of the great heterogeneity of Koreans in terms of anthropological types.[37] He even referred to the "pure, fair-haired villages north of Seoul," whatever those may have been.[38] Northeast of P'yŏngyang and south of Pusan he discerned a Malayan type.[39]

ETHNO-PSYCHOLOGICAL CHARACTERISTICS OF NORTHERN KOREANS IN RUSSIAN SOURCES FROM THE SECOND HALF OF THE NINETEENTH TO THE BEGINNING OF THE TWENTIETH CENTURIES

In his impressively researched *Statistical and Economic Study of Korea*, Russian scholar N. V. Kiuner of the Vostochnyi Institut (Oriental Institute) in Vladivostok[40] cites some fragments allegedly from the works of sixteenth-century Korean scholar Yi Hwang, better known under the pen name Yi T'oegye (1501–1571), stereotyping Koreans from different regions. Upon closer inspection, Kiuner's source is in fact a *French* scholar citing Yi T'oegye; alas, the French scholar does not cite the text, but it seems clear enough that he based his remarks on a Korean text in literary Chinese (*hanmun*) that he *thought* belonged to Yi T'oegye, so we include the information here in the hopes that readers might identify the original source.[41] The mysterious Korean author chose the bull as the symbol of Hamgyŏng Province, representing the stupidity of the population that was "rather more Chinese, both in language and customs." The alleged stupidity of the Hamgyŏng population was reflected in the fact that in this province the people died of various accidents more often than in other provinces: Children would drown or be burned alive; travelers would fall to their deaths as they walked along broken bridges; and old men would freeze to death or get lost in the snow. Villagers would build their huts in dangerous places at the feet of bare mountains despite the fact that their houses were regularly washed away by avalanches. Those who managed to survive would build their homes anew in the same places.[42]

As the symbol for P'yŏngan Province, the Korean mystery author chose the Korean horse. Like a Korean horse, the people of P'yŏngan Province were small yet feisty and courageous; they were not as tall as people from other provinces but were brave and fearless. They were stubborn and persistent, did not know flattery and low intrigues, and though not particularly communicative, were loyal to the end. Their toughness and wildness were sometimes close to brutality, and cases of premeditated murder, rare though they were in Korea, happened in P'yŏngan Province much more often than in other parts of the country.[43]

Proceeding from the characteristics enumerated by Yi T'oegye (or whoever the Korean author was) for the people living in the different provinces of Korea, Kiuner came to the conclusion that the most important point was that the prevailing moral qualities of the population in different parts of the peninsula were, he supposed, inherited from distant ancestors, northern and southern representatives of the Mongolian race. The supposed perfidy, falsity, and inconstancy of the people from Chŏlla Province were alleged to be well-preserved, typical qualities of the Malayan race, whereas open-heartedness, fearlessness, and a kind of intellectual underdevelopment were characteristics of the peoples of Inner Asia of Mongolian ancestry. Therefore, according to Kiuner, we can discern in the "unflattering but fair opinion" of "Yi T'oegye" about his compatriots proof of the dual origins of the modern Korean people.[44]

The Russian orthodox missionaries left a considerable amount of data and materials on Korea and Koreans including: Archimandrite Khrisanf (Schetkovskii; 1869–1906), Archimandrite Pavel (Ivanovskii; 1874–1919), Archimandrite Irinarkh (Shemanovskii), Father-Superior Vladimir (Skrizhalo),

Monk Palladii (Seletskii), and Archimandrite Feodosii (Fedor Ivanovich Perevalov; 1875–1933). Archimandrite Khrisanf's 1905 travelogue is particularly germane to our purposes here. Khrisanf writes that it was his "desire to acquaint myself as intimately as possible with the Koreans, their customs and mores" that motivated his journey.[45] Archimandrite Khrisanf in his travelogue also pointed to the regional character differences among Koreans:

> The character of the people in the northern province is significantly different from the character of the Koreans in the central provinces; whereas the latter give the impression of being—and in fact are—cowed and timid beings, the former, to the contrary, conduct themselves with dignity and even with a certain amount of pride. Among the Koreans of the central provinces I never encountered and never heard any contradictions or defiance, and everything that the European says they take on faith without any debate; the Koreans of Hamgyŏng Province, by contrast, always, no matter what you start to talk to them about, think things over from the start, ask and ask again several times, and constantly state their opinion, sometimes even getting into arguments. One notes among the latter a strong tendency to the critical method of thinking; among the former—credulity and dullness. The northern Koreans are keen of character, somewhat coarse and restless; but ours [meaning the Koreans in Seoul where the Orthodox Korean mission was] are soft, peaceful, and sickly sweet and smooth-tongued. From the missionary point of view, the soil for the spread of Christianity among the northern Koreans is considerably better and more fruitful than among the central Koreans. The northern Koreans can master Christianity and be good Christians in a rather more solid way, and rather more intelligently, while our Koreans are ready to change their faith like gloves; in the qualitative aspect missionary success should be on the side of the former, but in the quantitative aspect, on the side of the latter.[46]

According to Zhdan-Pushkin and others, the populations from different parts of the Korean peninsula have specific character traits in regards to both intellect and morals. Thus, people from the four northern provinces and Kangwŏn Province, especially from North and South P'yŏngan provinces, were supposedly endowed with better intellectual abilities than other Koreans. Their courage and restive nature sometimes manifested itself in indignation. In addition, the ruling dynasty considered them to be secret enemies of the state.

Inhabitants of Hwanghae Province, by contrast, were said to be intellectually limited. They were accused of extreme stinginess and lack of conscientiousness. The population of Kyŏnggi Province where the capital was situated, and of North and South Ch'ungch'ŏng provinces, was light-minded and inconsistent, fond of life, and full of joy and pleasure. The people from Chŏlla Province were considered impudent, hypocritical, and cheating, pursuing their own interests only for the sake of profit and were ready to shamelessly betray each other. The Cheju Island people, belonging to South Chŏlla Province and a place of exile for criminals, were known for their rudeness. In Kyŏngsang Province, the people stuck to the values of old more than in other provinces. Luxury and wastefulness were rarely met with there; on the contrary, the spirit of thriftiness reigned everywhere and this supposedly explained why there were so many well-off families and how even modest inheritances could pass from father to son over long periods of time. There were more people interested in research there than anywhere else. Quite often one could see a young person who, having worked the whole day in the fields, sits down to read in the evening and even into the night.[47]

Curiosity and Hospitality

There seems little doubt that the first impressions of a person, people, or country are the most vivid even if afterwards they turn out to be false. So what did the Russians who came to Korea for the first time notice in the "character" of Koreans? Books and articles by Russian authors are unanimous in pointing to the limitless curiosity aroused in Koreans by all strangers, though obviously most Koreans were seeing a white person for the first time in their lives. Thus, the very first Russian to visit Kyŏnghŭng in northernmost Hamgyŏng writes: "Soon a massive crowd formed, surrounding us on all sides .... In fact, this impudent curiosity with which they observe you from head to foot had already become unbearable, and they feel you, take things right out of your pocket or hands, and practically tear them to pieces."[48]

Dadeshkaliani writes: "The Koreans are witty, lively, impressionable, inquisitive. During my stay in Korea I was a true martyr; I ended up in some village and became the focal point of a throng of a hundred people; I had to answer a mass of questions, give information about distant regions, explain the meaning and use of every thing that was on my person; frequently things would go so far that I simply had to undress, in order to show the inner parts of European clothing."[49]

Delotkovich describes similar throngs from his first days in Korea: "As soon as I entered the room a big crowd of people gathered and it was difficult to breathe. In the room of one square *sazhen'* [1 *sazhen'* = 7 feet] I counted 29 persons, big and small. Everyone says he will be leaving after having a look at me, but as soon as one leaves another appears in his place."[50] Then, he says, "As soon as I entered the town there came cries of 'Orasi' ('Russian'), 'orasi chun' ('a Russian is coming') from all sides, and the people followed me *en masse*, blocking the way completely."[51] Strel'bitskii likewise writes of having to "push aside the throng and, after barricading ourselves behind the gates, free ourselves from our obliging, but extremely importunate, hosts."[52]

Hospitality is another feature of Koreans that is unanimously recognized (and appreciated) by the Russian authors who visited the northern regions of the country. In his morbid short story, "Masha the Korean," set in a Korean village in the South Ussuri *krai* and published in 1887, A. Ia. Maksimov describes a scene where two lecherous Russian soldiers barge into a Korean home to ogle Masha, the comely Korean girl living there with her aging parents. Despite their rudeness, they are greeted with the "spirit of cordial hospitality, so typical of Koreans."[53] Lubentsov writes:

Hospitality is one of the most attractive traits of Koreans. If a stranger stops near a *fanza* [peasant hut], a host comes out and keeps asking him to enter and honor him with his visit. Refusal on the part of a stranger is considered an insult to the host and will not be forgotten for a long time; fellow villagers will remind him of it, saying that he was not courteous enough to a stranger. Hospitality is truly unlimited and a stranger can live in a *fanza* for weeks and even months and the host will provide shelter and food. Many Koreans make use of it, especially lately when the Korean population has become so remarkably mobile. During the last Japanese-Chinese war many inhabitants of the regions enveloped by war escaped to places far from the war theater and took advantage of people's hospitality there. The same happened during the cholera which swept P'yŏngan Province in late summer and early autumn. Finally, during our trip many Koreans from the southern and western provinces fled out of fear of the Japanese to northeastern parts of Korea and even to Russia and China where they made use of the hospitality of their compatriots.[54]

Strel'bitskii, whose expedition and travel narrative are dominated by military objectives and whose work ends with a recommendation to more or less occupy and annex the far north of Korea, writes of the incredible kindness and assistance that the Koreans provided: "It was positively touching to see how eagerly and painstakingly the natives would spend entire days in order to lighten somewhat for us a difficult ascent or conceal for our wheels the ungracious rocks of their homeland. . . . I suppose the routes in Korea would become a great deal more convenient if 'distinguished foreigners' passed through more often."[55] Other Russian authors who note Korean hospitality are Ragozin, who wrote, "Koreans are hospitable to the extreme,"[56] and Nasekin, who notes, "Hospitality is observed by everyone as one of the most sacred duties."[57] In the opinion of Selivanovskii, excessive hospitality on the part of Koreans had led to a situation in Korea where there were many spongers who took advantage of traditional hospitality and managed to live at somebody else's expense. One could cross the whole country without a coin in his pocket.[58]

Above all, hospitality was shown to Russian travelers by Korean local and provincial administrators who, due to their official duties, were to make sure that nothing untoward happened to the strangers from Russia. Thus, they did their best to assist them in their trips through Korea. Delotkevich writes: "At about 20 verst's [1 verst' = .66 miles] from our lodging for the night I met the head [R. nachal'nik K. Moksa] of Kilju. . . . He is a thoughtful old man and he has sent his assistant several times to me to find out whether I have enough food and to inquire after my health."[59]

Finally, N. Nasekin noticed the same kind of hospitality among Korean settlers on Russian territory. He wrote that during trips and when moving to other places, Koreans gave food and shelter not only to their compatriots but also to the Russians and Chinese; if travelers had some food with them, their hosts would cook it, adding their own spices. A traveler could stay as long as he wanted and, according to Korean etiquette, he was to warn that he could not pay for the shelter. If he kept silence it meant he would pay; the latter concerned coaching inns and eating houses, as in the villages they did not take money.[60]

Neo-Confucian Patriarchy and Ethics: The Place of Women

In the second half of the nineteenth century, Korea was a patriarchal society with a centuries-old traditional way of life. The natural economy, weak contacts between the provinces and the center, and regionalism reflected the everyday life of the Koreans. The Russian scholars, travelers, military men, and missionaries, all of whom were well-educated and familiar with European civilization and culture, discovered in Korea what seemed to be a primordial and patriarchal society quite different from the Russia that had changed after the abolition of serfdom in 1867. Lubentsov writes:

> One of the most characteristic features of Korean everyday life is its patriarchy and the cult of ancestors. The forefather of the family is honored from generation to generation and every year the head of the family reveres his memory by conducting a ceremonial rite. However, lately this patriarchy is starting to lose its meaning, a fact which is partially demonstrated by the following anecdote. A new *kunshiu* [Kunsu] arrived in the area and upon his arrival addressed the people with a speech describing his way of thinking and said: "I revere God and honor my ancestors." One of the Koreans shook his head. The *kunshiu* asked: "And who do you revere most?" "My bull." "Why?" "My bull works and feeds me, but my ancestors do not give me anything, even though we have to spend money for funeral rites in their honor!"[61]

Yet Lubentsov points to the exclusive importance of ancestral belonging in Korean society and writes: "The greatest solidarity is characteristic of the members of the same ancestral line. Thus, when a Korean becomes bankrupt, if his debts are not paid by his close relatives, they are to be paid by members of the same ancestral line, even if they are the most distant relatives and have never seen the person in debt."[62]

The famous Russian writer Nikolai Georgievich Mikhailovskii (1852–1906), better known perhaps by his pen name Garin-Mikhailovskii, accompanied Korf and Zvegintsev on their expedition of 1898, and later published a hugely popular account of his travels under the title *In and About Korea, Manchuria, and the Liaodong Peninsula*.[63] Garin-Mikhailovskii recorded interesting ethnographic observations and sketches of daily life in the far north of Korea, and made numerous remarks on Korean ancestor worship and on the inordinate predilection of Koreans for digging up their dead and reburying them in more auspicious grave sites. "(22 September) From Musan they take birch bark, in which they wrap up the deceased when they move them from one grave to another. Given the love of Koreans for transporting such dead people around, this is a decent branch of trade—the bones don't rot inside the birch bark."[64] Selivanovskii was amazed at the mutual assistance among the Koreans, as not only relatives and friends but also strangers hurry to render assistance to those suffering from misfortune. New settlers are readily given ploughs, seeds, and other things and are assisted in building a house and other buildings. All around support is rendered to those in need during weddings, funerals, illnesses and especially after floods, fires, earthquakes, and other natural disasters.[65]

Superiority of men over women, the absolutism in the rights of a husband and total lack of rights for Korean women made educated Russians wonder and many Russian authors were highly critical regarding the relationships between spouses and condemned the situation of Korean women in Korean society. One of the first things commented on was the way in which Korean women—particularly those of the upper classes—were sequestered away in the inner quarters of the houses and generally kept out of sight and under wraps. During his foray into Kyŏnghŭng, Przheval'skii saw only men: "Incidentally, there were only men in the crowd; I did not see one woman during the whole time I was in Kygen-Pu [Kyŏnghŭng]."[66]

Prince Dadeshkaliani seemed positively frustrated that he could not turn his gaze more effectively to Korean women:

However lax the Korean man may be in family life, the Korean woman is that much faithful and moral; you cannot buy her off or tempt her with anything; woe is she who shows weakness: she can be beheaded by her husband or a relative with impunity. The strictness of Korean women's morals has led to a situation where all Europeans living in Korea are forced to send off to Japan for wives. Unfortunately, I was unable to create for myself any understanding, whether of the type or costume of these Oriental Penelopes: they do not reveal themselves to outsiders and appear on the streets only in covered palanquins or on foot, but covered from head to toe in a white blanket. I saw only married women from the simple folk, who dress themselves in anything at all and who have lost all feminine charm from their heavy labours. But judging from the type of the men, and their tall height, it is probable that the women of Korea, too, are not devoid of attractiveness.[67]

But Russian travelers were also quick to notice that many of the strictures on women in evidence in Seoul were relaxed in the northeast. Delotkovich records: "Starting from Von-zan [Wŏnsan], the women and girls in the villages do not wear any mantles. Among them I saw not only pretty ones, but even a few of very fine appearance. If one encountered pleasant faces, though, in the majority of cases they were disfigured by smallpox. In Chan-ban [probably Chŏngp'yŏng] Korean women clustered around me in such a significant number that I left without even eating."[68] When Arkhimandrit Khrisanf arrived in Hamhŭng, a huge crowd surrounded him and his party as usual:

Here even the women go around completely in the open . . . no sooner had we entered the inn, than the entire village gathered around us, even the women. In the central provinces, and especially in Seoul, Korean etiquette does not allow women to appear openly on the streets and especially not to mix in the company of men; here, though, obviously, this etiquette did not exist, not only for the common folk, but even for the wives of the officials, as in Hamhŭng we stopped at the home of an official and his wife walked around completely openly, sat with us and observed our luggage with exactly the same curiosity as everybody else. From the missionary point of view this is a most important circumstance: it offers the possibility to spread the word of God freely even among women, in the hands of whom lies the raising of children . . . for the Seoul women one needs a female missionary as well as a separate, closed place in the sanctuary, whereas here, neither the one nor the other is necessary.[69]

And when Khrisanf arrived in Pukch'ŏng, it was market day: "It was remarkable that the vendors were almost exclusively women in bright, colorful attire; we hardly noticed any male vendors at all. This is exactly the opposite from Seoul. Entering and exiting the city we encountered many women riding on horseback, on oxen and cows, with various goods produced in the countryside."[70] Khrisanf continues, "As usual a substantial crowd of people gathered and among them nearly all had been more than once in Vladivostok, even the women; one woman spoke tolerably well in Russian."[71]

Seven years earlier, on the Russian side of the border, Shreider paid a visit to one of the Korean villages, where he noticed that some of the older customs were already falling away.

> I took advantage of the opportunity—one that seldom falls upon the European—to take a close look at the Korean woman, who is usually hidden away according to the customs of this tribe, in the depths of their uncomfortable halves, whither nobody is allowed to penetrate, and whence they, back home in Korea, have no right to leave without the permission of the head of the family, especially during the day. But obviously this custom is not observed so strictly here. In Korea, though—no more than 175 *verst's* from the village where I was now, that is—the traveler rarely succeeds in meeting a woman on the street.... The women here are rather pretty: they are tall, stately, well-proportioned, although with a noticeably fat waist; with the regular lines of a matt face, they yield nothing to European women in their external appearance. Occasionally one encounters even real beauties.[72]

The notion that Korean women did not have names was widely commented on by Russian travelers, starting with Przheval'skii already in 1869: "It is amazing that Korean women have no name, and are called by their kin relation, for example: mother, auntie, grandmother, etc."[73] Shreider, in his rambling account of his three years in the South Ussuri *krai*, writes:

> No woman is as disenfranchised and voiceless a creature as the Korean woman. The Korean woman is a slave in the full sense of this word, a humiliated being, who does not even have her own name!... If you ask a Korean man the name of his wife, sister, mother, daughter, bride, niece, grandmother, etc., he will not understand you at all: the Korean woman, as I have already said, has no name at all. "Tu-iun-shan's mother," "Kim's wife," "Pin-ian's grandmother"—this is what you will hear in answer to your question.[74]

N. Nasekin writes: "Among Koreans, as among other Asian peoples, the situation of women in the family and society is humiliating and insultingly subordinate.... Women do not have names."[75]

All the Russian travelers were men, and not surprisingly, the Russian traveler's gaze turned to the physical charms (or lack thereof) of Korean women.

> Compared to the men, the women are much smaller in stature, in which they remind of their Japanese fellow tribeswomen. The women wither quickly, which on the one hand can be attributed to the heavy role of work which falls on women of the simple folk, and on the other, to the ceruse, which is in great vogue among Korean ladies. Whiteness is considered a mark of beauty among the women, and even the word "pretty" in Korean includes a particle indicating white color (ko-pun-ge [kobun ke] "pretty" where "pun" means whiteness).[76] We were able to see on more than one occasion women of the upper class covered in a thick layer of ceruse.[77]

Maksimov's story written in 1887, "Masha the Korean girl," fetishizes Korean feminine beauty as follows: "In the open doors stood a shapely, charming girl, with black fiery eyes, and with a happy laugh.... The girl's full, round face breathed the health and freshness of innocence; her long, tightly plaited braids, the glory of Korean women, hung like black serpents almost down to her heels ... her blouse barely conceal[ed] her virgin breasts and her full, classical shoulders."[78] When one of the two lecherous Russian soldiers introduced above continues to stare at her, Masha "felt that he was admiring her half-open torso and breasts.... 'Didn't I tell 'ya, Laskin? Let me tell 'ya now: I've never seen a girl like her in my whole life. And how about those clothes— you can see practically everything that's for dinner. Can't take my eyes off her. See what a beauty she is? But why is she being so shy and awkward?'"[79]

Garin-Mikhailovskii's gaze falls often on the Korean women he encounters; sometimes he sees in them women no different than the Russian women back home:

> (20 September) A pretty, white-faced Korean is walking by. She is carrying a jug on her head, and her gait is somehow special as she maintains her balance. Biblik's face breaks into a most blissful smile: "Damn, she's pretty...."[80]

> (24 September) I sat down to observe a group of Korean women who were waiting for the ferry.... They are all well-proportioned, and there is much

grace in them, but their faces are not pretty. Their costume is similar to the Russian lady's.... The elegant manners, the hairdo—this is a group of our Russian ladies.[81]

Literacy

The Russian sources contain a number of interesting observations on Korean literacy habits, starting with some general notes on Korean language and script: "The Korean language is absolutely original and in its nature has nothing common with Chinese, Manchu, or Japanese, although it has taken in quite a few words borrowed from these dialects. The Korean alphabet is also hieroglyphic, but much simplified, with no more than 28 sound-producing signs."[82] Al'ftan had the following to say about Korean reading practices:

Literacy in Korea is very widespread. There is a school in every hamlet, and one rarely meets a Korean who does not know how to read and write. Frequently in the evenings from a dimly lit peasant hut, jam-packed with little kids sitting on their haunches wherever they can find space, one hears the frenzied singing of a strange, monotonous tune of two or three notes. This means that a lesson is in full swing. This peculiar method of teaching literacy via singing, insofar as we know, exists among only three peoples: the Koreans, the Japanese, and the Chinese. They learn not only reading, but also counting via singing. And this method will be with them forever. I happened once to see how they brought a piece of paper to the *nachal'nik* [head] of a province for him to sign. The *kun'-shu* [Kunsu] or *kvan-tsarsa* [Kwanch'alsa] himself, having turned over the long sheet of paper, upon which something was written in large letters in vertical columns, parallel with short margins, from right to left, immediately struck up a little song. The Koreans present, who were also interested in the contents of the letter, clustered around him, and without any sense of embarrassment in his presence, also set to reading the letter, loudly echoing their *nachal'nik*. Every morning, when my Korean interpreter was calculating his expenses, he would almost always get carried away and break into an aria, until a burst of laughter brought him back to his senses.[83]

And Garin-Mikhailovskii, too, renders a description of Korean *viva voce* reading practice:

(18 September) The noise from the unpacking died down, dinner was cooking, and somewhere behind me some pleasant tenor was singing some oriental song. Like the pattern of the flowers in their mountains and valleys, it suits them, and fits the sensitive, but squeezed and meek souls of the Korean. There is something tender and melancholy that seizes you by the soul in this monotonous melody. The individual roulades and notes are comprehensible and have a strong effect, but all together require translation for our ear—this is material only for that composer who would like to study the music of the Orient. P. N. arrived and explained that it wasn't singing, but reading, and that here, when they read, they sing, and that the person reading was one of the best readers in the town.[84]

Most of the Russian observers claim widespread literacy in the vernacular script: "The Russian Koreans are almost all literate in Russian and Korean (ŏnmun)."[85] Korf and Zvegintsev advised using "ŏnmun only" for notices in case of a military occupation, as "all Koreans are literate."[86] Garin-Mikhailovskii provides a nice confirmation of the (allegedly) gendered nature of vernacular script usage at his time of writing:

(14 September) The heir is a completely degenerate person, who does not need even his wife. Great hopes lie on the illegal son of the Korean king, who is being educated in Japan. He is 22 now. He is a very bright and educated man. He "knows all foreign writing systems, and knows ours, both the men's and the women's." The men's script is Chinese writing, and the women's is the Korean script, simplified for the common folk. Half the Koreans know the women's script, and the other half are illiterate.[87]

Later, Garin meets an old scholar who is adept at storytelling: "(17 September) Incidentally, it became clear that the nobleman knows only Chinese writing, but not Korean women's writing, which makes of him an illiterate living among the common folk. But it is understood to be improper for a nobleman to know the women's writing of the simple folk."[88]

But the Orthodox missionary Khrisanf implies, after conversations with an American missionary in a northeastern village, that literacy in the vernacular script may not be so widespread after all: "According to the missionary, the people here are coarse, and—what is surprising—do not like book learning, and this is why one can encounter many illiterates among the Hamgyŏng Koreans, something one does not find in the central and southern provinces."[89]

Selivanovskii writes that scholars were very much respected in both Korea and China, and that mainly they studied the works of Chinese men of wisdom. Until (the Kabo Reforms of) 1894, state posts were given to the scholars who had passed special examinations, although quite often exam passes and state posts could be acquired with money rather than scholastic achievement. Ordinary people would buy cheap books of verse, stories, fairy tales, and dramas.[90]

Alleged Shortcomings in Habits and Character: Drinking and Smoking

The Russian authors did not fail to comment on what they perceived as weaknesses and shortcomings in the Koreans. Lubentsov thought that one major shortcoming of the Koreans was their passion for alcoholic drinks and smoking tobacco. Smoking tobacco is described by the Russian authors as an inveterate habit of nearly everyone. Already in 1869, Przheval'skii wrote: "They all smoke, even the women."[91] During more ceremonious meetings with Korean local officials, pipe smoking was almost de rigeur. Thus, when Przheval'skii met the satto (magistrate) in Kyŏnghŭng, he described the meeting as follows: "He was a rather good-looking middle-aged man of 41 years, called Iun'-Khab [probably Yun Hap] and held the rank of captain, satti [sic] in Korean ... two pipes were brought out and lit up ... then they brought a geographic atlas of Korean authorship.... His knowledge concerning Russia was so extensive, that he even knew about the torching of Moscow by the French. When my translator was unable to understand and translate this, Iun'-Khab took some ash from the pipe bowl, placed it on the map where it said Moscow, and said "Frantsuzy" [the French]."[92]

In his story, "Masha the Korean girl," Maksimov describes a bizarre scene of reunion between father, mother, and daughter—all three kiss (surely a fantasy!) and sit down to smoke a pipe upon their reunion.[93] Ten years later, pipe smoking is part of Shreider's unflattering portrait of the Korean porters in Vladivostok: "They cannot get them to overcome their simply incomprehensible laziness and cease their dolce far niente with the pipe that never leaves their mouth. Thanks to this, it is rare for Kauli [the local Russian term for Koreans, from Chinese "Gaoli"] to join the ranks of people and achieve material well-being and security."[94]

Back in Korea itself, Khrisanf writes: "As soon as they have eaten, they light up their pipes and belch horribly. Korean men and women love to smoke: a non-smoking Korean man or woman is a rarity."[95] According to Selivanovskii, a small chibouque with a long stem and a purse with tobacco was an accessory of nearly every Korean.[96]

Regarding opium smoking the opinions differ. For instance, Lubentsov wrote that "despite the proximity of China it is unknown in Korea."[97] But Selivanovskii assumed that, despite the strict prohibitions, many people smoked opium, mixing it with tobacco.[98] Khrisanf writes: "They smoke locally grown tobacco, which is cultivated all throughout Korea. . . . Pipe-smoking, by the way, is not so terribly evil and one can fight it relatively more easily than the other harmful and difficult-to-eradicate predilection growing in Korea—opium."[99] He continues, "Our Koreans here [in Seoul] with Russian citizenship who work as court interpreters are almost all opium addicts. . . . Idleness, wine, opium, gambling, and debauchery of every nature swallow up the days and nights of the lives of capital dwellers. . . . They told me that Koreans consider the best way to quit smoking opium to be drinking."[100]

As for drinking, here, too, the first comment comes from Przheval'skii, who happened upon a funeral in a Korean village in the South Ussuri krai ". . . they offered me the tastiest of beverages—warmed vodka with honey; I forced myself to try a swallow—a terrible abomination."[101] The same beverage is alluded to by Maksimov in his short story, "Masha the Korean Girl," as the "favorite beverage of Koreans—warmed vodka with honey."[102] Dadeshkaliani, in a description of a typical Korean meal, writes: "All of this is washed down with a handsome quantity of rice vodka."[103] And Lubentsov notes that many of the local officials he met were fond of drink: "The governor [in Kyŏngsŏng] was obviously a great lover of alcoholic beverages."[104] He adds, "Incidentally, all Koreans in general seem to be distinguished by this feature. We were able to meet quite a few drunks, especially in the cities."[105] More generally, Lubentsov finds that "One great deficiency of the Koreans is their love for alcoholic beverages and smoking tobacco. Both are typical also of women, especially in P'yŏngan Province. Drunkenness is extremely widespread, especially on holidays. Vodka [suri, suli] is prepared in every fanza and its cost is negligible."[106]

Finally, Garin-Mikhailovskii describes an encounter with a Chinese peddler of Chinese rice vodka along the Sino-Korean border:

> (16 September) In our fanza we find an old Chinese man.... "He didn't show you the most important thing," said P. N., "Chinese vodka, khanshin, as the Russians call it, or khodzhiu as the Chinese say, or tanu-stsur in Korea. This vodka is what he trades in the most of all. In Korea the sale of vodka is permitted unrestrictedly and is not assessed any excise." I tried this vodka—it has a very strong fusel smell and a rather bitter taste. "It's very strong," says P. N., "if you light it with a match, it will burn." I light a match, but the match dies out, and the vodka doesn't want to burn. "He poured lots of water in." The Chinese smiles. "This is cheap vodka," he says.[107]

RUSSO-KOREAN CONTACTS IN THE RUSSO-KOREAN "CONTACT ZONE"

Among other things, the Russian travel narratives are full of indications of the extent and spread of Russian cultural influence in northeastern Korea, and of the general goodwill towards Russia and Russians felt by Koreans in that region. It is clear from the different accounts that many Koreans have traveled to and/or worked in Vladivostok or other areas of the Russian Far East, and it is not unusual to meet Koreans who speak tolerably good Russian. Thus, Delotkovich writes already in 1886, as he was approaching Sŏngjin: "From here many Koreans go to Vladivostok, completing the journey in 4–5 days in good weather. From Pukchan [Pukch'ŏng] a great many people go to Vladivostok, too, which takes 6 or 7 days of travel time."[108] He continues:

> The city Khordian" [Hoeryŏng] lies on the upper reaches of the river Tomon-gam [Tuman-gang or Tumen River]. From here it is 170 verst's to Kyekhyn [Kyŏnghŭng]. I met a Korean with the surname Chuprov, called Pëtr, and in Korean Kim-tu-shej [probably Kim Tu-sŏng]. Chuprov lives in Kyekhyn, but spends most of his time in Ianchikhe, our Korean village close to Novokievsk. Chuprov served as interpreter for two and half years with our border komissar in the South Ussuri krai, Mr. Matiunin,[109] and reads, speaks, and writes

Korean and Russian very well, and also speaks Chinese. Chuprov wants to find work as an interpreter in Seoul with our *chargé d'affaires*, Mr. Veber. The Korean authorities approve of Chuprov, especially the *pussa* Sheo-khin-shiun [probably Sŏ Hyŏng-sun], who has known Chuprov for eight years, and also the duty collector, Pkhan-khan-diu [probably P'an Han-ju].[110]

Al'ftan tells a similar tale:

At the present time, when a defeated China has been pushed to the side, a period of almost open battle between two influences has started in Korea: Russian and Japanese.... The people in the north living in constant contact with us have already been able to get accustomed to us. Many Koreans have spent time in Russia in the Ussuri *krai*, have earned some money here, and returned home to Korea with good memories of our *krai*. In almost every village up to 100 *verst's* from our border one can meet Koreans who speak Russian. And upon meeting us, all of them shouted with joy, "*Zdravstvui, kapitana!*" [sic: "Greetings, Captain!"][111] Expressed in this greeting is the pride at being able to greet someone in Russian, and a genuine good will with respect to us Russians. Many of these Koreans were able to conduct themselves half-decently in Russian. Further to the south the number that have spent time in Russia and knowing Russian gradually dwindles, and finally, to the south of Kil'chu (200 *verst's* from our border) we hardly encountered any at all. About the Japanese, people from our border as far as Ken-shen [Kyŏngsŏng] (150 *verst's* from the border) knew little and were not particularly interested.[112]

Whereas north of Kyŏngsŏng the Koreans paid little mind to the Japanese, south of Kyŏngsŏng the rise in anti-Japanese feelings was palpable for our Russian observers, and concomitant with that sentiment they reported a pronounced pro-Russian attitude. "The situation is different to the south of the city of Ken-shen [Kyŏngsŏng]. The further one gets from it, the sharper and more pronounced is the attitude of the people to the Japanese. In Kil'chzhiu we met a very interesting Korean.... According to him, the entire people now await help only from Russia."[113]

Lubentsov was positively puzzled by the pro-Russian sentiments he witnessed: "The further we got from Russian territory, the more cordially [*radu-*

shnee] and sincerely [*zadushevnee*] we were greeted, and the more respectfully they treated us. I have positively no idea to what to attribute this."[114] Garin-Mikhailovskii's diaries are full of episodes where Koreans express positive feelings for Russia and Russians. A railroad engineer by training, Garin shares the following conversation with a Korean eager for railroad technology for Korea:

> (17 September) "Ah, we're already building a road like that, but without the knowledge we won't be able to use it." I answered that the Koreans are a talented people, and that once they start learning technology, they will learn it just as quickly as the Japanese, and surpass the Europeans.
> "Northern Korea will get science from Russia."
> "If Korea wants it. Russia counts Koreans as her brothers."
> "*We* want it, but we don't know about the others."[115]

Garin, too, records instances of spontaneous expressions of Russophilia:

> (18 September) A white Korean ran out of one of the *fanzas* and, extending his hand, shouted in Russian: "Greetings, greetings, come to my *fanza!*" This was a Korean who had returned from working in Russia. I treated him to a cigarette, shook his hand, and we parted, as his entire store of knowledge was limited to the phrase above.[116]

Often, Garin puts expressions of pro-Russian sentiment in the mouths of the Korean characters he describes:

> (17 October) The name of the Russian in Korea is sacred. Russia has done too much for us and is too magnanimous for us not to value this. The Russian is our most honored guest. We are between two open maws: on the one side, Japan, on the other, China. If neither one nor the other swallows us up, it will, of course, be thanks only to Russia.[117]

The Orthodox priest and missionary Archimandrite Khrisanf records similar experiences along his journey: "In the northern province bordering Russia (Kham-gion-do) [Hamgyŏng-do], which I have traveled throughout, starting from the south, I noticed a strong influence from Russia. . . . Some of the

Koreans command Russian, and one finds Russian goods in the Korean stores; they wear Russian clothing and old soldiers' uniforms purchased in Vladivostok in the open-air market."[118] Khrisanf also records, "We left Yŏnghŭng early in the morning. . . . We went 40 li and stopped to feed the horses in the large village of Ch'owŏn. In this village we heard the Russian word *khleb* ("bread") for the first time from a native of the village—the owner of the inn who, as it turned out, had been in Vladivostok several times on business. The Koreans really love Russian bread, and as soon as they arrive in Vladivostok the first word they learn is *khleb*."[119]

The following episode, also from Khrisanf, took place in Hongwŏn: "The inhabitants of the city are frequently in Vladivostok on business, and some of them know a few words of Russian and are quite flattering in their remarks about Russians. We pushed on further, and after passing a few li from the city, three Koreans caught up to us, one of whom recognized me as a Russian priest and immediately starting speaking with me in a broken version of Vladivostok Russian; he called himself by the Russian name "Andrei" and, apparently, was very pleased to meet us."[120] By the time Khrisanf had got as far north as the pass at Maullyŏng, "Here you can 'smell Russia' already. All the local Koreans have been in Vladivostok many times and praised the kindness of Russia. For those Koreans who know Russians well, the word 'Russian' has become a synonym for 'good.'"[121]

After the division of Korea into North and South and in the context of the new Cold War, expressions like these of pro-Russian feeling were seized upon by Soviet commentators and woven into the Soviet discourse of "internationalism" and "friendship of peoples," especially "friendship of Russia with all peoples."[122] This was especially true of passages from Garin-Mikhailovskii, whose birth centenary in 1952 occasioned a flurry of publications about him as well as new editions of his works, and also coincided with the Korean War. Another example is Zaichikov; citing G. Kennan, who wrote about Korea in 1905, Zaichikov comments:

We should note that the fraternal relation to the Korean people and the high appraisal of their moral qualities were characteristic for almost all Russian travelers in Korea. And this is all the more important to underline, namely, that for the majority of western European and American "tourists" in Korea, as well as for the Japanese expansionists, a derisive relation toward this nation was characteristic, and a view of the Korean nation as an inferior one, incapable of progress or independent existence. The slander of the American racists toward the Korean people went so far as monstrous expressions like the rotten product of a degenerate oriental civilization.[123]

Kolos writes: "In the works of N. G. Garin we find a clear expression of how, already in the nineteenth century, a great feeling of friendship to the Russian people had formed and ripened in the consciousness of the laboring masses in Korea. The first thing that caught Garin's attention after he became acquainted with Koreans was their especially good relations toward Russia."[124]

BACK TO THE QUESTION OF NORTH-SOUTH DIFFERENCES

We have already related some of the claims made by Europeans, both Russian and non-Russian, as well as Koreans (the mystery premodern author cited by Kiuner from Rouelle), about differences in character and physique between southern and northern Koreans. Let us now examine a few more such claims and their resonances in later Soviet writing. One point worth noting here is that, to the Russians writing these travelogues (and, one assumes, to the Koreans they were working with), the "south" included P'yŏngan Province. Thus, Zvegintsev writes: "Over the pass ['Togurion-Miti' to the south of Kanggye], I unfortunately came to the conclusion that my interpreters also poorly understand the locals here and that the locals, for their part, poorly understand them; the very appearance of the locals changed, their eyes became more slanted, and they were smaller in stature."[125] Garin-Mikhailovskii, too, when his party finally crossed over into P'yŏngan Province from Paektusan and the source of the Yalu River, writes: "(11 October) In the evening the *fanza* filled with Koreans. They talked politics, about the flow of things. . . . I double-checked my earlier information. I could sense a certain difference between the southern and northern Koreans. The southerners are darker, there eyes are more severe, and burn with little fires, their speech is fast, passionate. . . . But they are just as hospitable and well-disposed."[126]

Views like these were picked up and elaborated by Soviet researchers in the 1950s and 1960s as part of the new discourse on the "friendship of peoples" and in support of the USSR's ally, North Korea.

There does in fact exist a difference between southern and northern Koreans. They differ from each other in their physical type, in their language, and in their culture. The southerners are somewhat smaller in stature, and the Mongolian type is expressed more strongly with them.... We should only note that the differences in physical types noted by Garin related to the inhabitants of the eastern and western provinces of North Korea. Between the population of these locales in Korea, apparently, there also exist differences in physical type, perhaps as a result of the closer ties which have existed since ancient times between the northwest seashore and the south of Korea. The northeast of Korea remained relatively isolated for an extended period of time.[127]

Finally, Kolos writes in his commentary on Garin-Mikhailovskii and the Korean folktales that Garin-Mikhailovskii collected:

The history of Korea tells us that since ancient times the most populated places on the Korean peninsula were the northern regions. The northern Korean tribes were more advanced, and here, earlier than with other ethnic groups of Korea, are noted the development of both government and culture. Chinese writing and culture penetrated here first, effecting a great and positive influence on the development of the culture of Korea. It is precisely here, in the North, whence flow the currents of Korean history [citing a DPRK source]. We daresay: everything that is typical and characteristic in general for the Korean, his life and culture, is, in the first instance, characteristic for the northern Korean. By dint of this, the rather limited territorial study of Korea and its culture in the case observed here is nonetheless not too narrow in its coverage, and has a pan-Korean significance.[128]

CONCLUSIONS: THE BEAR AND THE SWAN?

The excerpts from Russian travel narratives in the Russo-Korean "contact zone" cited above are but a small portion of the data we have collected for this project, and could easily be amplified to include economy and trade, religion, music and dance, etiquette, food, language and dialect, administrative structure, descriptions of individual Korean local officials, etc. But from what we have demonstrated thus far, it should be clear that the Russian writers during this period left a rich body of descriptive and factual material about Korea and

Koreans on the whole, with special emphasis on the northern provinces adjoining Russia.

But just as important as the facts and observations offered up by the Russians are the rhetorical devices and discourse in which they are couched. Thus, and perhaps unsurprisingly, the Russian sources on Korea, like British and French works on the "Orient" from this period, reveal many of the same "Orientalist" tropes and images familiar to us now from Said's analysis. Soviet Garin scholar Kolos is eager to point out that Garin-Mikhailovskii "polemicized with bourgeois philosophy, science, and with bourgeois exoticizing literature (R. Kipling, P. Loti)" and "angrily condemned racist theory,"[129] but the Korea that Garin-Mikhailovskii writes about is a surreal place, veiled in Romantic imagery—it is a *skazka* (fairy tale)-like land much like the Korean fairy tales he so lovingly recorded during the Korf & Zvegintsev expedition. In the forward to his book *Koreiskie Skazki* (Korean Folktales),[130] Garin-Mikhailovskii writes, "Entire sheafs of violet and orange rays from the yellow sun, just setting in all its glory, filled this distant place; the sun glittered and flashed one last time before disappearing, like an apparition, in the shafts of the fast-approaching twilight. And everything around me—this remote place, these people and their lives—seemed like a fairy tale, too."[131] He continues, "Ah, what magical children, locked to this day in their own fairy tale world!"[132] On another occasion he adds, "The Korean needs ... nothing: he needs tales of happiness. And tales and stories are dearer to him than heavy coins or a scrawny patch of field."[133]

This romantic imagery extends to other, less literary writers like Lubentsov, saying, "Like a forbidden fruit, she [Korea] was imagined with much enigmatic fascination."[134] Another dominant descriptive strategy is the infantilization of the Koreans, as expressed in the words of Strel'bitskii: "It felt as though all around us was a crowd of curious children; but affectionate, artless children."[135] Garin-Mikhailovskii, too, writes: "(27 September) I remember the words of one Russian tourist—that the Korean loves the stick and that one needs to conduct oneself with great dignity with him, and to beat him from time to time. I am ashamed of such Russian tourists. What animal would take it into his head to resort to the fist among these children!"[136] And the missionary Khrisanf complains, with respect to Korean curiosity: "The Koreans are like children, and absolutely everything interests them, starting with my clothing and finishing with how we walk and sleep. . . . They are simply children, and the most naïve ones, at that."[137] David N. Wells, in his study of Russian narratives of travel in Japan, notes the same imagery, and relates it to a Russian paternalism—a Russian assumption of superior culture: "To Goncharov the Japanese are like children . . . they must look now to European instructors to find a way out of their impasse."[138]

Another classic "Orientalist" trope found in Garin-Mikhailovskii is his frequent description of Korean men in Korean garments as somehow feminine or lady-like: "Twenty or thirty Koreans in their lady-like white blouses, their lady-like hats with the broad brims and their high narrow crowns, surrounded us, sitting on their haunches."[139] These images of femininity, softness, whiteness, and infantilism converge in the image of the swan: "They call the Koreans cowards. Because of their white attire and their timidity the Russians call the Koreans white swans. . . . Yes: like swans, the Koreans are incapable of fighting among themselves, of spilling human blood; like swans, they can only sing their songs and tales. To take everything from them, even life itself, is as easy as to do the same with children or swans—all one needs is a trusty rifle and a good eye."[140]

Some of the Russian writers (admittedly few) deploy rather blatant racist imagery at times, the most egregious being Shreider, who refers to Koreans as weak, stupid, semi-human, half-dead, and half-asleep, their homes "constant sources and hotbeds of all manner of infectious diseases."[141] Shreider adds, "This is a strange creature—children of the 'land of eternal beggars,' as if they were completely devoid of nerves and blood. What you see before you is not living people, but walking mummies. And even in their external appearance they are similar to dried out skeletons. You look at them, and the thought creeps into your head that their place is not here, among living people, but somewhere in a museum or anatomical theater."[142]

But while the Russian authors are clearly guided by certain stereotypes, these stereotypes are more cultural than racial, and this, in turn, implies that the Russian observers saw the possibility for Koreans to transcend their current difficulties. Like Georgiev, the Russian orientalist scholar studied by Nathaniel Knight, most of the Russian writers "show little concern for representing the contemporary 'other' and creating the cognitive apparatus for domination."[143] Thus, there is much sympathy for the Koreans' plight at the turn of the twentieth century, as well as optimism for Korea's future. Grounds for optimism can be found close to home, in a comparison of the fates of the Koreans on either side of the Russo-Korean border; in Lubentsov's evaluation: "Many accuse the Koreans of laziness, but the best counter-evidence of this is the flourishing situation of the Korean settlements both close to Blagoveshchensk and in the South Ussuri *krai*: namely, literally the poorest Koreans, who had nothing but their healthy hands and the heads on their shoulders settled within Russian territory in the 1860s."[144] Garin tempers his at times idyllic images of a Korea stuck in a fairy tale past with bright visions of its potential: "The time will come when your valleys will be green with gardens and vineyards, and the people's labor will be vindicated ten times more than now. Then Korea will be rich."[145] Perhaps most optimistic of all is Lubentsov, whose research on P'yŏngan and Hamgyŏng provinces revealed so much of the latent economic potential of these regions: "Korea has significant potential energy, and, finding itself on the crossroads of the Old and New Worlds, can look forward to a brilliant future and perhaps, not too far in the future, this country will leave behind its condition of poverty and nothingness and make of itself one of the richest and most blessed corners of the Pacific rim."[146]

It is this combination of standard European racial, but mostly cultural stereotypes, and cautious presumptions of superiority, with the sympathies of a Russian nation that itself is ambivalent in its own identity as to its European and "Oriental" components, that make the Russian narratives of travel in Korea unique and valuable.

NOTES

1. Pratt, *Imperial Eyes: Travel Writing and Transculturation*, 6.
2. Tiagai, *Po Koree: Puteshestviia 1885–1896 gg.*, 6–7. Some useful surveys of Russian published sources on Korea from the Tsarist era are: Adami, "Die Geschichte der Koreaforschung im zaristischen Russland"; Adami, *Die russische Koreaforschung: Bibliographie 1682–1976*; Kontsevich, "O razvitii traditsionnogo koreevedeniia v tsarskoi Rossii (Istoriko-bibliograficheskii ocherk)"; and Ko Songmu, "Chejŏng rŏsia esŏ ŭi han'gugŏ mit han'guk yŏn'gu." A survey of specifically ethnographical literature is Dzharylgasinova, "Iz istorii rossiiskogo etnograficheskogo koreevedeniia."
3. Zaichikov, "N. G. Garin-Mikhailovskii i ego puteshestvie vokrug sveta," 15.
4. Kolos, "N. G. Garin-Mikhailovskii o Koree i sobrannye im koreiskie skazki," 206–207.
5. Unterberger, *Primorskaia oblast'*, 1856–1898.
6. Unterberger, *Priamurskii krai, 1906–1910 gg.*

7. Nadarov, "Iuzhno-Ussuriiskii krai v sovremennom ego sostoianii."

8. Ragoza, "Kratkii ocherk pereseleniia Koreitsev v nashi predely"; idem, "Pos'etskii uchastok"; idem, "Kratkii istoricheskii ocherk pereseleniia Koreitsev v nashi predely"; and Vebel', "Poezdka v Koreiiu."

9. Rittikh, *Pereselencheskoe i krest'ianskoe delo v Iuzhno-Ussuriiskom krae.*

10. For the valuable Korean linguistic (dialect) data in Nasekin, see King, "Russian Sources on Korean Dialects."

11. Nasekin, "Koreitsy Priamurskogo kraia."

12. Pesotskii, *Koreiskii vopros v Priamur'e.*

13. Nedachin, "Koreitsy-kolonisty. K voprosu o sblizhenii Koreitsev s Rossiei," 198.

14. Nedachin, *Pravoslavnaia tzerkov' v Koree: k 10-letiiu eia sushchestvovaniia;* and idem, "K voprosu o priniatii Koreitsev v khristianstvo."

15. Busse, *Pereselenie krest'ian morem v Iuzhno-Ussuriiskii krai v 1883–1893 gg.*

16. Putsillo, *Opyt russko-koreiskogo slovaria.*

17. See King, *Russian Sources on Korean Dialects* for more details on Putsillo himself, as well as a detailed analysis of the dialect materials in his dictionary.

18. Przheval'skii, "Inorodcheskoe naselenie v Iuzhnoi chasti Primorskoi oblasti," 195.

19. Vagin, "Koreitsy na Amure."

20. King, "Blagoslovennoe: Korean Village on the Amur, 1871–1937."

21. Knight, "Grigor'ev in Orenburg, 1851–1862," 75.

22. Brower and Lazzerini, eds., *Russia's Orient,* Preface: xviii.

23. Knight, "Grigor'ev in Orenburg, 1851–1862," 97.

24. Brower and Lazzerini, eds., *Russia's Orient,* Preface: xix.

25. Wells, *Russian Views of Japan,* 13–14.

26. Kim and King, *Istoriia, kul'tura i literature Kore saram,* 4–9.

27. Zuber, "Ekspeditsiia v Koreiu: Iz zapisok byvshego flotskogo ofitsera M. G. Zubera," 232–33.

28. Delotkovich, "Dnevnik Pavla Mikhailovicha Delotkovicha," 162.

29. Selivanovskii, *Kak zhivut i rabotaiut Koreitsy,* 12–13.

30. Lubentsov, *Khamkenskaia i pkhienanskaia provintsii Korei,* 168.

31. Ibid., 166.

32. As L. R. Kontsevich notes, this three-volume compendium is a truly encyclopedic work about Korea, and is based on a comprehensive survey of published sources available at the time, as well as on original research conducted specifically for the purposes of the book. This work contains data on the history of Korea, its industrial potential, trade, finances, state administrative structure, military forces, population, religions, language, literature, and education. Statistical tables, maps, international

agreements, the Korean system of chronology, and measurements of weight and height are also included in appendices. The enduring importance of this work can be seen from its numerous translations and editions; a Japanese translation (Nōshōmushō & Sanrinkyoku 1905); a North Korean translation (Chosŏn Minjujuŭi Inmin Konghwaguk Kwahagwŏn 1959); a Soviet abridged edition (Institut Narodov Azii 1960); and a South Korean translation (Kim Pyŏngnin 1983).

33. *Korean Repository* (1892), 269.

34. *Opisanie Korei*, 337.

35. Kirillov, *Koreia. Mediko-antropologicheskii ocherk*, 2.

36. Ibid., 5.

37. Ibid., 10.

38. Ibid., 11.

39. Ibid., 12.

40. For a short history of this institution, see Serov, "Vostochnyi Institut (1899–1909 gg.)."

41. The source cited by Kiuner was Rouelle (1907). We were unable to locate anything in Yi T'oegye's works resembling the source cited.

42. Kiuner, *Statistiko-geograficheskii i ekonomicheskii ocherk Korei*, 232, and Rouelle, "Les coréens jugés par un de leurs sages," 50.

43. Rouelle, "Les coréens jugés par un de leurs sages," 52–53.

44. Ibid.

45. Khrisanf, *Ot Seula do Vladivostoka*, 1.

46. Khrisanf, *Iz pisem Koreiskago missionera*, 9–10.

47. Zhdan-Pushkin, "Koreia: Ocherk istorii uchrezhdenii, iazyka, nravov, obychaev i rasprostraneniia khristianstva," 133.

48. Przheval'skii, *Puteshestvie v Ussuriiskom krae, 1867–1869*, 97.

49. Dadeshkaliani, "Kratkii ocherk sovremennogo sostoianiia Korei kniazia Dadeshkaliani," 55.

50. Ibid., 26.

51. Ibid., 28. Delotkovich complains frequently about the spectacle that was made of him, but then realizes: "My guide, it turns out, was a scoundrel. All along the way he had been collecting money from the crowds for showing me to them." Ibid., 160.

52. Strel'bitskii, *Iz Khunchuna v Mukden i obratno po sklonam Chan"-Bai-Shan'skago khrebta*, 31.

53. Maksimov, *Na dalekom vostoke: Razskazy i ocherki*, 51.

54. Lubentsov, *Khamkenskaia i pkhienanskaia provintsii Korei*, 175.

55. Strel'bitskii, *Iz Khunchuna v Mukden i obratno po sklonam Chan"-Bai-Shan'skago khrebta*, 119.

56. Ragozin, *Koreia i Iaponiia*, 18–19.

57. Nasekin, "Koreitsy Priamurskogo kraia," 27; *Opisanie Korei*, 1: 346–47.

58. Selivanovskii, *Kak zhivut i rabotaiut Koreitsy*, 30.

59. Delotkovich, "Dnevnik Pavla Mikhailovicha Delotkovicha," 41.

60. Nasekin, "Koreitsy Priamurskogo kraia," 28.

61. Lubentsov, *Khamkenskaia i pkhienanskaia provintsii Korei*, 175.

62. Ibid., 174.

63. Baron N. A. Korf and Staff-Captain A. I. Zvegintsev headed up an expedition to Korea in 1898, the results of which were published in 1904 as Korf & Zvegintsev, *Voennyi obzor Severnoi Korei*. This expedition, much larger in scale than previous Russian expeditions, also led to the compilation of a new map of Korea, described in detail in Korf, *Severnaia Koreia: Sbornik marshrutov* (1901). Zvegintsev and his team engaged in geological and botanical research, and also compiled detailed information on the locations, sizes, and economy of Korean communities near the border between Russia, China and Korea, especially on the Chinese side of the border.

64. Garin-Mikhailovskii, *Iz dnevnikov krugosvetnogo puteshestviia: Po Koree, Man'chzhurii i Liaodunskomu poluostrovu*, 133.

65. Selivanovskii, *Kak zhivut i rabotaiut Koreitsy*, 30.

66. Przheval'skii, *Puteshestvie v Ussuriiskom krae, 1867–1869*, 97.

67. Dadeshkaliani, "Kratkii ocherk sovremennogo sostoianiia Korei kniazia Dadeshkaliani," 57.

68. Delotkovich, "Dnevnik Pavla Mikhailovicha Delotkovicha," 145.

69. Khrisanf, *Ot Seula do Vladivostoka*, 76–77.

70. Ibid., 79.

71. Ibid., 81.

72. Shreider, *Nash Dal'nyi Vostok*, 156.

73. Przheval'skii, "Inorodchesko naselenie v Iuzhnoi chasti Primorskoi oblasti," 199.

74. Shreider, *Nash Dal'nyi Vostok*, 166.

75. Nasekin, "Koreitsy Priamurskogo kraia," 27–29.

76. This is a folk etymology, as the phrase *kobun ke* "pretty thing" is from the descriptive verb *kopta* "be pretty."

77. Lubentsov, *Khamkenskaia i pkhienanskaia provintsii Korei*, 168.

78. Maksimov, *Na dalekom vostoke: Razskazy i ocherki*, 46.

79. Ibid., 52.

80. Garin-Mikhailovskii, *Iz dnevnikov krugosvetnogo puteshestviia: Po Koree, Man'chzhurii i Liaodunskomu poluostrovu*, 126.

81. Ibid., 137–38.

82. Dadeshkaliani, "Kratkii ocherk sovremennogo sostoianiia Korei kniazia Dadeshkaliani," 54.

83. Al'ftan, "Poezdka v Koreiu podpolkovnika general'nogo shtaba Al'ftana v deka-bre 1895 i ianvare 1896," 245–46.

84. Garin-Mikhailovskii, *Iz dnevnikov krugosvetnogo puteshestviia: Po Koree, Man'chzhurii i Liaodunskomu poluostrovu*, 119.

85. Zvegintsev, "Poezdka v severnuiu Koreiu," 503.

86. Korf and Zvegintsev, *Voennyi obzor Severnoi Korei*, 63.

87. Garin-Mikhailovskii, *Iz dnevnikov krugosvetnogo puteshestviia: Po Koree, Man'chzhurii i Liaodunskomu poluostrovu*, 93.

88. Ibid., 113.

89. Khrisanf, *Ot Seula do Vladivostoka*, 76.

90. Selivanovskii, *Kak zhivut i rabotaiut Koreitsy*, 37.

91. Przheval'skii, "Inorodcheskoe naselenie v Iuzhnoi chasti Primorskoi oblasti," 198.

92. Przheval'skii, *Puteshestvie v Ussuriiskom krae, 1867–1869*, 100.

93. Maksimov, *Na dalekom vostoke: Razskazy i ocherki*, 47.

94. Shreider, *Nash Dal'nyi Vostok*, 16.

95. Khrisanf, *Ot Seula do Vladivostoka*, 23.

96. Selivanovskii, *Kak zhivut i rabotaiut Koreitsy*, 29–30.

97. Lubentsov, *Khamkenskaia i pkhienanskaia provintsii Korei*, 175.

98. Selivanovskii, *Kak zhivut i rabotaiut Koreitsy*, 29–35.

99. Khrisanf, *Ot Seula do Vladivostoka*, 23.

100. Ibid., 25.

101. Przheval'skii, *Puteshestvie v Ussuriiskom krae, 1867–1869*, 94.

102. Maksimov, *Na dalekom vostoke: Razskazy i ocherki*, 49.

103. Dadeshkaliani, "Kratkii ocherk sovremennogo sostoianiia Korei kniazia, 58.

104. Lubentsov, *Khamkenskaia i pkhienanskaia provintsii Korei*, 60.

105. Ibid., 71.

106. Ibid., 169.

107. Garin-Mikhailovskii, *Iz dnevnikov krugosvetnogo puteshestviia: Po Koree, Man'chzhurii i Liaodunskomu poluostrovu*, 105–106.

108. Delotkovich, "Dnevnik Pavla Mikhailovicha Delotkovicha," 156.

109. N. G. Matiunin served as the border commissar in the South Ussuri *krai* from 1880–1895, and later served as a commercial agent in Korea and Manchuria, as *chargé d'affaires* in Seoul from 1898, and as consul in 1889. Thus, he had frequent occasion to visit Korea and published at least two short accounts of his impressions there (see Matiunin, "Nashi sosedi na krainem Vostoke").

110. Delotkovich, "Dnevnik Pavla Mikhailovicha Delotkovicha," 163.

111. Note that the flavor of the Russian is somewhat pidgin-like, with its informal *ty*-form imperative and spurious *–a* on *kapitan*.

112. Al'ftan, "Poezdka v Koreiu podpolkovnika general'nogo shtaba Al'ftana v dekabre 1895 i ianvare 1896," 256–57.

113. Ibid., 258.

114. Lubentsov, *Khamkenskaia i pkhienanskaia provintsii Korei*, 120.

115. Garin-Mikhailovskii, *Iz dnevnikov krugosvetnogo puteshestviia: Po Koree, Man'chzhurii i Liaodunskomu poluostrovu*, 112.

116. Ibid., 116. Zaichikov also notes, "Behind us is a crowd of little kids and all kinds of people. They are all friendly, polite, and well-disposed. You can hear the affectionate *arasa* (Russian)." Zaichikov, "N. G. Garin-Mikhailovskii i ego puteshestvie vokrug sveta," 26.

117. Garin-Mikhailovskii, *Iz dnevnikov krugosvetnogo puteshestviia: Po Koree, Man'chzhurii i Liaodunskomu poluostrovu*, 252; Kolos, "N. G. Garin-Mikhailovskii o Koree i sobrannye im koreiskie skazki," 210; and Zaichikov, "N. G. Garin-Mikhailovskii i ego puteshestvie vokrug sveta," 26.

118. Khrisanf, *Iz pisem Koreiskago missionera*, 8–9.

119. Khrisanf, *Ot Seula do Vladivostoka*, 73.

120. Ibid., 78.

121. Ibid., 83.

122. See Tillett, *The Great Friendship*.

123. Zaichikov, "N. G. Garin-Mikhailovskii i ego puteshestvie vokrug sveta," 27.

124. Kolos, "N. G. Garin-Mikhailovskii o Koree i sobrannye im koreiskie skazki." 209.

125. Zvegintsev, "Poezdka v severnuiu Koreiu," 514.

126. Garin-Mikhailovskii, *Iz dnevnikov krugosvetnogo puteshestviia: Po Koree, Man'chzhurii i Liaodunskomu poluostrovu*, 229.

127. Zaichikov, "N. G. Garin-Mikhailovskii i ego puteshestvie vokrug sveta," 438 and also in note 68.

128. Kolos, "N. G. Garin-Mikhailovskii o Koree i sobrannye im koreiskie skazki," 221.

129. Ibid., 208.

130. This collection contains sixty-four Korean folktales recorded from Korean informants during the journey; originally there were more, but one of Garin's notebooks was lost. Garin's Korean folktales continued to be reprinted and translated into other languages well into the 1950s (see bibliography for reprints and translations). Another participant in the Korf & Zvegintsev expedition was Sergei Nikolaevich Syromiatnikov, who collected objects of material culture and a number of Korean books, all of which are now housed in the library of the Oriental Faculty, St. Petersburg University: see Kontsevich, *Izbrannye raboty*, 548; and Trotsevich, "Opisanie Koreiskikh pis'mennykh pamiatnikov, khraniashchikhsia v biblioteke vostochnogo fakul'teta

S.-Peterburgksogo universiteta." Garin-Mikhailovskii's folktales remain a valuable source to this day, both for the stories themselves, as well as for the linguistic forms he recorded in them.

131. Garin-Mikhailovskii, *Koreiskie skazki*, Forward.

132. Ibid.

133. This quote is cited in Kolos, "N. G. Garin-Mikhailovskii o Koree i sobrannye im koreiskie skazki," 213.

134. Lubentsov, *Khamkenskaia i pkhienanskaia provintsii Korei*, 37.

135. Strel'bitskii, *Iz Khunchuna v Mukden i obratno po sklonam Chan"-Bai-Shan'skago khrebta*, 29.

136. Garin-Mikhailovskii, *Iz dnevnikov krugosvetnogo puteshestviia: Po Koree, Man'chzhurii i Liaodunskomu poluostrovu*, 154.

137. Khrisanf, *Iz pisem Koreiskago missionera*, 4–5.

138. Wells, *Russian Views of Japan, 1792–1913*, 18–19.

139. Garin-Mikhailovskii, *Koreiskie skazki*, Forward.

140. Ibid.

141. Shreider, *Nash Dal'nyi Vostok*, 17.

142. Ibid., 281.

143. Knight, Nathaniel. "Grigor'ev in Orenburg, 1851–1862," 82.

144. Lubentsov, *Khamkenskaia i pkhienanskaia provintsii Korei*, 248. Isabella Bird Bishop makes similar remarks about the stark contrast between Korean communities in Korea and Russia in *Korea and Her Neighbours.*

145. This is cited in Kolos, "N. G. Garin-Mikhailovskii o Koree i sobrannye im koreiskie skazki,"212.

146. Lubentsov, *Khamkenskaia i pkhienanskaia provintsii Korei*, 252.

11

Images of the North in Occupied Korea, 1905–1945

MARK E. CAPRIO

Images that the Japanese created of Korea following Japan's annexation of the peninsula from 1910 initially presented the territory as a single homogeneous region, rather than as a territory comprised of diverse regions. The Japanese government characterized residents as "Korean" with little consideration for regional uniqueness. This characterization followed a similar practice employed by Meiji Japan to define other peripheral territories annexed from the late nineteenth century, including the Ryukyu Kingdom (Okinawa), Ezo (Hokkaido), and Taiwan. It reversed a Tokugawa-era trend that had divided domains (han) and peripheral areas such as the Ryukyu Islands and Ezo into smaller territories.[1] The practice further coincided with Meiji-era policy that consolidated multiple domains into a single prefecture. In Korea's case, the Japanese developed an expansive vocabulary to promote the Korean peninsula as a homogeneous zone—the hantō (peninsula), its people as senjin (Korean people), and their union as naisen (Japan and Korea).

Occasionally, however, distinctions emerged as Japanese began traveling to different parts of the peninsula. Magazines that published travel experiences described these adventures as trips to hokusen (northern Korea) or to nansen (southern Korea). Informants identified characteristics of the landscape, people, and culture in their writing. Japanese migration to Korea provided a second factor which also encouraged regional definition. Their initial concentration in the south promoted discussion that contributed to the formation of a northern image by questioning why the north was so unappealing to Japanese. Japanese expansion into the Asian continent in the late 1930s increased the value of, and subsequently Japanese interest in, Korea's northern provinces primarily due to their proximity to the war Japan was fighting in northeast China.

Japanese images of Korea as a collection of regions, rather than as a single homogeneous region thus emerged as a process that depended highly on Japan's realization of the northern Koreans' attributes to the empire. This realization encouraged speculation as to how these Koreans differed from people of the south and why these differences came into existence, despite the lingering Japanese official view of the Korean peninsula as a single region in and of itself. This chapter examines the Japanese development of this northern image as a practical response to the changing conditions within the Japanese Empire and the forces that threatened its frontiers. Though influenced by negative social Darwinist-driven doctrine and traditional Korean images of northern Korea and its residents, the perilous challenge brought by conflict on the Chinese mainland forced the Japanese to emphasize the importance of the area's natural attributes and the need to nurture strong cooperative ties with the northern Koreans.

JAPAN AND REGIONAL IDENTITY

During the Age of Empire (1875–1914) much of the world was imperially consolidated by a small number of colonial powers.[2] A number of nations absorbed smaller kingdoms that existed within their traditional borders to form larger nation-states. These nations also added territories along their peripheries to strengthen their national security. The French example is illustrative. From the 1870s, France initiated two processes: to "make French" the peoples of its southern provinces and to assimilate tribes in its Algerian colony. Both methods promised to assimilate residents as French men and women.[3] The theoretical conclusion to accomplishing this was their de-regionalization and their incorporation into the nation as French with no cultural distinction. Also at this time, forces in contemporary Italy, Germany, and Japan initiated similar processes to geographically, politically, and culturally consolidate peoples and territories into greater nation-states. They also extended their sovereignty over neighboring territories with the stated—but less frequently pursued—intention to assimilate the residents as imperial subjects.[4]

An important task facing nation-building efforts was the central government felling regional divides to create an "imagined community" of citizens equal in status and stature. This required replacing regional distinctions such as local dialects, customs, and mannerisms with unified national counterparts. The state created national institutions—the most important being compulsory education—to engage its constituents in this rather intense process of de-regionalization. It also devised ways to remind its subjects of their national allegiance in the form of national holidays, memorials, songs, and symbols.[5] The state's efforts to integrate people under its jurisdiction met with mixed results; regionalism often was strengthened by local efforts to preserve local culture.[6]

Threats by Western powers drove Japan's determination to demonstrate itself as homogeneous. By assimilating everyone residing within its redefined national borders, including Ainu and Ryukyan tribes and the outcast *burakumin* group, Japan in theory attempted to create a multi-ethnic nation state. Cultural integration followed political integration as the Meiji government established education and military institutions to teach the people what it meant to be Japanese. The burgeoning media reinforced these messages in its increasingly popular publications. The government guided this centralization process by establishing ministries to direct and monitor institutions that disseminated (in the case of education) and evaluated (such as the media) the content of these messages.[7]

Regional distinction and discrimination, however, survived despite efforts to erase regional differences.[8] In addition to distinctions between the Japanese homeland and its peripheral additions, divisions remained between residents of different islands, as well as among residents of a single island. On Honshu, Japan's main island, distinctions remained between "back side" (*ura Nihon*) residents of prefectures that straddled the Sea of Japan and "front side" (*omote Nihon*) residents of prefectures along Japan's Pacific Ocean coast.[9] Distinctions between Japan's east (Tokyo region) culture and its west (Osaka region) culture linger to this day. Indigenous groups residing in territories officially annexed after the Meiji Restoration, such as Okinawa and Hokkaido, have experienced occasional cultural revivals that sought to resurrect traditional language and customs. Both have maintained their distinct regional status. Visitors and migrants to these prefectures considered the indigenous residents different from the "Japanese" and refused to allow their children to study with indigenous students in the same classroom. One travel guide authored by the renowned Japanologists Basil Hall Chamberlain and W. B.

Mason characterized Hokkaido, four decades after its incorporation, as a geographically and culturally foreign land.

> The characteristics of Yezo [Hokkaido], both natural and artificial, differ in many respects from those of the Main Island [Honshu] of Japan. The climate is colder, the country newer, the people less polished and more independent.... In many places, too, relics of the Stone Age, which for this island has only recently passed away, are to be met with.[10]

It categorized Japan's northernmost island as a "different sub-region from Japan proper," an area distinguished by its wildlife (even the Ezo bear was a different species), plant life, and minerals. This diversity was certainly not welcomed at a time when nationalist definitions stretched biological and cultural differences to encourage people to adopt one homogeneous national identity.

Following Japan's annexation of Korea in 1910, the Meiji government identified the peninsula as one homogeneous region as opposed to a collection of distinct areas. It also considered the peninsula's residents homogeneous; people who in ancient times shared racial ties with the Japanese until a historical break separated them.[11] This characterization of the Japanese-Korean relationship justified, in the minds of the Japanese, their government's decision to assimilate Koreans at a time when social Darwinists criticized the policy. Japan could succeed at incorporating the Koreans by building on the shared historical and cultural roots linking Korea and Japan.

While most writing by Japanese (and later Koreans) defined the *naisen* relationship in terms of two homogeneous peoples, occasionally writers considered Korea as a region within Japan's network of regions. Nitobe Inazō's (1862–1933) comparison of Koreans and Japanese people targeted biological classification. While pondering the question of whether the difference between "the Kyushu man and the Chosenese (Korean) was likely to be less than the Kyushu man and his North-eastern compatriots," he expressed his surprise at learning just how close his "surmise" had been. Nitobe wrote:

> A professor in Keijo who has studied the Chosenese anatomy, tells me that there was very slight difference between the two races, and this difference is still slighter between the Chosenese and the inhabitants of the Kei-Han

district [around Kyoto and Osaka]—and not of Kyushu as I had imagined. The Kei-Han people are more different from our own Northwesterners than they are from the Chosen peninsular.[12]

Ukita Kazutani, editor of the magazine *Taiyō* (The Sun), compared Korean assimilation to the process that had integrated Japan's Kyushu and Tōhoku regions into the greater Japanese nation-state. The fit was not perfect in either case as residents maintained their regional dialects and customs. Despite their cultural peculiarities the people of these regions were nonetheless still considered Japanese. Likewise, the Japanese could recognize Korean peculiarities and still consider their Korean neighbors to be fellow subjects.[13] Others described the Korean language in similar terms. One 1938 report rendered the language a dialect (*hōgen*) of *kokugo* (Japanese, but literally the "national language"), adding that if the Japanese people could recognize a Kagoshima (in southern Kyushu) dialect and an Akita (in northwestern Honshu) dialect as variations of Japanese, they could also recognize a Korean dialect as such.[14] In all cases observers considered the homogeneous Korean peninsula as a distinct region contrastable with the collage of regions spread across the diverse Japanese archipelago.

Korea's March First independence demonstrations in 1919 jolted Japanese confidence over the ease of their assimilation task. The shock of witnessing Koreans taking to the streets of Keijō (Seoul) to demand their freedom from Japanese rule encouraged deeper inquiries into their images of the Korean people. Yet these inquiries (at least initially) retained the images of the Korean peninsula's regional homogeneity. One individual affected by this event was Hosoi Hajime (1886–1934), a reporter who had also worked in Japan's Government-General offices in Keijō. Hosoi blamed the demonstrations on the failure of the "naïve Japan" (*wakaki Nihon*) to fulfill their roles as the Korean people's "elder brothers." "We show no signs of love (*jinai*) or chivalry (*kyōyū*), but only menace (*ihaku*) toward the Korean people," he wrote. The experience of witnessing the Korean demonstration destroyed his enthusiasm for assimilation. His arguments against the policy, stretched over a six-part article carried in the nationalist magazine *Nihon oyobi Nihonjin* (Japan and the Japanese), reflected his perception of "Korea" as a homogeneous entity. He warned the Japanese against extending Japan's prefecture system (*fuken seido*) to the peninsula. Should it do so, Japan would have to admit Korea as a distinct region that might be called "Seihokudō" (Northwest Province) or "Seikaidō" (Western Sea Province). This vision was, in Hosoi's mind, "naïve."[15]

Torii Ryūzō (1870–1953), one of the founders of the Asia Society (Ajia gakkai), almost two decades later offered a more positive twist to Hosoi's thinking by suggesting that Korea be renamed the "Northern Japan Region" (Hoppō Nippon). Torii wrote that when he crossed into Korea after his extended trip through Manchuria, he felt that he had returned home to Japan. The mountains, rivers, and fields, along with the farm villages, he described as "very Japanese" (Nihonteki). The "Japan" that he saw at this time, however, reminded him of the Japan of Manyōshū poetry days (750–1100), rather than Japan of the present. He proposed that Korea be incorporated as Japan's "Hoppō Nippon," alongside the Kinai (Osaka-Kyoto area), Kyushu, and Chūgoku (Hiroshima) regions.[16] Torii's idea of Korea as a homogeneous region was perhaps influenced by his research on Korean pottery that he reported over a decade earlier. Here he refuted a conventional belief that striped and plain designs separated northern and southern Korean artisans. Rather, he argued this difference to be intra-regional; both designs could be found within established areas of Korea's northern and southern provinces.[17]

On occasion rulings by the Japanese government corrected attempts to distinguish the Korean peninsula regionally. A 1929 proposal issued by the Korean Political Participation Deliberation Committee (Chōsen sansei shin-gikai kōseiin) to admit Koreans into Japan's National Assembly motivated one such occasion. A group of seventeen Japanese submitted this petition to the Japanese Diet with the idea of putting colonial assimilation rhetoric into practice. Part of their proposal required the Japanese to permit regional assemblies (chihō gikai), as was authorized in Japan proper. The decision handed down by the Japanese Diet rejected their petition on the grounds that Korean participation would sway legislative decisions and thus prove "harmful" to the assembly. Regarding the formation of regional assemblies, the decision argued that since Korea was a "single region" (ichi chihō) it seemed more appropriate for the people to form a single assembly, rather than multiple regional assemblies across the peninsula.[18]

The Japanese also imagined the Korean peninsula as homogeneous territory in comparisons they made with Japan's backward regions, particularly ura Nihon and Hokkaido. These comparisons were rather popular at the time annexation discussion peaked in 1910, and no doubt encouraged by images that portrayed the regimes as similar in their level of development. Kita Sadakichi noted that Japanese experiences in assimilating Hokkaido's Ainu tribes would prove useful in assimilating Koreans.[19] Fujimura Hiromasa encouraged the development of a more practical trade relationship between Korea and Japan's underdeveloped areas; the potential existed for renewing past contacts between these regions. At present, he bemoaned, Korea had no connection with either Hokkaido or *ura Nihon*, as the spokes of Korea's trade and commerce with Japan connected to Japan's Kanto (Tokyo) and Kansai (Osaka) districts. These roads had bypassed Japan's underdeveloped areas. Transportation ties needed to be developed to promote Korean interactions with Hokkaido and prefectures along the Sea of Japan (K. East Sea).[20]

GEOGRAPHICAL AND HISTORICAL IMAGES OF KOREA'S NORTHERN REGION

Subscribers to social Darwinist and scientific colonial thinking believed people to be a product of their environment, that geographical, biological, and historical factors honed a people's psychological and social development. This thinking gained importance in Europe in the nineteenth century, during the Age of Reason, as science assumed greater importance over religion and superstition. People like the Frenchman Gustave Le Bon (1841–1931) used scientific thinking to attack philosophical ideas born during the Renaissance which assumed that all peoples had equal potential to be elevated to the level of the civilized should they receive enlightened guidance from a civilized people. Le Bon argued instead that people were products of their biological inheritance: "Like the individual human organism which is composed of living cells that are constantly reproducing and dying, so a race is composed of individuals who perform a similar function. The dead, like the living, leave their indelible mark on the character of their race." Thus "mental gaps" separated the civilized from the barbarians and rendered cross-group integration impossible. Educating an inferior people in the hope of changing their traditional habits would bear feeble results. Assimilation, Le Bon concluded, was "one of the most harmful illusions that the theorists of pure reason have ever engendered."[21] Such ideas encouraged research aimed at categorizing people racially and ethnically based on their biological attributes and shortcomings. Japanese scholars adapted this framework to demonstrate Japan's superiority and justify the subjugation of the people they colonized.[22]

Regional distinctions existing across the Korean peninsula appear to have been influenced by this thinking. Indeed, many of the volumes of statistics compiled by the Government-General were categorized to differentiate the Japanese, Korean, and other foreign peoples. Japanese officials also arranged this data to distinguish Koreans by province. These charts consistently placed Kyŏnggi at the top before listing Korea's other provinces, moving northward from South Chŏlla to North Hamgyŏng. The Government-General published this data in the Chōsen sōtokufu nenpō (Korean Government-General Annual), and divided the data by population, education, health, crime, and other similar categories. The compilers of these volumes did not bother to analyze these figures to distinguish regional distinction. The information no doubt proved useful to scholars, including those who contributed to the Korean Journal of Medicine (Chōsen igakkai zasshi). Most studies characterized Korea and Koreans in homogeneous terms. However, (as we shall see later) a small number, particularly those that examined quality of life aspects such as illness, birth, and death rates, included a component that considered regional differences.

Travelers provided another source of regional characterization. Over the first decade the peninsula's southern half received more attention, due probably to the fact that the majority (over 80 percent in 1917) of Japanese expatriates resided in southern provinces.[23] As Japan's empire expanded, and its wartime needs married the resources available in the northern provinces, more Japanese (34.8 percent by 1942) migrated to the northern provinces.[24] This demographic change encouraged more interest in, which in turn encouraged increased coverage of, the region by the Japanese media. This period also witnessed increases in police, medical, and education facilities that the Japanese linked to those in the peninsula's southern provinces and in the homeland by improved transportation networks. These developments reflected two interrelated changes in the Japanese Empire from the late 1920s. First, Japan's expansion onto the Asian continent extended the empire's frontier beyond the Yalu River. The northern provinces, though still threatened by leftist insurgents, gained a buffer in the Manchurian puppet state created by the Japanese government. From the late 1930s the Government-General committed itself to strengthening these intraimperial ties by developing Senman (Korean-Manchurian) ties. A second important development involved the change in emphasis from Korea's agricultural to mineral assets. This change emphasized the northern provinces' resources over those of the southern provinces and directly related to Japan's deepening involvement in its continental interests and concerns, which soon came to include war.[25]

Japanese definitions of Korea's "north" varied. Travelers generally defined their journey to northern Korea from the perspective of Keijō; anything north of the capital constituted northern Korea. Academic studies offered different definitions of "northern Korea." One survey drew the peninsula's inhabitable (jinrui kakyō) border at South P'yŏngan Province, the area of "Kan minzoku kokka katsudō" (activity of the Korean people state) to be distinguished by the highlands of Korea's northern area that bordered Manchuria.[26] Descriptions left by Japanese of their travels to the north began with their departure at Seoul's Namdaemun (South gate) station, where they boarded either the early morning or early afternoon Senmansha (Korea-Manchuria) line that took them through Kaesŏng and P'yŏngyang en route to Sinŭiju and the Manchurian border. Many travelers divided their discussions of the north by the city's attractions—Kaesŏng food, P'yŏngyang women—as if oblivious to the provincial borders they had crossed. These travel logs appeared regularly in popular magazines such as Chōsen oyobi Manshū (Korea and Manchuria) published in Korea and the Chūō kōron (Central Review) and Nihon oyobi Nihonjin both produced in Japan.

This writing often highlighted the north's unique terrain, harsh weather, and unbridled wildlife. The northern region's continental and mountainous geography created a sense of mystique and contributed to its image as a dangerous habitat. Its border with Manchuria and the Soviet Union, until the early 1930s the empire's extreme frontier, allowed foreigners relatively easy access to and from Korea.[27] This characterization earned the region the reputation as a magnet for foreign ideas, beginning with Christianity and later communism and anarchism.[28] Mizutō Bō noted that the north's abundant beautiful women appeared more comfortable associating with foreigners than the southern Korean. His trip log also contained a rather long description of the wolf threat that kept people inside at night.[29] Companies and institutions that dispatched Japanese employees to the peninsula for extended periods of time recognized this relocation as a particularly burdensome one. Japanese workers dispatched to Korea received an extra salary stipend; those sent to the northern provinces received an additional 30 percent "hardship" stipend, and those to the areas along the Yalu and Tamen River an additional 7 percent on top of the initial hardship stipend.[30]

History also influenced regional differences throughout the Korean peninsula. Japanese historians traced Korean personality differences back to Korea's ancient three kingdoms period. They identified a northern Koguryŏ identity that contrasted with the Paekche and Silla identities of Korea's southwest and southeast regions. Inaba Kunsan (1876–1940) agreed that understanding Korea in a broad sense required understanding Korea's ancient history.[31] Inaba's two-part article contested what he felt to be a misguided Korean belief that Korean cultural roots lay in Kyŏngju, the capital of Silla Kingdom. Instead, he argued that since two of the three ancient kingdoms, Paekche and Koguryŏ, were heavily influenced by Manchurian culture the stronger influence came from the north rather than from the south. His essays, released just as Japan was beginning to strengthen its continental interests, contended that Koreans shared a "Senman" (Korean-Manchurian) cultural foundation that united them as descendents of Tan'gun.[32] Inaba's portrayal of the Korean people in terms of their ancient roots reflected comments made by Japanese visitors to Korea who imagined their experiences as a trip back to Japan's ancient past. Nitobe Inazō wrote after his 1906 visit to Korea that he felt as if he "were living three thousand years back in the age of [Japan's] Kami. . . . [The people] belong not to the twentieth century or the tenth—or indeed the first century. They belong to a prehistoric age."[33]

A NORTHERN PERSONALITY

The Japanese established assimilation as their colonial administrative policy soon after annexing Taiwan in 1895. Regarding Korea, the discussion focused on how best to assimilate Koreans (as opposed to whether or not to assimilate the people) even before Korea's annexation had become official in late August 1910. Particularly, the Japanese officials discussed the pace—gradual or accelerated—at which this policy should be carried out. The Japanese saw their task as assimilating a homogeneous Korean people, and had little apparent sympathy for regional distinction.[34] Indeed, scientific investigation conducted by members of the Chōsen igakkai, with rare exception, concluded with apparent confidence that their results characterized the Korean people as a whole without regard to regional variation.[35] The studies that did consider Korean regional distinctions tended to be authored (or co-authored) by Korean researchers.

Two surgeons, Kirihara Shinichi and Paek Inje, employed by the Government-General hospital, conducted one such study in 1922 that classified Koreans and Japanese by blood type ratios. Of particular interest is the background of Paek. Paek, who hailed from Chŏngju in North P'yŏngan Province, was a descendent of Paek Kyŏnghae, one of few northerners to successfully overcome the bureaucratic discrimination against northern yangban and gain official appointments during the Chosŏn period (1392–1910).[36] Yet, the Kirihara-Paek study supported traditional Chosŏn discrimination by demonstrating the northerner as inferior to Korea's southerner. The medical team first established the racial ranking of Japanese and Koreans by calculating "biochemische indexes" (seibutsugaku keisu). Mimicking a Western experimental model, the study categorized a population's civilization level by ranking the ratio of different blood types. Studies previously conducted under this framework, some using Japanese as subjects, had concluded the following three-tiered racial categorization: the "European group" (2.3–4.5) occupied the most advanced tier; Middle Eastern and Slavic peoples (1.3–1.5) occupied the middle tier; and Asian and African peoples (0.5–1.1) occupied the lowest tier. That Kirihara and Paek's study found Japanese (1.7) to be superior to Koreans (1.1) is not surprising; demonstrating Japanese superiority reflected an apparent goal of the journal in general, and this study in particular. The interesting part of this study was the researchers' decision to calculate regional differences among Koreans. Here they found the peninsula's southern provinces to be more advanced than its northern provinces. The biochemische index for residents of South Chŏlla Province (1.41) placed them in the middle tier, higher than their North Chŏlla cousins (1.08), who were more advanced than residents of North P'yŏngan (0.83).[37]

We now understand studies of this ilk—based on an agenda to display racial superiority under the guise of scientific objectivity—to be unsound.[38] As with many other studies adapted by Japanese scientists, Kirihara and Paek sought to objectively prove Japanese superiority over Koreans. Most interesting here is the question of why this study chose to examine and report regional differences. It would also be particularly interesting to learn what influence Paek may have exerted to extend the research design to this dimension. Paek's reaction to the study's results verifying stereotypes that Japanese held against the Koreans, as well as those that Koreans had historically maintained against people of his ancestral region, would also be of interest. Scientific objectivity prevented the two scientists from including any such thoughts in their rather bland summary that described the experimental procedures and results but avoided commentary that explained these results in any great detail.

We find such commentary in the writing of another northerner, Pak Sanghŭi, who offered a rather detailed view of the northern Korean personality in his August 1927 article "Unique Characteristics of the Northwestern Korean" (Chōsen seihokujin no tokushitsu), which appeared in a special issue of the journal Chōsen oyobi Chōsen minzoku (Korea and the Korean Race).[39] The timing of Pak's article is important. It came at a critical turning point in Japan's China policy, just four months after the army general Tanaka Giichi assumed the position of prime minister. This administrative change signaled a diplomatic adjustment to Japan's China policy—from "economic" to "military"—as a means to quell the rise in Chinese anti-Japanese sentiment.[40] Pak's thoughts also appeared four months after Ugaki Kazushige began a seven-month spell as interim governor general to replace Saitō Makoto, who served as a delegate to the Geneva arms limitations conference. Ugaki would later establish a reputation as a promoter of industrial development during his official term as governor general that began in 1931. The increasing importance of northern Korea in the Japanese Empire encouraged more Japanese to migrate to the region. Pak, a native of P'yŏngyang who wrote in Japanese, appeared to target Japanese readers who either resided in northern Korea or who had plans to migrate there. He proposed that by informing the Japanese of the northwestern Koreans the Japanese people could better understand themselves: "Understanding the mind of an individual or the special circumstances of a particular person allows the observer to examine more completely and with greater impartiality their own selves and to see how a person is reflected in the mirror of others."[41]

Pak, a Tokyo dispatcher (tokuhain) for the Korea Thought Correspondence Company (Chōsen shisō tsūshinsha), had little positive to say of his fellow northwesterners. He wrote, from the beginning of the Chosŏn period and perhaps earlier, these people had developed a personality that oscillated

between two extremes (*kyokutansei no ryōsō*). While they tended to settle disputes with "fist and knuckles" (*genkotsu no kōshisha*), they were also moved by
"distressful folk songs" (*shūshinka*). Pak wondered why these people, who had
been subjected to the same monarchal rule, could not appreciate the more
tranquil songs (*taiheika*) enjoyed by the southern and central Koreans. He
believed one factor to be the geographical and historical conditions that the
people had endured over the centuries. Their wild mood swings flowed in
concert with the wild fluctuations of northern Korean temperatures that provided "three days of cold and four days of hot temperatures." This phenomenon, he observed, became more acute the further north one traveled.[42]

"Artificial" (*jin'iteki*) elements also molded this northwest Korean psyche.
Pak explained that historically, the "evil [Chōsen] government" (*akasei*) unlaw-
fully blocked talented northerners from receiving positions of influence on
the grounds that "the northwesterner had nothing important" (*seihokujin nasu
nakare jūyō*) to offer. The government sent its most brutal administrators to
this region and squeezed the people bloodless. This had led to the 1812 Hong
Kyŏngnae Rebellion, 120 years before Pak tweaked this discriminatory history
to explain the northern Koreans' unnatural personality extremes. The resentment from the discrimination itself advanced their "male turbulent side"
(*danseiteki no gekidōsei*), while the grief they experienced gradually developed
their contrasting "female sentimentality side" (*joseiteki no kanshōsei*).[43]

The northern people's ability to harmonize their extreme personality
swings saved them from succumbing to the "weak and lazy abyss of self-
abandonment." Their lack of trust in central administrations nurtured a
strong feeling of "self-reliance" (*jikatsu kannen*), an attitude of independence
that distinguished them from residents in the central and southern parts of
the peninsula. The northwestern Koreans did not recognize the time-honored
Confucian hierarchies determined by status, age, and gender differences.
Northwestern women, unlike women of Kyŏnggi, did not require incentives
to encourage their participation in farm chores. Indeed, they outperformed
their male counterparts in this work. The northerners' personalities, however,
complicated companionship relations. They felt little need to adapt to new
situations. They preferred to pretend to know something rather than admit
ignorance.[44]

Pak's composite picture of the northwest Koreans was of a people unable
to compromise, of people with "zero ability to get along in life" (*shoseijutsu wa*

zero), and of people lacking in cooperation skills. Efforts to negotiate with them inevitably resulted in disruption. The personality extremes manifested in disjointed images maintained by Japanese officials. The region's Japanese residents first saw the northwestern Korean as an assassin, a person prepared to ruthlessly kill Japanese and pro-Japanese Koreans. On the other hand, Japanese residents in Korea also saw people of the northern region as supportive of Japan's efforts on the peninsula. Pak explained that neither image alone represented the true picture of the northwestern Korean. This bi-polar disposition enabled northerners to assume either image at any given time. Their violent disposition was transitional. Pak illustrated the differences by offering the example of Korean behavior at popular demonstrations: the Koreans standing and yelling at the front lines were most likely from the northwestern provinces; those who remained behind to negotiate and clean up the mess were most likely from the central and southern provinces.[45]

The work of both Paek Inje and Pak Sanghŭi introduced to their Japanese audiences characteristics of northern Korea. We can only ponder why two northern Korean authors would present such negative characterizations of their home region, and what impact their writing had on Japanese audiences. Both Koreans having left their region may help explain the first concern. Having found apparent success elsewhere they viewed their home region from a different light, not only in comparison with the more enlightened south, but also with the Japanese. Colonial occupations encouraged the indigenous to rethink their national allegiances, causing many to adopt the colonial message. The Government-General journal *Chōsen* welcomed contributions by Koreans that criticized Korea and its people; particularly contributions that targeted Koreans who maintained aspirations for Korean independence and sovereignty. In this light it seems plausible that Koreans—and particularly those who left the northern region—might accept and even promote disparaging images of their home region when given the chance.

THE IMAGE OF THE NORTH AS WILD AND UNCIVILIZED

Images left by Paek and Pak also portrayed residents of the northern provinces as underdeveloped. Pak's essay suggested the people were wild and potentially dangerous. As noted above, the Japanese did not initially find these provinces particularly attractive. They were inconveniently situated far from the Japanese homeland, they were viewed as more dangerous than southern provinces, and the weather was much less inviting. Japanese citizens required incentives (such as extra pay) to migrate to the region. For many residents, their tenure tended to be transitory rather than permanent. In 1941, Yi Sŏkhun (1907–195?), a native of Chŏngju in North P'yŏnan, addressed the region's unpopularity in his short story "Quiet Storm" (Shizuka no arashi). Yi begins his story by describing a meeting to decide the regions to which Korean volunteers would travel to lecture residents on the wartime situation. Participants chose their working areas by the rail lines that passed through the provinces. His main character, Pak Taemin, chose the Hamgyŏng line that runs from Wŏnsan to Hoeryŏng—a city in North Hamgyŏng Province's northern extreme—after realizing the lack of interest in this northern route. Volunteers quickly claimed the southern rail lines. But, as Secretary Yamamoto jokingly observed, "Nobody has claimed the Hamgyŏng line." The volunteers offered: "It's too cold," "It's too scary," "It's too noisy up there," before Pak finally volunteered to go. The secretary adjourned the meeting by announcing that those not in attendance would join Pak as punishment for their absence.[46]

Yi's short story gave this negative image a positive twist. Pak, who aspired to becoming a writer, purposefully chose this rail line. To him it was the more attractive route and allowed him to avoid the Kyŏnggi line which ran through his home province. His choice to travel to the north reflected his reasoning for participating in these lectures: to venture to the unknown to encounter an "ideologically deep experience" (shisōteki ni shinkoku na keiken). Traveling to the north would provide him with a challenge unattainable in more familiar territory.

The disparaging images of the north presented by Yi reflected the lack of interest by Japanese in this region. Soon after annexation, contributors to the Korea-based magazine, Chōsen oyobi Manshū, addressed the question of why the Japanese favored the southern provinces over the northern provinces. In October 1913 Inoue Kōsai, a manager employed by the Oriental Development Company, noted the need for Japanese residents to spread to the north, as well as the south, to develop Korea throughout. He attacked some of the reasons offered by Japanese who refused to migrate to northern Korea. While noting that many thought the south to be more convenient (benri) than the north, Inoue still expressed surprise that people avoided the north to the extent that they did. He listed some of its advantages: as the north's population density was smaller, it had more available farmland. Inoue acknowledged that the comparatively colder weather was an important, but not an insurmountable factor. The north was not as cold as parts of China. Also, there were other professions available in the region besides farming. As a solution, he urged the government to offer added incentives in the form of transportation and housing assistance to Japanese citizens who opted to move to the region.[47] Matsuda Shirō, section chief for *Higashi takushokumin* (Eastern Colonists), echoed this opinion in his report, adding that Japanese moving to northern Korea faced climactic circumstances similar to those encountered by residents who moved to Japan's northern (Hokuriku) and northeast (Tōhoku) regions.[48] Inoue's article explicitly stated what Matsuda implied: despite the inconvenience it was the duty of the Japanese to migrate to the region. The government, for its part, must encourage this migration by offering assistance to cover the added costs.

Pak Taemin's interest in the north was precisely what the Japanese had found unattractive. Areas north of Kyŏnggi had gained an infamous reputation among the Japanese as dangerous. The *Seoul Press* wrote that South P'yŏngan had long been known as a province inhabited by people possessing stronger wills than their southern brethren, people who were by no means friendly towards Japanese. The newspaper noted (incorrectly) that Resident General Itō Hirobuimi's assassin, An Chunggŭn (1879–1910), was native to South P'yŏngan Province, as were a "majority of the conspirators against the Korean Premier." Miyanaga S., whose article contained reflections made during his trip to northern Korea, explained the region's anti-Japanese reputation as one harbored primarily by its unemployed population: "There now exists no such thing in P'yŏngan as a general and deep-rooted anti-Japanese sentiment among the productive classes of this population. But some of the unproductive people, largely students, are still dreaming of the impracticable [Korean independence]."[49] Here he suggested the solution lay within Japan's power, that employing Koreans would curtail their anti-Japanese behavior. In November 1921 Kitakan Sanjin (probably a pseudonym) penned an article that appeared in *Chōsen oyobi Manshū*, which argued the problem to be more fundamental: "Korea's special product, not found anywhere else, is insubordinate people (*futeijin*). They reside particularly in the north where they can cross over the border from China and Siberia."[50]

An Chunggŭn, who claimed his domicile as P'yŏngyang,[51] anchored a long list of northern Koreans who made Japanese headlines for their attempts to assassinate Japanese officials and disrupt Japanese operations on the peninsula. Two of his three cohorts, Cho Kilsŏn and Yu Kangno were native to South Hamgyŏng Province. Of the defendants in the 105-person incident, an alleged plot to assassinate Governor General Terauchi Masatake during his 1910 trip through North and South P'yŏngan provinces, all but three were listed as hailing from the north.[52] In September 1919 Kang Ugyu (1855–1920), hurled a bomb at Saitō Makoto's carriage as Satiō entered Keijō to assume his duties as governor general. Kang was listed as being from South Hamgyŏng Province, as were three of his four cohorts Ch'oe Chanam, Hŏ Hyŏng, and O T'aeyŏng.[53] By contrast, just under half (fifteen) of the Koreans who signed the March First Declaration of Independence were from Korea's northern provinces.[54] It was the north, however, that rejuvenated the fading movement in the days following King Kojong's funeral.[55] Finally, major figures in the post-March First Korean Independence movement, including Syngman Rhee, Yŏ Unhyŏng, Kim Ku, and Kim Il Sung, were Koreans from the north who had earned infamous anti-Japanese reputations.

The region's residents considered the north's continental geographic location to be a major contributing factor to the image of Korea's northern provinces as dangerous. Tsuboi Sachio, who rose through the ranks of the Japanese police force after graduating from Keijō Imperial University's law department, remembered "north Korea" (kita Chōsen but here specifically Hamgyŏng Province) as a distant region where "from long ago . . . administrative efforts did not extend." After annexation, he continued, "many Koreans fled to foreign lands but crossed back in winter when the Tumen River froze over." Tsuboi described this border as a "confusing condition" (konmei jōtai) that served as a venue for a military spy war. Russian and Japanese spies exploited Korean "peasant spies" (hakushō supai) and had them gather "trivial information" (samatsu no jōhō). In other districts policemen patrolled in pairs; in the north they patrolled in groups of up to one hundred.[56]

The initial lack of interest among the Japanese to migrate to the north may also have resulted from the region being less developed than Korea's southern provinces, particularly regarding transportation, education, and employment. This may have resulted from Japan's interests over its initial decades of rule centering on developing Korea's agricultural over its industrial potential.

Initially, Japan restricted Korea's industrial development to limit competition. Following the March First movement in 1919, the Government-General began to review this policy, and eventually modified the Factory Law that had curtailed industrial development on the peninsula.[57]

Greater infrastructural attention to the region by Japanese authorities blazed trails and encouraged an influx of Japanese settlers. By 1926 almost half (44.1 percent) of the peninsula's police force patrolled the northern provinces. Close to a quarter of the Japanese police force (23.5 percent) was stationed in the two border provinces.[58] In addition, from 1920 the Japanese government stationed two elite military divisions in northern Korea.[59] Sakai Toshio believes that the stronger police presence was one factor that influenced Japanese place of residence. He noted that the Japanese began to settle in his village, Pukchin in North P'yŏngan, in greater numbers after the Japanese residency general in 1909 situated a police bureau (keisatsuchō) in the region to quell righteous army (ŭibyŏng) insurgencies operating there.[60] Japanese statistics suggest that northern provinces may not have needed this high concentration of police. Police records show the region having a lower crime rate per capita. In 1926 the two border provinces, North Hamgyŏng and North P'yŏngan, accounted for 10.5 percent of the population but just 8.4 of special law (tokuhō), and 8.1 of criminal law (keihō) offenses. By contrast, per capita crime was slightly higher in South Hamgyŏng and South P'yŏngang (13.6 percent of the population committed 15.8 and 14.3 percent of special and criminal law respectively).[61] However, it was in violent crime where the northern provinces particularly stood out. In 1926 almost half of all violent crimes (47.8 percent) were committed in the northern provinces. North P'yŏngan alone was responsible for 16.5 percent of violent crime, and nearly twice the number of homicides (107) as in any other province.[62] Special crime violations, which covered thought crimes, rose dramatically during the war years to 42.3 percent (perhaps due to stricter police vigilance to prevent leftist activity), while criminal violations remained relatively steady (29.7 percent) in the northern provinces.[63]

In addition to crime victimization, health and education concerns provided additional concerns for prospective Japanese migrants. Members of the Korean Medical Association began surveying regional health standards from the early 1920s. One survey, titled "Korean Population Effects" (Chōsen no jinkō genshō), began in 1921 and repeated every five years. These studies examined the life and death rates, population density, and literacy by province, with the

Map 11.1 Birth Rates (per 1,000 people)

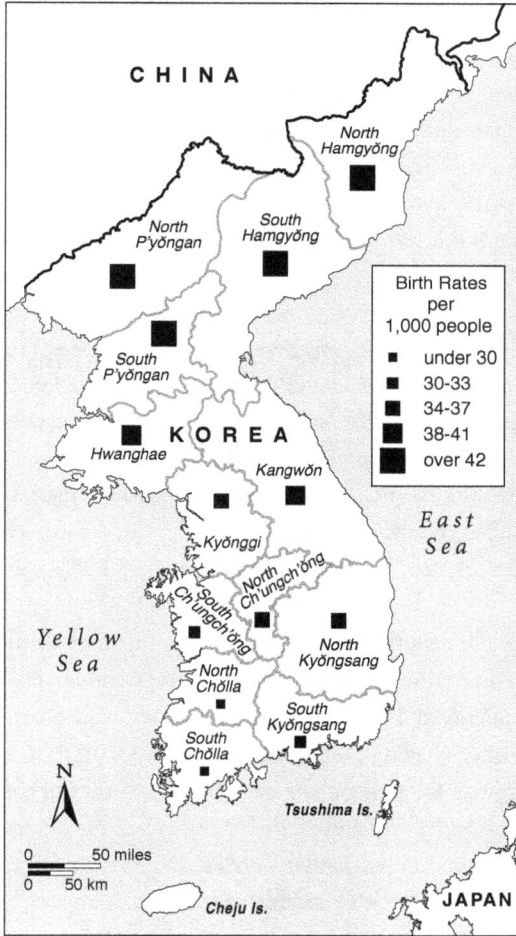

CHINA

North
Hamgyŏng

North
P'yŏngan

South
Hamgyŏng

Birth Rates
per
1,000 people

▪ under 30
▪ 30-33
▪ 34-37
▪ 38-41
▪ over 42

South
P'yŏngan

KOREA

Hwanghae

Kangwŏn

Kyŏnggi

East
Sea

North
Ch'ungch'ŏng

Ch'ungch'ŏng

South
Ch'ungch'ŏng

Yellow
Sea

North
Chŏlla

North
Kyŏngsang

South
Kyŏngsang

South
Chŏlla

N

Tsushima Is.

0   50 miles
0   50 km

Cheju Is.

JAPAN

Source: Ch'oe Hŭiyŏng, "Chōsen in okeru shusseiritsu
oyobi shibōritsu ni kan suru shakai seibutsu gakuteki
kōsatsu," 104. This map was slightly altered for clarity
purposes.

idea that these factors had been influenced by natural factors such as climate, as well as artificial factors such as the people's level of culture (bunka no teido). Ch'oe Hŭiyŏng linked the results of his study to his subjects' development, and in part to the northwestern provinces:

> People of the informed class [chishiki kaikyū] have fewer children. People with lower education have more children. In the same regard, people of a region with a developed culture have lower death rates than those of underdeveloped [mikaichi] regions. [Based on this] we can judge the level of education spread in Korea by looking at North P'yŏngan and North Hamgyŏng's high birth rates and North and South Kyŏngsang's low death and birth rates.[64]

Had his results been reported in a more popular Japanese publication (and this possibility cannot be ruled out) we can imagine these statements influencing decisions regarding residence made by prospective Japanese migrants to the Korean peninsula. Ch'oe, who was a member of the preventive medicine research group in the Department of Hygiene at Keijō Imperial University, illustrated his results by including maps that clearly demonstrated Korea's northern provinces (North and South P'yŏngan and North Hamgyŏng) as distinctly different from the southern provinces (North and South Kyŏngsang).[65]

A number of Ch'oe's findings, like those of Kirihara Shinichi and Paek Inje, suggested that Koreans who lived in the provinces closest to Japan enjoyed more civilized lifestyles. His survey showed North and South Kyŏngsang provinces having the highest literacy rates, with North and South Chŏlla and Kangwŏn following close behind. The northernmost provinces of North Hamgyŏng, and North and South P'yŏngan had the lowest literacy rates (Map 11.2). We do not know whether Korea's traditionally negative images of northerners influenced Ch'oe's experimental design in any way. However, the criteria he used to group his results deserve scrutiny. Was, for example, the difference between his most literate provinces (over eighty per one hundred people) and his least literate provinces (under seventy-four per one hundred people) as significant as his maps suggest? Also, his figures placing Kyŏnggi Province literacy (seventy-four to seventy-six per one hundred people) among the lower levels raise speculation over his study's overall validity given the region's traditionally high concentration of Korea's literati population.

Map 11.2 Literacy Rates (per 100 people)

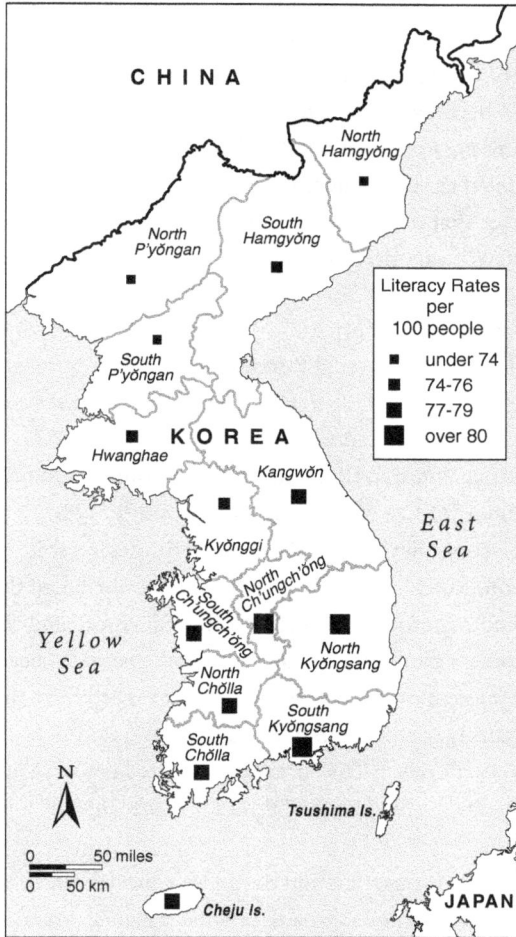

Source: Ch'oe Hŭiyŏng, "Chōsen in okeru shusseiritsu oyobi shibōritsu ni kan suru shakai seibutsu gakuteki kōsatsu," 115. This map was slightly altered for clarity purposes.

THE "ERA OF NORTHERN KOREA"

Ch'oe Hŭiyŏng published his study just months before the outbreak of war with China in July 1937, when Japanese and Chinese troops clashed at the Marco Polo Bridge. Japanese troops engaged in the war on the Asian continent encouraged the Japanese government to intensify efforts to develop its interests in northern Korea. Japanese written accounts of northern Korea's industrial assets began appearing during the first decade of Japanese rule. As early as 1914, among a series of articles that appeared in *Chōsen oyobi Manshū*, Ogawa Unpei noted the Government-General's decision to prioritize southern development over that of the northern provinces. He argued instead for the development of Wŏnsan, over Pusan, as an industrial port and military base, explaining that the northern city would prove to be safer than the southern port should war come to the region.[66] A little over a decade later Zenshō Eisuke, a scholar who researched Korea's social and cultural structure, realized that the development of "Korea's conventional market was being developed to a greater extent in the peninsula's northwest."[67] Other articles appearing in various journals illustrated North P'yongan's industrial development and potential.[68] In 1935, following his month-long trip throughout the peninsula, the economist Takahashi Kamekichi declared in the magazine *Kaizō* (Conversion) Korea's "rebirth" (*umefukeru*). He attributed the peninsula's industrial development to its connection with Manchuria and that Korea had transformed from a "purchaser of Japanese products [to its becoming] a factory base." The content of Korea's exports had advanced from the agricultural to the manufacturing sector. Both developments pointed to the advancement of the northern territories.[69] This attention reflected growing Japanese attention towards Korea as a peninsula of diversity rather than as a homogeneous entity.[70]

Following Japan's expansion onto the Asian continent in 1931, many articulated in stronger terms the long-held view that Japan's survival depended on it gaining predominance in the region, and the international community recognizing its interests as such. Resource-starved Japan required the northern Korean region as a supply base for industrial and military materials. The European powers had secured African territories, and the United States had fed off Latin American territories for this purpose. The Asian continent should serve as Japan's supply base.[71] The strategic location of the Korean peninsula as the bridge between the Japanese archipelago and the Asian continent increased the Korean colony's value, as well as its risk. The natural resources available in Korea's northern provinces, the proximity to Manchuria and China, and the reputation northern Koreans had as being inhospitable to Japanese people and policy required the Government-General to exert special attention toward the region. After Ugaki Kazushige, whose administration has been remembered for its emphasis on Korean industrialization, replaced Saitō Makoto as governor general, the Japanese administration increased its efforts to develop Korea's northern provinces.[72]

In 1934, three years after assuming office, Governor General Ugaki made two speeches that outlined the necessity of Korea's industrial development.[73] He presented the first of these speeches in January 1934, less than a year after the League of Nations accepted the Lytton Commission Report that condemned Japan's intrusion into Manchuria. Here Ugaki emphasized Korea's critical role in the empire and Japan's important task of assimilating the Korean people. His prediction that the peninsula would one day come to be known for its industrial, rather than for simply its agricultural contributions, reflected the Korean colony's new role in the Japanese Empire. The situation in Manchuria, Ugaki emphasized, "heightened the peninsula's significance and mission."[74]

Ugaki's September 1934 speech targeted Korea's northern provinces. Imperial harmony rested first with the Japanese and Korean people assimilating as a nation of 90 million brethren (dōhō), rather than stubbornly maintaining separate Korean and Japanese identities. Japanese-Korean harmony also required cooperation from peninsular Koreans, as well as overseas Koreans in Manchuria, the Russian Far East, and China. This latter task targeted the northern Koreans, and particularly those residing along the northern border. Developing these people was the key to nurturing better relations with Koreans living abroad, particularly those residing in areas north of the Yalu River. Ugaki listed some of the problems that the region faced: much of the land remained forested (and thus unexploited) and was ill prepared for farming; and the region's transportation networks remained underdeveloped. Advancing these industries would make Korea less dependent on Japanese financial assistance and move the colony to self-sufficiency. Using the textile industry as an example, he advised that Koreans raise sheep in the north and produce cotton in the south. This peninsular conveyor belt would place the cotton at the Korean ports closest to Japan's textile mills where finished products could be produced for export back to Korea.[75]

Three years later Korea's northern provinces received an additional boost as Japan's continental military efforts intensified following the July 1937 Marco Polo Bridge Incident. This development prompted Korea's Government-General to draft an extensive plan to strengthen "*naisen ittai*" (literally Japan-Korea, one body), to quicken the pace of assimilation. Governor General Minami Jirō issued a draft of this plan one year later, in September 1938.[76] Most of this document's proposals advised that the administration prepare Koreans to meet the needs of the present circumstances. The Government-General was instructed to intensify its efforts to educate the people on their responsibilities as subjects of the Japanese Empire in the precarious wartime situation. It was to organize special training sessions, enlist Korean participation in group activities (such as radio calisthenics), and strive to curb potential health and social problem areas. In follow-up discussions arranged to evaluate this report, Vice-Governor General Ōno Rokuichirō, summarized the campaign's ambition as developing the image of the waters separating Korea and Japan as a land-locked lake, rather than an open sea.[77]

The report echoed the emphasis placed by Ugaki on developing Korean industry and military facilities, and strengthening Korean-Manchurian relations. These interlinked ambitions again demonstrated the paramount importance that the Japanese administration had placed on the northern provinces. It detailed a plan for developing this region that "corresponded to the special characteristics of northern Korea." The potential for war existed all along Korea's northern border with China, as well as the Soviet Union. This threat, coupled with the region's valuable assets—specifically coal mines, and industrial as well as electricity-generating capacity—made the region the "root and core of national security."[78] Thus northern Korea had to be fortified by solid military and surveillance operations. It also required increased transportation, medical, and educational institutions to prepare the region's residents for the critical roles they would play should the war come to the region. Communist presence in the region, and particularly in the border provinces, required the Japanese government to intensify education efforts and guide the people intellectually, while reinforced police vigilance protected the Korean people from the bearers of illegal leftist thought.

There was sufficient reason for concern. The report noted North Hamgyŏng as particularly vulnerable to communist influence. Extra security forces were required at the Korean peninsula's extreme north to prevent border crossings by communist agitators. The region's proximity to the war zone, and its value to the war effort, required army, navy, and air force sites to be relocated in the north. This rendered the region vulnerable as a "prime target for air strafing as well as a battleground for direct fighting." The report advised that defense plans be drafted to protect the region from these threats.[79]

These developments encouraged Kawaai Akitake in 1941 to dub this period as the "era of northern Korea" (hokusen jidai).[80] Greater emphasis on industrial development increased employment opportunities, which in turn increased Japanese interest in the region. This shift targeted the advantages held by Korea's northern provinces over those of the south. The homeland also facilitated Japanese travel to the north and provided living arrangements once residents arrived. The opening of the Wŏnsan-P'yŏngyang rail line facilitated travel from Japan to Korea's northern inlands. Itagaki Tadaji wrote in 1926 that this development cut costs—but added time—to allow for transporting products between Nagoya and P'yŏngyang, via the port of Tsuruga on the Japanese coast. He also noted the railway advantage in helping resolve the national security and the food supply problems.[81] The Government-General also increased the region's health facilities by situating two of the peninsula's six national hospitals (one each in North and South Hamgyŏng) there.[82] The increasing rate of students transferring out of northern schools (41.2 percent), however, suggests that a high percentage of the Japanese population was transitory rather than permanent.[83]

It is difficult to access whether this increase in interest in the northern provinces affected Japanese images of the northern Koreans. The wartime situation concentrated attention on war-related matters. Precious print media could no longer be spared for matters that detracted from the main message of Koreans being united as one body with the Japanese. The 1938 report on strengthening naisen ittai had emphasized many of the dangers highlighted previously. The region remained susceptible to ideological suasion—now Communism rather than Christianity; its continental border provided space for both communist agitators and anti-Japanese terrorists to slip into Korea and cause trouble. Japanese overextension into the Asian continent required the fortification of this region to ensure that Japan's lifeline to the continent remained connected.

The Japanese succeeded in maintaining this up until the end of World War II. Japanese negative experiences following the Soviet occupation of northern Korea—their having to flee to southern Korea for repatriation or being transported to Siberia to perform hard labor—left many with bitter feelings toward the northern Koreans as well as the Russians, feelings no doubt exasperated by the bitter relations that continue to prevail between North Korea and Japan.

CONCLUSION

The value of examining images of a people over a particular region or cultural group in this exercise is a revelation of truth perception rather than of absolute truth itself. An enhanced understanding of these perceptions is valuable, as human action is greatly influenced by human perception. The subjectivity of perception helps us understand shifts in image, which in turn helps us understand adjustments in human action. On occasion, image examination reveals changes in value priority.

This chapter has traced the transformation of images created by the Japanese during their colonial occupation over Korea from 1910–1945. There is little evidence suggesting that the Japanese accepted the Chosŏn era descriptions of northern Koreans as less civilized than their southern counterparts. Most often the Japanese described the Korean territory as a homogeneous region, inhabited by a homogeneous people who as a whole they depicted as inferior. Rhetorically this image of homogeneity strengthened the Japanese belief that it would be easy to assimilate the Korean people, despite the severe criticism that this policy faced at the time. Korean homogeneity, along with shared cultural and social similarities, would allow the Japanese to succeed where others had failed.[84]

In practical terms, however, the image of Korean homogeneity gradually came to be challenged. Koreans participated actively in introducing traditional northern-southern images to the Japanese. The images introduced to the Japanese appeared to differ from those formed during the Chosŏn Dynasty. Rather than imply the northerner's intellectual incapability, informants introduced the northern Koreans as psychologically unstable, a people bordering on personality disorders, to explain the high involvement of northern Koreans in the more newsworthy crimes of the period. Further study of personal documents reveals that these images may have influenced decisions by Japanese residents in Korea to remain in the more stable areas of southern Korea. This study suggests that development and opportunity trumped any fears that the Japanese people may have harbored regarding the region's safety.

How Japanese images of Korea and the Korean people transferred to American and Soviet occupiers in the aftermath of "liberation" presents another angle for future research. US documents suggest their influence. A 1944 report titled "Survey of Korea," for example, noted "marked differences between the attitude of 'hostile' northern and 'docile' southern Koreans toward the Japanese."[85] These images proved useful after the two Koreas went to war in 1950. As one popular weekly magazine put it, the northerner was "mainly mountain villagers, hardy folk, more warlike than the rice-growing South Koreans."[86] The extent to which the global superpowers exploited these images, or created new ones, to further their parochial interests on the Korean peninsula during the Cold War remains an interesting topic deserving future consideration.

NOTES

1. Following the 1603 Battle of Shimonoseki, the Tokugawa government divided hostile domains for control purposes. The island of present-day Hokkaido was divided into two regions: the Matsumae domain to the south of present-day Sapporo, and Ezo inhabited by Ainu tribes to its north. In the Ryukyu Kingdom the Satsuma domain separated the northern part of Okinawa from its southern half and the surrounding islands.

2. Hobsbawm, *The Age of Empire*, 59. Hobsbawm writes: "Between 1876–1915 about one-quarter of the globe's land was distributed or redistributed as colonies among a half-dozen states."

3. Weber, *Peasants into Frenchmen*. This policy enjoyed greater success in French proper than in Algeria and France's other colonized territories. At the turn of the twentieth century, assimilation faced heavy criticism from people who believed it impossible to integrate culturally different peoples.

4. Caprio, "Koreans into Japanese." Here I address European assimilation efforts (Chapter 1) and Japanese efforts in Okinawa, Hokkaido, and Taiwan (Chapter 2), before considering the Korean example.

5. Anderson, *Imagined Communities*.

6. This is the lesson gained from many of the examples introduced in Hobsbawm and Ranger, eds., *The Invention of Tradition*.

7. Carol Gluck's *Japan's Modern Myths* offers a comprehensive study of this process. For the development of Japan's education system see Marshall, *Learning to be Modern*. For Japan's media see Huffman, *Creating a Public*. Takashi Fujitani's *Splendid Monarchy* traces the role of the imperial throne in Japanese development.

8. Research on regional responses to the Meiji Restoration include Meiji ishin shinshigakkai, ed., *Meiji ishin no chiiki to minshū*; and Lewis, *Becoming Apart*.

9. The most respected Japanese dictionary, the *Kōjien*, notes these terms: "Pacific Ocean side" and "Sea of Japan side" as originating during the Meiji Period. The Pacific Ocean side is used to distinguish Japan's advancement.

10. Chamberlain and Mason, *Handbook for Travellers*, 505.

11. Kita Sadakichi's research on this topic was extensive. Some of his ideas are recorded in *Kankoku no heigō to kokushi*, "Chōsen minzoku to wa nani zoya," and "Nissen ryōminzoku dōgenron."

12. Nitobe Inazō, "Assimilation of the Chosenese," 667.

13. Ukita Kazutani, "Kankoku heigō no kōka ikan," 6.

14. Yamada Kanto, *Shokuminchi Chōsen ni okeru Chōsengo shorei seisaku*, 48–49.

15. Hosoi Hajime, "Chōsen no tōchi," 35. Hosoi serialized this article for the journal *Nihon oyobi Nihonjin* from October 1 to December 15, 1920.

16. Torii Ryūzō, "Watakushi no miru Chōsen," 38. Torii's characterization of Korea as an ancient country was far from unique. Many Japanese imagined Korea as a place in Japan's ancient past and reported feelings of "nostalgia" (*natsukashii*) when traveling across the peninsula.

17. Torii Ryūzō, "Yūshi izen ni okeru Chōsen to sono shūnen no kankei."

18. Takihisa Yonejiō, "Chōsen ni tai suru sanseiken jisshi ni kan suru seigansho."

19. Kita Sadakichi, "Kankoku no heigō to rekishi." Peter Duus explores Kita's research in greater detail in *The Abacus and the Sword*, 415–16.

20. Fujimura Hiromasa, "Chōsen tai ura Nihon keiyū Hokkaido senrō ni tai suru kōsatsu," 110–11.

21. For discussion on Gustave Le Bon's ideas see Betts, *Assimilation and Association in French Colonial Theory*, 64–69.

22. One of Japan's most ardent scientific colonial followers was Gotō Shinpei who served in the Taiwan Government-General offices. The Japanese government formed medical associations (*igakkai*) in Taiwan, Korea, and Manchuria soon after expanding into these territories. Their research was published in journals sponsored by these research institutions.

23. Chōsen sōtokufu, *Chōsen sōtokufu nenpō*, 1917: 22–23.

24. Chōsen sōtokufu, *Chōsen sōtokufu nenpō*, 1942: 36–37.

25. This change is reflected in the professions of Japanese residents in Korea. Those engaged in agriculture professions fell from 8 to just over 3 percent between 1926 and

1942. Japanese involved in industrial professions rose from 12.6 to 40.2 percent over this same period. Chōsen sōtokufu, *Chōsen sōtokufu nenpō*, 1928: 46–55 and 1944: 28–33.

26. Ōkurasho kanrikyoku, *Nihonjin no kaigai katsudō ni kansuru rekishiteki chōsa Chōsen hen*, 37.

27. Ibid., 37–38.

28. Horiuchi Minoru. "Nitteika, Chōsen hokubu chihō ni okeru anakizumu undō," 81.

29. Mizuto Bō, Hokukan ryokō zassō," 38–39.

30. As recorded in an interview by Hildi Kang in her *Under the Black Umbrella: Voices from Colonial Korea*, 56.

31. Inaba Kunsan, "Chōsen no rōdō mondai, minzoku mondai oyobi Senman bunka kankei ni oite" (Part I and II). Inaba appears to have been influenced by Kita Sadakichi's writing, much of which appeared in the journal *Minzoku to rekishi* (Ethnicity and History). Kita tended to characterize the Koreans has a homogeneous entity against the equally homogeneous Japanese. Their origins resulted from assimilations of various tribes in Manchuria. In a 1921 article titled "Nissen ryōminzoku dōgenron," he argued that the two people descended from the same family branch, a thesis that suggested assimilation as an appropriate administrative policy.

32. Inaba Kunsan, "Chōsen no rōdō mondai" (Part I), 13.

33. Nitobe Inazō, "Primitive Life and Presiding Death in Korea," 327–28.

34. The Japanese often used European examples with equal disregard for regional differences to justify their decision to implement an assimilation policy. In the case of Scotland, where lowland and highland responses to English rule differed dramatically, the Japanese government's examination of regional distinction might have benefited their assessment of Korea.

35. An example of this research was conducted by Kubo Takeshi. His work appeared in the *Chōsen igakkai zasshi* throughout the 1910s and into the 1920s. Summaries that appeared in *Chōsen oyobi Manshū* reached the non-medical population, as well.

36. See Sun Joo Kim, "Negotiating Cultural Identities in Conflict."

37. Kirihara Shinichi and Paek Inje, "Nitchōjinkan ni okeru ketsueki shokubetsu hyakubunnritsu no sai oyobi ketsueki shokubetsu tokūyusei no den ni tsuite," 276, 280–81.

38. See arguments in Gould, *The Mismeasure of Man*.

39. Pak Sanghŭi, "Chōsen seihokujin no tokushitsu."

40. This debate is often framed as a difference between Foreign Minister Shidehara Kijurō's "soft and spineless" economic diplomacy—increased economic expansion would quell anti-Japanese sentiment—and Tanaka Giichi's tough military solution. Japanese policy moved toward the latter military response and eventually engulfed a

continental war that dramatically increased the importance of Korea's northern provinces in the empire.

41. Pak Sanghŭi, "Chōsen seihokujin no tokushitsu," 112.

42. Ibid., 114–15.

43. Ibid.

44. Ibid., 117–20.

45. Ibid., 112–13.

46. Yi Sŏkhun's story is found in Kurokawa Sō, ed, "Gaichi" no Nihongo bungakusen 3: Chōsen, 176–91. Biographical information on Yi is found on pages 371–72 of this volume. He was killed in the Korean War.

47. Inoue Kōsai, "Hokusen imin tokubetsu hogō ni tsuite," 22–24.

48. Matsuda Shirō, "Tōhoku, Hokuriku, oyobi Kyushu chihō to Chōsen imin mondai," 39–40.

49. Miyanaga S., "A Flying Visit to Pyongyang," 2. An hailed from the north, but from Hwanghae Province rather than South P'yŏngan. This English language newspaper's primary audience was Korea's foreign residents. Its mission appeared to be to inform this population of the positive changes taking place in Korea under Japanese rule, particularly regarding the Korean people's attitude toward the Japanese. This was evident in the second part of this article published on June 7, 1910, which was devoted entirely to the Dōjin Hospital that the Japanese had established in P'yŏngyang four years earlier.

50. Kitakan Sanjin, "Chōsen no futei senjin," 81.

51. See An's testimony in Kim Chŏngju, Chōsen tōchi shiryō, 27.

52. A list of defendants is found in Kang Chaeŏn and Kita Hiroaki, eds., Hyakugonin jiken shiryōshū, 33–68.

53. Defendants are listed in Kim Chŏngju, Chōsen tōchi shiryō, 809.

54. Ibid., 697–711.

55. Frank Baldwin's account of the events surrounding the March First Independence movement demonstrates that the more violent reactions began in P'yŏngan Province after the initial demonstration had quieted in early March. See his "The March First Movement: Korean Challenge and Japanese Response," 91–93.

56. Tsuboi Sachio, Aru Chōsen sōtokufu keisatsu kanryō no kaisō, 88–93. Tsuboi was sent to North Hamgyŏng Province in May 1939.

57. Soon-Won Park, Colonial Industrialization and Labor in Korea: The Onoda Cement Factory, 33–36.

58. Chōsen sōtokufu, Chōsen sōtokufu nempō, 1926: 354–55.

59. As noted in Peattie, "Introduction," 89.

60. Sakai Toshio, Nihon tōchika no Chōsen hokuchin no rekishi, 89.

61. Chōsen sōtokufu, Chōsen sōtokufu nenpō, 1926: 367.

62. Chōsen sōtokufu keimukyoku, Chōsen keisatsu no gaiyō, 1926, 97. South Kyŏngsang,

with fifty-eight murders, ranked second.

63. Chōsen sōtokufu, *Chōsen sōtokufu nenpō*, 1942: 246–47.

64. Ch'oe Hŭiyŏng, "Chōsen in okeru shusseiritsu oyobi shibōritsu ni kan suru shakai seibutsu gakuteki kōsatsu," 113.

65. Ibid.

66. Ogawa Unpei, "Kita Chōsen no keiei wo ronsu," 16–18.

67. Zenshō Eisuke, "Chōsen shuyō shigai no sangyō seiryoku."

68. For example, the April 1926 issue of *Chōsen* carried an article by Kōchi Menseki titled "Heian hokudō ni okeru nōgyō narabi fukuhyō no shōhei." In February 1930, it carried Yoshida Yūjirō's "Heian hokudo no menyō shiyō."

69. Takahashi Kamekichi, "Chōsen wa umarefukeru," 47–48.

70. *Chōsen* devoted its August 1933 issue primarily to northern Korean issues.

71. The journal *Gaikō jihō* (Foreign Affairs) carried several articles in the 1920s on Japan's Monroe-shugi (Monroeism) that argued the need for Japan to develop its sphere of influence on the Asian continent, just as the US controlled its sphere in South America by virtue of the Monroe Doctrine.

72. While the Terauchi Masatake and Hasegawa Yoshimichi eras came to be known as "military rule" (*budan seiji*), and the Saitō Makoto era as "cultural rule" (*bunka seiji*), Ugaki Kazunari's administration was sometimes referred to as "industrial rule" (*sangyō seiji*).

73. Ugaki Kazunari, "Chōsen tōchi no taidō" and "Chōsen no shōrai."

74. Ugaki Kazunari, "Chōsen tōchi no taidō."

75. Ugaki Kazunari, "Chōsen no shōrai."

76. Chōsen sōtokufu, "Chōsen sōtokufu jikyoku taisaku chōsakai shimon tōshinsho."

77. Chōsen sōtokufu "Chōsen sōtokufu jikyoku chōsakai gijiroku," 307.

78. Chōsen sōtokufu "Chōsen sōtokufu jikyoku taisaku chōsakai shimon tōshinsho," 427.

79. Ibid., 434.

80. Kawaai Akitake, "Hokusenron," 1.

81. Itagaki Tadaji, "Heigen tetsudō to Gensankō," 39–41

82. Chōsen sotokufu, *Chōsen sōtokufu nenpō*, 1942: 268. The remaining four hospitals were located in Kyŏnggi (3) and South Kyŏngsang (1).

83. Ibid., 201. Sakai Toshio attributes this high turnover to the high percentage of administrators dispatched to the region. See his *Nihon Tōchika no Chōsen hokuchin no rekishi*, 133.

84. By contrast, the Japanese occasionally described their task in Taiwan as an effort to assimilate a plurality of peoples. Gotō Shinpei, "The Administration of Formosa (Taiwan)," 533.

85. War Department, Military Intelligence Service, "Survey of Korea," in Yi Kilsang, (ed.) *Haebang chŏnhusa charyojip I: migunjŏng chunbi charyo*, 67. I examine post-liberation views of Koreans by American occupation forces in "Japanese and American Images of Koreans: A Tale of Two Occupations."

86. "North Korean Target: Cold and Tough," 22.

Glossary

Adong pangŏn chŏngbyŏn sŏl 我東方言正變說 An Opinion on the Rights and Wrongs of Our Nation's Dialects

ahăygwa 아희과 with the child

Ajia gakkai アジア學會 Asia Society

akusei 惡政 the evil [Chosŏn] government

amhŭk sidae 암흑 시대 (or amhŭkki 암흑기) a dark age

benri 便利 convenient

budan seiji 武斷政治 military rule

bunka no teido 文化の程度 level of culture

bunka seiji 文化政治 cultural rule

burakumin 部落民 Japan's debased people

Ch'aemiga 採薇歌 Song of Picking Herbs

ch'aengmun 柵門 palisade settlement

Ch'ambong 參奉 superintendent of a royal tomb or shrine

Ch'amp'an 參判 vice minister of six ministries, Jr. 2

Ch'amŭi 參議 third minister of six ministries, Sr. 3

Changdaehyŏn kyohoe 장대현교회 Central Presbyterian Church

changno 장로 elder

Changnyŏng 掌令 third inspector of the Office of the Inspector-General, Sr. 4

Chang Poksŏn chŏn 張福先傳 Biography of Chang Poksŏn

changsach'ŭng 壯士層 military misfits

Chean-baek 齊安伯 Lord of Chean

chibang insa 地方人士 local personage

chihō gikai 地方議會 regional assemblies

chingyong 징용 the labor draft instituted by imperial Japan whereby Koreans were made to work in Japanese factories and elsewhere in support of the Japanese war effort

chinsa 進士 lower civil service examination degree-holder

Chinwisa 陳慰使 Condolence Embassy

chishiki kaikyū 知識階級 informed class

chogong ch'aekpong che 朝貢冊封制 tribute-investiture system

ch'ŏllima 千里馬 a thousand-li horse, a horse that can gallop one thousand li in one day

chŏn 錢 monetary unit; 10 chŏn = 1 yang

ch'ŏndang 天堂 heaven or paradise

chŏndosa 전도사 evangelist

ch'ŏngbaengni 清白吏 honest government officer

Ch'ŏngbuk 清北 the region north of the Ch'ŏngch'ŏn River

Ch'ongdokpu 총독부 Government-General

Chŏnggamnok 鄭鑑錄 Book of Chŏng Kam

chŏnggyŏk 正格 proper form

Chŏngju chinsa chemyŏngan sŏ 定州進士題名案序 preface to the record of the chinsa exam passers from Chŏngju

Chŏngŭm 正音 Correct Sounds (journal)

chŏngŭm 正音 correct pronunciation

chŏngŭn 丁銀 70 percent silver 30 percent lead

ch'ŏng yŏbi 請旅費 cover various official travel expenses

ch'ŏngyojik 清要職 reputable and prestigious posts or positions

Ch'ŏnjamun 千字文 Thousand Character Classic

Chŏnjŏk 典籍 librarian at the Royal Confucian Academy, Sr. 6

chŏnsŏ 全書 complete works

ch'ŏnŭn 天銀 pure silver

Chonwi 尊位 subdistrict head

chŏp 接 section in the Tonghak organization

chŏpchu 接主 section leader in the Tonghak organization

chŏptae 接待 reception

chosa 조사 assistant

Chōsen 朝鮮 Korea

Chōsen igakkai 朝鮮醫学會 Korean Medical Association

Chōsen igakkai zasshi 朝鮮醫學會雜誌 Korean Journal of Medicine (journal)

Chōsen no jinkō genshō 朝鮮の人口現象 Korean population effects

Chōsen oyobi Chōsen minzoku 朝鮮及朝鮮民族 Korea and the Korean Race (journal)

Chōsen oyobi Manshū 朝鮮及滿州 Korea and Manchuria (journal)

Chōsen sansei shingikai kōseiin 朝鮮參政審議會構成員 Korean Political Participation Deliberation Committee

Chōsen shisō tsūshinsha 朝鮮思想通信社 Korea Thought Correspondence Company

Chōsen sōtokufu nenpō 朝鮮總督府年報 Korea Government-General Annual

ch'osi 초시 one who passed the lowest (local) level of the national civil service examination; more generally a title of respect for a rural elite somewhat akin to a squire.

Chosŏn esŏ kajang chŏnghwakhan ŭm ŭl kŭnyang chŏnhayŏ 조선에서 가장 正確한 音을 그냥 전하여 preserved intact the most exact sounds in Korea

chosŏn'gŭl 조선글 Korean writing

Chosŏn kidokkyo kyoyuk yŏnmaeng 조선기독교교육연맹 Korean Protestant Education League

Chosŏn ŏhak 조선어학 Korean

Linguistics

Chosŏn ŏhak yŏn'guhoe
조선어학연구회 Research Society for
Korean Linguistics

Chosŏn ŏmun chŏngni kisŏnghoe 朝鮮
語文整理期成會 Action Committee for
the Rationalization of Writing in Korean
Script

Chosŏnmal kyubŏmjip 조선말규범집
Compendium of Korean Language
Norms

Chosŏnŏ ch'ŏlchabŏp 조선어철자법
Korean Orthography

Chosŏnŏ hakhoe 조선어학회 Korean
Language Society

Chosŏnŏ munbŏp 조선어문법 Korean
Grammar

Chosŏnŏ sinch'ŏlchabŏp 조선어신철자법
New Korean Orthography

Chosŏnŏ yŏn'guhoe 조선어연구회
Korean Language Research Society

Chuhan Miguk Kongsa 駐韓美國公使
minister of the Legation of the United
States

Chungch'ubu or Chungch'uwŏn 中樞府
or 中樞院 Office of Ministers-without-
Portfolio

Chunggan Tusi ŏnhae 重刊杜詩諺解
Poems of Du Fu in Korean Vernacular,
reprint

Ch'unsaengmun sagŏn 春生門事件
Incident of the Ch'unsaeng Gate

Chūō kōron 中央公論 Central Review
(journal)

ch'up'a 秋波 flirtatious glances

ch'uri 秋鯉 autumn carp

Chuyŏk yŏnŭi 周易演義 Explication of
The Book of Changes

Chwarang 佐郎 assistant section chief
of six ministries, Sr. 6

Ci ke lie zhuan 刺客列傳 Biographies
of Assassin Retainers, a chapter in the
Shi ji

Daitō gappōron (DTGR) 大東合邦論
Theory of the Great East Federation

danseiteki no gekidōsei 男性的の激動性
male turbulent side

dōhō 同胞 brethren

Duzhihuishisi 都指揮使司 Regional
Military Commissions of Ming China

fanza (R) peasant hut

fuken seido 府県制度 prefecture system

futeijin 不逞人 insubordinate people

Gaikō jihō 外交時報 Foreign Affairs
(journal)

genkotsu no kōshisha 拳骨の行使者 those
who wield fist and knuckles

haebang konggan 해방 공간 post-
Liberation "space"

Haedong chegukki 海東諸國記 Record of
Countries Across the Sea to the East

Haesŏ kaeja 海西丐者 A Beggar from
Hwanghae Province

Haesŏ kyoan 海西教案 Catholic
persecutions or disturbances in
Hwanghae Province

Hagyu 學諭 third proctor at the Royal
Confucian Academy, Jr. 9

Hakpu 學部 Ministry of Education

Hamgyŏng iin chŏn 咸鏡異人傳
Biographies of Outstanding Men from
Hamgyŏng Province

han 藩 domain

hăna 하나 one

Han-Ch'ŏng t'ongsang choyak 韓淸(靑) 通商條約 Korean-Chinese Agreement on Commerce and Trade in 1899

Hando taein 漢都大人 a master of the central capital

han'gŭl 한글 vernacular Korean script or indigenous script

Han'gŭl mach'umbŏp t'ongir-an 한글마춤법통일안 Unified Han'gŭl Orthography

hanmun 漢文 literary Chinese

Hansŏngbu 漢城府 Seoul Magistracy

hantō 半島 peninsula

higashi takushokumin 東拓殖民 Eastern colonists

hōgen 方言 dialect

Hogun 護軍 third deputy commander of the Five Military Commands, Sr. 4, to which the Chosŏn court appointed Jurchens

Hojo 戶曹 Ministry of Taxation

hokusen 北鮮 northern Korea

hokusen jidai 北鮮時代 northern Korea era

Hongbŏm 洪範 Great Principles to Order the World, a chapter in the *Shu jing*

hongsam 紅蔘 red ginseng

Hoppō Nippon 北方日本 Northern Japan Region

hŭgin 黑人 black people

hŭgŭi 黑衣 black clothing

Hullyŏn togam 訓鍊都監 Military Training Command

Hundo 訓導 instructor of a district

Hurhan Wudiha (C. Gukan Wangdihe) 骨看兀狄哈 Jurchen tribe

husi 後市 after-market

hwahwa chi se 花花之世 beautiful and flowering world

Hwangjoga 黃鳥歌 Song of the Nightingale

Hwang Kojip 黃固執 Obstinate Hwang

Hwang Kojip chŏn 黃固執傳 Biography of Hwang Kojip

Hwangmyŏng t'onggi 皇明通記 A Comprehensive History of the Ming Dynasty

Hwangsŏng sinmun 皇城新聞 Capital Gazette

Hwayang mun'gyŏllok 華陽聞見錄 Records of Things Heard and Seen at Hwayang

hyakushō supai 百姓スパイ peasant spies

hyangan 鄉案 local yangban association or the yangban roster

hyanghwa 向化 immigrant

hyangim 鄉任 official of the local elite bureau

hyangjang 鄉長 director of the local elite bureau

hyang t'ongsa 鄉通事 local interpreters

Hyogi Turyŏn chŏn 孝妓斗蓮傳 Biography of Turyŏn a Filial Female Entertainer

hyŏndaein 現代人 modern people

Hyŏngam 縣監 magistrate, Jr. 6

Hyŏngjo 刑曹 Ministry of Punishments

ichi chihō 一地方 single region

idan 異端 heretical

ihaku 威迫 menace

Ijo P'ansŏ 吏曹 Minister of Personnel

Ilchinhoe 一進會 Advance in Unity
Society

Injo panjŏng 仁祖反正 King Injo's
Restoration of 1623

irŏn 一言 a unitary language

Iryun haengsilto 二倫行實圖 Illustrated
Conduct of the Two Bonds

jikatsu kannen 自活觀念 a strong feeling
of self-reliance

jin'ai 仁愛 love

jin'iteki 人爲的 artificial

jinrui kakyō 人類可居 inhabitable

Jiyu byōdō keirin 自有平等經綸 World of
Liberty and Equality (journal)

joseiteki no kanshōsei 女性的の感傷性
female sentimentality side

kabo 甲午 the kabo year in the sixty-
year cycle, 1894 in particular

Kaehwa-dang 開化黨 enlightenment
party

Kaizō 改造 Conversion (magazine)

Kam 監 superintendent of the Kija
Shrine

Kamja 감자 Sweet Potatoes, a Kim
Tongin's short story

kamja 감자 potatoes

Kamnigyo yŏnhoe 감리교연회
Methodist Conference

Kamsa 監司 provincial governor, Jr. 2

Kamyŏng 監營 Provincial Governor's
Office

kangnae 江內 the land south of the rivers

kangoe 江外 the land beyond (or north
of) the rivers

Kan minzoku kokka katsudō 韓民族國家
活動 state activities of the Korean
people

karo (p'urŏ) ssŭgi 가로 (풀어) 쓰기
de-syllabified horizontalized Korean
script

kasa 歌辭 long vernacular verses

Kauli (C. Gaoli; K. Koryŏ) 高麗 local
Russian term for Koreans

Kawachi Yoshihiro 河內良弘 a Japanese
historian

kŏygul 기굴 cave

keihō 刑法 criminal law

keisatsuchō 警察廳 police bureau

khanshin (R) (C. *khodzhiu*; K. *tanu-stsur*)
Chinese vodka

khleb (R) bread

Kidok sinbo 基督新報 New Journal of
Christianity (journal)

Kija 箕子 legendary transmitter of
Chinese civilization to Korea

Kilmongga 吉夢歌 Song of Auspicious
Dreams

kimun 紀聞 hearsay accounts

kisaeng 妓生 professional female
entertainer

kobun ke 고분 게 pretty thing

Kobusa 告訃使 Obituary Embassy

kogong 雇工 temporary laborers

kohyang 고향 the ancestral home, often
the centuries-old seat of a family

Koju (see Oebae) 孤舟 literally a lone
boat, a pen name of Yi Kwangsu

kokugo 國語 Japanese, literally the
"national language"

Kokumin dōmeikai 國民同盟會 Anti-

Russian National League

Kokuryūkai 黑龍會 Black Dragon Society or Amur River Society

kongch'ul 공출 the imperial Japanese grain-requisition system in Korea

Konghuin 箜篌引 Song of Husband Not Crossing the River

Kongja tŭng T'aesan chang 孔子登太山章 Confucius Ascended Tai Mountain, a chapter in Mencius

kongnap 公納 tribute

kongyongŭn 公用銀 silver for public use

konmei jōtai 混迷狀態 confusing condition

kopta 곱다 be pretty

kosin 告身 office warrant issued to recipients of Chosŏn government posts

krai (R) region

kudang 舊黨 old crowds

kugŏhak 국어학 Korean language studies

kukkyŏng 國境 country's boundary

kŭmjam 金簪 gold ornamental hairpin

Kŭmwiyŏng 禁衛營 Capital Garrison

kŭn 斤 unit of weight about 600 grams; 1 kŭn of ginseng was worth 25 yang of silver in the early eighteenth century

kungma chi hyang 弓馬之鄉 region of archery and horsemanship

kungmun 國文 national script

Kungmun ch'ŏlcha ch'ŏpkyŏng 국문철자첩경 Shortcut to Korean Spelling

Kunsu (R. nachal'nik) 郡守 local magistrate of undefined rank

kwa 과 a particle in the Korean language

kwabŏl 科閥 families that produced a considerable number of munkwa passers

Kwanbuk munhŏllok 關北文獻錄 Literature of Hamgyŏng Province

Kwanbuk puja 關北夫子 master of Hamgyŏng Province

Kwanbuk sisŏn 關北詩選 Selected Poems from Hamgyŏng Province

Kwanch'alsa 觀察使 provincial governor, Jr. 2

Kwangmu 光武 reign title of the TaeHan Cheguk (Great Han Empire)

Kwan'gok p'algyŏng 寬谷八景 Eight Scenic Places in Kwan'gok

kwanmoje 官帽制 official hat system

Kwansŏ kimun 關西紀聞 Hearsay from P'yŏngan Province

Kwansŏ munhŏllok 關西文獻錄 Literature of P'yŏngan Province

Kwansŏ taejok 關西大族 prominent lineage of P'yŏngan Province

Kwansŏ t'ongji 關西通志 Comprehensive Gazetteer of P'yŏngan Province

kwanye 官隸 local clerks

kwihwa 歸化 immigrant

kwŏnsa 권사 a category of female church leader

kyohoe chŏkt'akcha 教會籍托者 church exploiters

kyoin 教人 believers; Christian believers or Catholics

kyokutansei no ryōsō 極端性の兩相 a personality that oscillated between two extremes kyŏl 結 a constant measure of crop yield produced by an area that varied from 2.2 to 9.0 acres depending on the fertility of the land

Kyŏngguk taejŏn 經國大典 Great Code of Administration

Kyŏngminp'yŏn ŏnhae 警民編諺解 Instructions for the People in Vernacular Korean

kyŏngŏbŏp 경어법 honorific usage

kyŏngsang 京商 Seoul merchant

Kyosŏgwan 校書館 Office of Editorial Review

kyouĭ 交倚 chair

kyōyū 俠勇 chivalry

li 里 unit of distance approximately 3.3 miles (449.17 m) or a subdistrict

Lu You (1125–1210) 陸游 a Chinese poet

Maeksuga 麥秀歌 Mourning Yin Melody

mal 斗 unit of volume; 1 mal = 10 toe = 1.57 gallons (5.96 liters)

Manho 萬戶 provincial military post to which Chosŏn court appointed Jurchens

mansang 灣商 Ŭiju merchant

Mansen 滿鮮 Manchurian-Korean

Manyōshū 万葉集 Eighth-Century Japanese Poetic Anthology

Mencius 孟子 one of the Four Books of Confucianism

mikaichi 未開地 undeveloped lands

minjungjŏk 民衆的 popular or populist

Minzoku to rekishi 民俗と歷史 Ethnicity and History (journal)

mo chibang 모지방 a certain unnamed province

mokpi 木匪 timber bandits

Moksa 牧使 (R. nachal'nik) magistrate of undefined rank

Monroe-shugi モンロー主義 Monroeism

mose 帽稅 hat tax

mugŭm 默音 silent letter

mugwa 武科 military examination

mumyŏng 무명 unknown

mun 文 monetary unit; 100 mun = 10 chŏn = 1 yang

munch'e 문체 writing style

Munhoe sŏwŏn 文會書院 Munhoe Private Academy

munin 文印 travel permit

munjip 文集 collected literary works

munkwa 文科 higher civil service examination

munoehan 문외한 outsider or non-specialist

munp'a 門派 branch of the Tonghak

musi 無視 flouting

Myohyangsanji 妙香山誌 History of Myohyang Mountain

nachal'nik (R) head, chief

Naesamch'ŏng 內三廳 Three Internal Offices

naisen ittai 內鮮一体 Japan-Korea one body

Namnam, pungnyŏ 南男北女 literally "In the south—men and in the north—women," hence "Korean men are more handsome in the southern provinces while women are more beautiful in the north"

nanbang 亂放 firing guns at will

nansaphan 난삽한 confusing and abstruse

nansen 南鮮 southern Korea

natsukashii 懐かしい nostalgic

Nihon oyobi Nihonjin 日本及日本人 Japan and the Japanese (magazine)

Nihonteki 日本的 very Japanese

Nogŏltae ŏnhae 老乞大諺解 The "Old Cathayan" in Vernacular Korean

nokpong 祿俸 stipend

Nongbusa 農夫詞 Song of Farmers

Noron 老論 Patriarch Faction

Numuhe 奴木哈 a man of the Uryangkhad tribe who used a forged office warrant

Odoli (C. Woduoli, Wuduli) 斡朵里, 吾都里 Jurchen tribe

Oebae (see Koju) 외배 loan boat, a pen name of Yi Kwangsu

oegwan 外官 provincial official

ŏgam 語感 language feelings

ogi 吾箕 "our P'yŏngyang"

ŏgŭn pulbyŏn 語根不變 unchanging word stems

omote Nihon 表日本 front (Pacific Ocean) side of Japan

ŏnmun 諺文 vernacular Korean script

Ŏnmun'guk 언문국 Vernacular Script Office

Ŏnmunji 諺文志 A Study of the Ŏnmun

osŏ 吾西 "our P'yŏngan Province"

Owi 五衛 Five Military Commands

Ŏyŏngch'ŏng 御營廳 Royal Guards Command

Paettaragi 배따라기 Kim Tongin's short story, The Boatman's Song

p'algye 八戒 Eight Admonitions

Palsŭngam 髮僧庵 literally "cell of a monk with unshaven head"; sobriquet of Kim Hongyŏn

Palsŭngam ki 髮僧庵記 An Account of a Monk with Unshaven Head

pangchŏm 방점 "side-dots" used to designate pitch accent in Late Middle Korean

panggi 方技 witchcraft

pangjang 坊長 ward chiefs

P'ansŏ 判書 minister of six ministries, Sr. 2

patch'im 받침 syllable-final consonant in the Korean language

P'ilsŏn 弼善 first tutor of the Crown Prince Tutorial Office, Sr. 4

p'o 包 subsection in the Tonghak organization

Pogong changgun 保功將軍 military prestige title, Jr. 3 (lower)

p'ogun 砲軍 commander of local expedition troops

ponbadak 본바닥 home ground

pon'ga 本家 family

Pongyo yŏksa 本敎歷史 History of Our Religion

pont'o 本土 home village

ponŭm 본음 original sounds

p'osu 砲手 gunmen

pukchŏp 北接 northern section of the Tonghak

Pukp'yŏnggwan 北平館 Hall of Northern Peace

Pukto nŭngjŏn chi 北道陵殿誌 Records of Tombs and Shrines in Hamgyŏng Province

Pumago 夫馬庫 local agency that

supplied men and horses for diplomatic missions

Pumanho 副萬戶 provincial military post to which the Chosŏn court appointed Jurchens

pun 分 monetary unit; 100 pun = 10 chŏn = 1 yang

Pusa 府使 (R. nachal'nik) magistrate of undefined rank

Pusajik 副司直 sixth rank military office of the Five Military Commands to which the Chosŏn court appointed Jurchens

Pusajŏng 副司正 eighth rank military office of the Five Military Commands to which the Chosŏn court appointed Jurchens

p'yesagun 廢四郡 four abolished districts

p'yogi 표기 orthographic representation

p'yoho 標號 diacritic marks or differentiating marks

Pyŏlchang 別將 special commander

P'yŏnganbuk-to Chaep'anso P'ansa 平安北道 裁判所 判事 judge of the Provincial Court in North P'yŏngan Province

P'yŏngan Kamyŏng chunggan 平安監營 重刊 republished by the Provincial Governor's Office in P'yŏngan Province

P'yŏngan pangŏn 平安方言 P'yŏngan dialect

P'yŏngbuk pangŏn ch'ŏnjamun 平安方言千字文 Thousand Character Classic in P'yŏngan Dialect

Pyŏngjo 兵曹 Ministry of Military Affairs

Pyŏngma Chŏltosa 兵馬節度使 provincial military commander, Jr. 2

Pyŏngma p'yŏngsa 兵馬評事 provincial military inspector

p'yŏn'gokhan 偏曲한 distorted, biased

Pyŏngsa 兵使 provincial military commander, Jr. 2

Pyŏngyŏng 兵營 Provincial Military Command

pyŏnjang 邊將 military official in border region

p'youi 表意 semantographic or ideographic

p'youihwa 表意化 semantographize

p'youm 表音 phonographic

sadaebu 士大夫 scholar-official

saengwŏnsi 生員試 lower civil service examination

Sahŏnbu 司憲府 Office of the Inspector-General

sahwan 使喚 personal servant

saip'yo 사이표 intercalary sign in the Korean language

saisiot 사이시옷 intercalary s in the Korean language

Sajik 司直 fifth rank military office of the Five Military Commands to which the Chosŏn court appointed Jurchens

Sajŏng 司正 seventh rank military office of the Five Military Commands to which the Chosŏn court appointed Jurchens

Sajŏnghan chosŏnŏ p'yojunmal moŭm 사정한 조선어 표준말 모음 Revised Compendium of Standard Korean

samatsu no jōhō 瑣末の情報 trivial information

samsumi 三手米 surtax for three combat forces

sangguk 上國 the country to the north or Ming China

sangguk cha 上國者 Chinese

Sanghogun 上護軍 first deputy commander of the Five Military Commands, Sr. 3 (lower), to which the Chosŏn court appointed Jurchens

sangjang 上將 general

sangmu chi hyang 尙武之鄕 military-honoring region

sangyō seiji 産業政治 industrial rule

Saŏp 司業 second assistant master at the Royal Confucian Academy, Sr. 4

sarang 사랑 salon of literati

sasang 私商 private merchant

sasang ŭihak 四象醫學 theory of four physical constitutions

satto 使道 local official of undefined rank

Saŭnsa 謝恩使 Embassy Expressing Gratitude for Imperial Grace

sawi 詐僞 fraudulent

Sayŏgwŏn 司譯院 Bureau of Interpretation

seibutsugaku keisu 生物學係數 biochemische index

Seihokudō 西北道 Northwest Province

seihokujin nasu nakare jūyō 西北人勿爲重要 the northwesterner had nothing important [to offer]

Seikaidō 西海道 Western Sea Province

senjin 鮮人 Korean people

Senman 鮮滿 Korean-Manchurian

Shi ji 史記 Records of the Grand Historian

Shi jing 詩經 Book of Odes, one of the five Confucian classics

shisōteki ni shinkoku na keiken 思想的に深刻な經驗 ideologically deep experience

Shizuka no arashi 靜の風 the short story, Quiet Storm

shoseijutsu wa zero 處世術はゼロ zero ability to get on in life

Shugo 守護 governor of Tsushima

Shu jing 書經 Book of History, one of the five Confucian classics

shūshinka 愁心歌 distressful folk songs

Sigangwŏn 侍講院 Crown Prince Tutorial Office

simsŏngnon 心性論 learning of mind and heart

sini 神異 miracles

Sinyak chyŏnsyŏ 신약젼셔 New Testament

sipchang 什長 chief miner

siryongsŏng 實用性 practicality

sŏ 序 preface

Sŏbuk minsim 西北民心 The Sentiment of the Northwestern People, a chapter in *Sŏngho saesŏl*

Sŏbuk musa 西北武士 The Military Officials from the Northwestern Region, a chapter in *Sŏngho saesŏl*

Sŏgyŏngbu 西京賦 Song of the Western Capital

Sŏgyŏng chuin 西京主人 host of the western capital

Sŏgyŏngji 西京志 Gazetteer of the

Western Capital

Sŏgyŏng sihwa 西京詩話 A Talk on Poetry From the Western Capital

Sohak 小學 Elementary Learning

Sok kŭnsarok 續近思錄 Reflections on Things at Hand, Continued

Sŏl P'illim 薛弼林 Stripling, a British citizen who operated an illegal mine in Unsan in 1900

Sŏl taein 설대인 Master Sŏl

sŏm 石 unit of volume; 1 *sŏm* = 15 (or 20) *mal* = 1 *picul* of grain by volume = 89.464 (or 119.285) liters

Sŏ Ma kisa sa 書馬騎士事 Story of Horseman Ma

Sŏnggyun'gwan 成均館 Royal Confucian Academy

Sŏngho saesŏl 星湖僿說 Yi Ik's Trivial Remarks

sŏngnihak 性理學 learning of nature and principle

songsang 松商 Kaesŏng merchant

sŏryang 西糧 western provisions tax

Sŏu 西友 Friends of the West (journal)

sŏwŏn 書院 private academy

Sŏyun 庶尹 deputy magistrate of P'yŏngyang, Jr. 4

ssimyŏng sajŏk 氏名事蹟 record of families

sugu 守舊 reactionary

sujŏn yusa 收錢有司 money-collecting agents

suli (see *suri*) (R) vodka

sumi 收米 rice surcharge

Sunginjŏn 崇仁殿 Kija Shrine

Sŭngmunwŏn 承文院 Office of Diplomatic Correspondence

Sungyang kigu chŏn 崧陽耆舊傳 Hagiographies of Kaesŏng's respected elders

suri (see *suli*) (R) vodka

suryŏng 守令 district magistrate

Taedo 大道 The Korean Evangel (journal)

taedong 大同 uniform land tax

Taehanin chyŏnggyobo 대한인졍교보 The Journal of the Korean Russian Orthodox Church

Taehogun 大護軍 second deputy commander of the Five Military Commands, Jr. 3, to which the Chosŏn court appointed Jurchens

taejak 代作 ghostwriting

T'aejong sillok 太宗實錄 Veritable Record of King T'aejong

Taema-do 對馬島 name for Tsushima in Chosŏn

taemyŏng ŭiri 大明義理 loyalty to the Ming Dynasty

Taesŏnsaeng 大先生 Great Master

taiheika 太平歌 tranquil songs

Taiyō 太陽 The Sun (magazine)

Tallyŏnsa 團練使 military escort

Tang 湯 a legendary emperor of the ancient Shang Dynasty

Tangak-kun 唐岳君 Lord of Tangak

Tangojŏn 當五錢 monetary unit equal to 5 *yang* of copper cash

t'angp'yŏng 蕩平 the politics of impartiality

tangsanggwan 堂上官 offices of rank senior third or above or ministerial rank

Tan'gun 檀君 legendary founder of the first Korean state Chosŏn

tigŭt kugaeŭmhwa 디귿 구개음화 t-palatalization

to 道 province

Tōa dōbunkai (K. Tonga tongmunhoe) 東亞同文會 East Asia Common Culture Society

t'och'ak sŏnggwan 土着姓貫 indigenous surname groups

tohak 道學 learning of the Way

tojang 도장 name chops

Tŏkch'ŏn-gun 德泉君 Prince Tŏkch'ŏn

tokuhō 特法 special law

Tōkyō tokuhain 東京特派員 Tokyo special dispatch

Tomanho 都萬戶 provincial military post to which the Chosŏn court appointed Jurchen elites

Tonga ilbo 동아일보 East Asia Daily

Tongbuk-myŏn Ch'ŏmjŏlchesa 東北面僉節制使 garrison commander in the northeastern region

Tongdo pin 東都賓 guest from the eastern capital

Tongguk yŏji sŭngnam 東國輿地勝覽 Survey of the Geography of Korea

tonggul 동굴 cave

Tonghak 東學 Eastern Learning or its followers

Tongjisa 冬至使 Winter Solstice Embassy

Tong Mongke Temur (?–1433) 童猛哥帖木兒 Odoli chieftain

t'ongsu 通首 unit heads of households

tongyang p'yŏnghwa 東洋平和 the peace of East Asia

Tosach'ŏng 都事廳 Office of the Inspector

Tosan sŏwŏn 陶山書院 Tosan Private Academy

tot'ae 淘汰 being forcibly wiped out

Tsushima 對馬 island between Japan and Korea

t'uhwa 投化 immigrant

Tumen (K. Tuman) 豆滿 Tumen River

tumin 頭民 leaders of villages

Tunam chŏnsŏ 遯菴全書 Complete Works of Sŏnu Hyŏp

tuŭm pŏpch'ik 두음법칙 head-sound rule

ŭibyŏng 義兵 righteous armies; Korean soldiers who were mobilized around the turn of the twentieth century in response to Japanese aggression on the Korean peninsula

Ŭijŏngbu 議政府 State Council

ŭimi 의미 meaning

umarefukeru 生れ更ける rebirth

ŭpchi 邑誌 local gazetteers

ura Nihon 裏日本 back (Sea of Japan) side of Japan

urigŭl 우리글 "our script"

Uryangkhad 兀良哈 Jurchen tribe

Uyun 右尹 third magistrate of the Seoul Magistracy, Jr. 2

verst' (R) a Russian measuring unit; 1 *verst'* = .66 miles (1.0668 km) = 2 Korean li

Waegwan 倭館 Japan House

wakaki Nihon 若き日本 naïve Japan

walcha 闊者 chivalrous swordsman or knight-errant known for unrestrained personality

wei 衛 guard or commanderies

wŏlbuk 월북 "gone north"; designation for those writers native to what is now South Korea who migrated—or less commonly were taken involuntarily—north of the thirty-eighth parallel to present-day North Korea after liberation

wŏn 元 a monetary unit of Korea

Wŏnduu 元杜尤 Horace G. Underwood (1859–1916)

wŏn'ŭm 原音 original sound

Yain (see Yŏjin) 野人 general term for both the tribal groups that relocated to the peninsular northeast, and that also lived north of Chosŏn, and their members

Yain'gwan 野人館 buildings for state gatherings with Jurchen elites

Yalu (K. Amnok) 鴨綠 Yalu River

yang 兩 monetary unit; 1 *yang* = 10 *chŏn* = 100 *pun* or *mun*

Yanggwan 洋館 missionary compound

yangniin 楊里人 people residing in some Jurchen villages

yaso kyoin 耶蘇教人 people affiliated with Christian churches

yehak 禮學 study of rituals and rites

Yejo 禮曹 Ministry of Rites

Yesu kyohoe 예수교회 Protestant Church

Yesu syŏnggyo chyŏnsyŏ 예수셩교젼셔 New Testament

Yŏjin (see Yain) 女眞 general term for both the tribal groups that relocated to

the peninsular northeast, and that also lived north of Chosŏn, and their members

yŏjŏndosa 여전도사 biblewomen

yŏkhak 易學 learning of divination

yŏkkwan 譯官 interpreter

Yŏkkyŏng (C. Yi jing) 易經 Book of Changes

Yŏksŏl 易說 Discussions on The Book of Changes

Yŏmbul pogwŏnmun 念佛普勸文 Selected Prayers to Buddha

yŏnbyŏn 沿邊 the area close to land's edge

Yŏngmun yuch'wi 易文類聚 Collections of Divinatory Writings

yŏngno 驛路 government post roads

Yŏnhaeju 沿海州 Maritime Province of Siberia

Yŏnhaengdo 燕行圖 Illustration of Chosŏn Envoy to Qing

Yuandousha 元多沙 man of the Uryangkhad tribe who traded in Chosŏn and under whose name other Jurchens traded in Chosŏn

yukchin 六鎭 six garrisons

Zhaonan 召南 Odes of Zhao and the South in The Book of Odes

Zhihui 指揮 guard commander

Zhihuishi 指揮使 guard commander

Zhou Wenmo 周文謨 Chinese priest who came to Korea in 1794 to disseminate Catholicism

Zhunan 周南 Odes of Zhu and the South in The Book of Odes

Bibliography

Adami, Norbert R. "Die Geschichte der Koreaforschung im zaristischen Russland" [History of Korean Studies in Tsarist Russia]. *Bochumer Jahrbuch zur Ostasienforschung* (1980): 1–97.

———. *Die russische Koreaforschung: Bibliographie 1682–1976* [Russian Research on Korea: Bibliography 1682–1976]. Wiesbaden: Reichert, 1976.

Al'ftan, V. A. "Poezdka v Koreiu podpolkovnika general'nogo shtaba Al'ftana v dekabre 1895 i ianvare 1896" [The Journey to Korea of Lieutenant-Colonel Al'ftan of the General Staff in December 1895 and January 1896]. *Sbornik materialov po Azii*, sb. LXIV. Voenno-uchenyi Komitet Glavnogo Shtaba. Originally written in 1896. Reprinted in Tiagai (1958): 220–65.

An Chunggŭn. "An Ŭngch'il yŏksa" [Autobiography of An Ŭngch'il]. In *An Chunggŭn ŭisa chasŏjŏn* [Autobiography of An Chunggŭn], edited by Yi Ŭnsang. Seoul: An Chunggŭn ŭisa sungmohoe, 1970.

———. "Tongyang p'yŏnghwaron" [On the Peace of East Asia]. In *An Chunggŭn ŭisa chasŏjŏn* [Autobiography of An Chunggŭn]. Seoul: Pŏmusa, 2000.

Anderson, Benedict. *Imagined Communities: Reflections on the Origin and Spread of Nationalism*. London: Verso Press, 1983/1991.

Applegate, Celia. "A Europe of Regions: Reflections on the Historiography of Sub-National Places in Modern Times." *American Historical Review* 104, no. 4 (Oct. 1999): 1157–82.

Baird, Mrs. Wm. H. "The Future of Unmoon." *The Korea Mission Field* 6, no. 8 (August 1, 1910): 204–6.

Baird, Richard H. *William M. Baird of Korea: A Profile*. Oakland, CA: family manuscript, 1968.

Baldwin, Frank. "The March First Movement: Korean Challenge and Japanese

Response." PhD diss., Columbia University, 1969.

Ball, Rodney. "Spelling Reform in France and Germany: Attitudes and Reactions." *Current Issues in Language and Society* 6, no. 3 & 4 (1999): 276–80.

Baxter, James C. *The Meiji Unification Through the Lens of Ishikawa Prefecture*. Cambridge, MA: Harvard University Council on East Asian Studies, 1994.

Bayly, C. A., Sven Becker, Matthew Connelly, Isabel Hofmeyr, Wendy Kozol, and Patricia Seed. "AHR Conversation: On Transnational History." *American Historical Review* 111, no. 5 (December 2006): 1440–64.

Belsky, Richard. *Localities at the Center: Native Place, Space, and Power in Late Imperial Beijing*. Cambridge and London: Harvard University Asia Center, 2005.

Berezin, N. *Chao-sian'. Strana utra. Koreia, ee priroda, zhiteli i ikh proshloe I sovremennoe sos-toianie* [Choson. Land of the Morning. Korea, Her Nature, Inhabitants, and Their Past and Present Situation]. St. Petersburg: Obshchestvannaia Pol'za, 1904.

Betts, Raymond F. *Assimilation and Association in French Colonial Theory, 1890–1914*. New York: Columbia University Press, 1961.

Bishop, Isabella Bird. *Korea and Her Neighbours*. New York and Toronto: F. H. Revell, 1897.

Blair, William Newton. *Gold in Korea*. New York: Presbyterian Church in the USA, 1957.

Blommaert, Jan, ed. *Language Ideological Debates*. Berlin: Mouton de Gruyter, 1999.

Blommaert, Jan. "The Debate Is Closed." In Blommaert, *Language Ideological Debates*, 425–38.

———. "The Debate Is Open." In Blommaert, *Language Ideological Debates*, 1–38.

Booker, M. Keith. *Techniques of Subversion in Modern Literature*. Gainesville: University of Florida Press, 1991.

Bourdieu, Pierre. "Le Fétichisme de la Langue." *Actes de la Recherche en Sciences Sociales* 4 (1975): 2–32.

Brokgauz-Efron. *Iaponiia i ee obitateli. S prilozheniem ocherka "Koreia i Koreitsy"* [Japan and Her Inhabitants. With an Appended Essay, "Korea and the Koreans"]. St. Petersburg: Brokgauz-Efron, 1904.

Brower, David and Edward J. Lazzerini, eds. *Russia's Orient: Imperial Borderlands and Peoples, 1700–1917*. Bloomington and Indianapolis: Indiana University Press, 1997.

Busse, Fedor Fedorovich. *Pereselenie krest'ian morem v Iuzhno-Ussuriiskii krai v 1883–1893 gg.* [The Resettlement of Peasants by Sea to the South Ussuri Krai, 1883–1896]. St. Petersburg: Tip. "Obshchestvennaia pol'za," 1896.

Caprio, Mark E. "Japanese and American Images of Koreans: A Tale of Two Occupations." In *Trans-Pacific Relations: America, Europe, and Asia in the Twentieth Century*, edited by Yoneyuki Sugita, Richard Jensen, and Jon Davidann, 105–24. Westport, CT: Praeger, 2003.

———. "Koreans into Japanese: Japan's Assimilation Policy, 1910–1945." PhD diss., University of Washington, 2001.

The Catholic Church in Korea. Hong Kong: Imprimerie de la Societé des Missons-Étrangéres, 1924.

Ch'a Ch'ŏllo. *Osanjip* [Collected Works of Ch'a Ch'ŏllo]. In *Han'guk munjip ch'onggan*, Vol. 61. Seoul: Minjok munhwa ch'ujinhoe, 1991.

Ch'ae Chegong. *Pŏnamjip* [Collected Works of Ch'ae Chegong]. In *Han'guk munjip ch'onggan*, Vol. 236. Seoul: Minjok munhwa ch'ujinhoe, 1999.

Ch'ae Chŏngmin. "Ch'ansongga ch'ulp'an ŭl pandaeham" [I Oppose the Publication of the Hymnal]. *Chŏngŭm* 32 (1939): 1891–96.

———. "Chosŏnŏ t'ongil kwa sŏnggyŏng ch'ŏlcha ŭi han'gŭlsik kaejŏng pulgaron" [Why *Han'gŭl*-Style Reform Is Not Acceptable for Bible Spelling and the Unification of the Korean Language]. *Chŏngŭm* 24 (1938): 1607–9.

———. "Han'gŭlhakp'a ŭi kyojŏng ŭl chesi" [Suggested Revisions to the *Han'gŭl* School]. *Chŏngŭm* 25 (1938): 1650–53.

———. "Kang Pyŏngju ssi ege chaech'a munŭiham" [Yet Another Set of Questions for Mr. Kang Pyŏngju]. *Chŏngŭm* 26 (1938): 1680–83.

———. "Kidokkyo palchŏn kwa Chosŏn muncha kye ŭi changnae" [The Development of Protestantism and the Future of the Korean Writing System]. *Chŏngŭm* 30 (1938): 1819–22.

———. "Ŏnmun ŭi changchŏm kwa tanchŏm" [Strengths and Weaknesses of the Ŏnmun]. *Chŏngŭm* 34 (1940): 1961–62.

———. "Tokcha ŭi sori: han'gŭl sinch'ŏlcha ŭi yangchŏm kwa kyŏlchŏm" [Readers' Voices: Pluses and Minuses of the New *Han'gŭl* Spelling]. *Han'gŭl* 20 (1935): 15–17.

———. "Uri ch'onghoe ka sinch'ŏlcha ch'aeyongham ŭl tŭtko" [On Hearing that Our Presbyter Has Adopted the New Spelling]. *Chŏngŭm* 21 (1937): 1443.

———. "Uri hyŏngje ŭi kuŏŭm ŭl malsalt'i malla" [Don't Annihilate the Vernacular Sounds of Our Brethren!]. *Chŏngŭm* 23 (1938): 1551–54.

———. "Yi T'aebaek kwa Parhae kungmun" [Li Taibo and Parhae National Script]. *Chŏngŭm* 22 (1938): 1516–17.

Chamberlain, Basil Hall, and W. B. Mason. *Handbook for Travellers in Japan.* London: Kelly & Walsh, 1913.

Chandra, Vipan. "An Outline Study of the Ilchin-hoe of Korea." *Occasional Papers on Korea* 2 (March 1974): 43–72.

Chang Chiyŏn. "Ch'uksa" [A Congratulatory Remark]. *Sŏu* 1 (1906): 5.

Chang Hakkŭn. "Sejong-Sŏngjong nyŏn'gan ŭi sindo sut'am chŏngch'aek" [The Policy of Searching for New Islands from the Reign of King Sejong to the Reign of King Sŏngjong]. *Haesa nonmunjip* 28 (1988): 9–30.

Chang Hyŏnsuk. "Hwang Sunwŏn, 'Minjok hyŏnsil kwa isang kwa ŭi koeri': Tanp'yŏnjip *Kirŏgi* rŭl chungsim ŭro" [The Ideal and the Real in the Nation in Hwang Sunwŏn's Story Collection *Wild Geese*]. In *Hwang Sunwŏn yŏn'gu*, 189–220. Seoul: Munhak kwa chisŏngsa, 1993.

———. *Hwang Sunwŏn munhak yŏn'gu* [A Study of the Literature of Hwang Sunwŏn]. Seoul: Si wa sihaksa, 1994.

Chang Kyusik. *Ilcheha Han'guk kidokkyo minjokchuŭi yŏn'gu* [A Study of Christian Nationalism in Colonial Korea]. Seoul: Hyean, 2001.

Chang Yŏnggil. "P'yŏngan pangŏn ŭi pi-gugaeŭmhwa yoin e taehan il koch'al" [A Study on the Causes of Non-palatalization of P'yŏngan Dialect]. *Tongak ŏmun nonmunjip* 29 (1994): 315–25.

Chang Yusŭng [Jang Yoo-seung]. "Chosŏn hugi sŏbuk chiyŏk munin chiptan ŭi sŏnggyŏk—P'yŏngan-do wa Hamgyŏng-do ŭi chiyŏk chŏngch'esŏng ch'ai rŭl chungsimŭro" [The Characteristics of Literati in the Northern Region—Focusing on the Regional Identities of P'yŏngan and Hamgyŏng Provinces and Their Differences]. *Chindan hakpo* 101 (2006): 391–425.

———. "Chosŏn sidae Hamgyŏng-do chiyŏk ŭi munin chiptan kwa munhak hwaltong" [Hamgyŏng Literati and Their Literary Activities During the Chosŏn Period]. In *Che 2 hoe segye han'gukhak taehoe nonmunjip*. Sŏngnam: Han'gukhak chungang yŏn'guwŏn, 2005.

———. "17–18 segi Hamgyŏng-do chiyŏk ŭi munjip p'yŏnch'an kwa sŏjŏk kanhaeng" [Compilation and Publication of Literary Works in Hamgyŏng Province in the Seventeenth and Eighteenth Centuries]. *Sŏjihakpo* 27 (2003): 45–77.

Charr, Easurk Emsen. *The Golden Mountain: The Autobiography of a Korean Immigrant, 1895–1960*. Second Edition, edited with an introduction by Wayne Patterson. Urbana and Chicago: University of Illinois Press, 1961.

"Chibam Hwang Sunsŭng chŏn" [Life of Hwang Sunsŭng]. *Sŏbuk hakhoe wŏlbo* 6 (November 1, 1908): 21–24.

Cho Hŏnyŏng. "Soi rŭl pŏrigo 'Han'gŭl t'ongiran' ŭl chijihaja" [Let Us Discard Small Differences and Support the "Unified Orthography"]. *Han'gŭl* 24 (1935): 8–10.

Cho Kwang. "An Chunggŭn yŏn'gu ŭi hyŏnhwang kwa kwaje" [The Reality of Study of An Chunggŭn and Future Tasks]. *Han'guk kŭnhyŏndaesa yŏn'gu* 12 (2000): 180–222.

Cho, Seungbog. *A Phonological Study of Korean, With an Historical Analysis*. Uppsala: Almqvist & Wiksells, 1967.

Ch'oe Chinok. "Chosŏn sidae P'yŏngan-do ŭi saengwŏn chinsasi hapkyŏkcha silt'ae" [Analysis of Saengwŏn and Chinsa Examination Passers from P'yŏngan Province During the Chosŏn Dynasty]. *Chosŏn sidaesa hakpo* 36 (2006): 211–51.

Ch'oe Hyŏnbae. "Chibang yuse ŭi u: ŏmun undong? Chŏngch'i undong?" [The Folly of the Provincial Speaking Tour: Language and Writing Campaign? Political Campaign?]. *Han'gŭl* 22 (1935): 24–27.

———. "Kidokkyo wa han'gŭl" [Protestantism and *Han'gŭl*]. *Sinhak nondan* [Theological Forum] 7 (1962): 51–80.

Ch'oe Hŭiyŏng. "Chōsen in okeru shusseiritsu oyobi shibōritsu ni kansuru shakai seibutsu gakuteki kōsatsu" [A Social-Biological Study of the Birth and Death Rate in Korea]. *Chōsen igakkai zasshi* (February 1937): 101–25.

Ch'oe Kiyŏng and Pak Maengsin, eds. *Hanmal Ch'ŏndogyo charyojip* [Collected Sources on Catholic History in the Last Decade of the Chosŏn Dynasty]. 2 vols. Seoul: Kukhak Charyowŏn, 1997.

Ch'oe Kiyŏng. *Han'guk kŭndae kyemong sasang yŏn'gu* [A Study of Enlightenment Thought in Modern Korea]. Seoul: Ilchogak, 2003.

Ch'oe Sin. *Hagamjip* [Collected Works of Ch'oe Sin]. In *Han'guk munjip ch'onggan*, Vol. 151. Seoul: Minjok munhwa ch'ujinhoe, 1995.

Ch'oe Sŏgu. "Haesŏ kyoan ŭi yŏn'gu" [A Study of Catholic Persecutions in Hwanghae Province]. In *Han'guk kyohoesa ŭi t'amgu*, Vol. 2, 413–61. Seoul: Han'guk kyohoesa yŏn'guso, 1991.

Ch'oe T'aeyŏng. "Ch'ogi pŏnyŏk sŏngsŏ yŏn'gu II" [A Study of Early Bible Translations, II]. In *Han'gŭl sŏngsŏ wa kyŏre munhwa: Ch'ŏnjugyo wa kaesin'gyo ŭi mannam*, edited by Kŭrisŭdogyo wa kyŏre munhwa yŏn'guhoe, 269–302. Seoul: Kidok kyomunsa, 1985.

Chŏn Yŏngt'aek. "Kidokkyo wa Chosŏn muncha" [Protestantism and Korean Writing]. *Han'gŭl* 37 (1936): 2–4.

Chŏng Ho. *Changamjip* [Collected Works of Chŏng Ho]. In *Han'guk munjip ch'onggan*, Vol. 157. Seoul: Minjok munhwa ch'ujinhoe, 1995.

Chŏng Sŏkchong. "Hong Kyŏngnae nan ŭi sŏnggyŏk" [The Nature of the Hong Kyŏngnae Rebellion]. *Han'guksa yŏn'gu* 7 (1972): 151–206.

Chŏng Wŏnyong. *Pukhaeng surok* [Records on Hamgyŏng Province]. Kyujanggak collection, ko 4794.

Ch'ŏngsŏn'go [Selected List of Chosŏn Officials] Edited by Changsŏgak. Seoul: T'amgudang, 1972.

Ch'ŏnjugyo P'yŏngyang kyogusa p'yŏnch'an wiwŏnhoe. *Ch'ŏnjugyo P'yŏngyang kyogusa* [History of the Catholic Church in P'yŏngyang]. Seoul: Pundo ch'ulp'ansa, 1981.

Chōsen sōtokufu. "Chōsen sōtokufu jikyoku chōsakai gijiroku" [Record of the Proceedings of the Korean Government-General Investigation on Strategy for the Present Circumstances]. In *Ilcheha chibae chŏngch'aek charyojip* [Compilation of Materials on Control Policy under Imperial Japan], edited by Sin Chubaek, Vol. 16. Seoul: Koryŏ sŏrim, 1993.

———. *Chōsen sōtokufu nenpō* [Korean Government-General Statistics Annual], 1917, 1926, 1928, 1942, and 1944. Keijō: Chōsen sōtokufu.

———. "Chōsen sōtokufu jikyoku taisaku chōsakai shimon tōshinsho" [The Korean Government-General Report on the Inquiry Investigation into the State of Affairs]. *Ilcheha chibae chŏngch'aek charyojip* [Compilation of Materials on Control Policy Under Imperial Japan], edited by Sin Chubaek, Vol. 15. Seoul: Koryŏ sŏrim, 1993.

Chōsen sōtokufu keimukyoku. *Chōsen keisatsu no gaiyō*, 1927 [Japanese Police Summary, 1927]. Keijō: Chōsen sōtokufu keimukyoku, 1927.

Chosŏn minjujuŭi inmin konghwaguk kwahagwŏn. *Chosŏn chi: ch'oyŏk* [Description of Korea: Abridged Translation]. P'yŏngyang: Kwahagwŏn ch'ulp'ansa, 1959.

Chosŏnŏ hakhoe. "Han'gŭl t'ongil undong e taehan pandae ŭmmo konggaejang [Open Letter Concerning the Plot in Opposition to the *Han'gŭl* Unification Movement]. *Han'gŭl* 22 (1935): 14–19.

"Chosŏnŏ hakhoe ŭi kongham igŏn" [Two Open Letters from the Chosŏnŏ hakhoe]. *Han'gŭl* 37 (1936): 8–9.

Chu Ch'ŏjŏng. *Kwanbuk sisŏn* [Selected Poems from Hamgyŏng Province]. Originally compiled in 1714. Kyujanggak collection, ko 3441 15.

Chu Sigyŏng. "Han nara mal" [The Korean Language ("Han-nation-ese")]. *Pojung ch'inmok hoebo* 1 (June 1, 1910): 86–92.

Ch'ubung. *Myohyangsanji* [History of Myohyang Mountain]. Kyujanggak collection, Ilswae ko 915.18–Se63m.

Chŭngbo munhŏn pigo [Documents on Korea Compiled for Reference, Supplemented and Revised]. Compiled by Pak Yongdae et al. in 1908. Reprint. Seoul: Han'gukhak chinhŭngwŏn, 1987.

Chunggan Tusi ŏnhae [Poems of Du Fu in Korean Vernacular, Reprint Edition]. Reprint of 1632 edition. Korea: 1999.

Clark, Allen D. *A History of the Church in Korea*. Seoul: Christian Literature Society, 1972.

Coulmas, Florian. "The Far East." In *Handbook of Language and Ethnic Identity*, edited by Joshua Fishman, 399–413. Oxford and New York: Oxford University Press, 1999.

Craig, Albert. *Chōshū in the Meiji Restoration*. Lanham, MD: Lexington Books, 2000. Originally published in 1961 by Harvard University Press.

Crossley, Pamela Kyle, Helen Siu, and Donald Sutton. *Empire at the Margins: Culture, Ethnicity, and Frontier in Early Modern China*. Berkeley: University of California Press, 2006.

Da Ming huidian [Collected Statutes of the Great Ming]. Yangzhou: Jiangsu guangling guji keyinshe, 1989.

Dadeshkaliani, K. N. "Kratkii ocherk sovremennogo sostoianiia Korei kniazia Dadeshkaliani, sostoiashchego pri kantseliarii priamurskogo general-gubernatora (1885 g.)" [Short Sketch of the Current Situation of Korea by Prince Dadeshkaliani, Attached to the Chancellery of the Priamur Governor-General (1885)]. *Sbornik materialov po Azii*, sb. 23: 61–118. Skt. Peterburg: Voenno-uchenyi Komitet Glavnogo Shtaba, 1886. Reprinted in Tiagai (1958): 48–96.

Delotkovich, Pavel Mikhailovich. "Dnevnik Pavla Mikhailovicha Delotkovicha na puti peshkom iz Seula v Pos'et cherez severnuiu Koreiu, s 6 Dekabria 1885 g. po 29 Febralia 1886 g." [Diary of Pavel Mikhailovich Delotkovich on His Journey by Foot from Seoul to Pos'et Across Northern Korea, from December 6, 1885 to February 29, 1886]. *Izvestiia Imp. R. G. O.* 24 (1886): 294–315. Also printed in *Sbornik materialov po Azii*, sb. 38 (1887): 128–67. Skt. Peterburg: Voenno-uchenyi Komitet Glavnogo Shtaba, and again in *Izvestiia Imp. R. G. O.* 25 (1889): 294–315. Reprinted in Tiagai (1958): 11–48.

"Diary from Fr. Byrne." Dated May 8, 1923. In Mission Diaries, Korea, Box 1. Maryknoll Mission Archives, New York.

"Diary of Maryknoll in Peng Yang, August 1925 to March 1927." In Mission Diaries, Korea, Box 1. Maryknoll Mission Archives, New York.

Douglass, William A. "A Western Perspective on an Eastern Interpretation of Where North Meets South: Pyrenean Borderland Cultures." In *Border Identities: Nation and State at International Frontiers*, edited by Thomas M. Wilson and Hastings Donnan, 62–95. Cambridge: Cambridge University Press, 1998.

Duara, Prasenjit. *Rescuing History from the Nation: Questioning Narratives of Modern China*. Chicago: University of Chicago Press, 1995.

Duncan, John. "*Hyanghwain*: Migration and Assimilation in Chosŏn Korea." *Acta Koreana* 3 (2000): 99–113.

Duus, Peter. *The Abacus and the Sword: The Japanese Penetration of Korea, 1895–1910*. Berkeley: University of California Press, 1995.

Dzharylgasinova, Roza Shataevna. "Iz istorii rossiiskogo etnograficheskogo koreevedeniia" [From the History of Russian Ethnographic Korean Studies]. *100 let Peterburgskomu Koreevedeniiu: Materialy mezhdunarodnoi konferentsii, posviashchennoi stoletiiu Koreevedeniia v S.-Peterburgskom universitite.* 14–16 oktiabria 1997 g. (tesizy), 99–101. St. Petersburg, 1997.

Eleventh Annual Report of the Korea Woman's Conference of the Methodist Episcopal Church. Seoul: Methodist Publishing House, 1909.

Epstein, Stephen. "Elusive Narrators in Hwang Sunwŏn." *Korean Studies* 19 (1995): 104–11.

Fenkl, Heinz Insu. "Buried in a Stained Sweater: The Politics of Misogyny in Hwang Sunwŏn's 'Sonagi.'" Paper presented to the conference "Gender in Korean Literature, Culture, and Society," University of Southern California, 1996.

Forbes, Jack D. "Frontiers in American History and the Role of the Frontier Historian." *Ethnohistory* 15 (Spring 1968): 203–35.

Friedman, Edward. "A Failed Chinese Modernity." *Daedalus: China in Transformation* 122, no. 2 (Spring 1993): 1–17.

Fujimura Hiromasa. "Chōsen tai ura Nihon keiyū Hokkaido senrō ni taisuru kōsatsu" [Deliberating on a Sea Lane between Korea and Hokkaido on the Japan Sea Side of Japan]. *Chōsen* (February 1926): 110–18.

Fujitani, Takashi. *Splendid Monarchy: Power and Pageantry in Modern Japan.* Berkeley: University of California Press, 1996.

Fulton, Bruce. "Analysis of a Debate: Kim Yunsik, Hwang Sunwŏn, and 'Hak' [Cranes]." Seminar paper, Seoul National University, 1997.

———. "Hwang Sunwŏn tanp'yŏn sosŏl yŏn'gu" [A Study of the Short Fiction of Hwang Sunwŏn]. PhD diss., Seoul National University, 1999.

———. "The Wŏlbuk Writers." In *The Columbia Companion to Modern East Asian Literature,* edited by Joshua Mostow, 81–83. New York: Columbia University Press, 2003.

Gal, Susan. "Multiplicity and Contention among Language Ideologies." In *Language Ideologies: Practice and Theory,* edited by Bambi B. Schieffelin, Kathryn A. Woolard, and Paul V. Kroskrity, 317–31. New York: Oxford University Press, 1998.

Gale, James Scarth. *A Korean-English Dictionary (Han-yŏng chajŏn).* First edition. Yokohama: Kelly & Walsh, 1897.

———. *A Korean-English Dictionary.* Yokohama: Fukuin Printing Co., 1911.

———. *Korean Sketches.* New York: Fleming H. Revell, 1898.

Galton, Francis. *Hints to Travelers.* London: Royal Geographic Society, 1878.

Garin-Mikhailovskii, N. G. *Iz dnevnikov krugosvetnogo puteshestviia: Po Koree, Man'chzhurii i Liaodunskomu poluostrovu* [From My Notebooks of a Trip Around the World: In and

About Korea, Manchuria and the Liaodong Peninsula]. Edited and with introduction and commentary by V. T. Zaichikov. Moskva: Gos. izd-vo geog. lit-ry, 1950.

―――. N. G. *Garin-Mikhailovskii: Sobranie sochineniia* [N. G. Garin-Mikhailovskii: Collected Works]. Vol. 5: Po Koree, Man'chzhurii i Liaodunskomu poluostrovu; Vokrug sveta; Koreiskie skazki; skazki dlia detei; P'esy; Vospominaniia, Stat'i 1894–1906. Moscow: Gosudarstvennoe Izdatel'stvo Khudozhestvennoi Literatury, 1958.

Garin-Mikhailovskii, Nikolai Georgievich. *Koreiskie skazki* [Korean Folktales]. Skt. Peterburg: Znanie, 1904. Reprint, Moscow: Gos. izd-vo detskoi lit-ry, 1952 and 1956.

―――. *Po Koree, Man'chzhurii i Liaodunskomu poluostrovu* [In and About Korea, Manchuria, and the Liaodong Peninsula]. Skt. Peterburg: Znanie, 1904. (Translated into Korean and published in 1980 as *Chŏ kŏsi paektusan-ida: Chosŏn, 1898 nyŏn* by Minjoksa, and again in 1981 as *Chosŏn 1898 nyŏn* by Tandae ch'ulp'anbu).

Gel'mersen, P. A. "Zametka o Koree" [A Note on Korea]. *Izvestiia Imperatorskogo Russkogo Geograficheskogo Obshchestva* 5, no. 5 (1869): 202–204.

Gluck, Carol. *Japan's Modern Myths: Ideology in the Late Meiji Period*. Princeton, NJ: Princeton University Press, 1985.

Gotō, Shinpei. "The Administration of Formosa (Taiwan)." In *Fifty Years of New Japan*, edited by Okuma Shigenobu and Marcus B. Huish, 530–53, London: Smith, Elder and Co., 1909.

Gottschang, Thomas R., and Diana Lary. *Swallows and Settlers: The Great Migration from North China to Manchuria*. Ann Arbor: Center for Chinese Studies, University of Michigan Press, 2000.

Gould, Stephen Jay. *The Mismeasure of Man*. New York: W. W. Norton, 1996.

Grave, V. V. *Kitaitsy, Koreitsy i Iapontsy Priamur'ia* [The Chinese, Koreans, and Japanese of the Amur Region]. (Trudy komandirovannoi po vysochaishemu poveleniiu Amurskoi Ekspeditsii, vyp. XI). Skt. Peterburg: Tipografiia V. F. Kirshbauma, 1912.

Grayson, James H. *Early Buddhism and Christianity in Korea: A Study in the Implantation of Religion*. Leiden: E.J. Brill, 1985.

Guentcheva, Rossitza. "Symbolic Geography of Language: Orthographic Debates in Bulgaria (1880s–Today)." *Language & Communication* 19 (1999): 355–71.

Ha Tongho, ed. *Kungmunnon chipsŏng* [Compendium of Essays on Korean Writing]. In *Yŏktae Han'guk munbŏp taegye che 3 pu che 3 ch'aek*. Seoul: T'ap ch'ulp'ansa, 1985.

Ha Tongho. "Kugŏ ch'ŏlcha ch'yŏpkyŏng, haeje" [The Shortcut to Korean Spelling, a Bibliographical Note]. *Han'gŭl* 151 (1973): 35–56.

Haesŏ chich'ik chŏngnye [Regulations on Diplomatic Expenditures for Hwanghae Province]. Kyujanggak collection, 16041.

Han Hoesŏn. *Yujaejip* [Collected Works of Han Hoesŏn]. National Library of Korea collection, han kojo 46–ka 2238.

Han Mongp'il. *Yuhŏn yugo* [Collected Works of Han Mongp'il]. National Library of Korea collection, han kojo 46–ka 1531.

Han Myŏnggi. *Kwanghae-gun: t'agwŏrhan oegyo chŏngch'aek ŭl p'yŏlch'in kunju* [King Kwanghae: A King Who Adopted an Excellent Foreign Policy]. Seoul: Yŏksa pip'yŏngsa, 2000.

Han Sŏkchi. *Myŏngsŏllok* [Book of Illustrating Good]. National Library of Korea collection, ko 1572–18.

Han Sŏngu. "Ŭiju pangŏn ŭi ŭmunnonjŏk yŏn'gu" [A Phonological Study of Ŭiju Dialect]. PhD diss., Seoul National University, 2003.

Han Sŭnggon. *Kugŏ ch'ŏlcha ch'yŏpkyŏng* [Shortcut to Korean Spelling]. P'yŏngyang: Kwangmyŏng sŏgwan, 1908.

"Han'gŭl ch'ŏlchabŏp sibi e taehan sŏngmyŏngsŏ" [Declaration Concerning the Han'gŭl Spelling]. *Chosŏn ilbo* (July 7, 1934). Reproduced in *Kungmunnon chipsŏng*, edited by Ha Tongho, 482–84. Seoul: T'ap ch'ulp'ansa, 1985.

Hatada Takashi. *Ilbonin ŭi Han'gukkwan* [Japanese Views on Korea]. Translated into Korean by Yi Kibaek. Seoul: Ilchogak, 1983.

Hayashi Yūsuke. "Isshinkai no zenhanki ni kansuru kisoteki kenkyū" [Basic Study on the First Half Period of the Ilchinhoe]. In *Chōsen shakai no shiteki tenkai to higashi Ajia* [Historical Development of the Korean Society and East Asia], edited by Takeda Yukio, 494–526. Tōkyō: Yamakawa shuppansha, 1997.

Hayes, Louise B. "The Korean Bible Woman and Her Work." *The Korea Mission Field*, XXX: 7 (July 1935), XVIII: 11 (November 1922), and XIX: 11 (November 1923).

Heath, Shirley Brice. "Language Ideology." *International Encyclopedia of Communications*, Vol. 2, 393–95. New York: Oxford University Press, 1989.

Hevia, James L. *Cherishing Men from Afar: Qing Guest Ritual and the Macartney Embassy of 1793*. Durham, NC: Duke University Press, 1995.

Hŏ Mok. *Kiŏn* [Collected Works of Hŏ Mok]. In *Han'guk munjip ch'onggan*, Vol. 99. Seoul: Minjok munhwa ch'ujinhoe, 1992.

Hobsbawm, Eric. *The Age of Empire, 1875–1914*. New York: Vintage Books, 1987.

Hobsbawm, Eric, and Terence Ranger, eds. *The Invention of Tradition*. Cambridge: Cambridge University Press Canto edition, 1994.

Hong Hŭiyu. "1811–1812 nyŏn P'yŏngan-do nongmin chŏnjaeng kwa kŭ sŏnggyŏk" [The Peasant War in P'yŏngan Province in 1811–1812 and Its Nature]. In *Ponggŏn chibae kyegŭp ŭl pandaehan nongmindŭl ŭi t'ujaeng*, 47–120. P'yŏngyang: Kwahagwŏn ch'ulp'ansa, 1963.

Honig, Emily. *Creating Chinese Ethnicity: Subei People in Shanghai, 1850–1980*. New Haven, CT: Yale University Press, 1992.

Horiuchi Minoru. "Nitteika, Chōsen hokubu chihō ni okeru anakizumu undō" [The Anarchist Movement in Northern Korea Under Japanese Imperial Rule]. *Chōsen minzoku undōshi kenkyū* 5 (1988): 59–86.

Hosoi Hajime. "Chōsen no tōchi" [Korean Administration]. *Nihon oyobi Nihonjin* (October 11, 1920): 30–39.

Huffman, James L. *Creating a Public: People and Press in Meiji Japan*. Honolulu: University of Hawai'i Press, 1997.

Hunmin chŏngŭm ŏnhae haerye [Hunmin chŏngŭm in Vernacular Korean, Examples and Explanations]. Seoul: Taejegak, 1979.

Hwang Kyujŏng. "Sŏnggyŏng ŭi ch'ŏlcha kaejŏng ŭl ch'okham" [I Urge Reform of the Bible Spelling]. *Han'gŭl* 37 (1936): 14–15.

Hwang, Kyung Moon. *Beyond Birth: Social Status in the Emergence of Modern Korea*. Cambridge, MA: Harvard University Asia Center, 2004.

———. "From the Dirt to Heaven: Northern Koreans in the Chosŏn and Early Modern Eras." *Harvard Journal of Asiatic Studies* 62, no. 1 (June 2002): 135–78.

Hwang Sunwŏn. "Abŏji." In *Mongnŏmi maŭl ŭi kae*. Seoul: Yongmunsa, 1948; Bruce and Ju-Chan Fulton, trans. "My Father." In *Lost Souls: Stories*, 240–46. New York: Columbia University Press, 2009.

———. "Ch'ŏngsan kari" [Potassium Cyanide]. In *Hak* [Cranes]. Seoul: Chungang ch'ulp'ansa, 1956.

———. "Harabŏji ka innŭn tessang" [A Sketch of My Grandfather]. Originally published under the title "Tessang" [A Sketch]. *Sasanggye* [The World of Thought] 7, no. 10 (October 1959): 325–37.

———. "Iri to." *Paengmin* [The People] 6, no. 1 (February 1950): 218–28; J. Martin Holman, trans. "Even Wolves." In *Shadows of a Sound: Stories by Hwang Sun-wŏn*, edited by Holman, 45–55. San Francisco: Mercury House, 1990.

———. *Irŏbŏrin saram tŭl*. Seoul: Chungang munhwasa, 1958; Bruce and Ju-Chan Fulton, trans. In *Lost Souls: Stories*, 269–348. New York: Columbia University Press, 2009.

———. *K'ain ŭi huye*. Seoul: Chungang munhwasa, 1954; Suh Ji-moon and Julie Pickering, trans. *The Descendants of Cain*. Armonk, NY: M.E. Sharpe, 1997.

———. "Kŭnŭl" [Grandfather's Shadow]. *Ch'unch'u* [Spring and Autumn] (March 1942): 123–33.

———. "Majimak chan" [One Last Drink]. *Hyŏndae munhak* [Contemporary Literature] 20, no. 10 (October 1974): 12–26.

———. "Mongnŏmi maŭl ŭi kae." *Kaebyŏk* [Genesis] 77 (March 1948): 80–103; Bruce and Ju-Chan Fulton, trans. "The Dog of Crossover Village." In *Lost Souls: Stories*, 247–68. New York: Columbia University Press, 2009.

———. "Mul han mogŭm" [A Drink of Water]. In *Kirŏgi* [Wild Geese], 219–33. Seoul: Myŏngsedang, 1951.

———. "Nae kohyang saram tŭl" [The People of My Ancestral Home]. *Hyŏndae munhak* 7, no. 1 (March 1961): 12–27.

———. "Nosae." In *Kirŏgi*, 181–208. Seoul: Myŏngsedang, 1951; Kim Chong-un and Bruce Fulton, trans. "The Mule." In *A Ready-Made Life: Early Masters of Modern Korean Fiction*, 179–91. Honolulu: University of Hawai'i Press, 1998.

———. *Nŏ wa na na man ŭi sigan* [Time for You and Me Alone]. Seoul: Chŏngŭmsa, 1964.

———. "Nun." In *Kirŏgi*, 251–56. Seoul: Myŏngsedang, 1951; Bruce and Ju-Chan Fulton, trans. "Snow." *Korean Culture* 22, no. 3 (Fall 2001): 10–11.

———. "Paeyŏk tŭl." In *Hwang Sunwŏn tanp'yŏnjip*. Seoul: Hansŏng tosŏ, 1940; Bruce and Ju-Chan Fulton, trans. "The Players." In *Lost Souls: Stories*, 43–55. New York: Columbia University Press, 2009.

———. "Pibari." *Munhak yesul* [Literary Arts] 3, no. 10 (October 1956): 12–25; Bruce and Ju-Chan Fulton, trans. "Pibari." In *Lost Souls: Stories*, 57–83. New York: Columbia University Press, 2009.

———. "Pulgasari." *Munhak yesul*, vol. 3, no. 1 (January 1956): 24–39; Bruce and Ju-Chan Fulton, trans. "Deathless." In *Lost Souls: Stories*, 271–88. New York: Columbia University Press, 2009.

———. "P'ungsok." In *Hwang Sunwŏn tanp'yŏnjip* [Short Stories by Hwang Sunwŏn]. Seoul: Hansŏng tosŏ, 1940; Bruce and Ju-Chan Fulton, trans. In *Lost Souls: Stories*, 122–30. New York: Columbia University Press, 2009.

———. "Pyŏl." *Inmun p'yŏngnon* [Humanities Review] (February 1941); Edward Poitras, trans. "Stars." In *The Stars and Other Korean Short Stories*, 81–99. Hong Kong: Heinemann Asia, 1980.

———. "Samagwi." In *Hwang Sunwŏn tanp'yŏnjip*. Seoul: Hansŏng tosŏ, 1940; Bruce and Ju-Chan Fulton, trans. "Mantis." In *Lost Souls: Stories*, 108–21. New York: Columbia University Press, 2009.

———. "Sanai." *Munhak yesul* 1, no. 1 (July 1954): 6–14; Bruce and Ju-Chan Fulton, trans. "A Man." In *A Man*, 43–56. Seoul: Jimoondang, 2003.

———. "Sonagi." In *Hak* [Cranes]. Seoul: Chungang ch'ulp'ansa, 1956; Edward Poitras, trans. "The Cloudburst." In *The Stars and Other Korean Stories*, 133–48. Hong Kong: Heinemann Asia, 1980.

———. *T'al* [Masks]. Seoul: Munhak kwa chisŏngsa, 1976.

———. "Tume." In *Hak* [Cranes]. Seoul: Myŏngsedang, 1956; Bruce and Ju-Chan Fulton, trans. "A Backcountry Village." *Koreana* 7, no. 3 (Winter 1993): 53–57.

Hwang Sunwŏn *yŏn'gu* [Studies on Hwang Sunwŏn]. In *Hwang Sunwŏn chŏnjip* [Collected Works of Hwang Sunwŏn], rev. ed., Vol. 12. Seoul: Munhak kwa chisŏngsa, 1993.

Hwang Taehwa. *Chosŏnŏ pangŏn yŏn'gu* [A Study of Korean Dialects]. Han'guk munhwasa, 2000.

Hyŏn Chin'gŏn. "Sul kwŏnhanŭn sahoe." *Kaebyŏk* 17 (November 1921): 136–47; Kim Chong-un and Bruce Fulton, trans. "A Society That Drives You to Drink." In *A Ready-Made Life: Early Masters of Modern Korean Fiction*, 7–16. Honolulu: University of Hawai'i Press, 1998.

Ilsŏngnok [Record of Daily Reflection]. 86 vols, edited by Seoul taehakkyo Kyujanggak. Seoul: Seoul taehakkyo Kyujanggak, 1992.

Im Ch'angt'aek. *Sŭngakchip* [The Collected Works of Im Ch'angt'aek]. In *Han'guk munjip ch'onggan*, Vol. 202. Seoul: Minjok munhwa ch'ujinhoe, 1998.

Im Chongch'il. *Tunojip* [Collected Works of Im Chongch'il]. National Library of Korea collection, uch'on ko 3648–64–9.

Inaba Kunsan. "Chōsen no rōdō mondai, minzoku mondai oyobi Senman bunka kankei ni oite" [Considering the Relation Between Korea's Labor Issues, Its Ethnic Issues, and the Korean-Manchurian Culture]. Part I in *Chōsen* (September 1927): 6–17 and Part II in *Chōsen* (October 1927): 16–26.

Inoue Kōsai. "Hokusen imin tokubetsu hogō ni tsuite" [Regarding Special Protection to Northern Korean Immigrants]. *Chōsen oyobi Manshū* (October 1913): 22–24.

Institut narodov Azii (Akademiia nauk SSSR). *Bibliografiia Iaponii. Literatura, izdannaia v Rossii s 1734 po 1917 g.* [Bibliography of Japan: Literature Published in Russia from 1734 to 1917]. Moscow: Nauka, 1965.

———. *Opisanie Korei: sokrashchennoe pereizdanie* [Description of Korea: Abridged Re-Edition]. Moskva: Izdatels'tvo vostochnoi literatury, 1960.

Itagaki Tadaji. "Heigen tetsudō to Gensankō" [The P'yŏngyang-Wŏnsan Railway and Wŏnsan Port]. *Chōsen* (May 1926): 39–55.

Iudin, I. M. *N. G. Garin-Mikhailovskii: Zhizn' i literaturno-obshchestvennaia deiatel'nost'* [N. G. Garin-Mikhailovskii: Life and Literary and Social Work]. Leningrad: Nauka, 1969.

Jang Yoo-seung. *See* Chang Yusŭng.

Johnson, Sally. "The Cultural Politics of the 1998 Reform of German Orthography." *German Life and Letters* 53, no. 1 (2000): 106–25.

———. "On the Origin of Linguistic Norms: Orthography, Ideology, and the First

Constitutional Challenge to the 1996 Reform of German." *Language in Society* 31 (2002): 549–76.

Kaksa tǔngnok (KSTN) [Compilation of Correspondence Between Local Government and Central Bureaus]. Seoul: Kuksa p'yŏnch'an wiwŏnhoe, 1981.

Kang Chaeŏn and Kita Hiroaki, eds. *Terauchi Chōsen sōtokufu bōsatsu misui hikoku jiken: Hyakugonin jiken shiryōshū dai 1 kan* [Defendants of the Governor General Terauchi Assassination Attempt Incident: Collection of Materials for 105 Incident, Volume 1]. Seoul: Koryŏ sŏrim, 1986.

Kang, Hildi. *Under the Black Umbrella: Voices from Colonial Korea, 1919–1945.* Ithaca, NY: Cornell University Press, 2001.

Kang Sŏkhwa. *Chosŏn hugi Hamgyŏng-do wa pukpang kyŏnggye ǔisik* [Northern Border Perceptions and Hamgyŏng Province in the Late Chosŏn Period]. Seoul: Kyŏngsewŏn, 2000.

Kang Taehǔi. "Ch'ae Chŏngmin ssi ǔi kǔl ǔl ilko" [After Reading Ch'ae Chŏngmin's Article]. *Han'gǔl* 3 (1938): 13–15.

Kapp, Robert A. *Szechwan and the Chinese Republic: Provincial Militarism and Central Power, 1911–1938.* New Haven, CT: Yale University Press, 1973.

Karlsson, Anders. "The Hong Kyŏngnae Rebellion 1811–1812: Conflict between Central Power and Local Society in Nineteenth-Century Korea." PhD diss., Stockholm University, Institute of Oriental Languages, 2000.

Kawaai Akitake. "Hokusenron" [North Korea Thesis]. *Chōsen* (February 1941): 3–17.

Kawachi Yoshihiro. *Mindai Joshinshi no kenkyū* [Studies in Jurchen History During the Ming Period]. Kyoto: Dōhōsha, 1992.

Kennan, G. "Korea: A Degenerate State." *Outlook* (Oct. 7, 1905): 409.

Kho, Song-moo. *See* Ko Songmu.

Kholodovich, A. A. "O proekte reformy Koreiskoi orfografii 1949 g." [On the Project to Reform Korean Orthography of 1949]. *Uchenye Zapiski LGU* 236 (Seriia vostokoved-cheskikh nauk, vyp. 6) (1958): 19–31.

Khrisanf, Episkop (Shchetkovskii). *Iz pisem Koreiskago missionera* [From the Letters of a Korean Missionary]. Kazan': Tipografiia Imperatorskago Universiteta, 1904.

———. *Ot Seula do Vladivostoka (Putevyia zapiski missionera)* [From Seoul to Vladivostok (A Missionary's Travel Notes)]. Moscow: Pechatnia A. I. Snegirevoi, 1905. Reprinted in Pozdniaev, 1999.

"Kidokkyo kyoyuk yŏnmaeng kyŏrǔi" [Decision of the Korean Protestant Education League]. *Han'gǔl* 4–8 (1936): 15.

Kim Chŏm. *Sŏgyŏng sihwa* [A Talk on Poetry from the Western Capital]. Originally compiled in 1728. Supplemented in 1733. Reprint in *Han'guk sihwa ch'ongp'yŏn*, edited by Cho Chongŏp. Seoul: T'aehaksa, 1996.

Kim, Chong Bum. "Christianity in Colonial Korea: The Culture and Politics of Proselytization." PhD diss., Harvard University, 2004.

Kim Chonghoe, ed. *Hwang Sunwŏn*. Seoul: Saemi, 1998.

Kim Chonghoe. "Munhak ŭi sunsusŏng kwa wan'gyŏlsŏng, ttonŭn munhakchŏk sam ŭi k'ŭn mobŏm: 'Na ŭi kkum' esŏ *Mal kwa sam kwa chayu kkaji*" [A Great Exemplar of the Literary Life and of the Purity and Perfectibility of Literature: From "My Dream" to *Language, Life and Freedom*]. *Chakka segye* 24 [Hwang Sunwŏn Feature] (Spring 1995): 18–25.

Kim Chŏngju. *Chōsen tōchi shiryō* 5 [Materials for Korean Administration, Vol. 5]. Tokyo: Shūkō shobō, 1996.

Kim Chongjun. "Ilchinhoe chihoe ŭi hwaltong kwa hyangch'on sahoe ŭi tonghyang" [Activities of the Advance in Unity Society and Conditions of the Local Societies]. MA thesis, Seoul National University, 2001.

Kim Chŏngjung. *Yŏnhaengnok* [Record of Travel to China]. Originally written in 1712 and translated by Chŏng Yŏnt'ak. Seoul: Minjok munhwa ch'ujinhoe, 1976.

Kim Chunsik. "Han'gŭl kyojŏngbu nŭn han'gŭl tokchae kigwan" [The Han'gŭl Revision Office Is a Han'gŭl Dictatorship]. *Chŏngŭm* 25 (1938): 1656–58.

Kim Chup'il. "17, 18 segi kugŏ ŭi kugaeŭmhwa wa kwallyŏn ŭmun hyŏnsang e taehan t'ongsironjŏk yŏn'gu" [An In-Depth Study of Phonological Phenomena in Relation to Palatalization of Korean Language in the Seventeenth and Eighteenth Centuries]. PhD diss., Seoul National University, 1994.

Kim Chuwŏn. "Kugŏ pangŏn punhwa wa paltal" [Differentiation and Development of Korean Dialects]. In *Han'guk munhwa sasang taegye* 1: 429–45. Kyŏngsan: Yŏngnam taehakkyo ch'ulp'anbu, 2000.

———. "18 segi Hwanghae-do pangŏn ŭi ŭmun hyŏnsang" [Phonological Phenomena of Hwanghae Dialect in the Eighteenth Century]. *Kugŏhak* 24 (1994):19–44.

———. "18 segi P'yŏngan-do pangŏn ŭl panyŏng hanŭn *Yŏmbul pogwŏnmun* e taehayŏ" [On *Yŏmbul pogwŏnmun* that Reflects P'yŏngan Dialect in the Eighteenth Century]. In *Ŭmsŏnghak kwa ŏnŏhak*, 429–45. Seoul: Seoul Taehakkyo ch'ulp'anbu, 1996.

Kim, Dong-Un. *See* Kim Tongŏn.

Kim, German N. "Koryŏ saram ŭi yŏksa, munhwa, ŏnŏ e kwanhan saryo p'yŏnch'an-jŏk koch'al [Bibliographic Survey of Materials on the History, Culture, and Language of the Koryŏ Saram]. *Izvestiia Koreevedeniia Kazakhstana*, vyp. 5 (1998): 92–121.

———. *Istoriia immigratsii Koreitsev, kn. 1: Vtoraia polovina XIX v.–1945 g.* [History of

Korean Immigration, Vol. 1: Second Half of the Nineteenth Century–1945]. Almaty: Daik Press, 1999.

Kim, German N. and Ross King. *Istoriia, kul'tura i literature Kore saram: Istoriografiia i bibliografiia* [History, Culture and Literature of the Kore Saram: Historiography and Bibliography]. Almaty, 1993.

Kim, Gwi-Ok [Kim Kwiok]. "Life Experiences and Culture of the People from Hamgyŏng Province During the Japanese Colonial Rule." A paper presented at the conference "The Northern Region, Identity, and Culture in Korea" held at Harvard University on October 20, 2005.

Kim Ihyŏp. *P'yŏngbuk pangŏn sajŏn* [Dictionary of North P'yŏngan Dialect]. Seoul: Han'guk chŏngsin munhwa yŏn'guwŏn, 1981.

Kim Iyang. *Kim Iyang munjip* [The Collected Works of Kim Iyang]. National Library of Korea collection, han kojo 46-ka 1872.

Kim Kwiok, *See* Kim, Gwi-Ok.

Kim Ku. *Paekpŏm ilchi* [Autobiography of Kim Ku]. Seoul: Samjungdang, 1990.

Kim, Michael. "The Apparition of the Rational Public." PhD diss., Harvard University, 2004.

Kim Myŏngsik. "Han'gŭl undong kwa p'asyo ŭisik" [The *Han'gŭl* Movement and Fascist Consciousness]. *Chŏngŭm* 22 (1938): 1495–99.

Kim Ni. *Yudangjip* [Collected Works of Kim Ni]. Changsŏgak collection, K4–6374.

Kim Ŏk. "Sat'uri onghoron" [On Embracing Dialect]. *Chŏngŭm* 28 (1938).

Kim Pyŏngik. "Sunsu munhak kwa kŭ yŏksasŏng: Hwang Sunwŏn ŭi ch'oegŭn ŭi chagŏp" [Pure Literature and Its Historicity in the Recent Works of Hwang Sunwŏn]. In *Hwang Sunwŏn yŏn'gu*, 21–35. Seoul: Munhak kwa chisŏngsa, 1993.

Kim Pyŏngje. *Chosŏn ŏnŏ chirihak sigo* [A Preliminary Study of Linguistics and Geography of Korea]. P'yŏngyang: Kwahak paekkwa sajŏn chonghap chu'lp'ansa, 1988.

———. "Han'gŭl t'ongiran pip'an e taehan yakkan ŭi kŏmt'o wa tappyŏn" [A Response to and Some Considerations of the Criticisms of the *Han'gŭl* Unified Orthography]. *Chosŏn chungang ilbo*, (September 13–October 14, 1934).

———. *Pangŏn sajŏn* [Dictionary of Dialects]. P'yŏngyang: Sahoe kwahagwŏn ch'ulp'ansa, 1980.

Kim Pyŏngnin (trans.). *Ku Hanmal ŭi sahoe wa kyŏngje: puyŏlgang kwa ŭi choyak* [Society and Economy in the Last Decades of Chosŏn Korea]. Seoul: Yup'ung ch'ulp'ansa, 1983. (Abridged translation of *Opisanie Korei* by the Ministerstvo Finansov, Russia).

Kim Sŏnju. *See* Kim, Sun Joo.

Kim, Sun Joo [Kim Sŏnju]. "Chosŏn hugi P'yŏngan-do Chŏngju ŭi hyangan unyŏng kwa yangban munhwa" [The Management of the Local Yangban Roster and Elite Culture in Chŏngju, P'yŏngan Province, in the Late Chosŏn Period], *Yŏksa hakpo* 185 (March 2005): 65–105.

———. "In Defense of Regional Elite Identity and Culture." Unpublished paper.

———. *Marginality and Subversion in Korea: The Hong Kyŏngnae Rebellion of 1812*. Seattle: University of Washington Press, 2007.

———. "Negotiating Cultural Identities in Conflict: A Reading of Paek Kyŏnghae (1765–1842)'s Writings." *Journal of Korean Studies* 10, no. 1 (Fall 2005): 85–120.

Kim T'aegyŏng. *Sungyang kigu chŏn* [Hagiographies of Kaesŏng's Respected Elders]. In Kim Sŭngnyong, trans. *Songdo inmul chi*. Seoul: Hyŏndae sirhaksa, 2000.

Kim Tongin. "Han'gŭl ŭi chiji wa sujŏng: Chosŏnŏ hakhoe ŭi han'gŭl mach'umbŏp t'ongiran e taehayŏ" [Supporting and Amending *Han'gŭl*: on the Chosŏnŏ hakhoe's "Unified *Han'gŭl* Orthography"]. *Chungang ilbo* (August 14–24, 1934). Reproduced in *Kungmunnon chipsŏng*, edited by Ha Tongho, 485–502. Seoul: T'ap ch'ulp'ansa, 1985.

Kim Tongŏn [Kim, Dong-Un] and Ross King. "New Russian Materials on 'Kaehwagi' (Enlightenment Period) Korean." *Han'gŭl* 255 (2002): 205–62.

Kim Tongsŏn. "Hwang Kojip ŭi mihak, Hwang Sunwŏn kamun" [The Aesthetics of Hwang Kojip and the Family Background of Hwang Sunwŏn]. In *Hwang Sunwŏn chŏnjip*, rev. ed., Vol. 12, *Hwang Sunwŏn yŏn'gu*, 272–74. Seoul: Munhak kwa chisŏngsa, 1993.

Kim Wŏn'gyŏng. "Pukhan ŭi ch'ŏlchabŏpsa" [History of North Korean Orthography]. In *Pukhan ŭi Chosŏnŏ yŏn'gusa 1945–1990*, edited by Kim Minsu, Vol. 2: 96–116. Seoul: Nokchin, 1991.

Kim Yŏngbae. *Chŭngbo P'yŏngan pangŏn yŏn'gu* [Enlarged Study of P'yŏngan Dialect]. Seoul: T'aehaksa, 1997.

———. "Corean Primer ŭi ŭmun hyŏnsang" [Phonological Phenomena in *Corean Primer*]. *Han'gŭl* 179 (1983): 29–52.

———. "Iryun haengsilto ŭi wŏn'ganbon kwa chungganbon ŭi pigyo" [Comparison of the First and Second Editions of *Iryun haengsilto*]. *Tongbang hakchi* 71/72 (1991): 499–533.

———. *P'yŏngan pangŏn yŏn'gu* [A Study of P'yŏngan Dialect]. Seoul: Tongguk taehakkyo ch'ulp'anbu, 1984.

———. *P'yŏngan pangŏn yŏn'gu, charyo-p'yŏn* [A Study of P'yongan Dialect, Sources]. Seoul: T'aehaksa, 1997.

———. "P'yŏngan pangŏn yŏn'gu: kŭ hyŏnhwang kwa kwaje" [Present and Future of the Study of P'yŏngan Dialect]. In *Nambukhan ŭi pangŏn yŏn'gu*, edited by Kim Yŏngbae, 309–64. Seoul: Kyŏngun ch'ulp'ansa, 1992.

Kim Yŏnghwang. *Chosŏnŏ pangŏnhak* [Korean Dialectology]. P'yŏngyang: Kim Ilsŏng chonghap taehak ch'ulp'ansa, 1982.

King, Ross. "Blagoslovennoe: Korean Village on the Amur, 1871–1937." *Review of Korean Studies* 4, no. 2 (December 2001): 133–76.

———. "Dialect Elements in Soviet Korean Publications from the 1920s." In *NSL 7: Linguistic Studies in the Non-Slavic Languages of the Commonwealth of Independent States and the Baltic Republics*, edited by Howard I. Aronson, 151–83. Chicago: Chicago Linguistic Society, 1994.

———. "Experimentation with *Han'gŭl* in Russia and the USSR." In *The Korean Alphabet: History and Structure*, edited by Young-Key Kim-Renaud, 296–339. Honolulu: University of Hawai'i Press, 1997.

———. "Korean Language Studies in the USSR." *Ijung ŏnŏ hakhoe chi* [Bilingual Education for the Overseas Koreans] 8 (1991): 42–153.

———. "Language and National Identity in Korea." In *Language and National Identity in Asia*, edited by Andrew Simpson, 200–34. Oxford: Oxford University Press, 2007.

———. "Language, Politics, and Ideology in the Post-War Koreas." In *Korea Briefing*, edited by David R. McCann, 109–44. Boulder, CO: Westview Press, 1996.

———. "Nationalism and Language Reform in Korea: The *Questione Della Lingua* in Precolonial Korea." In *Nationalism and the Construction of Korean Identity*, edited by Timothy Tangherlini and Hyung-il Pai, 33–72. Center for Korean Studies Monograph Series, Berkeley: University of California Press, 1998.

———. "Russian Sources on Korean Dialects." PhD diss., Harvard University, 1991.

———. *Russian Sources on Korean Dialects.* 3 vols. Unpublished manuscript.

———. "A Soviet Korean Grammar from 1930." *Han'gungmal kyoyuk* [Korean Language Education] 3 (1991): 153–78.

———. "Western Missionaries and the Origins of Korean Language Modernization." *Journal of International and Area Studies* 11 (2005): 7–38.

Kirihara Shinichi and Paek Inje. "Nitchōjinkan ni okeru ketsueki shokubetsu hyakubunritsu no sai oyobi ketsueki shokubetsu tokuyusei no den ni tsuite" [Regarding Differences in the Blood Type Coefficient and Special Blood Type Characteristics of Japanese and Koreans]. *Chōsen igakkai zasshi* (November 1922): 273–94.

Kirillov, A. "Koreitsy sela Blagoslovennogo: Istoriko-etnograficheskii ocherk" [The Koreans of the Village Blagoslovennyi: A Historico-Ethnographic Essay]. *Priamurskie vedomosti*, nos. 58–59 (1895): Appendix. Khabarovsk.

Kirillov, N. V. *Koreia. Mediko-antropologicheskii ocherk* [Korea: A Medico-Anthropological

Study]. *Zapiski Priamurskogo Otdela IRGO* 9, vyp. 1 (1913): 117 + IV pp. Khabarovsk.

Kita Sadakichi. "Chōsen minzoku to wa nani zoya" [What is the Korean Race?].
Minzoku to rekishi (June 1919): 1–13.

———. "Kankoku no heigō to rekishi" [Korean Annexation and History]. In *Nichikan ryōkokugo dōkeiron* [The Common Origins of the Japanese and Korean Languages] edited by Nihon rekishi chiri gakkai. Originally published in 1910. Reprint, Tokyo: Ryūkei shosha, 1995.

———. "Nissen ryōminzoku dōgenron" [The Same Origin Theory of the Korean and Japanese Races]. *Minzoku to rekishi* (January 1921): 3–39.

Kitakan Sanjin. "Chōsen no futei senjin" [Korea's Lawless Koreans]. *Chōsen oyobi Manshū* (November 1921): 81–82.

Kiuner, N. V. *Statistiko-geograficheskii i ekonomicheskii ocherk Korei* [A Statistical and Economic Study of Korea]. *Izvestiia Vostochnogo Instituta* 12–13, vyp. 1 (1912). Vladivostok: Vostochnyi Institut.

Knight, Nathaniel. "Grigor'ev in Orenburg, 1851–1862: Russian Orientalism in the Service of Empire?" *Slavic Review* 59, no. 1 (2000): 74–100.

Ko Chaesŏp. "Hunmin chŏngŭm ŭi wŏlli rŭl musihanŭn sŏnggyŏng ch'ŏlchabŏp kaeak kyŏrŭi rŭl pakham" [I Refute the Decision to Change for the Worse the Bible Spelling, a Reform that Ignores the Principles of the *Hunmin Chŏngŭm*]. *Chŏngŭm* 21 (1937): 1444–48.

Ko Seunghee. *See* Ko Sŭnghŭi.

Ko Sŏkkyu. *Sipku segi Chosŏn ŭi hyangch'on sahoe yŏn'gu* [A Study of Local Society in Nineteenth-Century Chosŏn]. Seoul: Seoul taehakkyo ch'ulp'anbu, 1998.

Ko Songmu [Kho, Song-moo]. "Chejŏng rōsia esŏ ŭi han'gugŏ mit han'guk yŏn'gu" [Research on Korea and Korean Language in Imperial Russia]. *Han'gŭl* 169 (1980): 193–212.

Ko Sŭnghŭi [Ko Seunghee]. *Chosŏn hugi Hamgyŏng-do sangŏp yŏn'gu* [A Study of Commercial Development in Hamgyŏng Province During the Late Chosŏn Period]. Seoul: Kughak charyowŏn, 2003.

———. "The Regional Characteristics of Development in Hamgyŏng Province During the Late Chosŏn Period." A paper presented at the conference "The Northern Region, Identity, and Culture in Korea" held at Harvard University on October 20, 2005.

———. "18, 19 segi Hamgyŏng-do chiyŏk ŭi yut'ongno paltal kwa sangŏp hwaltong" [Economic Activities and the Development of Trade Routes in Hamgyŏng Province in the Eighteenth and Nineteenth Centuries]. *Yŏksa hakpo* 151 (1996): 71–108.

Ko Yŏnggŭn, ed. *Pukhan mit chaeoe kyomin ŭi ch'ŏlchabŏp chipsŏng* [Compendium of North

Korean and Overseas Korean Orthographies]. In *Pukhan mit chaeoe kyomin ŭi ŏmun charyo ch'ongsŏ* [Compendium of Materials on the Language and Literature of North Korea and Overseas Koreans], Vol.1. Seoul: Yŏngnak, 2000.

Kōchi Menseki. "Heian hokudō ni okeru nōgyō narabi fukuhyō no shōhei" [Regeneration of the Agriculture Industry in North P'yŏngan]. *Chōsen* (April 1926): 122–33.

Kolin, P. "Zheltyi vopros na russkom Dal'nem Vostoke" [The Yellow Question in the Russian Far East]. *Russkii vestnik* 1 (1898): 310–20.

Kolokol'nikov, V. *Koreia: strana utrennei iasnosti* [Korea: Land of the Morning Clarity]. Second edition. Moscow: A. S. Panafidina, 1909.

Kolos, V. M. "N. G. Garin-Mikhailovskii o Koree i sobrannye im koreiskie skazki: U istokov russko-koreiskoi druzhby" [N. G. Garin-Mikhailovskii on Korea and the Korean Tales He Collected: At the Origins of Russo-Korean Friendship]. *Nauchnye zapiski Dnepropetrovskogo un-ta* 74, no. 18 (1961): 208–222.

Kontsevich, L. R. "Bibliograficheskii ukazatel' rabot po Koreiskomu iazykoznaniiu" [Bibliographic Guide to Works on Korean Linguistics]. In *Voprosy grammatiki i istorii vostochnykh iazykov*, edited by Aleksandr Konstantinovich Borovkov, 187–238. Moscow-Leningrad: Izd-vo Akademii nauk SSSR [Leningradskoe otd-nie], 1958.

——. "Rŏsia esŏ ŭi chŏnt'ong-jŏk han'gukhak ŭi palchŏnsa, hyŏnhwang kwa munje-jŏm [History of the Development of Traditional Korean Studies in Russia, Its Current Status and Problematic Points]. *Ijung ŏnŏ hakhoe chi* 11 (1994): 125–70.

——. "Some Questions of the Traditional Korean Studies in Russia and the Soviet Union." *Ijung ŏnŏ hakhoe chi* 8 (1991): 242–54.

Kontsevich, Lev R. *Izbrannye raboty* [Selected Works]. Moscow: Izd. Dom "Muravei-Gaid," 2001.

——. "O razvitii traditsionnogo koreevedeniia v tsarskoi Rossii (Istoriko-bibliograficheskii ocherk)" [On the Development of Traditional Korean Studies in Tsarist Russia (Historico-Bibliographical Essay)]. *Rossiiskoe koreevedenie. Al'manakh* (MTsK MGU), vyp. 1 (1999):8–45. Moscow: Izd. Dom "Muravei-Gaid." Reprinted with some additions and corrections in L. R. Kontsevich (2001), 537–68.

"Korea Mission of the Presbyterian Church in the U.S.A." *The Korea Mission Field*, III (September 1908).

Korf, N. A. and A. I. Zvegintsev. *Voennyi obzor Severnoi Korei* [Military Survey of North Korea]. St. Petersburg: n.p., 1904.

Korf, N. A. ed. *Severnaia Koreia: Sbornik marshrutov* [Northern Korea: Collection of Routes]. Part of *Trudy osennei ekspeditsii 1898 g*, 1901. 256 pp.

Koschmann, Victor J. *The Mito Ideology: Discourse, Reform, and Insurrection in Late Tokugawa Japan, 1790–1864*. Berkeley: University of California Press, 1987.

Ku Wanhoe. *Hanmal ŭi Chech'ŏn ŭibyŏng* [Righteous Army in Chech'ŏn in the Last Decade of the Chosŏn Dynasty]. Seoul: Chimmundang, 1997.

"Kungmun chamoŭm yakhae" [Summary Explanation of the Consonant and Vowel Sounds of the National Script]. *Taedo/The Korean Evangel* 1, no. 6 (May 1909): 12–16. San Francisco: Korean Mission, Methodist Episcopal Church, South.

Kurokawa Sō, ed. *"Gaichi" no Nihongo bungakusen 3: Chōsen* [Outer Empire Japanese Language Literature Selection 3: Korea]. Tokyo: Shinjuku shobō, 1996.

Kwak Ch'unggu. "Han'gugŏ ŭmun kyuch'ik ŭi palsaeng kwa chŏnp'a." [The Emergence and Dissemination of Phonological Regulations in Korean Language]. In *Segye sok ŭi Chosŏnŏ (Han'gugŏ) taebi yŏn'gu*, 1–25, Yonyŏng minjok ch'ulp'ansa, 2001.

————. "Hyŏndae kugŏ moŭm ch'egye wa kŭ pyŏnhwa ŭi panghyang" [The Vowels in Modern Korean and the Directions of Their Changes]. *Kugŏhak* 41 (2003): 59–91.

————. "Kugaeŭmhwa kyuch'ik ŭi palsaeng kwa kŭ hwaksan" [The Emergence and Dissemination of Palatalization Rules]. *Chindan hakpo* 92 (2001): 237–68.

Kwansŏ chich'ik chŏngnye [Regulations on Diplomatic Expenditures for P'yŏngan Province]. Kyujanggak collection, 17197.

Kwansŏ chinsillok [Civil Service Examination Passers from P'yŏngan Province]. Kyujanggak collection, Sangbaek ko 920.051–G994.

Kwansŏ ŭpchi [Gazetteers of P'yŏngan Province]. In *Han'guk chiriji ch'ongsŏ ŭpchi*, Vols. 14–17, P'yŏngan-do 1–4. Seoul: Asea munhwasa, 1986.

Kwon, Hyuk-Chan, "Hwang Sunwŏn as a Political Writer: Reading Political Implications in His Short Stories." Paper presented at the annual meeting of the Western Conference of the Association for Asian Studies, Arizona State University, October 10, 2003.

Kwon Naehyun. *See* Kwŏn Naehyŏn.

Kwŏn Naehyŏn [Kwon Naehyun]. *Chosŏn hugi P'yŏngan-do chaejŏng yŏn'gu* [A Study of Financial Management of P'yŏngan Province in the Late Chosŏn Period]. Seoul: Chisik sanŏpsa, 2004.

Kwŏn Sangha. *Hansujaejip* [Collected Works of Kwŏn Sangha]. In *Han'guk munjip ch'onggan*, Vol. 151. Seoul: Minjok munhwa ch'ujinhoe, 1995.

Kwŏn Sŏkpong. "Ch'ŏng-Il chŏnjaeng ihu ŭi Han-Ch'ŏng kwan'gye ŭi yŏn'gu (1894–1899)" [A Study of Relations Between Chosŏn and Qing after the Sino-Japanese War (1894–1899)]. In *Ch'ŏng-Il chŏnjaeng ŭl chŏnhuhan Han'guk kwa yŏlgang*. Seoul: Chŏngsin munhwa yŏn'guwŏn, 1984.

Kwŏn T'aehwan and Sin Yongha. "Chosŏn wangjo sidae in'gu ch'ujŏng e kwanhan ilsiron" [On Population Estimates of the Chosŏn Dynasty]. *Tonga munhwa* 14 (December 1977): 287–330.

Kwŏn Yŏngmin. *Haebang chikhu ŭi minjok munhak undong yŏn'gu* [A Study of National Literature in the Immediate Post-Liberation Era]. Seoul: Seoul taehakkyo ch'ulp'anbu, 1986.

Kye Tŏkhae. *Ponggok Kye Ch'albang yujip* [Collected Works of Kye Tŏkhae]. Kyujanggak collection, kyu 4221.

Kyŏnggi chich'ik chŏngnye [Regulations on Diplomatic Expenditures for Kyŏnggi Province]. Kyujanggak collection, 17196.

Kyŏngguk taejŏn [Great Code of Administration]. Seoul: Asea munhwasa, 1983.

Labov, William. *Sociolinguistic Patterns*. Philadelphia: University of Pennsylvania Press, 1973.

Larsen, Kirk. "From Suzerainty to Commerce: Sino-Korean Economic and Business Relations During the Open Port Period (1876–1910)." PhD diss., Harvard University, 2000.

Lavely, William. "The Spatial Approach to Chinese History: Illustrations from North China and the Upper Yangzi." *Journal of Asian Studies* 48, no. 1 (Feb. 1989): 100–13.

Ledyard, Gari. "Cartography in Korea." In *The History of Cartography* 2, no. 2, edited by J. B. Harley and David Woodward, 235–344. Chicago: University of Chicago Press, 1994.

Lee, Jong Hyeong. "Samuel Austin Moffett: His Life and Work in the Development of the Presbyterian Church of Korea, 1890–1936." PhD diss., Union Theological Seminary, Richmond, Virginia, 1983.

Lewis, James Bryant. "The Pusan Japan House (Waegwan) and Chosŏn Korea: Early-Modern Korean Views of Japan Through Economic, Political, and Social Connections." PhD diss., University of Hawai'i, 1994.

Lewis, Michael. *Becoming Apart: National Power and Local Politics in Toyama, 1868–1945*. Cambridge, MA: Harvard University Press, 2000.

Li Ungyu, Sim Hoesŏp, and An Un. *Chosŏnŏ pangŏn sajŏn* [Dictionary of Korean Dialects]. Yŏnbyŏn: Yŏnbyŏn inmin ch'ulp'ansa, 1990.

Little, Daniel, and Joseph W. Esherick. "Testing the Testers: A Reply to Barbara Sands and Ramon Myers's Critique of G. William Skinner's Regional Systems Approach to China." *Journal of Asian Studies* 48, no. 1 (Feb. 1989): 90–99.

Lubentsov, A. G. *Khamkenskaia i pkhienanskaia provintsii Korei* [The Hamgyŏng and P'yŏngan Provinces of Korea]. Khabarovsk: Tip. Kantseliarii Priamurskago General'-Gubernatora, 1897. (Zapiski Geograficheskago Obshchestva, Priamurskii Otdel 2: 4). 297 pp.

Mahito, Ishimitsu, ed. *Remembering Aizu: The Testament of Shiba Gorō.* Honolulu: University of Hawai'i Press, 1999.

Maksimov, A. Ia. *Na dalekom vostoke: Razskazy i ocherki* [In the Far East: Stories and Sketches]. Skt. Peterburg: Tipografiia V. V. Komarova, 1887.

Man'gi yoram [Handbook of Government Affairs]. Compiled by Sim Sanggyu and Sŏ Yŏngbo in 1808. Reprint. Seoul: Minjok munhwa ch'ujinhoe, 1971.

Manaster-Ramer, Alexis. "The Korean Precursors of Generative Phonology." In *The Joy of Grammar,* edited by Diane Brentari, Gary N. Larson and Lynn A. MacLeod, 213–24. Amsterdam and Philadelphia: John Benjamins Publishing Company, 1992.

Marshall, Byron K. *Learning to be Modern: Japanese Political Discourse on Education.* Boulder, CO: Westview Press, 1994.

Matiunin, N. "Nashi sosedi na krainem Vostoke" [Our Neighbours in the Far East]. *Vestnik Evropy* 7 (1887).

Matsuda Shirō. "Tōhoku, Hokuriku, oyobi Kyushu chihō to Chōsen imin mondai" [The Tōhoku, Hokuriku, and Kyushu Regions and the Korean Migration Problem]. *Chōsen oyobi Manshū* (September 1914): 39–40.

Mény, Yves and Vincent Wright eds. *Centre-Periphery Relations in Western Europe.* London: George Allen & Unwin, 1985.

Michell, Tony. "Fact and Hypothesis in Yi Dynasty Economic History: The Demographic Dimension." *Korean Studies Forum* 6 (Winter–Spring 1979/1980): 65–92.

Ministerstvo, Finansov, ed. *Opisanie Korei* [Description of Korea]. 3 vols. Skt. Peterburg, 1900. Abridged edition in 1960, Moscow.

Mironov, G. M. *Poet neterpelivogo sozidaniia—N. G. Garin-Mikhailovskii: Zhizn', tvorchestvo, obshchestvennaia deiatel'nost'* [A Poet of Impatient Creation—N. G. Garin-Mikhailovskii: Life, Oeuvre, Social Works]. Moscow: Nauka, 1965.

Miyanaga S. "A Flying Visit to Pyongyang." *The Seoul Press* (June 5, 7, 1910): 2.

Mizuto Bō, "Hokukan ryokō zassō" [Memos on a Trip to Northern Korea]. *Chōsen oyobi Manshū* (October 1909): 38–39.

Moffett, Samuel A. *First Letters from Korea, 1890–1891.* Seoul: Presbyterian Theological Seminary Institute of Missions, 1975.

———. "A New Mission Station at Pyeng Yang." *The Church at Home and Abroad* 14 (August 1893): 107.

Mun Tŏkkyo. *Tonghojip* [Collected Works of Mun Tŏkkyo]. In *Han'guk munjip ch'onggan,* Vol. 7. Seoul: Minjok munhwa ch'ujinhoe, 2005.

Na Ch'aeun. "Kaeyŏk sŏngsŏ e issŏsŏ ŭi kugŏhakchŏgin munjechŏm: Ogyŏng ŭi munbŏpchŏgin munje rŭl chungsim ŭro" [Korean Linguistic Issues in the Revised

Translation of the Bible: Focusing on Grammatical Problems in the Pentateuch]. In
Han'gŭl sŏngsŏ wa kyŏre munhwa: Ch'ŏnjugyo wa kaesin'gyo ŭi mannam, edited by
Kŭrisŭdogyo wa kyŏre munhwa yŏn'guhoe, 21–48. Seoul: Kidok kyomunsa, 1985.

Nadarov, I. P. "Iuzhno-Ussuriiskii krai v sovremennom ego sostoianii" [The South
Ussuri Krai in Its Current Condition]. *Izvestiia Geograficheskago Obshchestva* 25, no. 3
(1889).

————. "Puteshestvie po Koree s dekabria 1885 g. po mart 1886 g. P. M. Delotkovicha"
[The Journey Through Korea from December 1885 to March 1886 of P. M.
Delotkovich]. *Izvestiia Geograficheskago Obshchestva* 25, no. 4 (1889): 294–315.

Nagashima Hiroki. "Isshinkai no katsudō to sono tenkai" [Ilchinhoe's Activities and
Development]. *Nenpō Chōsengaku* 5 (July 1995).

Nam Kit'aek. "Iryun haengsilto ŭi kugŏhakchŏk yŏn'gu" [A Linguistic Study of the *Iryun
haengsilto*]. *Yŏn'gu nonmunjip, Kangwŏn taehakkyo* 15 (1981): 77–102.

Nam Myŏnghak. *Oryongjae yugo* [Collected Works of Nam Myŏnghak]. National Library
of Korea collection, han kojo 46–ka 566.

Naquin, Susan, and Evelyn S. Rawski. *Chinese Society in the Eighteenth Century*. New Haven,
CT: Yale University Press, 1987.

Nasekin, N. "Koreitsy Priamurskogo kraia" [The Koreans of the Amur Region]. *Trudy
Priamurskogo otdela IRGO* 11 (1895): 1–36.

Nedachin, S. V. "Koreitsy-kolonisty. K voprosu o sblizhenii Koreitsev s Rossiei" [The
Korean Colonists. On the Question of the Rapprochement of Koreans with Russia].
Vostochnyi sbornik 1 (1913): 183–204. Petrograd: Obshchestvo Russkikh Orientalistov.

————. "K voprosu o priniatii Koreitsev v khristianstvo" [On the Question of the
Acceptance of Koreans into Christianity]. Paper read at the general meeting of the
Obshchestvo Russkikh Orientalistov. St. Petersburg: V. Skvortsov, 1913. 15 pp.

————. "Pravoslavnaia tzerkov' v Koree: k 10-letiiu eia sushchestvovaniia. Istoricheskii
ocherk" [The Orthodox Church in Korea, on the Occasion of Its Tenth Anniversary: A
Historical Sketch]. *Missionerskoe obozrenie* (St. P.) 16, no. 9 (1911): 27–43; no. 10: 258–
72; no. 11: 474–92; no. 12: 699–707. St. Petersburg.

————. *Pravoslavnaia tzerkov' v Koree: k 10-letiiu eia sushchestvovaniia. Istoricheskii ocherk* [The
Orthodox Church in Korea, on the Occasion of its Tenth Anniversary: A Historical
Sketch]. St. Petersburg: 1911. 59 pp.

Nitobe Inazō. "Assimilation of the Chosenese." In *Nitobe Inazō zenshū* [The Complete
Works of Nitobe Inazō], Vol. 23, edited by Yanaihara Tadao. Tokyo: Kyōbunkan, 1983–
87.

————. "Primitive Life and Presiding Death in Korea." In *Nitobe Inazō zenshū* [The

Complete Works of Nitobe Inazō] Vol. 12, edited by Yanaihara Tadao. Tokyo: Kyōbunkan, 1983–87.

"North Korean Target: Cold and Tough." *U.S. News and World Report* (October 13, 1950): 22–23.

Nōshōmushō and Sanrinkyoku. *Kankoku shi* [Description of Korea]. (Translation of *Opisanie Korei* by the Ministerstvo Finansov, Russia). Tokyo: Tōkyō Shoten, 1905.

O Ch'anghwan. *Koryŏ munjŏn* [A Grammar of Korean]. Khabarovsk: Dal'nevostochnoe Kraevoe Izdatel'stvo, 1930.

O Saenggŭn. "Chŏnbanjŏk kŏmt'o" [Overview]. In *Hwang Sunwŏn yŏn'gu*, 11–17. Seoul: Munhak kwa chisŏngsa, 1993.

O Sanggyu. *Koejŏngjip* [Collected Works of O Sanggyu]. National Library of Korea collection, ko 3, 648–52.

O Such'ang. *Chosŏn hugi P'yŏngan-do sahoe palchŏn yŏn'gu* [A Study of Social Development in P'yŏngan Province During the Late Chosŏn Period]. Seoul: Ilchogak, 2002.

———. "19 segi ch'o P'yŏngan-do sahoe munje e taehan chibangmin kwa chungang kwalli ŭi insik kwa chŏngch'aek" [Perceptions and Policies on P'yŏngan Province in the Early Nineteenth Century: Perspectives from the Local and the Center]. *Han'guk munhwa* 36 (2005): 125–56.

Ŏ Sukkwŏn, *Kosa ch'waryo* [Selected Essentials on Verified Facts]. Reprint of the 1585 edition. Seoul: Nammungak, 1974.

Ogawa Unpei. "Kita Chōsen no keiei ō ronsu" [Arguing for Northern Korean Administration]. *Chōsen oyobi Manshū* (March 1914): 16–18.

Ogura Shimpei. *Chōsen hōgen no kenkyū* [A Study of Korean Dialects]. Tokyo: Iwanami shoten, 1944.

Ōkurasho kanrikyoku. *Nihonjin no kaigai katsudō ni kansuru rekishiteki chōsa: Chōsen hen 37* [Historical Studies on Japanese Overseas Activities: Korea Edition I, 37]. Reprint. Seoul: Koryŏ sŏrim, 1995.

Ong, Chang Woei. "Men of Letters within the Passes: Guanzhong Literati from the Tenth to Eighteenth Centuries." PhD diss., Harvard University, 2004.

Paasi, Anssi. "Boundaries as Social Processes: Territoriality in the World of Flows." In *Boundaries, Territory, and Postmodernity*, edited by David Newman, 69–88. London: Frank Cass, 1999.

Paek Doo-hyeon, *See* Paek Tuhyŏn.

Paek Sŭngjong. *Han'guk ŭi yeŏn munhwasa* [History of Korea's Prophetic Culture]. Seoul: P'ŭrŭn yŏksa, 2006.

Paek Tuhyŏn [Paek Doo-hyeon]. *Hyŏnp'ung Kwak-ssi ŏn'gan chuhae* [Vernacular Korean

Letters from Hyŏnp'ung Kwak Family, Annotated]. Seoul: T'aehaksa, 2003.

Paik, George. "What is Han Keul?" *The Korean Mission Field* 31 (October 1935): 204–10.

Paik, Lak-Geoon George. *The History of Protestant Missions in Korea, 1832–1910.* Reprint. Seoul: Yonsei University Press, 1970.

Pak, B. D. "Izvestiia o Koree v Rossii v kontse XVII–nachale XVIII vv." [News of Korea in Russia at the End of the Seventeenth and Beginning of the Eighteenth Centuries]. *Uchenye zapiski Irkutskogo Pedagogicheskogo Instituta*, vyp. 39 (1970). Irkutsk: Irkutskii Pedagogicheskii Institut.

———. *Koreitsy v Rossiiskoi imperii* [Koreans in the Russian Empire]. Second edition. Irkutsk: Mezhdunarodnyi tsentr koreevedeniia Moskovskogo gos. universiteta im. M.V. Lomonosova: Mezhdunarodnyi tsentr aziatskikh issledovanii Irkutskogo gos. pedagog. in-ta, 1994.

———. *Rossiia i Koreia* [Russia and Korea]. Moscow: Nauka, 1979.

Pak Chaeyŏn. *"Nogŏltae" wa "Pakt'ongsa" wŏnmun ŏnhae pigyo charyo* [*Nogŏltae* and *Pakt'ongsa*, Original and Vernacular Editions for Comparative Studies]. Asan: Sŏnmun taehakkyo chung-han pŏnyŏk munhŏn yŏn'guso, 2003.

Pak Ch'ansik. "Hanmal Cheju chiyŏk ŭi ch'ŏnju kyohoe wa Cheju kyoan" [Catholic Churches and Catholic Persecutions in Cheju Island in the Last Decade of the Chosŏn Dynasty]. *Han'guk kŭnhyŏndaesa yon'gu* 4 (1996): 62–106.

Pak Ch'anuk. "Han'gugŏ sinmyŏng ko: chŏngsŏbŏp esŏ pon hanŭnim" [A Study of the Neologism for God: "Hanŭnim" from the Perspective of Orthography]. In *Han'gŭl sŏngsŏ wa kyŏre munhwa: ch'ŏnjugyo wa kaesin'gyo ŭi mannam*, edited by Kŭrisŭdogyo wa kyŏre munhwa yŏn'guhoe, 93–114. Seoul: Kidok kyomunsa, 1985.

Pak Chiwŏn. *Kugyŏk Yŏnamjip* [The Collected Works of Pak Chiwŏn]. 3 vols. Translated by Sin Hoyŏl and Kim Myŏngho. Seoul: Minjok munhwa ch'ujinhoe, 2005.

Pak Pyŏngch'ae. "'Chŏngŭm' haeje: Chosŏn ŏhak yŏn'guhoe wa Pak Sŭngbin haksŏl ŭl chungsim ŭro" [Introduction to *Chŏngŭm*: Focusing on the Research Society for Korean Linguistics and Pak Sŭngbin's Theories]. *Chŏngŭm* 1 (1978): 1–20.

Pak Saho. *Simjŏn'go* [Writings of Pak Saho]. Originally written in 1828 and translated by Kim Chongo. Seoul: Minjok munhwa ch'ujinhoe, 1977.

Pak Sanghŭi. "Chōsen seihokujin no tokushitsu" [Unique Characteristics of the Northwestern Korean]. In *Chōsen oyobi Chōsen minzoku* [Korea and the Korean Race], 112–123. Keijō: Chōsen shisō tsūshinsha, 1927.

———. "Han'gŭlsik ch'ŏlchabŏp pandae undong pogosŏ" [Report on the Movement in Opposition to the *Han'gŭl*-Style Spelling]. *Chŏngŭm* 7 (1935): 563–65.

Pak Sŭngbin. *Chosŏn ŏhak* [Korean Linguistics]. Kyŏngsŏng: Chosŏn ŏhak yŏn'guhoe, 1935.

Pak Sŭngdo. "Chŏngnidoen ch'ŏlchabŏp e ŭihan sŏnggyŏng" [The Bible in the Newly Adjusted Spelling]. *Chŏngŭm* 7 (1935): 553–60.

Pak Ŭnsik. "Nonsŏl" [Editorial]. *Sŏu* 1 (1906): 10.

Pak, V. "Iz istorii sobiraniia i izucheniia Koreiskogo fol'klora" [From the History of the Collection and Study of Korean Folklore]. In *Literatura i fol'klor narodov vostoka: Sbornik statei*, edited by Sorokin, V. F. and A. S. Sukhochev, 242–54. Moscow: Nauka, 1967.

P'aldo ŏsa chaegŏ samok [Handbook for Secret Inspectors to the Eight Provinces]. Kyujanggak collection, kyu 1127.

Pang Tongin. *Hanguk ŭi kukkyŏng hoekchŏng yŏn'gu* [Studies in the Demarcation of Korea's National Boundaries]. Seoul: Ilchogak, 1997.

Pang Ujŏng. *Sŏjŏng ilgi* [Records of the Pacification Campaign in P'yŏngan Province]. Reprint. Seoul: Kuksa p'yŏnch'an wiwŏnhoe, 1964.

Panov, A. *Rabochii rynok Priamur'ia* [The Labor Market in the Amur Region]. St. Petersburg: Izd. Kantselarii Komiteta po zaseleniiu Dal'nago vostoka, 1912.

———. "Zheltyi vopros i mery bor'by s 'zheltym zasil'em' v Priamur'e (Istoriko-statisticheskii ocherk)" [The Yellow Question and Measures for the Battle with the "Yellow Domination" in the Amur Region (Historico-Statistical Essay)]. *Voprosy kolonizatsii* 11 (1912): 171–84.

———. "Zheltyi vopros v Priamur'e. Istoriko-statistischeskii ocherk" [The Yellow Question in the Amur Region. Historico-Statistical Essay]. *Voprosy kolonizatsii* 7 (1910): 53–116.

Park, Chung-shin. *Protestantism and Politics in Korea*. Seattle: University of Washington Press, 2003.

Park, Soon-Won. *Colonial Industrialization and Labor in Korea: The Onoda Cement Factory*. Cambridge, MA: Harvard University Press, 1999.

Peattie, Mark R. "Introduction." In *The Japanese Colonial Empire, 1895–1945*, edited by Ramon H. Myers and Mark R. Peattie, 3–52. Princeton, NJ: Princeton University Press, 1984.

Perry, Elizabeth J. *Shanghai on Strike: The Politics of Chinese Labor*. Stanford, CA: Stanford University Press, 1993.

Pesotskii, V. *Koreiskii vopros v Priamur'e* [The Korean Question in the Amur Region]. Trudy komandirovannoi po vysochaishemu poveleniiu Amurskoi ekspeditsii, Vol. 11. Khabarovsk, 1913.

Pettid, Michael J. "Vengeful Gods and Shrewd Men: Responses to the Loss of

Sovereignty on Cheju Island." *East Asian History* 22 (December 2001): 171–86.

Pibyŏnsa tŭngnok [Record of the Border Defense Command]. 28 vols. Seoul: Kuksa p'yŏnch'an wiwŏnhoe, 1959–60.

Pollard, Harriet. "The History of the Missionary Enterprise of the Presbyterian Church, USA." MA thesis, Northwestern University, 1927.

Pozdniaev, D. ed. *Istoriia Rossiiskoi dukhovnoi missii v Koree: Sbornik statei* [History of the Russian Ecclesiastic Mission in Korea: A Collection of Articles]. Moscow: Izdatel'stvo Sviato-Vladimirskogo Bratstva, 1999.

Pratt, Mary Louise. *Imperial Eyes: Travel Writing and Transculturation*. London: Routledge, 1992.

Prokhorenko, F. "Russkaia dukhovnaia missia v Koree" [The Russian Ecclesiastic Mission in Korea]. *Vera i razum* 1 (1907): 30–48.

Przheval'skii, Nikolai Mikhailovich. "Inorodcheskoe naselenie v Iuzhnoi chasti Primorskoi oblasti" [The Non-Russian Population in the Southern Part of the Maritime Oblast']. *Izvestiia Imperatorskogo Russkogo Geograficheskogo Obshchestva* 5, no. 5 (1869): 185–201.

———. *Puteshestvie v Ussuriiskom krae, 1867–1869* [Travels in the Ussuri Krai, 1867–1869]. Self-published in St. Petersburg, 1870. Reprints. Moscow: Godusardstvennoe sotsial'no-ekonomicheskoe izdatel'stvo, 1937; Moscow: Gos. izd-vo geogr. lit-ry, 1947; and Vladivostok : Dal'navostochnoe kn. izd-vo, 1990.

———. *Usurii chihō no tabi* [Travels in the Ussuri Region]. Translated by Anekawa Iwane. Dairen: Dairen nichinichi shinbunsha, 1943.

Pukchŏng ilgi [Daily Records in Hamgyŏng Province]. Kyujanggak collection, kyu ko 25.

Putnam, Robert D. *Making Democracy Work: Civic Traditions in Modern Italy*. Princeton, NJ: Princeton University Press, 1993.

Putsillo, M. *Opyt russko-koreiskogo slovaria* [Attempt at a Russian-Korean Dictionary]. St. Petersburg: Tipografiia Gogenfelden & Co, 1874.

P'yŏngan-do nae kagŭp min'go chŏngnye chŏlmok [Regulations on the Min'go in P'yŏngan Province]. Kyujanggak collection, 17207.

P'yŏngyang sokchi [Gazetteer of P'yŏngyang, Continued]. In *Chosŏn sidae sach'an ŭpchi* 46. Seoul: Han'guk inmun kwahagwŏn, 1990.

Ragoza, A. "Kratkii istoricheskii ocherk pereseleniia Koreitsev v nashi predely" [A Short Historical Sketch of the Settlement of Koreans in Our Borders]. *Voennyi sbornik* 6 (1903): 206–22.

———. "Pos'etskii uchastok" [The Pos'et Region]. *Sbornik geograficheskikh, topo-graficheskikh i statisticheskikh materialov po Azii* 45 (1891): 47–135.

Ragozin, D. *Koreia i Iaponiia* [Korea and Japan]. Odessa: Izdanie L. Luk'ianova (Tipografiia B. Sapozhnikova), 1904.

Rhodes, Harry A. *History of the Korea Mission, Presbyterian Church U.S.A., 1884–1934*. Seoul: Chosen Mission Presbyterian Church U.S.A., 1935.

Rittikh, A. *Pereselencheskoe i krest'ianskoe delo v Iuzhno-Ussuriiskom krae* [Resettlement and the Peasantry in the South Ussuri Krai]. St. Petersburg: Ministerstvo Vnutrennykh Del, 1899.

Robinson, Kenneth R. "From Raiders to Traders: Border Security and Border Control in Early Chosŏn, 1392–1450." *Korean Studies* 16 (1992): 94–115.

———. "An Island's Place in History: Tsushima in Japan and in Chosŏn, 1392–1592." *Korean Studies* 30 (2006): 40–66.

Rodman, Margaret C. "Empowering Place: Multilocality and Multivocality." *American Anthropologist* 94, no. 3 (September 1992): 640–56.

Ross, John, trans. *Yesu syŏnggyo chyŏnsyŏ* [New Testament]. Kyŏngsŏng: Mun'gwang sŏwŏn, 1887.

Rossabi, Morris. *The Jurchens in the Yüan and Ming*. Ithaca, NY: China-Japan Program, Cornell University, 1982.

Rouelle, V. du. "Les coréens jugés par un de leurs sages" [The Koreans as Evaluated by One of Their Sages]. *Mélanges japonais* 13 (January 1907): 43–55.

Rumiantseva, O. "N. G. Garin-Mikhailovskii." In *N. Garin: Povesti i rasskazy* [N. Garin: Stories and Tales], 541–47. Moscow: Moskovskii rabochii, 1955.

Ryu Taeyŏng, O Sŏngdŭk, and Yi Manyŏl, eds. *Taehan sŏngsŏ konghoesa II* [History of the Korean Bible Society II]. Seoul: Korean Bible Society, 1994.

Sahlins, Peter. *Boundaries: The Making of France and Spain in the Pyrenees*. Berkeley: University of California Press, 1989.

Sakai Toshio. *Nihon tōchika no Chōsen hokuchin no rekishi* [The History of Korea's North P'yongan Under Japanese Rule]. Tokyo: Kusa no shisha, 2003.

Sasse, Werner. "Sprachreform und Koreanische Kulturgeschichte" [Language Reform and Korean Cultural History]. In *Twenty Papers on Korean Studies Offered to Professor W. E. Skillend*, edited by Daniel Bouchez, Robert C. Provine, and Roderick Whitfield, 299–310. Paris: Collège de France, Centre d'études coréennes, 1989.

Schieffelin, Bambi B. and Rachelle Charlier Doucet. "The 'Real' Haitian Creole: Ideology, Metalinguistics, and Orthographic Choice." In *Language Ideologies: Practice and Theory*, edited by Bambi B. Schieffelin, Kathryn A. Woolard, and Paul V. Kroskrity, 285–316. New York and Oxford: Oxford University Press, 1998.

Schmid, Andre. *Korea between Empires, 1895–1919*. New York: Columbia University Press, 2002.

Selivanovskii, I. *Kak zhivut i rabotaiut Koreitsy* [How the Koreans Work and Live].
Moscow: K. I. Tikhomirov, 1904.

Seoul taehakkyo Kyujanggak ed., *Kyujanggak sojang ŏmunhak charyo ŏhakp'yŏn*
[Kyujanggak Collections on Korean Language and Literature: Linguistics]. Seoul:
T'aehaksa, 2001.

Serov, V. M. "Vostochnyi Institut (1899–1909 gg.)" [The Oriental Institute (1899–1909)].
Izvestiia Vostochnogo Instituta (Dal'nevostochnogo Gosudarstvennogo Universiteta) 1
(1994): 14–36.

Shinshigakkai, ed. *Meiji ishin no chiiki to minshū* [Regions and the Masses of the Meiji
Restoration]. Tokyo: Yoshikawa kōbunka, 1996.

Shreider, D. I. *Iaponiia i iapontsy* [Japan and the Japanese]. Skt. Peterburg: Izd. A.F.
Debriena, 1895.

―――. *Nash Dal'nyi Vostok (Tri goda v Ussuriiskom krae)* [Our Far East (Three Years in the
Ussuri Krai)]. Skt. Peterburg: A. F. Devrien, 1897.

―――. *Strana voskhodiashchago solntsa* [Land of the Rising Sun]. Skt. Peterburg: Izd.-vo
O.N. Popovoi, 1898.

Silberman, Bernard S. *Ministers of Modernization: Elite Mobility in the Meiji Restoration,
1868–1873*. Tucson: University of Arizona Press, 1964.

Silverstein, Michael, and Urban, Greg, eds. *Natural Histories of Discourse*. Chicago:
University of Chicago Press, 1996.

Sin Ch'angsun. *Kugŏ kŭndae p'yogibŏp ŭi chŏn'gae* [Development of Modern Korean
Orthography]. Seoul: T'aehaksa, 2003.

Sin Hyŏnggi and O Sŏngho. *Pukhan munhak sa: hangil hyŏngmyŏng munhak esŏ chuch'e
munhak kkaji* [A History of North Korean Literature: From Anti-Japanese Revolutionary
Literature to Chuch'e Literature]. Seoul: P'yŏngminsa, 2000.

Sin Kwangsu. *Sŏkpukchip* [Collected Works of Sin Kwangsu]. In *Han'guk munjip
ch'onggan*, Vol. 231. Seoul: Minjok munhwa ch'ujinhoe, 1999.

Sin Kyŏng. *Chigamjip* [The Collected Works of Sin Kyŏng]. In *Han'guk munjip ch'onggan*,
Vol. 216. Seoul: Minjok munhwa ch'ujinhoe, 1998.

Sin Myŏnggyun. "Han'gŭl chŏngni rŭl pandaehanŭn kokhaeja ege" [To the Distorters
Opposing the Regularization of Han'gŭl]. *Chungoe ilbo* (September 5–23, 1929).
Reproduced in *Kungmunnon chipsŏng*, edited by Ha Tongho, 85–101. Seoul: T'ap
ch'ulp'ansa, 1985.

Sin Sŏnggwŏn. "Ro-Il ŭi hanbando punhal hoekch'aek" [Plot to Divide the Korean
Peninsula by Russia and Japan]. In *Han'guksa*, Vol. 41. Kwach'ŏn: Kuksa p'yŏnch'an
wiwŏnhoe, 1993.

Sinjŭng Tongguk yŏji sŭngnam [Augmented Survey of the Geography of Korea]. Seoul: Myŏngmundang, 1959.

Sliunin, N. Sovremennoe polozhenie nashego Dal'nego Vostoka [Current Situation of Our Far East]. St. Petersburg: Tipografiia Red. period. Izdanii Ministerstva finansov, 1908.

Sŏk Chuyŏn. Nogŏltae wa Pakt'ongsa ŭi ŏnŏ [The Language of the Nogŏltae and Pakt'ongsa]. Seoul: Kugŏ hakhoe, 2003.

Sok taejŏn [Great Code, Supplemented]. Reprint. Seoul: Kyujanggak, 1998.

Son Pyŏnggyu et al. Tansŏng hojŏk taejang yŏn'gu [The Study of Household Registers of Tansŏng]. Seoul: Sŏnggyun'gwan taehakkyo taedong munhwa yŏn'guwŏn, 2003.

Song Hyŏnho. Hwang Sunwŏn: sŏnbi chŏngsin kwa in'gan kuwŏn ŭi kil [Hwang Sunwŏn: A Scholarly Soul's Quest for the Salvation of Humankind]. Seoul: Kŏn'guk taehakkyo ch'ulp'anbu, 2000.

"Sŏnggyŏng ch'ŏlcha kaejŏng ŭi kyŏrŭi" [Decision in Favor of Reforming Bible Spelling (Editorial)]. Han'gŭl 49 (1937): 1–3.

Sŏnu Hyŏp. Tunam chŏnsŏ [Complete Works of Sŏnu Hyŏp]. In Han'guk munjip ch'onggan, Vol. 93. Seoul: Minjok munhwa ch'ujinhoe, 1992.

Spencer, J. E. "On Regionalism in China." Journal of Geography XLVI, no. 4 (April 1947): 123–36.

Stallybrass, Peter, and Allon White. The Politics and Poetics of Transgression. Ithaca, NY: Cornell University Press, 1986.

Strel'bitskii, I. I. Iz Khunchuna v Mukden i obratno po sklonam Chan"-Bai-Shan'skago khrebta (Otchet o semimesiachnom puteshestvii po Man'chzhurii i Koree v 1895–1896 gg.) [From Khunchun to Mukden and Back Again, Along the Changbaishan Mountain Range (Account of a Seven-Month Journey in Manchuria and Korea, 1895–1896)]. Skt. Peterburg: Voennaia Tipografiia, 1897.

Sŭngjŏngwŏn ilgi [Records of the Royal Secretariat]. 126 vols, edited by Kuksa p'yŏnch'an wiwŏnhoe. Seoul: T'amgudang, 1961–77.

Taejŏn hoet'ong [Comprehensive Collection of the Dynastic Code]. Reprint. Seoul: Pogyŏng munhwasa, 1990.

Takahashi Kamekichi. "Chōsen wa umarefukeru" [Korea's Rebirth]. Kaizō (April 1935): 47–63.

Takahashi Kimiaki. "Chōsen gaikō chitsujo to Higashi Ajia kaiiki no kōryū" [The Chosŏn Diplomatic Order and Interaction in Maritime East Asia]. Rekishigaku kenkyū 573 (1987:10): 66–76.

Takeuchi Yoshimi. Ajiashugi [Asia-ism]. Tokyo: Chikuma shobō, 1963.

Takihisa Yonejiō. "Chōsen ni taisuru sanseiken jisshi ni kansuru seigansho" [A Petition

Regarding the Effectuation of Political Participation Rights in Korea]. *Saitō Makoto kankei monjo* (reel 76), Japanese Diet Library (February 1929).

Tarui Tōkichi. *Daitō Gappōron* (DTGR) [Theory of the Great East Federation]. Reprint. Tokyo: Choryo shorin, 1975.

Tensin, M. A. "Predislovie" [Foreward]. In *Puteshestvie v Ussuriiskim krae, 1867–1869,* by N. M. Przheval'skii, 5–18. Moscow: OGIZ/Gosudarstvennoe Izdatel'stvo Geograficheskoi Literatury, 1947.

Tiagai, G. D. "Trudy russkikh issledovatelei kak istochnik po novoi istorii Korei" [Works of Russian Researchers as a Source for a New History of Korea]. *Ocherki po istorii russkogo vostokovedeniia* 1: 122–147. Moscow, 1953.

Tiagai, G. D. ed. *Po Koree: Puteshestviia 1885–1896 gg.* [In and About Korea: Travels 1885–1896]. Moscow: Izdatel'stvo Vostochnoi Literatury, 1958.

Tian, Xiaofei. "The Cultural Construction of the North and South in Early Medieval China." Ch. 7 in *Beacon Fire and Shooting Star: The Literary Culture of the Liang,* 502–557. Cambridge, MA: Harvard University Asia Center for Harvard-Yenching Institute, 2007.

Tillett, Lowell. *The Great Friendship: Soviet Historians on the Non-Russian Nationalities.* Chapel Hill: University of North Carolina Press, 1969.

T'ongmun'gwan chi [Record of the Bureau of Interpretation]. 4 vols. Reprint. Seoul: Sejong taewang kinyŏm saŏphoe, 1998.

Tongmun hwigo [Collection of Diplomatic Documents]. First compilation in 1788, with supplementary edition compiled in 1881. Reprint. Seoul: Kuksa p'yŏnch'an wiwŏnhoe, 1978.

Tongmun yuhae [Korean-Manchu Dictionary]. Originally published in 1748. Reprint. Seoul: Yŏnse taehakkyo ch'ulp'anbu, 1958.

Torii Ryūzō. "Watakushi no miru Chōsen" [The Korea that I See]. *Chōsen* (January 1939): 37–39.

———. "Yūshi izen ni okeru Chōsen to sono shūen no kankei" [Korea and Its Regional Relations in Prehistoric Times]. *Chōsen* (September 1923): 1–28.

Trotsevich, A. F. "Opisanie Koreiskikh pis'mennykh pamiatnikov, khraniashchikhsia v biblioteke vostochnogo fakul'teta S.-Peterburgksogo universiteta" [Description of the Korean Written Monuments Housed in the Library of the Oriental Faculty of St. Petersburg University]. *Vestnik Tsentra Koreiskoi Kul'tury,* vyp. 2 (1997): 117–35. Skt. Peterburg.

Tsuboi Sachio. *Aru Chōsen sotokufu keisatsu kanryō no kaisō* [Recollections of One Bureaucrat in the Korean Government-General Police]. Tokyo: Sōshisha, 2004.

Ugaki Kazunari. "Chōsen no shōrai" [Korea's Future]. *Ugaki Kazunari monjo* [Official

Papers of Ugaki Kazunari]. Japanese National Diet Library, keisei shiryō shitsu (microfilm) (September 1934).

———. "Chōsen tōchi no taidō" [The Great Road of Korean Administration]. *Chūō kōron* (January 1934): 85–87.

Ukita Kazutani. "Kankoku heigō no kōka ikan" [What are the Effects of Korean Annexation]. *Taiyō* (October 1, 1910): 1–6.

Underwood, H. G., James Scarth Gale, and Homer Hulbert. *Han-Yŏng Chajŏn= A Concise Dictionary of the Korean Language: In Two Parts, Korean-English and English-Korean.* Student edition. Yokohama: Kelly & Walsh; London: Trübner; New York: A.D.F. Randolph, 1890.

Underwood, Lillias H. *Fifteen Years among the Top-Knots.* Originally published by Boston: American Tract Society, 1904. Translated into Korean by Sin Pongnyong and Ch'oe Sugŭn. Seoul: Chimmundang, 1999.

Unterberger, P. *Priamurskii krai, 1906–1910 gg.* [The Amur Krai, 1906–1910]. St. Petersburg: Tip. V. F. Kirshbauma, 1912.

———. *Primorskaia oblast', 1856–1898* [The Maritime Oblast', 1856–1898]. St. Petersburg: Tip. V. F. Kirshbauma, 1900.

Vagin, V. "Koreitsy na Amure" [The Koreans on the Amur]. *Sbornik istoriko-statisticheskikh svedenii o Sibiri i sopredel'nykh ei stranakh* 1 (1875): 1–29.

Van Gulik, Robert. *The Chinese Nail Murders.* Chicago: University of Chicago Press, 1977.

Vebel', F. I. "Poezdka v Koreiiu" [A Trip to Korea]. *Sbornik Materialov po Azii,* sb. XLI. Skt. Peterburg: Voenno-uchenyi Komitet Glavnogo Shtaba, 1890. Reprinted in *Russkii vestnik* 234 (1894): 115–53 and in Tiagai (1958): 96–134.

Wagner, Edward W. "The Civil Examination Process as Social Leaven: The Case of the Northern Provinces in the Yi Dynasty." *Korea Journal* 17, no. 1 (January 1977): 22–27.

———. *The Literati Purges: Political Conflict in Early Yi Korea.* Cambridge, MA: East Asian Institute, Harvard University, 1974.

War Department, Military Intelligence Service. "Survey of Korea," In *Haebang chŏnhusa charyojip I: migunjŏng chunbi charyo* [Collection of Historical Documents Around the Time of Liberation I: Materials of United States Administration Preparation] edited by Yi Kilsang. Seoul: Hyŏnju munhwasa, 1992.

Weber, Eugen. *Peasants into Frenchmen: The Modernization of Rural France, 1870–1914.* Stanford, CA: Stanford University Press, 1976.

Weems, Benjamin B. *Reform, Rebellion, and the Heavenly Way.* Tucson: University of Arizona Press, 1964.

Wells, David N. *Russian Views of Japan, 1792–1913: An Anthology of Travel Writing.* London and New York: Routledge Curzon, 2004.

Wigen, Kären. "Culture, Power, and Place: The New Landscapes of East Asian Regionalism."*American Historical Review* 104, no. 4 (Oct. 1999): 1183–201.

———. *The Making of a Japanese Periphery, 1750–1920.* Berkeley: University of California Press, 1995.

Woodruff, Phillip. "Status and Lineage among the Jurchens of the Korean Northeast in the Mid-Fifteenth Century." *Central and Inner Asian Studies* 1 (1987): 117–54.

Woolard, K. "Language Ideology: Issues and Approaches." *Pragmatics* 2, no. 3 (1992): 235–50.

Woolard, K. A. and B. B. Schieffelin. "Language Ideology." *Annual Review of Anthropology* 23 (1994): 55–82.

Yamada Kanto. *Shokuminchi Chōsen ni okeru Chōsengo shorei seisaku: Chōsengo wo mananda Nihonjin* [Japan's Korean Encouragement Policies in Colonial Korea: Japanese Who Learned the Korean Language]. Tokyo: Fuji shuppan, 2004.

Yang Chusam and Chŏng T'aeŭng, eds. *Min Hyu sŏnsaeng silgi* [True Account of Hugh Miller]. Seoul: Taeyŏng sŏngsŏ konghoe, 1937.

Yangyŏk silch'ong [Actual Assessment of Military Taxation]. Originally published in 1748. Reprint. Yŏgang ch'ulp'ansa, 1984.

Yi Ap. *Yŏnhaeng kisa* [Travel Record to China]. Originally written in 1777 and translated by Yi Sik. Seoul: Minjok munhwa ch'ujinhoe, 1976.

Yi Chaehyŏng. *Songamjip* [Collected Works of Yi Chaehyŏng]. In *Han'guk munjip ch'onggan*, Vol. 179. Seoul: Minjok munhwa ch'ujinhoe, 1996.

Yi Chema. *Tongmu yugo* [Collected Works of Yi Chema], edited by Yi Ch'angil. Seoul: Ch'ŏnggye ch'ulp'ansa, 1999.

Yi Chion. *Pin'gyo munjip* [Collected Works of Yi Chion]. National Library of Korea collection, ko 3648–62–485.

Yi Ch'ŏlsŏng. *Chosŏn hugi taech'ŏng muyŏksa yŏn'gu* [A Study of Foreign Trade with Qing in the Late Chosŏn Period]. Seoul: Kukhak charyowŏn, 2000.

———. "T'ongsinsa wa yŏnhaengsa ŭi pigyo yŏn'gu" [A Comparative Study of Chosŏn Envoys to Japan and China]. In *T'ongsinsa Waegwan kwa Han-Il kwan'gye* [Korean Envoys to Japan, Japan House, and the Relations between Korea and Japan], edited by Han-Il kwan'gyesa yŏn'gu nonjip p'yŏnch'an wiwŏnhoe, 75–115. Seoul: Kyŏngin munhwasa, 2005.

Yi Chonggwŏn. "Chosŏnjo kugyŏk pulsŏ ŭi kanhaeng e kwanhan yŏn'gu" [A Study of Buddhist Texts Translated into Vernacular Korean During the Chosŏn Period]. MA thesis, Sungkyunkwan University, 1988.

Yi Chunghwan. T'aengniji [A Guide to Select Villages]. Seoul: Chosŏn kwangmunhoe, 1912.

Yi Hun'gu. Manju wa Chosŏnin [Manchuria and Koreans]. P'yongyang: Sungsil chŏnmun hakkyo kyŏngjehak yŏn'gusil, 1932.

Yi Hyŏnhŭi. "Chosŏn wangjo sidae ŭi Pukp'yŏnggwan Yain: kŭ sumuch'aek iltan" [Jurchens at the Hall of Northern Peace During the Chosŏn Period: One Aspect of the Loose Rein Policy]. Paeksan hakpo 11 (Dec. 1971): 107–47.

Yi Ik. Sŏngho saesŏl [Yi Ik's Trivial Remarks]. In Kojŏn kugyŏk ch'ongsŏ, Vol. 110. Seoul: Minjok munhwa ch'ujinhoe, 1977.

Yi Inyŏng. Han'guk Manju kwan'gyesa ŭi yŏn'gu [Studies in the History of Korean-Manchu Relations]. Seoul: Ŭryu munhwasa, 1954.

Yi Kahwan. Kŭmdae simun ch'o [The Collected Works of Yi Kahwan, a Draft]. In Kŭn'gi sirhak yŏnwŏn chehyŏn chip, Vol. 2. Seoul: Sŏnggyun'gwan taehakkyo Taedong munhwa yŏn'guwŏn, 2002.

Yi Kimun. Kugŏ ŭmunsa yŏn'gu [A Study of Korean Phonology]. Seoul: Han'guk munhwa yŏn'guso, 1972.

Yi Kŭk-ro. See Yi Kŭngno.

Yi Kŭngno [Yi Kŭk-ro]. "Pak Sŭngbin ssi ege hapchak kyosŏp chŏnmal [A Full Account of My Negotiations with Mr. Pak Sŭngbin Concerning Cooperation]. Han'gŭl 22 (1935): 27.

Yi Kwangdŏk. Kwanyangjip [The Collected Works of Yi Kwangdŏk]. In Han'guk munjip ch'onggan, Vol. 209. Seoul: Minjok munhwa ch'ujinhoe, 1998.

Yi Kwangnin. "Kaehwagi Kwansŏ chibang kwa kaesin'gyo" [P'yŏngan Province and Protestantism in the Period of Enlightenment]. Sungjŏn taehakkyo nonmunjip 5 (1974): 435–47; and idem, Han'guk kaehwa sasang yŏn'gu, 239–54. Seoul: Ilchogak, 1979.

Yi Kyuhŏn. Sajin ŭro ponŭn kŭndae Han'guk: sanha wa p'ungmul, Vol. 2 [Modern Korea through Photographs: Mountains and Rivers and Customs, Vol. 2]. Seoul: Sŏmundang, 1986.

Yi Mijae. "Sahoejŏk t'aedo wa ŏnŏ sŏnt'aek" [Social Attitudes and Linguistic Choices]. Ŏnŏhak 12 (1990): 69–77.

Yi Myŏnggyu. "Kugaeŭmhwa e taehan munhŏnjŏk koch'al" [Bibliographical Study of Palatalization]. MA thesis, Seoul taehakkyo, 1974.

———. "Kugaeŭmhwa e taehan t'ongsi-jŏk yŏn'gu" [A Diachronic Study of Palatalization]. PhD diss., Soongsil University, 1993.

Yi Ok. Yi Ok chŏnjip [The Complete Collection of Yi Ok's Writing]. Seoul: Somyŏng, 2001.

Yi Okkŭm. "Chosŏnjo honam sach'alp'an e kwanhan sŏjijŏk yŏn'gu" [A Bibliographical Study of Buddhist Temple Publications in Chŏlla Province During the Chosŏn Period]. MA thesis, Sangmyung Women's University, 1988.

Yi Paeyong. "Kuhanmal Miguk ŭi Unsan kŭmgwang ch'aegulkwŏn hoektŭk e taehayŏ" [A Study of American Acquisition of the Unsan Mine in the Last Decade of the Chosŏn Dynasty]. PhD diss., Ehwa Womans University, 1971.

Yi Pongsu. "Ch'ae Chŏngmin ssi ege irŏnham" [A Word to Ch'ae Chŏngmin]. Han'gŭl 41 (1937): 35–36.

Yi Sanghyŏp. Chosŏn chŏn'gi pukpang samin yŏn'gu [A Study on Population Relocation Policy in the Early Chosŏn Period]. Seoul: Kyŏngin munhwasa, 2001.

Yi Sihang. Hwaŭnjip [Collected Works of Yi Sihang]. Kyujanggak collection, ko 3248–423.

Yi Sŏngju. "Sinp'yŏn ch'ansongga ŭi munhwajŏk ŭiŭi" [The Cultural Significance of the Newly Edited Hymnal]. Han'gŭl 40 (1936): 10–14.

Yi Sŏngnin [Yi Sŏk-rin]. "Tokcha ŭi sori: Kim Myŏngjin ssi ŭi pansŏng ŭl ch'okham: Kyŏngsŏng parŭm ŭl choch'ŭryŏnŭn" [Readers' Voices: I Urge Kim Myŏngjin to Reflect on His Ways—Who Allegedly Is Striving to Follow Kyŏngsŏng Pronunciation]. Han'gŭl 11 (1935): 13–16.

———. "Tokcha ŭi sori: 'ㅡ ㅓ' rŭl tŏ ssŏssŭmyŏn . . ." [Readers' Voices: If We Were to Write "ㅡ ㅓ . . ."]. Han'gŭl 25 (1935): 14.

———. "T'ongiran ŭi hanchaŭm ch'ŏri nŭn kwayŏn P'yŏngan-do pangŏn ŭl musihan kŏsin'ga?" [Does the Treatment of Chinese Character Readings in the Unified Orthography Really Flout P'yŏngan Province Dialect?]. Han'gŭl 46 (1937): 7–10.

Yi T'aedong, ed. Hwang Sunwŏn. Seoul: Sŏgang taehakkyo ch'ulp'anbu, 1997.

Yi Tŏksu. Sŏdang sajae [Collected Works of Yi Tŏksu]. In Han'guk munjip ch'onggan, Vol. 186. Seoul: Minjok munhwa ch'ujinhoe, 1997.

Yi Tongha. "Ch'oe Myŏngik: segye ŭi p'ongnyŏk kwa chishigin ŭi sooe" [Ch'oe Myŏngik: The Alienation of the Intellectual in a Violent World]. In Wŏlbuk munin yŏn'gu [Studies of the Wŏlbuk Writers], edited by Kwŏn Yŏngmin, 131–44. Seoul: Munhak sasangsa, 1989.

Yi Ŭnjŏng. "'Iryun haengsilto' ŭi kugŏhakchŏk yŏn'gu" [A Linguistic Study of "Iryun haengsilto"]. MA thesis, Sookmyung Women's University, 2000.

Yi Wanŭng. Chōsengo hatsuon oyobi bunpō [Korean Pronunciation and Grammar]. Keijō: Chōsengo Kenkyūkai, 1926.

———. Chungdŭng kyogwa Chosŏnŏ munjŏn [Middle School Textbook in Korean Grammar]. Kyŏngsŏng: Chosŏnŏ yŏn'guhoe, 1929.

Yi Wŏnbae. *Kwiamjip* [Collected Works of Yi Wŏnbae]. Kyujanggak collection, kyu 5209.

Yi Yo. *Yŏndo kihaeng* [Travel Record to China]. Originally written in 1656 and translated by Yi Minsu. Seoul: Minjok munhwa ch'ujinhoe, 1976.

Yi Yŏngho. *Han'guk kŭndae chise chedo wa nongmin undong* [Land Tax and Peasant Movements in Modern Korea]. Seoul: Seoul taehakkyo ch'ulp'anbu, 2001.

————. "Taehan cheguk sigi Yŏnghaktang undong ŭi sŏnggyŏk" [Yŏnghaktang Movements During the Great Han Empire and Their Characteristics]. *Han'guk minjok undongsa yŏn'gu* 5 (1991): 5–36.

Yi Yonghyu. *Hyehwan chapchŏ* [The Miscellaneous Works of Yi Yonghyu]. In *Kŭn'gi sirhak yŏnwŏn chehyŏn chip*, Vol. 2. Seoul: Sŏnggyun'gwan taehakkyo Taedong munhwa yŏn'guwŏn, 2002.

Yi Yunjae. "P'ilgyŏng haksaeng kkaji sŏndong hanŭnya? Chŏngŭmji ŭi kyŏngmang ŭl kyeham" [Do They Have to Incite Students? A Warning Concerning the Rash Folly of the Journal *Chŏngŭm*]. *Han'gŭl* 22 (1935): 20–24.

————. "Sŏnggyŏng ch'ŏlcha rŭl kaejŏnghara" [Reform the Bible Spelling]. *Han'gŭl* 37 (1936): 4–7.

Yoshida Yūjirō. "Heian hokudo no menyō shiyō" [North P'yŏngan's Sheep Breeding]. *Chōsen* (February 1930): 125–32.

Yu Pongyŏng. "Wangjo sillok e nat'anan Yijo chŏn'gi ŭi Yain" [Jurchens of the Early Yi Dynasty in the Veritable Records]. *Paeksan hakpo* 14 (June 1973): 87–164.

Yu Sŏngnyong. *The Book of Corrections: Reflections on the National Crisis During the Japanese Invasion of Korea, 1592–1598*. Translated by Byonghyon Choi. Berkeley: Institute of East Asian Studies, University of California, 2002.

Yu Sŭngju and Yi Ch'ŏlsŏng. *Chosŏn hugi chungguk kwa ŭi muyŏksa* [History of Trade with China in the Late Chosŏn Period]. Seoul: Kyŏngin munhwasa, 2002.

Yu Sŭngju. *Chosŏn sidae kwangŏpsa yŏn'gu* [A Study of Mining History During the Chosŏn Dynasty]. Seoul: Koryŏ taehakkyo ch'ulp'anbu, 1993.

Yun Ch'iho. "Sinch'ŏlchabŏp e taehan ugyŏn kii" [A Second Foolish Opinion on the New Spelling]. *Chŏngŭm* 4 (1934): 313–15.

————. "Sinch'ŏlchabŏp e taehaya" [On the New Spelling]. *Chŏngŭm* 2 (1934): 92.

Yun Pyŏngt'ae. "Chosŏn sidae P'yŏngyang ŭi inswae munhwa" [Print Culture of P'yŏngyang During the Chosŏn Dynasty]. *Koinswae munhwa* 1 [1993]: 45–91.

Yun Sŏnja. "Han-Il happyŏng chŏnhu Hwanghae-do ch'ŏnju kyohoe wa Wilhelm sinbu" [The Catholic Churches in Hwanghae Province Before and After the Annexation of Korea and Father Wilhelm]. *Han'guk kŭnhyŏndaesa yŏn'gu* 4 (1996): 107–31.

Yun Tusu. *P'yŏngyangji* [Gazetteer of P'yŏngyang]. National Library of Korea collection, han kojo 62–177.

Zaichikov, V. T. *Koreia* [Korea]. Second edition, 45–79. Moscow: Gos. izd-vo geogr. lit-ry, 1951.

———. "N. G. Garin-Mikhailovskii i ego puteshestvie vokrug sveta" [N. G. Garin-Mikhailovskii and His Journey Around the World]. In, *Iz dnevnikov krugosvetnogo puteshestviia: Po Koree, Man'chzhurii i Liaodunskomu poluostrovu*, edited by N. G. Garin-Mikhailovskii, 3–35. Moskva: Gos. izd-vo geog. lit-ry, 1950.

———. "Vklad russkikh uchenykh v issledovanie Korei" [Contribution of Russian Scholars to Research on Korea]. *Voprosy geografii* 8 (1948): 37–60. Reprint in Zaichikov (1951).

Zenina, L. V. "Uchenyi, uchitel', chelovek, grazhdanin: 120 let so dnia rozhdeniia Nikolaia Vasil'evicha Kiunera" [Scholar, Teacher, Person, Citizen: 120 Years Since the Birth of Nikolai Kiuner]. *100 let Peterburgskomu Koreevedeniiu: Materialy mezhdunarodnoi konferentsii*, 8–18. St. Petersburg: Sankt-Peterburgskii Universitet, 1997.

Zenshō Eisuke. "Chōsen shuyō shigai no sangyō seiryoku" [Korea's Important Urban Industrial Influence]. *Chōsen* (February 1926): 47–68.

Zhang Cunwu. *Qing Han zong fan mao yi, 1637–1894* [Tributary Trade Between Qing and Chosŏn, 1637–1894]. Taibei: Zhong yang yan jiu yuan jin dai shi yan jiu suo, 1978.

Zhdan-Pushkin, P. I. "Koreia: Ocherk istorii uchrezhdenii, iazyka, nravov, obychaev i rasprostraneniia khristianstva" [Korea: Sketch of the History, Language, Mores, Customs, and Spread of Christianity]. *Sbornik istoriko-statisticheskikh svedenii o Sibiri i sopredel'nykh ei stranakh*, Vol. 1 (Appendix). St. Petersburg, 1875.

Zuber, M. G. "Ekspeditsiia v Koreiu: Iz zapisok byvshego flotskogo ofitsera M. G. Zubera" [An Expedition to Korea: From the Notes of Former Naval Officer M. G. Zuber]. *Vsemirnyi puteshestvennik* 6 (June 1874): 223–43. St. Petersburg.

Zvegintsev, A. "Poezdka v severnuiu Koreiu" [A Trip to Northern Korea]. *Izvestiia IRGO* 36:5 (1900): 502–18.

Contributors

SUN JOO KIM is professor of Korean history at Harvard University. She is the author of *Marginality and Subversion in Korea: The Hong Kyŏngnae Rebellion of 1812* (2007). She is currently working on a research monograph, *Resurrecting the Forgotten: The Life and Work of Yi Sihang (1672–1736) in Late Chosŏn Korea*, and a collaborative book project, *Law and Order in Nineteenth-Century Korea* with Jungwon Kim, assistant professor at University of Illinois at Urbana-Champaign.

KENNETH R. ROBINSON is senior associate professor of history at the International Christian University, in Tokyo. He earned his Master's Degree in East Asian Studies from Stanford University and his PhD in History from the University of Hawai'i. Robinson's current research focuses on Korean-Japanese interactions and on Korean maps of Chosŏn and Japan in the Chosŏn period.

KWON NAEHYUN is associate professor at Korea University in South Korea. He is the author of the book, *Chosŏn hugi P'yŏngan-do chaejŏng yŏn'gu* [A Study of Financial Management of P'yŏngan Province in the Late Chosŏn Period] (2004). Recently, he has been participating in the computerization of household registers of the late Chosŏn Dynasty and in the study of reviewing the daily life of villages through such work. He is also involved in a study of the distinctive features of P'yŏngan Province from a social and economic viewpoint.

JANG YOO-SEUNG received his PhD degree in Korean literature from Seoul National University in 2010. He is currently a translator at the Institute for the Translation of Korean Classics (Han'guk kojŏn pŏnyŏgwŏn) in South Korea. His main research interests lie in Korean literature written in classical Chinese during the Chosŏn period.

JUNG MIN is professor of Korean literature at Hanyang University in South Korea. Ever since completing his doctoral degree from Hanyang University in 1990, he has established himself not only as a meticulous scholar but also a leading public intellectual. He has been interested in such research subjects as the theory of writings in the Chosŏn Dynasty, literature in the eighteenth century, aesthetics of poems written in classical Chinese (hansi), Chosŏn literati's perceptions of space through their travelogues, and comparative studies of paintings and literature.

PAEK DOO-HYEON specializes in Korean language and literature, all types of documents written in vernacular Korean during the Chosŏn period in particular. He is currently professor of Korean linguistics at the Kyungpook National University, in South Korea. He is the author of nine books and more than eighty articles. He has also been collecting old Korean documents and making them known to the public, so that invaluable linguistic and historical assets are recognized, studied, and preserved.

ROSS KING is professor and head of the Department of Asian Studies at the University of British Columbia, in Vancouver, Canada. His major research interests are Korean language and linguistics (including Korean historical linguistics, Korean dialectology, history of Korean linguistics and linguistic thought), Korean language pedagogy, and the history of Korean literary culture.

YUMI MOON is assistant professor at Stanford University. She obtained her PhD degree in History of East Asia from Harvard University in 2006. She is currently working on a book manuscript tentatively entitled, *Populist Collaborators: The Ilchinhoe and the Japanese Colonization of Korea, 1896–1910.* Her future research interests lie in exploring transnational cultural exchanges in East Asia and beyond and the formation of political, economic, and social infrastructures that mediated those exchanges.

BRUCE FULTON is the inaugural holder of the Young-Bin Min Chair in Korean Literature and Literary Translation in the Department of Asian Studies at the University of British Columbia in Vancouver, Canada. He has co-translated several anthologies of modern Korean short fiction, most recently *Lost Souls: Stories by Hwang Sunwŏn* (2009) and *The Red Room: Stories of Trauma in Contemporary Korea* (2009); edited the Korea section of the *Columbia Companion to Modern East Asian Literature* (2003); and is general editor of the Modern Korean Fiction series published by the University of Hawai'i Press. He is co-recipient of several translation awards and grants, including the first Asian literature–related residency at the Banff International Literary Translation Centre.

DONALD N. CLARK is professor of history and co-director of East Asian Studies at Trinity University in San Antonio, Texas. He earned his PhD in East Asian History at Harvard University in 1978. In the course of his academic career he has lived in and visited Korea many times, as a Fulbright Fellow, exchange professor, and participant in numerous conferences. He is the author of many books, including *Christianity in Modern Korea* (1986), *Culture and Customs of Korea* (2000), and *Living Dangerously in Korea* (2003), as well as co-authored works and editions on Korean history, politics, and society. A short version of his doctoral dissertation on Ming-Korean relations appears as a chapter in Volume VIII of the *Cambridge History of China*.

GERMAN KIM is one of the leading experts on Korean diasporas in Central Asia. He received his PhD from Kazakh National University. Currently he is director of the Center of Korean Studies and professor of world history at KazNU. He has written and edited a large number of books and published over one hundred papers. Of those, the most significant are: *History of Korean Immigration. Vol.1. Second Half of XIX c.-1945.* (in Russian and Korean), 1999 (2005); *History of Korean Immigration 1945-2000. Vol.2, Part 1 and Part 2*, Almaty 2006; *History of Education of Koreans in Russia and Kazakhstan*, Almaty, 2000; and *Koryo Saram: Koreans in the Former USSR* (co-edited with Ross King), *Korean and Korean American Studies Bulletin*, Vol.12, No.2/3, 2001.

MARK E. CAPRIO is professor in the College of Intercultural Communications at Rikkyo University, Tokyo, Japan. His research interests include Japan-Korean relations over the twentieth century, particularly the period of Japanese colonial occupation, and the present North Korean nuclear issue. He has published a monograph titled *Japanese Assimilation Policies in Colonial Korea, 1910-1945* (2009), and an edited volume titled *Democracy in Occupied Japan: The U.S. Occupation and Japanese Politics and Society* (2007). He has also written on post-liberation Korean repatriation from Japan and on contemporary North Korea-United States-Japan relations.

Index

www.ingramcontent.com/pod-product-compliance
Lightning Source LLC
Chambersburg PA
CBHW021807270326
41932CB00007B/83